NOTES ON THE ROMANS.

NOTES AND REFLECTIONS

ON THE

EPISTLE TO THE ROMANS.

BY

ARTHUR PRIDHAM.

"THY TESTIMONIES ARE WONDERFUL: THEREFORE DOTH MY SOUL
KEEP THEM."—PSALM CXIX. 129.

Third Edition, Revised and Enlarged.

WIPF & STOCK · Eugene, Oregon

Wipf and Stock Publishers
199 W 8th Ave, Suite 3
Eugene, OR 97401

Notes and Reflections on the Epistle to the Romans
By Pridham, Arthur
ISBN 13: 978-1-59244-499-1
Publication date 1/27/2004
Previously published by William Yapp, 1864

PREFACE.

THIS work has, in the present edition, been both altered and enlarged.[1] Retaining still its original character, as a help to inquiring disciples rather than an elaborate and critical commentary, the changes and additions which have been made since its first publication have had for their sole end the practical edification of the reader.

The study of inspired *words* is, when soberly pursued, a direct aid to spiritual profit; and a work of this description would be seriously defective, if in its construction this feature were entirely wanting. While, therefore, it holds an entirely subordinate place, there will be found, it is hoped, in the notes to this edition, a sufficient amount of verbal criticism to satisfy the fair demands of educated Christians. Grateful mention should be made, in connection with this subject, of the "Novum Testamentum Sinaiticum," recently edited by Tischendorf, and to

[1] This remark, though generally applicable, relates more especially to chaps. ii. iv. v. viii. and x.

which frequent references will be found in the course of the work.

But it is better to offend a critic, than to disappoint a hungering soul. And this must be my apology for passing lightly over many a scholar's topic, while enlarging with what, to some readers, may seem a disproportionate freedom, on points of practical interest. My desire is the profit of God's saints.

When the first edition of these Notes appeared, there were already many symptoms visible of the approaching end.[2] That in the interval these signs have greatly multiplied, and that the opposing powers of light and darkness will soon be marshalled for the day of decision, must be apparent to all who draw their divination from the fount of Truth.

May the sustaining power of the word of grace be abundantly proved by those who, with a due sense of the evil of the times, are "looking for the mercy of our Lord Jesus Christ unto eternal life."[3]

[2] 1 Pet. iv. 7.   [3] Jude 20, 21.

June, 1864.

CONTENTS.

	Page
INTRODUCTION	ix
CHAPTER I.	1
CHAPTER II.	26
CHAPTER III.	44
CHAPTER IV.	57
CHAPTER V.	76
CHAPTER VI.	107
CHAPTER VII.	126
CHAPTER VIII.	148
CHAPTER IX.	204
CHAPTER X.	239
CHAPTER XI.	272
CHAPTER XII.	334
CHAPTER XIII.	364
CHAPTER XIV.	390
CHAPTER XV.	417
CHAPTER XVI.	442

INTRODUCTION.

THE Epistle to the Romans may be distributed, with respect to its contents, into three great divisions. The first of these is comprised in the first eight chapters, and is essentially *doctrinal* in its character, although, like all other teaching which is truly Divine, it addresses itself to the *conscience* of the reader not less forcibly than to his understanding.

Indeed, the habit of regarding doctrine as something essentially distinct from what is practical is one which, though not unusual amongst Christians, is both erroneous in its principle and plainly of injurious tendency. For all true Christian practice is *obedience*, and therefore is but sound doctrine in its just effect. Men theorize; God never does. His doctrines are also His commands. What He reveals belongs equally to the consciences and hearts of men. It is by studying, therefore, the testimonies of His Spirit that faith acquires its needed knowledge of that "will of God," which it is the object of pure doctrine to make known, and the joy and blessing of the child of God to do.[1]

[1] John xiii. 17; xv. 10; 1 John v. 3, 4.

Accordingly, in the following pages, I have endeavoured so to treat the doctrinal portions of this Epistle, as to present immediately to a Christian reader the practical bearing of the truth which the doctrines convey.

The second branch of the Epistle begins at the ninth chapter, and closes with the eleventh. This division may with some propriety be termed *dispensational*. Its subject is the mystery of Divine wisdom in the dealings of God with the natural seed of Abraham, and with the nations of the earth as viewed in their relation to Israel. It thus stands in close relation to the preceding part, while it will be found to have a peculiar character of its own. It is a very deep and solemn view of the sovereignty of God, as the fulfiller, in wisdom and prudence, of the counsels of His holy will, which is presented in these chapters. The fixed and abiding principles of the Divine government, and the conditions of human blessing, are stated here at large. Although, therefore, it is with Israel as its proper subject that this division of the Epistle is chiefly concerned, its scope extends much further. For it includes, as essential features, the election of the true Church, on the one hand, and, on the other, the character and destiny of the visible professing body, considered in its relation to the dispensational government of God.

The last division commences at the twelfth chapter, and concludes the Epistle. It is more directly *practical* than either of the preceding parts. But, while abounding in exhortation, and addressing itself, on the doctrinal grounds already established in the former part of the Epistle, to the believer, as a manual of godly conversation, it contains besides a large addition of positive instruction on subjects not treated in the earlier chapters.

I have noticed these leading divisions of the Epistle, as being such as would obviously strike the mind of every careful student of the Word. But I need hardly say that the Epistle, to be studied *profitably*, should be studied as a *whole*. And ample indeed will be the reward which the prayerful meditation of this marvellous writing will bring, under the blessing of God, to one who, in simple dependence on Him who inspired its author, shall give himself to the close and thoughtful study of its contents.

The times in which our lot is cast are remarkable. To most Christians there are some features, at least, in the living picture of the present hour which suggest solemn thoughts and uneasy forebodings. It is well to have, in such a case, a mind firmly stayed upon God; and one object of the following work is to remind the inquiring believer of those truths which can alone confer stability upon the soul. The confidence with which Antichristian doctrines are asserted at the present day, even within the precincts of the nominal fold of Christ, is a fact too notorious to require further notice. We are, indeed, close upon the final times. Nor is there anything more worthy of regret, to those who better know the value of God's word, than the practical looseness with which that word is held—often even by real Christians—through the largely-prevalent influence of the neological element in the growing mind of the day.[2] It is a time when man is sifting everything within his reach, and, with the characteristic pride of that sciential conceit which really *knoweth* nothing,[3] is often found displacing Divine truth, without scruple, to make room for his own most false and self-deluding theories.

Nor is his the only sieve at work. God is, I surely believe, dealing with the souls that are to find a place in His garner in the day of the Lord which is at hand. It has been under the hopeful impression that no exposition of solid and pure doctrine, how feebly done soever, could be wholly out of season at such a time, that the following pages were originally put together, which are now, with some enlargement, afresh commended to the Christian reader in the name of our common Lord.

[2] Modern religious literature shows but too often and too distinctly with what readiness the most shallow sophistries are accepted in the stead of truth. The time is already come for the warning contained in 2 Tim. iv. 3, 4, to have its manifold exemplification even in this favoured land.

[3] 1 Tim. vi. 4.

NOTES AND REFLECTIONS

ON THE

EPISTLE TO THE ROMANS.

CHAPTER I.

VERSES 1–7 contain the introductory greeting of the apostle. He was at that time personally unknown to the Church at Rome. His sole claim to their regard and attention was his being a vessel and a minister of that grace of God, in the fellowship of which he knew and rejoiced over them as "called of Jesus Christ." Accordingly, he announces himself, first, *generally*, as a servant of Christ; and, secondly, as a called apostle; as one, moreover, especially "separated unto the Gospel of God." This last expression deserves our best attention, as it contains in a word what is characteristically the subject of this most precious Epistle.

The Gospel is emphatically the message of God.[1]

---

[1] The expressions, "Gospel of God," and "Gospel of Christ," occur in nearly equal frequency in Scripture. It is not, I think, only that we should ever be reminded of the equality of the Father and the Son, that the Spirit of God thus varies the expression. It is the Gospel of *God*, as having its source in His eternal counsel, as being declaratory of His gracious love to man, and as ministered by the Holy Ghost. It is the Gospel of *Christ*, inasmuch as He is its precious burden. It is His, too, as preached in His name, by His servants, at His command.

It is the revelation, by the Holy Ghost sent down from heaven, of Christ as the wisdom and the power of God.[2] The Father is known only through the record which He has given of His Son. Love now tells forth its own effective demonstration by the word of grace. And thus it is that in the Gospel, which is the ministration of Divine righteousness, there is unfolded to the human soul, when quickened by the power of the Spirit, the marvellous display of what God really is.

The unsearchable riches of Christ, which form the subject-matter of the Spirit's testimony, are nothing less than the revelation of the Divine fulness, as it is opened mediately to the eye of faith in the person of the Son. For the *Man* who mediates is one with the God whom He declares.[3] In Christ all the fulness of the Godhead dwells; it dwells in the Son "bodily."[4] The Holy Ghost, as the Divine witness of the finished grace of Jesus, is sent of the *Father* in His name. Though He comes as the messenger of Jesus, yet it is as proceeding from the Father.[5] Hence, in Acts ii. 33, the descent of the Spirit as the Divine power of testimony is referred by Peter immediately to the Father as the fulfiller of promise.

It is most needful to remember that it is by the active power of the *Holy Ghost,* who dwells in each member of Christ's mystic body, as well as in the one living Church,[6] that the special manifestation of God is now made to faith, even as He was declared in the *Son* while here in the days of His flesh. "God

---

[2] 1 Cor. i. 24. [3] 1 Tim. ii. 5. [4] Col. ii. 9. [5] John xvi. 7, xvi. 26.
[6] On this subject, the reader is referred to my *Notes on the Ephesians.*

was in Christ, reconciling the world," &c.⁷ The same God is now invisibly present by the Spirit, who, in demonstrating the person of the crucified and glorified Christ to be the perfect Truth, displays and magnifies the glory of God who raised Him from the dead. Thus the words of Jesus, "Glorify thy Son, that thy Son also may glorify thee,"⁸ begin to receive their fulfilment when the Spirit of Christ brings to the lips of believing sinners the utterance of that saving confession of the Lord which is to the glory of God the Father.⁹

The apostolate, then, of Paul, was for the setting forth of *God*,—for the publishing and open demonstration (to all who will receive His testimony) of Divine love and mercy, as now brought nigh to a ruined world in Jesus, and through His finished work.

But (verse 2) this had been the subject of earlier promise. The prophets had spoken of these things. *All prophecy* had been the utterance of the Spirit of Christ,¹ and *all* the promises found their object in His most blessed Person. Hence, the "glad message of God"² is none other than the annunciation of His having come in whom all the promises of God are yea and Amen. Not, indeed, as it was, when once the angels of God celebrated in strains of triumphant anticipation the incarnation of the Only-begotten, as the birth of Him who was both Israel's hope and the desire of the nations.⁸ Human sin, by the contemptuous rejection of Jesus, had (though in unconscious furtherance of the Divine counsel) turned the glory of Jehovah's Christ to shame. But now *from heaven*

---

⁷ 2 Cor. v.   ⁸ John xvii.   ⁹ Rom. x.; Phil. ii. 11.
¹ Gal. iii. 8; 1 Pet. i. 11.   ² εὐαγγέλιον Θεοῦ.   ⁸ Luke ii. 8–14.

the light of a risen and exalted Prince of life shines forth in saving grace to Jew and Gentile alike.[4]

He is, indeed, the same Messiah of whom the prophets spake; but the manner in which He is now revealed in the Gospel is not according to the general burden of Jewish prophecy. The prophets did, indeed, give utterance to the testimony of the Spirit, concerning both the sufferings of Christ and the glories which should follow. But there was a vein of richness in the deep and exhaustless mine of Divine counsel which it was not given to the Jewish prophets to open. *Their* subject is Christ, first humbled and then glorified, in its bearing on the nation of Israel, and the Gentiles *mediately* through them. It needed the descent of the Holy Ghost from heaven to minister, both from the words of the old prophets, and by the new and special utterances of apostolic testimony, the truth which formed and which now keeps and feeds that "Church of God," wherein the names of Jew and Gentile are alike unknown.[5]

It is not, then, in ocular manifestation to all flesh as the King of glory—the apparent source of *earthly* blessing—the true David—Israel's King while God's Son—wielding the sceptre of earthly rule before His ancients gloriously—that Jesus now appears. These things, indeed, shall be surely seen in their appointed time. But now it is as despised and abhorred of the nation and its rulers, rejected and slain—cast forth as an abominable branch by the authorities[6] of this world, but received up into glory in completion of the mystery of godliness,[7] and there awaiting, on the

---

[4] Col. iii. 11.
[5] 1 Pet. i. 1–12.
[6] ἄρχοντες, 1 Cor. ii. 6–8.
[7] 1 Tim. iii. 16.

Father's throne, the hour of His glorious appearing;[8] it is thus that He stands now revealed to faith as the Branch of the Lord, beautiful and glorious, and the Fruit of the earth, excellent and comely, for the remnant of electing mercy,[9] the called vessels of redemption, who now, as God's true worshippers in the Spirit, find their glory and their joy in Him.[1]

It is, then (verses 3, 4), "concerning *His Son*" that God now speaks, to all men without distinction, in the Gospel of His grace; setting Him forth both as the living fulfilment of His precious thoughts of peace towards His people, and as a pledge of that unalterable day of judgment when the victory of truth will be complete, and *every* knee shall bow to Him.[2] It is meanwhile the glory of believers to acknowledge Him as "Jesus Christ *our* Lord." In these verses we have both a recital of His generation after the flesh, and a declaration of the essential glory of His Person. He was "made of the seed of David according to the flesh," but "declared to be the Son of God with power, according to the Spirit of holiness, by the resurrection from the dead" (verse 4).[3]

The resurrection was the effectual justification of

[8] Tit. ii. 13; Rev. iii. 21.
[9] Isa. iv. I do not refer to this passage as if it received its proper fulfilment in the calling of the Church. Far from it; it is most clearly Jewish in its character. But its application in principle to the people of God now is, I think, plain. While we are watchfully to guard against a false division of the Word, it is one of our most precious privileges, as having the Spirit, the unction from the Holy One, to draw the marrow and fatness of Christ for the nourishment of our souls from every part of God's Word.
[1] Phil. iii. 3.   [2] John xx. 20; Acts xvii. 31.
[3] Acts xxvi. 23, εἰ παθητὸς ὁ Χριστός, εἰ πρῶτος ἐξ ἀναστάσεως νεκρῶν φῶς μέλλει καταγγέλλειν τῷ λαῷ καὶ τοῖς ἔθνεσιν, where the place assigned to the Resurrection, as the necessary means and condition of the shining of the true light, is strikingly shown. Compare 1 John ii. 8.

the title of Jesus as the Son of God. The act of omnipotent power which raised the dead Son of Man, vindicated at the same moment the glory of His Divine person as the Eternal Son of God. By the grace of God He died. He was crucified in weakness, He suffered in the flesh. "He lives,"[4] says the same apostle, "by the power of God."[5]

But this is not all. He was, indeed, quickened and raised, as having yielded up His spirit to the Father. But He also *arose*. He could say in the days of His flesh, "Destroy this temple, and in three days *I* will raise it up."[6] "I have power to lay down my life, and I have power to take it again." He made Himself capable of death when He took flesh. He died, to fulfil the Father's commandment, in willing, gracious love to lost sinners. He died, moreover, that the Scriptures might be fulfilled. For the same purpose He *revived*. Death could not hold Him in its grasp—it was not *possible*, as Peter says.[7] The spirit of holiness is not subject to the bondage of death. Because He was verily *man*, the Christ could die—could be slain, and *was* slain, in the obedient yielding of Himself to death. But He who suffered thus in the flesh was none other than the Living God —the Quickening Spirit. "He must rise," as well as die, according to the Scriptures.[8] Hence the question of the angel addressed to those who, forgetful of His former words, thought still to find their lifeless Master, though on the third day: "Why seek ye the *Living*[9] among the dead?"

[4] 2 Cor. xiii. 4.
[5] The distinction in this passage between the intrinsic and Divine personal vitality of Christ, and the application of the same quickening principle to the Church in grace, is clear and striking.
[6] John ii. 19.   [7] Acts ii. 24.   [8] John xx. 9.   [9] τὸν ζῶντα.

The divine Sonship of the crucified Jesus is thus affirmed by the event of His resurrection. The apostle's present subject does not lead him here beyond this particular view of the resurrection as a doctrine. Jesus, thus "justified in the Spirit," is declared to be the Lord of all. As such He is owned in the Church. "To us there is one Lord, Jesus Christ, *by whom* are all things."[1] As we are ourselves "by Him," so all true worship of the Father is by Him—all service, all faith, all hope to God-ward, is by Him. All gifts and measures of grace and blessing reach us by His means; a truth acknowledged in the following verse, "by whom (says the apostle) we have received grace and apostleship."

Having presented this supreme credential of His office, there follows next a statement of the scope and objects of His work. It was "among all the Gentiles" that He was to act. The end was the obedience of faith to God. But all the work was for the *name* of Jesus. The Lord having personally gone into the heavens, His name is, for faith, His own effective representative; and is thus given under heaven as the sole means of salvation among men.[2] God calls on man to obey *Himself* by thus receiving Jesus as the Lord. The Name of Jesus is, to the believer, the revelation of the living God. But verse 6 presents Jesus as Himself acting thus in calling and quickening at His will the chosen vessels of His grace.[3] They were "the called of Jesus Christ." The apostle well knew the meaning

---

[1] 1 Cor. viii. 6. [2] Acts iv. 12.
[3] Compare John v. 21, xv. 16, and x. *passim*.

of this, as himself a Christ-chosen and Christ-called vessel of Divine mercy.[4]

Verse 7 concludes the greeting. They were "beloved of God," and "called saints," or holy ones.[5] To be a *saint* is the eternal condition of the believer as accepted in the Beloved, seeing that he is sanctified, as well as washed and justified, in the name of the Lord Jesus, and by the Spirit of God.[6] All shared this holy title, and to all alike the Spirit addresses this Divine salutation of grace and peace —words which express the permanent aspect of God in Christ towards His people. For as grace gives them their true standing in His sight, so peace is the abiding condition of those whom God has called to the knowledge of Himself in Jesus, so long as they walk humbly in the faith. The nature and manner of the grace of God, and the strong foundation of that peace which "passeth knowledge," while it is freely preached to all, will be opened fully to our view as we proceed.

It is to be noted that the greetings in the Epistles are always from the Father and the Son, exclusive of the Holy Ghost. In the Revelation alone the Spirit is included;[7] and then, not as the "one Spirit,"[8] the Divine power of the Church's unity and fellowship in love, but as the seven-fold display of Omnipotent might—the seven spirits of God as the eternal and almighty Governor of His creation. But in the Epistles the Spirit is never presented as an object

---

[4] Acts ix.; 1 Tim. i. 16.
[5] Κλητοῖς ἁγίοις. Ephes. i. 6; 1 Cor. vi. 11; and i. 30.
[6] The subject of evangelical sanctity has been examined at some length in my *Notes on the Epistle to the Hebrews*, chap. ix. and x.
[7] Rev. i. 4. [8] Ephes. iv.

of our present worship.[9] He is always (even when not expressed by name) assumed to be *in* and *with* the redeemed people of God, both individually, and as collectively forming and abiding in the one body of Christ. Thus, in writing to Timothy or Titus, the same exclusive form of greeting is observed, since the Holy Ghost dwelt in them severally, even as He did in the Church collectively, whether at Rome, or elsewhere.[1]

Verses 8–15. The prosperous state of the Church at Rome was not only a cause of joyful thanksgiving to the apostle on their behalf; it had awakened in him also a longing wish to visit them. He had *heard* of their faith. His desire now was to be himself a witness of that faith, a partaker and a helper of their joy. This was a right desire—a genuine yearning of Christ in him towards his brethren—and in due time God would bring it to pass. Meanwhile, in the wisdom of His love, He finds a vent for the ardent zeal which filled the heart of His servant in the preparation of this marvellous Epistle. Doubtless, Paul would rather have at once visited them. Had he been allowed his earnest desire *then*, he would have deemed himself to be effectually furthering the Gos-

---

[9] Compare 1 Cor. viii. 6.

[1] Let it be observed once for all, to avoid misapprehension, that inasmuch as in the unity of the Divine Nature the Holy Ghost is truly *God*, to worship Him can never be *wrong* in principle. But, since, in the gracious operation of the Divine counsels, the Spirit now acts in an especial character as the revealer and glorifier of Jesus —of the Father in the Son—He is rather to be known and reckoned on as the living and indwelling source of all true worship and communion, than regarded *objectively* by our faith. Hence, no doubt, the peculiar structure of 1 Cor. viii. 6, while in chap. xii. of the same Epistle we have so full and detailed a view of His sovereignty, which is exercised in governing, as well as animating the body of Christ.

pel. And so, indeed, he would. But the God of *all* grace had a more extensive work for him to do, and one of incalculably wider extent in blessing.

He had wished to be with them, to give and to receive a present refreshment and comfort.[2] Moreover, he desired to impart some special gift[3] for their fuller establishment in the faith. But the thought of Divine love and wisdom, which found its faint reflection in the heart of the apostle, was wider and more wise toward His Church (not at Rome only) than could be fully compassed by the active ministry of His servant then. The thwarted desires of Paul gave occasion to the Spirit of God to add to the other Scriptures of truth, this full and comprehensive summary of Christian doctrine—to present thus to the entire Church a gift, not of present, passing effect only, but which should build up, and feed, and instruct the saints, to the end of their appointed pilgrimage of faith and patience in the world. Moreover, by giving utterance, in this exordium, to the longings of Christ's love in his own spirit towards these unknown brethren, he was unconsciously preparing an after-blessing to himself. It was after having thus prepossessed the affections of their hearts, that he found a welcome as from God, when,

---

[2] "By the mutual faith," &c., verse 12. With this may be compared, the similar sentiment expressed in 2 Cor. ii. 24. It is most instructive to observe how genuine grace leads even an inspired apostle to avoid and disclaim any thing like magisterial assumption. For his *doctrine* he claims an unreserved acceptance as the ministry of God, while *personally* he is a partaker of a "common" faith and hope. He is thus as capable of receiving refreshment through the faith and grace of those to whom he ministered, as of furthering their joy by the faithful discharge of his own stewardship. Where God is truly owned, His *order* reigns together with His peace. Comp. Matt. xxiii. 8; Philemon 20; Eph. v. 21; Phil. ii. 3–5; 1 Peter v. 3.

[3] χάρισμα.

towards the close of his career, on drawing nigh to that city as a prisoner in bonds, his tried and wearied spirit found in the cordial greetings of those who came forth from the city of the oppressor to meet him, as not ashamed of his chain, a cheering expression of that comfort with which God knows how to comfort them that are cast down.[4]

Verse 16 brings within reach the proper subject of the Epistle—the Gospel.[5] He was not ashamed of it—it was rather his glory and his joy.[6] He was God's servant; and that which he ministered was the *power* of God, as a Saviour, to every one who believed. He *knew* it to be this. For the Gospel which he ministered to others he had first proved and tasted in his own soul. It was in the joyful assurance of personal reconciliation that he spake as an ambassador of Christ. Filled with a worthy sense of his vocation, and sustained in cloudless peace of soul as one who rested upon God's unchanging mercy, he was indifferent to the special field in which he might be called to labour. For it was God who appointed him his sphere of service, and who, leading him from place to place as a triumphant herald of His Christ, made manifest the power of His knowledge thus in every place.[7] If, therefore, he came to Rome, he would come as the bearer of a truth which, though it was the only word of life and saving wisdom, was the only knowledge utterly unknown in that great metropolis of human pride and power. He need not, therefore, be ashamed, who went about

---

[4] Acts xxviii. 14, 15.
[5] The words τοῦ X. are omitted in all the best MSS.
[6] Gal. vi. 14; Acts xx. 24. [7] 2 Cor. ii. 14.

with the consciousness that where he went, he was dispersing through the city of death, the pure and plenteous rivers of the water of life. While ready to become the servant of all, yet, when he contemplates the end and glory of his mission, he finds himself upon a vantage-ground of Divine truth and power, of which he well might make his boast. But, in the exercise of his commission, he must follow the order of Divine appointment. His testimony is accordingly addressed "to the Jew first, and also to the Greek."

The Gospel is the message of God's grace to sinners. As such, it is unlimited in its range and objects. It is addressed to *man* as under sin. But, though Israel had stumbled at God's elect stone, and, by rejecting Jesus Christ come in the flesh, had forfeited, as far as lay in them, the national blessings of the New Covenant; still, to *them*, as the natural heirs of the promises, Christ was ever to be *first* proclaimed. Not any longer, indeed, as Israel's Messiah merely, but as God's appointed heir of all things;[8] as His Righteousness and free Salvation, offered, in the fulness of absolute mercy, to all, without distinction, whether near or afar off.[9] The Jew was now, not less than the uncircumcised alien, to be addressed as a lost *man*. He is a sinner, ruined under the law's condemnation. It is to such that Christ is preached, both as the Lamb of God, the appointed sacrifice for sin, and as the end of the law for righteousness. Circumcision is of no avail: their souls are forfeit, and their freely offered ransom is the precious blood of Jesus.

[8] Heb. i. 2.   [9] Eph. ii. 17.

It is not, therefore, now, the preëminence of the Jew as the dispenser of blessing to the Gentile—himself being first established in the full possession of the promises made to the fathers,—that is to be asserted. This will be exhibited in due time, as the apostle teaches further on.[1] But now the Jew, if blessed at all, must find his blessing in the Gospel of the *grace* of God, which speaks to man *as* man—speaks, therefore, to all, though the long-suffering of Divine mercy sends the message first to the natural seed of Abraham. By this is at once displayed both the faithfulness of the God of Jacob, and the marvellous manner and extent of the grace thus ministered—a grace that had its beginning exactly at the place where the chiefest sin had been displayed: "That repentance and remission of sins should be preached in His name among all nations," but, "*beginning* at Jerusalem."[2]

Verse 17. "For therein," &c. Grace was God's primal promise to fallen man. But as the world grew on in wickedness that promise was forgotten, with the God who spake it, by all but the faithful few of God's elect. It is now republished, no longer as a distant promise, but as an effected work. God shows no longer indistinctly what He *will* be, but plainly what He *is*. The Gospel is the revelation of God's righteousness as a Saviour. Christ *died* to justify Him as the God of saving mercy. He brought thus to its close the work which the Father had given Him to do. He *lived* the season of His earthly days, to glorify, by pure obedience, the God from whom He had come forth—thus for ever condemning man

[1] *Infra*, chap. xi.   [2] Luke xxiv. 47.

as a sinner, by His own display of perfect human righteousness as the devoted Servant of Jehovah. He obeyed unto *death*, and by dying made a sacrificial end of sin, that the satisfied will of the blessed God might become the direct means of salvation to His believing people. The effect therefore of the resurrection of Christ is to bring in everlasting righteousness, by revealing openly the triumphant Victor over sin and death. The believing sinner thus becomes a righteous man, by accepting, in Christ, the free gift of *Divine* righteousness. In this two-fold sense the Gospel is the revelation of the righteousness of God. It vindicates, in judgment, the holiness of the God of grace; while it places upon the sinner who believes the perfect title of the Just One Himself.

But nature is born blind, and cannot of itself discern what God reveals. The righteousness of God is manifested, not to the natural senses, but to the faith of His elect. Moreover, it is from, or by, faith,[3] *i. e.* it is communicated in the way of testimony and promise, and finds its resting-place in the hearts of those alone in whom the word preached is mixed with faith.[4] It is the quickening power of the Holy Ghost that effects this. A sinner's conversion is, in other words, an act of *God*, who works, not by enlightening the natural faculties, but by Himself shining in the heart to give the light of the knowledge of His own glory in the face of Jesus Christ.[5] Faith is God's gift, as much as the living righteous-

---

[3] ἐκ πίστεως εἰς πίστιν. "Faith-wise and unto (or, for) faith," may perhaps nearly express the meaning.
[4] Heb. iv. 2. [5] 2 Cor. iv. 6.

ness on which that faith lays hold. "Unto you it *is given* on the behalf of Christ, not only to believe on Him, but also," &c.[6] The word thus received is spirit and is life; God being thus known—known as a Saviour, and that through and in the Lord Jesus Christ. But this knowledge is eternal life;[7] and so it is written, "The just shall *live* by faith."[8]

At verse 18, the apostle commences his general argument for the demonstration of the riches of Divine wisdom and glory in the Gospel, by reviewing the past history and the actual condition of *man* as God's creature. This is done, first, generally, by contemplating him according to the original and natural responsibilities of the creature. The same object is then (chaps. ii. and iii.) placed in another and a stronger light, by an investigation of the nature and result of that distinctive standing which attaches to the Jew by virtue of the legal covenant.

Verses 18, &c. "For the wrath of God is revealed," &c. The Gospel draws aside the veil which had wrapped the nations of the world in natural ignorance and doubt; and discovers in the light of the risen Christ what the true position of the world is as already judged of God.[9]

Divine wrath is revealed from heaven against

---

[6] Phil. i. 29; comp. Acts xvi. 14, and Eph. ii. 8.   [7] John xvii. 3.
[8] Ὁ δὲ δίκαιος ἐκ πίστεως ζήσεται. This quotation is thrice repeated in the New Testament, each time, apparently, with a different force, according to the context:—

In Gal. iii. 11, it is cited as a peremptory witness against the thought of justification by law. In Heb. x. 38, its application is plainly not to the original reception of life (as quoted above in the text), but to the continuance of that life, its growth and energies, as dependent upon the daily exercise of the once-justifying faith— the living, by the faith of the Son of God, on the part of one who died daily. (Gal. ii. 20.) Compare John vi. 57; 1 Pet. i. 5, &c.
[9] Compare John iii. 18, 36.

human sin. This was, in itself, no new revelation. It was the reässertion of a truth which men had known from the beginning. The wrath of God had acted in vengeance more than once of old; but now the eternal principle of Divine judgment against sin is anew stated, in conjunction with the testimony to the grace which delivers from it. Moreover, in the administration of the Divine government of the world, it was in rare examples only that this principle had been openly illustrated. God had *winked* in time past,[1] as the same apostle says, while darkness remained as yet unbroken by the shining of the Light of life. But now He suffers no more the nations to walk in their own ways, but commandeth *all* men *everywhere* to repent. The Gospel is thus both a startling and emphatic warning of danger, and the faithful assurance of deliverance and safety to those who accept the warning.

It deals with man as he ever has been (as fallen) in *God's* sight, but as now shown to *himself* in the mirror of his own conscience, through the word of Divine truth.[2] His condition is now declared to be one of natural and entire alienation from God. He is regarded as ungodly and profane, as *simply wicked*, and that by the necessity of his birth. He is sinful by nature, and therefore, naturally, "a child of wrath,"[3] seeing that God can only recompense sin

[1] Acts xvii.
[2] It may be necessary to warn some readers against the common notion, that in the present chapter the apostle is drawing a picture of Roman manners merely. No doubt the qualities of our corrupted nature were displaying themselves in fearful distinctness in that city, at the time when he thus wrote; but it is man *as a species* whose apostasy he is here describing, and not the result of that apostasy in a particular instance.
[3] Eph. ii. 3.

by judgment. As a creature, he has utterly fallen from his true place; coming short of the glory of the Creator, who is glorified only by the obedient dependence of the creature on Himself. Failing in this, man's life is but a perpetual dishonour to the Creator, and a continual provocation of Divine holiness to that "wrath," which is the natural expression of God's hatred of all sin. These things had been but partially revealed before. The process of human probation had been incomplete until the advent and rejection of the Son of God in the flesh. But now the darkness was past, and the true light had shone forth, discovering *reprobation* to be the fixed and eternal estimate, on God's part, of what fallen man really is.

But this case of human reprobation is stated now in detail.[4] The wrath of God is directed against *all* human ungodliness and unrighteousness, and that on the ground of their holding the truth in unrighteousness.[5] There was originally in every man a natural knowledge of the God who had created him. But this truth, together with the claim which it involves of general obedience, has from the first been practically disregarded by the world. The high thoughts of men, bent on their own pleasure, erect themselves against the truth of God. *Ignorance* is not the *primary* cause of human opposition to God. It is the instinctive force of evil desire, which leads man to gratify the nearer and more importunate lusts of the

---

[4] Verses 18–23.
[5] τῶν τὴν ἀλήθειαν ἐν ἀδικίᾳ κατεχόντων. The versions differ in their representation of these words. On the whole, perhaps the common version is to be preferred, though the sense of hindrance or obstruction appears likewise to be involved.

flesh and of the mind, without reference to the will of God. But to act independently of God is practically to deny Him. Atheism is involved, in principle, in the very first departure of the creature from the position of simple dependence upon the Creator. It is the assertion of an independent will, and thus the exercise, as it were, of an independent *life*. But man is God's creature—his life is God's breath. Hence, to live without God—in defiance or even in forgetfulness of God—is virtually Atheism. It is the heart-Atheism of the fool, who, under many forms of outward profession, still says within *his heart*, "There is no God."[6]

But this is utterly without excuse. God has not left Himself without witness, that man should say, "Who and what is He?" Creation is for ever the universal witness of His power and Godhead. The evidence of God[7] as Himself filling all things in creative and sustaining power, is present to every eye and to every heart, which is not fenced by the madness of willing ignorance against these manifestations of the Divine glory. Accordingly (verse 21), the knowledge of God which was originally common to mankind is charged against the idolatrous Gentiles as the very essence of their guilt. "When they *knew* God, they glorified Him not as God," &c. The apostasy of man from God is an action of the will. The sense of dependence, of grateful homage and allegiance to God-ward, was what man could no longer brook, when once awakened by Satan to a consciousness of his *own* powers. This was the case originally, when

---

[6] Ps. xiv., liii.   [7] τὸ γνωστὸν τοῦ Θεοῦ.

in Eden, ere yet the fatal transgression had been done, the poison of the serpent's tongue had already corrupted the pure mind of God's creature by the suggestion of self-secured, self-dependent happiness. "Ye shall be as gods!" was the bait then offered by the tempter to a creature yet unfallen. And such continues still to be the dream which amuses, while it *proves* the heart-sickness of the natural man. Deluded by their vain imaginings, men readily forget, while dreaming thus, that the powers and the very will itself, which foolishly affects an independence of the Creator, exist and continue only by the sufferance of God.

The corrupt desires of the will of man, acting upon his imagination, and reäcted on by a darkened conscience, produced the varied forms of idolatrous worship; for the same heart which is by nature fundamentally averse from holiness, is constitutionally prone to religious observance. There is an innate and indwelling consciousness of personal insufficiency, which forces man, although reluctantly, to own some power mightier than himself. A god, in some shape, is a principal necessity of man. His natural desire, in his first apostasy from truth, is a god after his *own heart*. The image of himself is the outward expression of this. But the tendency of a mind once alienated from God is ever downwards. Birds, and quadrupeds, and creeping things display, when represented in idolatrous imagery, the progressive stages of that deterioration and debasement of the poor godless mind of nature, which, when left to the unrestrained working of its own tendencies, is found to contain in itself no counteractive principle strong enough to arrest its descent into the lowest depths of infatuation and dishonour.

But when once the human will has begun to act deliberately apart from God, the reign of *ignorance* has already commenced. God alone is Light, and truth, if obeyed, can only lead to Him. His will being disregarded, the imaginations[8] of the human heart become substituted for the *wisdom* of God. But these imaginations not only act as an interceptive barrier to exclude the light and blessing of Divine knowledge; they become themselves the guide and directory of human action—conscience, meanwhile, being too weak of itself to force its way through the mists of human thought into the presence of Truth—of God, though it may, and does, act in a measure as a check upon the lawlessness of the natural will. Hence the Gentiles are said to have the *understanding* darkened,[9] and their ignorance is affirmed to be the cause of their moral alienation from the life of God—the hardness[1] of their hearts being the true cause of all the varied manifestations of evil which the course of human life presents.

But is man, thus sunk, aware of his condition? Nay, it is while professing themselves to be wise that the profoundness of their folly most appears.[2] The human mind *being* in darkness through its voluntary departure from God, who alone is Light, man's course lies naturally in the endless circle of folly and of sin. He is ever seeking, but never finding—aware of his poverty, yet dreaming continually of recovery and

---

[8] διαλογισμοί.   [9] Eph. iv. 18.   [1] πώρωσις.
[2] Φάσκοντες εἶναι σοφοὶ ἐμωράνθησαν. The peculiar force of the word φάσκοντες is rather to be felt than explained.

prosperity as coming from himself. Rooted, rush-like, in the mire of a corrupted nature, he grows up only to be withered by the breath of truth. Running in the laborious career of his vanity through all the perplexed and defiled paths of evil and madness,[3] he exhibits in himself every phase and variety of hopeless sin and cureless misery, so long as he remains in ignorance of Christ.

Verses 24, 25, display the retributive judgment, even now, of God the Holy One on His debased image. "*Wherefore* also God gave them up," &c.; filthiness and dishonour being the unchecked and ripened fruit of the lusts of nature, which man had chosen as his guide, in preference to the will of God. They had changed His truth into a lie, putting the creature into the place of the Creator. The utter debasement of the creature, and that through the development of its own perverted will, follows, as the sentence of Divine wisdom upon the self-dishonoured workmanship of His hands.

Verses 26, 27. "For this cause," &c. The things here spoken of are clearly regarded as the "recompense," even now, of the error of the creature in departing from the Creator. The world is thus represented as under a judicial bondage of sin and dishonour.[4] Men eat the fruit of their own ways— sometimes pleasant to the depraved taste of corrupted nature, but with prospect of Divine and eternal judgment at the end. The very lusts which govern and torment the slaves of sin are, as it were, the

[3] Eccles. ix. 3.
[4] But this should not be confounded, as is sometimes done, with the positive revelation of the wrath of God, as declared in *v.* 18.

earnest and token of that wrath of God, which, already revealed from heaven in the Gospel, will yet deal with the ungodliness and wickedness of unrepentant sinners *after* death.[5]

It is most needful to observe, that the extreme cases of unnatural sin are put here as God's *general verdict* on the condition of the human family, as collectively apostate. The existence of such enormities does not simply condemn the perpetrators of the specific crimes. The things themselves are but surface-spots, by which is indicated the condition, morally, of the mass to which they are found attached. The lusts of the *human heart* are here in question— not as isolated phenomena of wickedness, but as the judicial alternative of dishonour and uncleanness in which *man*, as apostate, is now placed, and wherein he is regarded from heaven as an object of wrath, because of his departure from the only presence where purity and honour may be found. Every attempt, therefore, on man's part, to beautify or purify himself, save by a return, in the faith of the Gospel, to God as a *Saviour*, is but a fighting against God — a practical refusal to own His truth and righteousness in thus awarding him this dishonoured place. But this is only to arm himself as an adversary against Him who is an avenger of His name according to the unknown power of His wrath.[6]

Let me add another word on this point. Divine mercy may act, and doubtless will act, through the death of Christ, in a measure far beyond and above all our thoughts; but with respect to the state of the *nations* of the world, it is that of hopeless apostasy

[5] Heb. ix. 27.   [6] Ps. xc. 11.

from God—shut up under sin—incapable, therefore, if left to themselves, of ever becoming free. God will gather from them, by the Gospel of His grace, a people for His name,[7] but their natural condition is one of willing alienation from Him. As it is elsewhere written, "The *whole world* lieth in wickedness," or "in the wicked one."[8]

Verses 28–32. "And even as they did not like to retain God in their knowledge," &c. The corrupted human will has indeed thrown off the yoke of God, but to recover their lost position is impossible to men. They are the slaves of a reprobate *mind*. Now, the mind of man cannot be light and dark at the same time; it is an active principle, which works out its ends according to the direction and bias under which it moves. But that bias is *fixed* for evil, and that, as we have seen, by the judgment of God. He has *given them up* to work an evil work. They are *filled* with evil. Not partially depraved, but filled with all iniquity. Most solemn, most fearful truth! But they also *know* that it is even so. Conscience affords light enough to keep perpetually before the mind the dark and uneasy dread of an unsatisfied responsibility towards God. Moreover, the eye is ever in presence of the material witness of the Divine glory;[9] yet it seeks not good, but evil. The prevalence and extent of moral corruption are known and reckoned on by man (all human legislation proceeds on the recognition of this), but acquiesced in, and furthered unceasingly, by the natural course and progress of human society (verse 32).

The moral light which, wherever Christianity is

[7] Acts xv. 14; Col. i. 23.   [8] 1 John v. 19.   [9] Ps. xix. 3.

outwardly professed, relieves the dark picture of human depravity presented in this chapter, to the eye of an actual observer of life as it now is, only serves to augment the weight of man's responsibility, and to bring nearer the threatenings of Divine wrath. For God is not glorified *as God*, except by an obedient recognition of His truth. Apostate *nature* refused to Him its grateful homage as the Creator of the world. Apostate *Christianity* (which is nature still, though under another name), while it outwardly acknowledges the mystery of godliness, evades the pressure of the Spirit's testimony on the conscience, and therefore disregards the saving ministry of grace. That which the world itself accepts and patronizes can have no power to deliver from the world.[1] The blood of Jesus is a fountain of healing and refreshment to the new-born soul alone.

The doctrine of this chapter, coupled with the same apostle's warning in 2 Tim. iii. and iv., cannot be too frequently kept before the minds of all who love the truth at a time when, under the infatuating power of him that deceiveth the whole world,[2] men are endeavouring, by a false combination of diluted evangelical doctrine with scientific and æsthetic culture, to raise man's fallen nature to a satisfactory condition, in forgetfulness or willing ignorance of what is written as to the total unprofitableness of the flesh. But fragments of Divine truth, borrowed from the word of God, and used, either as a decorative polish, or a corroborative aid, in strengthening and beautifying the structure of human society, do not alter the intrinsic nature and character of that to which

[1] Gal. i. 4.   [2] Rev. xii. 9.

they are applied. Social science is not saving truth; nor is the end of the Spirit's ministry the civilization of mankind. Such a use of Scripture forms, on the contrary, the most conclusive evidence of the world's guilt, not now simply as naturally apostate, but as denying practically the Lord that bought it. For the truth of redemption and grace, thus perverted from its proper use, becomes the means of perpetuating and commending the very things which that truth, *where obeyed*, has already destroyed.

I do not dwell upon the specifications of human iniquity with which this solemn chapter closes. They form the leading features of fallen human character, in which the Spirit of God vainly seeks to find any good thing,[8] while making inventory of that which fills the hearts of men. The victory of the depraved will of man over the light of conscience, to the perpetual dishonour and provocation of the Divine glory, is strikingly put in the concluding verse.

[8] Chap. vii. 18.

CHAPTER II.

THE broad picture of apostate human character, which has just been presented to our view, contains within it, representatively, the whole family of man. Religious perversity and moral pravity are found to result universally as the fruit of an unregenerate will. But although incapable of serving worthily the God who made him, and willingly ignorant and heedless of the solemn nature of his own responsibilities, man is yet an eager censor of his fellow-sinner.

This crowning proof of our natural obliquity is noticed for especial condemnation at the commencement of the present chapter, in which the eternal principles of Divine government are solemnly asserted in their reference to human conduct, considered in itself and apart from the specialties of covenanted grace and mercy.

Accordingly, there is pronounced, in the opening verse, an unqualified denunciation of the blind and foolish arrogance which is implied in *every instance* of human censure. Having been himself arraigned Divinely as a sinner, man is for ever incompetent to judge his fellow. For by so doing he would be passing sentence upon himself. The sins expressed by name at the end of the preceding chapter are but the varied phenomena under which *sin* itself, as indwelling in man, discovers itself to the outward eye. But it is clear that a righteous judgment upon human sin can only be pronounced by one who is himself exempt from blame.[1] It is then a thing altogether inexcusable that man, who is naturally sinful, should presumptuously occupy the seat of judgment. But because the heart is deceitful, as well as evil, men do in fact constantly bring themselves under the double condemnation of sin and of hypocrisy, by judging their neighbour, while themselves continuing in sin.

But (verse 2) although man's judgment of his fellow be but an aggravation of his own iniquity, there *is* a judgment which is according to righteousness—and God is the judge. We are sure that His judgment is according to *truth* against evil-doers. For He is a God of truth, and without iniquity; justice and equity are in His very nature.[2] God *is* holy; and as such He *is* against sin. His face is, therefore, against the *workers* of iniquity. But this last definition comprises man as a species, Jew and Gentile being alike included in the review of man, morally considered, as standing in relation to the everlasting principles of God's holiness.

Verses 3–5. "And thinkest thou this, O man," &c. The question here introduced presupposes in the man addressed an outward acknowledgment, at least, of God; and as such it forms a sort of connecting link in the apostle's argument, which is presently to pass

---

[1] The judgment of sin in the Church of God is wholly another matter. *There* it is not man in his natural state (ψυχικός) judging his fellow, and thus taking God's place in the midst of his own natural uncleanness. It is God himself accomplishing, through the obedience of man as spiritual (πνευματικός), as a new creature, *His own will*, who, because He is the Holy One, will not and cannot tolerate evil in His house.   [2] Deut. xxxii. 4.

from the general subject of human pravity and incompetency to judge, to the special instance of the Jew as the professed disciple and keeper of Divine truth. Self-righteousness is ever the parent of censoriousness.[3] But while noticing this, it is important to keep clearly in view the undiminished breadth of application which belongs both to this verse and to those which follow, aimed as they are at impenitent, self-sustained religiousness, under whatever outward form it may appear. Now an assumption of the place of judgment presumes an assent, on the part of the individual judging, to the truth of God as the *righteous* God. But is it really thus? Nay, the judge is also himself, in *his* way, the evil-doer. His own responsibilities to God must first be met, before he can be in a condition to act as judge in another's case.

This censorious spirit, then, is doubly offensive to God. First, it thrusts a sinful creature, himself under the sentence of death, into the place of that God who is ready to call for *his* account, and to award him his portion according to his deeds. It is, secondly, a flat denial of the testimony of the Spirit, which concludes *all* under sin. The man who judges is thus unconsciously recording against himself the very sentence which hereafter will be pronounced, out of his own mouth, against the despiser of God's truth.[4] And so the word, as to this, is, "Judge not, that ye be not judged." "With what measure ye mete, it shall be measured to you again."[5] "He shall have judgment without mercy, who showed no mercy," &c.[6] Yet such is the deceitfulness of the

[3] Luke xviii. 9.   [4] Matt. xii. 37.   [5] Matt. vii. 1, 2.   [6] Jas. ii. 13.

natural heart, that, notwithstanding these solemn and repeated warnings, men do still habitually think that they will escape the judgment of God. It is the lurking presence of this thought in the secret of their hearts that supports and sustains them in their evil way. For it is the habit of man to think for God. Because he is himself deceived by the spirit that now worketh in the children of disobedience,[7] he flatters his darkened conscience into an approving witness on his own behalf, by the severity with which he judges evil when it presents itself objectively to his notice in the ways of others. By thus trusting to his own heart, he spends his life in a delusive dream, and at the end of his days is as a fool.[8]

Nor is it folly only that is thus evinced. The utter *baseness*, as well as ignorance, of corrupted nature here makes itself conspicuously manifest. God is despised on account of His goodness! Proclaiming mercy to the penitent forsaker of his sins, His gracious testimonies are neglected by a generation which is pure in their own eyes, although unwashed from their uncleanness.[9] The riches of His goodness, and forbearance, and long-suffering, instead of leading the natural man to repentance, only turns to the increase of human sin. Because the sentence of recorded judgment seems to linger in its execution, the unrepentant heart of man becomes more and more emboldened in an evil work.[1] A lengthened impunity in the pursuit of men's natural desires begets a feeling of security,[2] which in its effect pre-

---

[7] Eph. ii. 2.   [8] Tit. iii. 3; Eph. ii. 2, 3; Prov. xiv. 12.
[9] Prov. xxx. 12.   [1] Eccles. viii. 11.   [2] 2 Pet. iii. 3, 4.

pares the world for its last fatal slumber, which the advent of the Judge alone will break.[3] Men live a life of self-pleasing at the expense of Divine long-suffering and kindness,[4] wilfully indifferent, meanwhile, to the testimonies which warn, and to the occasional acts of judgment which give yet more emphatic earnest of that day of reckoning which is to come.

But this is to treasure up wrath against themselves. God is not mocked, although He draw out long His patient sufferance of human evil. He must one day remind men, in a manner not to be mistaken, that truth and power are His own, and only His. He will convince incredulous sinners by the epiphany in glory of the Lord of judgment, that a life of carnal security is a life of proud rebellion against God; that to speak and to act as from themselves, is to cast off dependence upon Him who formed them for himself; that the utterance of the natural counsels of the heart, according to the assumed privilege of man's proper liberty, is a contumacious gainsaying of the word of Divine truth; and that their pleadings for themselves have been hard speeches[5] against the God in whom they live, and move, and have their being. There is a day fixed for the righteous judgment of God. He will be just in His award. Woe *then* to the man whose knowledge of Divine righteousness has to be learned through the sentence of eternal judgment, because he would not hearken to the voice of mercy in the day of patience, when God prayed him by His messengers to be at peace with Him.[6]

---

[3] 1 Thess. v. 2, 3.
[4] χρηστότης.
[5] Jude 11, 15.
[6] 2 Cor. v. 20.

Verses 6–10. God will render to every man according to his deeds. To those who have sought Him, He will then *show* himself to be a rewarder, even as already He is thus known by faith in the souls that wait on Him.[7] It will be noticed, that the children of God are here described, not with reference to the grace which has begotten them, but according to their moral characteristics as led of the Spirit. Taught divinely the intrinsic vanity of all that is corruptible, they seek for glory, honour, and incorruptibility,[8] in the day of God. It is the walk of faith which seems here to be generally described, without any dispensational limitation, though the objects specified are more distinctly set before the Christian as a risen man in Christ.[9]

It shall be well with the righteous in that day. To those, on the other hand, who have refused God, and despised His grace, He will then show himself to *be* God, and that vengeance belongeth unto Him. The character of such is thus described in verse 8: "To them that are contentious,[1] and do not obey the truth, but obey unrighteousness." They are contentious! The desires of the natural mind are in perpetual opposition to the will of God. Life passed in ignorance

[7] Heb. xi. 6, 26.
[8] ἀφθαρσία, as in 1 Cor. xv. 42, 50, &c. That which by the resurrection of Jesus was distinctly brought to light, (2 Tim. i. 10,) had been the hope of faith from the beginning. (Compare Luke xx. 38.)
[9] Col. iii. 1, 2; 2 Cor. iv. 17, 18.
[1] ἐξ ἐριθείας, "of contention," as contrasted with those who are ἐκ πίστεως, or "of faith," as a characteristic distinction. If, as is insisted by some modern scholars, we are to refer the above word to ἔριθος rather than to ἔρις, the expression in the text will be, "those who are factious or self-seeking"—morally the sentiments are near akin. I prefer, however, to adhere in this passage to the more usual interpretation, the contrast stated in the text being between the patient steadfastness of faith, and the petulant insubjection of the unregenerate will.

and unbelief, is a continual striving against God—the carnal mind is enmity against Him.[2] The test of this enmity is the word of truth. Man naturally refuses obedience to that word, because it is the declared expression of a will, to which the whole course of fallen nature stands opposed.

And now let us remark, further, that wherever Divine truth is declared, a man must either be its servant or its adversary. A neutral condition is an impossible thing. To *disobey* the truth is to *obey* unrighteousness. "He that is not for me is against me" is the word of the Incarnate Truth Himself. Unbelief, though nominally a negative thing, is really a positive and active sin. If I do not believe God's truth, it is because I *do* believe Satan's lie, which deceives the heart of the world; persuading men, whose present lives are without God, that they will fare well at the last, albeit the wrath of God is revealed in Scripture as awaiting all who do not repent and believe the Gospel.

Unbelief is the preference of self to God. The promptings of a fallen and corrupt nature are accepted and obeyed in preference to the voice of God. Unbelief is, therefore, a deliberate decision of the will. It is the taking up a position, apart from God, in which the soul seeks its rest in the creature—in the world.[3] The positive testimonies of the word of God are accordingly discredited and disregarded, in proportion usually to the vigour and activity of the natural will, and men's actual enjoyment of present things. Smitten and exhausted nature, worn down by disease, or wearied by long-tried experience of

[2] Chap. viii. 7.   [3] Luke xii. 15–21.

earthly vanity, is sometimes tamed into seeming subjection to the word of God. But a reluctant acquiescence in Divine truth, only so far as its recognition is commended by one's own sensations and experience, is a very different thing from *faith*. The word may act even distinctly as a mirror on a man's conscience, when brought to bear immediately upon his practical life; but it is a mirror which, when withdrawn, leaves blank the space which should be filled with God. The heart has no willing capacity for truth while man remains in his natural state: his affections ever tend to other aims than God. But this heart-preference of the creature is itself enmity against the Creator. Hence, he that will be the friend of the world, is declared to be the enemy of God.[4] And God will rid Him of His adversaries in due time. He endures with *much* long-suffering the vessels of wrath, but they are fitted for destruction at the end.[5]

The judgment of God having for its object man as a creature under responsibility to Him, Jew and Gentile find their common level here. There is no respect of persons with God. But there is a difference, and that a wide one, between the Jew and the Gentile, when regarded relatively to each other. The Gentile is a sinner, rebelling, through the depraved will of his nature, against God as manifested in His works, and witnessed to in the sinner's conscience. The Jew is a rebel against the same God as the Lawgiver. He is a sinner against light especially revealed—a breaker of covenant. By the law, therefore, which he has received, he must be judged in that day.

[4] Jas. iv. 4.   [5] Chap. ix. 22.

But is the case so hopeless for the Jew? The promise of the Law is life to the doer of the Law—to the doer of good,—as it is written: "The man that doeth them shall live in them."[6] But does the Law confer upon its subject any power of obedience to its precepts? By no means. The Law defines the will of God, and leaves the man whom it addresses to prove his claim on the Divine favour in the way of obedience. But in this he fails—inevitably fails—through the very necessity of his condition as naturally sinful. The Law thus becomes a minister of death and a witness of sin. External conformity does not reach the case; God's question is with the heart. A fair show may be made in the flesh, while the inward part remains as ever. The imaginations —yea, *all* the imaginations of the thoughts of man's heart continue to bear their unaltered character of evil[7] beneath the outward covering of legal profession. And it is those "secrets" which God will judge, by Jesus Christ, in the appointed day.

Verses 11–16. "For there is no respect of persons," &c. Human conduct will be impartially estimated in the presence of the righteous Judge. God will judge *sin*—in Jew and Gentile alike. But sinners will themselves, moreover, become witnesses to their own condemnation. The professed subjection of the Jew to the Law will prove the fact of his disobedience in the day when his heart's secret is disclosed; while the conduct of the Gentile who has avoided any moral evil of which the Jew may have been guilty, will constitute a separate verdict of judgment against the outward Jew. Those, on

[6] Gal. iii.   [7] Gen. vi. 5.

the other hand, who, in ignorance of the letter of Divine commandment, have sinned against such light as they have had, will "perish" by the sentence of the Holy One, without the special condemnation of the Law. "The *work* of the Law"[8] is said (verse 15) to be written on the Gentile heart. As a child is known by his doings, whether his work be fair and whether it be right,[9] so a Gentile, though untaught by Moses, has a monitor within him, by whose guidance he may ever keep the way of moral honesty and right.

This is a general principle of truth connected with the doctrine of conscience. There is that in every man which indicates the broad distinctions of right and wrong with clearness to his mind, and which makes him know the quality of the actions he performs. But the language of the apostle in this passage is susceptible of a more especial and confined interpretation. While it is generally true that conscience is to every man a faithful witness of moral good and evil, the force of the comparison is more apparently to show that, whereas the Law, by conferring nothing upon its subject but the obligation and responsibility of obedience, left the Jew without hope on failure of that obedience, Gentiles[1] individually might become subject to the fear of God, and so produce the fruits of obedience, such as the letter of the Law enjoins, to the shame and deeper condemnation of the carnal Jew. A Gentile was, as

---

[8] There is a manifest difference in principle between the force of this expression and that of the New Covenant promise recited in Heb. viii. 10.   [9] Prov. xx. 11.

[1] It is to be remarked that in the original, the word rendered "the Gentiles," in verse 14, is without the article. "Οταν γάρ ἔθνη τὰ μὴ νόμον ἔχοντα, κ. λ. ῎Εθνη seems to be used here nearly in the sense of ἐθνικοί, meaning simply men of other nations than Israel.

a man, capable individually of Divine favour. The grace and power of God, though it regarded the nation of Israel as its especial object, could, and doubtless did, work upon Gentile hearts in individual cases. Neither Job nor his friends were of Israel, and yet the tables of the Law could have added little to their knowledge of the truth of God. The case of the sons of Rechab,[2] where the moral obligation of a parental command, receiving its obedient recognition at the hands of those who knew not the law of Moses, is avouched in special evidence of Judah's sin, may also have been in the mind of the apostle while writing these words.[3]

[2] Jer. xxxv.
[3] The passage above noticed is by general acknowledgment one of no ordinary difficulty, and has received very opposite interpretations, according to the widely-different views of some who have attempted to expound it. But, though difficult, I cannot regard it as really *obscure*, to one who attentively considers the drift of the Apostle's argument. His question is as to the positive and ultimate adjudication of reward or punishment, according to the unerring decision of Divine truth, in the coming day. The Jewish legalist is accordingly stript of his factitious pretensions, and warned that, as a law-breaker, he may be confounded in that day, not only by the righteous verdict of the Law, which he has failed to keep, and by which, therefore, he is condemned already, but even by the example of superior morality on the part of those who never knew the Law. The Gentile, on the other hand, will stand or fall, according to the perfect sentence of the "Judge of all the world."

Such being the nature of the argument, the specialties of Divine election, redemption, and imputed righteousness, though manifestly involved in every instance of eventual acceptance with God, do not here come distinctly into view.

While, therefore, it is an obvious as well as *ruinous* error, to attempt to extract from this passage, in flat contradiction of the Apostle's doctrine in the sequel, a justification of the anti-Christian idea that human merit can, in any sense or under any circumstances, avail as a title to Divine acceptance, it is needful also to demur to the forced and unnatural construction put upon the passage by some evangelical interpreters, who seem to overlook the real drift of the passage, and in their anxiety to maintain sound doctrine, as they suppose, neglect or lose sight of the expression at the close of *v.* 14, where the Gentiles are said to be "a law unto themselves."

As to the difficulty which such writers find in accepting the com-

Verses 17-20, which present a life portrait of the legal Jew, are well worthy of attention. The distinctive attributes of such an one are ostensibly the same as those which attach to the spiritual man in Christ. The Jew trusts in God, though vainly. The justified believer does the same in truth.[4] The Jew knows the will of God in the letter of the commandment. The Christian knows it in the power of that Spirit which ministers both life and righteousness to the believer by the faith of Jesus.

The discerning approval of more excellent things, which is here ironically conceded to the self-deceived legalist, is elsewhere desired on behalf of those in whom God has begun His new work in Jesus Christ.[5] And so of the rest. The Jews' proud confidence of superior light and knowledge is to be succeeded by that full assurance of understanding which belongs to those who have received an unction from the Holy One, and know all things, &c.[6]

If, therefore, concessions are here made to the natural Israelite, it is for no other purpose than to demonstrate more completely the futility of all pretensions of a legal kind. The Judge of all the world will do right. He will confound the Jew's vain

---

mon translation of the former part of that verse, wherein Gentiles are said to "do by nature the things contained in the law," it does not appear to me a solid one. The same apostle elsewhere reminds us that "nature teaches" some things right and decent in themselves (1 Cor. xi. 14); nor does he affirm, in the present passage, that men are naturally capable of fully keeping the Law, but that some things which are contained in the Law are recognized by the natural conscience, and are observed or neglected according to the measure in which men practically obey their moral convictions of right and wrong. The essential difference between such a doing of things contained in the Law, and the "fulfilment" of the Law itself, will be more fully shewn at the close of the remarks on verses 26, 27.

[4] Chap. v. 11.   [5] Phil. i. 10.   [6] 1 John ii. 20.

boasting by the practice of the heathen. He will try the heathen by the standard of His own eternal truth. He will judge *sin*. But it is not as a warning only that the certainties of Divine judgment are declared. The plea of the Jew is found to be already traversed, and his claim completely disallowed, by the testimony of Jewish Scripture itself. A single glance at that word, which they professed to venerate as the oracles of Jehovah, ought to suffice to prove to Israel the utter groundlessness of all those hopes and expectations, whether of personal acceptance, or of national blessing, which were founded on the Mosaic covenant. For the Lawgiver had already decided also as the Judge. Even as it is written, "The name of God is blasphemed among the Gentiles through you."[7] The Gentiles, whom they still affected to despise, had become, through their sin, both the possessors of their inheritance, and the proclaimers of their shame. They are thus cited as God's witnesses, to the confusion of the Jew as under Law. To set up, therefore, a claim on the ground of legal obedience, is not only vain in itself, but is also a lie against God, whose word it is that contains the record of their sin (verses 21–24).

Nevertheless (verse 25), circumcision profits if the Law be kept. But the Law being wholly broken, circumcision becomes the mark of reprobation, instead of privilege and favour. It becomes *uncircumcision*. The Jew, that is, finds himself reduced again to the level of natural distance from God, only with the additional condemnation of having been tried specially under the covenant of works, and found reprobate.[8]

[7] Ezek. xxxvi. 20–23.   [8] Comp. Jer. vi. 30, and Amos ix. 7.

I do not dwell more particularly on the details of the general argument of the apostle in this most instructive chapter. With respect to the reference made (verses 26, 27) to the uncircumcision keeping the righteousness of the Law, it appears to me to be not only a continuation of the previous reasoning in the earlier verses, but to apply also more pointedly to Gentile converts to Christ, a part of whose characteristic description is to be fulfillers of the Law, according to the doctrine laid down in the sequel of this Epistle.[9] But, in order to make this appear more distinctly, it will be useful to recapitulate the several references made to the Law in this part of the apostle's argument, and to endeavour to determine their respective force.

First, there is enounced in verse 25, the general principle, that circumcision profits "if thou keep (or practise) the Law."[1] Secondly, after stating the alternative of practical failure on the Jew's part, he presents the moral counterpart of his first thesis in the question proposed in verse 26: "If the circumcision keep the *righteousness* of the Law," &c.?[2] This latter expression may, perhaps, be compared with Luke xviii. 21, and Phil. iii. 6; outward observance being, apparently, the point in question. But in the following verse, we have a description to which nothing less than the regenerate workmanship of God will fully correspond: "And shall not uncircumcision which is by nature, *if it fulfil the Law*, judge thee," &c.?[3] Such a perfecting of the Law as

---

[9] *Infra*, chap. viii.   [1] ἐὰν νόμον πράσσῃς.
[2] ἐὰν .... τὰ δικαιώματα τοῦ νόμου φυλάσσῃ.
[3] ἡ ἐκ φύσεως ἀκροβυστία τὸν νόμον τελοῦσα.

is here expressed belongs only to those who, by grace, find their standing in Him who is become to the believer the end[4] of the Law for righteousness. They, and they only, will sit in judgment on the works and ways of other men.[5]

The closing verses of this chapter are of deep and searching moral application to the conscience of every one who takes in hand to draw nigh professedly to God. The calling of the Jew was to holiness, for the Lord's name's sake. The exhortation, "Be ye holy, for I am holy,"[6] was written for those to whom Moses rehearsed it while as yet the separated people of Jehovah abode in the wilderness, receiving at the lips of the Lawgiver the statutes and ordinances which were to be their glory and their praise among the nations of the earth.

But outward observance, even when faithfully performed, could only secure the sanctification of the flesh. It had no power, in itself, to reach the conscience or to purify the heart. But God's standard of conformity for His worshippers must ever be His own holiness. Hence the national title and calling, though it indicated the purpose of future blessing (which in due time God would effect, when, under a better covenant than that of works, He should have sanctified the people once for all through the blood of redemption), proved only, while the Law remained, a memorial of failure and rebuke. Yet among the thousands of the fleshly nation, there were ever found and owned of God the numbered remnant who were Israelites indeed. To such (while the Law was the delight of their inner man, and was their meditation

---

[4] $\tau \acute{\epsilon} \lambda o \varsigma$. *Infra*, x. 4.   [5] 1 Cor. vi. 2, 3.   [6] Lev. xi. 44.

day and night, that they might keep the right way of the commandment), the word of *promise* was the sustaining aliment of their souls. They put their trust in God; they hoped in Him. And because their expectations were alone from Him, they were practically separate from all that which they knew to be unsanctioned by His name and contrary to His will.

But this made them strangers in the midst of their own brethren. The believing Nazarite, whose aim was purity of heart, and who sought the sanctification of practical obedience, would meet reproaches rather than praise from those who, while they kept iniquity between their breasts, yet wore externally the form and pattern of conformity to the Law. Such were the prophets, who spake in the word of the Lord to the rebellious and backsliding heart of the nation. He that departed from evil made himself a prey to those whose feet were swift to shed blood.[7] Still, the sure testimony of God remained. He knew them, and He hearkened to the words which they spake rightly of Him, while their brethren who cast them out were vainly saying, "Let the Lord be glorified."[8] They were His. To be revealed as His in the day when His jewels should be made up;[9] and, being found complete, should shine in the fair colours of Divine salvation. Their praise was not of men, but of God.

And let it never be forgotten by the Christian reader, that the principle just illustrated is exactly that which is of present exemplification in the faith of God's elect. The Jew inwardly is a man of God.

[7] Isa. lix., *passim*.   [8] Isa. lxvi. 5.   [9] Mal. iii. 16, 17.

Killed by the letter, which worketh death, he is revived by the power of God, who quickeneth the dead, reviving, by the word of faithful promise, the heart of the man who is of a contrite spirit.[1] Morally, the godly man stands ever upon the same ground, though in respect of positive calling and the measure and quality of the blessings which attach to such calling, differences of the widest description may and do exist in the respective dispensations. But it is *God* who is the aim, and the fear, and the hope, and the reward, in every case where faith, with much or little light, animates man's heart, and sets in motion the affections of the new-born life. Hence the exhortation to holiness, which has been above quoted in its application to the Jew under Law, is anew addressed by the Spirit[2] to those who had been begotten to the title of children, and the sure hope of an eternal inheritance, according to the abundant mercy of the God and Father of the Lord Jesus Christ; and who, therefore, stood already in the pure and perfect sanctification of the name of Christ.[3]

A Christian is, in strictness of speech, a Jew neither outwardly nor inwardly,[4] though by virtue of his faith he is a true child of Abraham.[5] His knowledge of God transcends exceedingly the measure of that which was enjoyed by the godly of old, who

---

[1] Isa. lvii. 15. [2] 1 Peter i. 16. [3] 1 Cor. i. 30, vi. 11.

[4] If any one should demur to the latter clause of this sentence, on the authority of such passages as Phil. iii. 3; Gal. vi. 16, &c., I have no wish to contest the point further than this: that while the Christian unquestionably enjoys in Christ the body and substance of all Jewish promise, his standing and calling are materially different from that of Israel. The nature and extent of this difference has been fully shown in the course of the present volume, and in those on the Hebrews and Ephesians.

[5] *Infra*, chap. iv., and Gal. iii. 26-29.

knew not nor possessed the Spirit of adoption. But he is a *man of God*, as was the Jew. Like him, too, he bears the name of God in testimony, for shame or for glory, according to the holiness of his way. And it is in this sense that, both in the present passage and elsewhere, the Jewish name is sometimes given to believers in the present dispensation. If we compare verse 29 with the similar expression in a later chapter of this epistle,[6] it will appear yet more distinctly that the apostle is here contemplating not an illustrative abstraction, but the true workmanship of God, as it already existed in vital contrast to the empty and death-laden profession of the "letter." Hence, while carefully keeping in view the proper bearing and the just dimension of the apostle's argument, the Christian reader of this chapter may find large matter for his own thoughtful meditation in pondering the word thus practically addressed to the conscience. May that praise which is of God and not of man be the coveted desire of His saints!

[6] Chap. vii. 5, 6.

CHAPTER III.

The futility of the Jew's claim, as resting in the Law, having been shown, the question now arises, Has, then, the Jew *no* preëminence, or is circumcision a pledge of no value? The first branch of this question is discussed in the present chapter; the second, in that which follows. And, first, in verses 1–8, there is a distinct assertion of the Jew's preëminence, and that not in one point, but "every way."[1] As the natural seed of Abraham, the Jew is the natural heir of blessing. *Naturally*, then, and *nationally*, he stands widely apart from the nations of the world, out of which God had called and separated Abraham before He confirmed to him the covenant of promise. Viewed as under Law, and therefore judged on his own merits, the Jew is, as has been shown, personally ruined, and nationally dishonoured and disowned. But Law is not promise. Abraham, however, received the *promises* of God;[2] and God is true, and cannot deny Himself. The excellency, then, of the Jew consists, first and chiefly, in that to him have been intrusted the oracles of God.

But then (verse 3), had not the nation in effect forfeited this distinction because of their unbelief?

[1] κατὰ πάντα τρόπον. A more detailed summary of Israel's preëminence is given by the apostle in chap. ix. 4, 5. [2] Gal. iii.

The promise was of faith, but the nation was found and declared to be a generation in whom there was no faith.[3] This had, indeed, been characteristically the national sin, from Moses downwards to the rejection of the Just One. Yet had not *all* thus sinned.[4] There never had been wanting a remnant who hoped in God, and whose faith was fed upon the word of promise. This remnant had been, as it were, the life of the nation. But there was a yet firmer basis, and more valid title, of the nation's hope than this. The grace which fed and sustained this faithful remnant was the unremoved, though dimly seen, foundation of Israel's preëminence. It was the fidelity of the God of promise that constituted the true security of the national blessing. Human unbelief cannot vacate Divine promises, because such promises are made unconditionally, and become vested in due order in their destined objects, according to the good pleasure of the Giver, in His own sure time. The broken covenant of works would prove the falsity of all human professions; but though every man be a liar, God is true. He thus becomes not only the condemning witness of the unprofitableness of the flesh, but the pledge also of Israel's future blessing, when the time for the national regeneration shall have come. The word of God, after having been tried by their sin to the uttermost, will yet verify itself in

[3] Deut. xxxii. 20; Matt. xvii. 17.
[4] εἰ ἠπίστησάν τινες. It is most interesting to observe how, both here and in Heb. iii. 16, the Spirit of God, ever keeping the integrity of the nation as the vessel of Divine promise in view, speaks of "some" failing, although, when describing the failure historically, there might be but Caleb and Joshua in a whole generation who failed not. All are not Israel who are of Israel. But Israel remains unbroken, through all changes, in the steadfast counsel of the faithful God of promise.

their conversion of heart to the Lord, when the Spirit shall be poured upon them from on high.[5] Then will the preëminence of the Jew be an acknowledged result of the sovereign grace of God, fulfilling in faithfulness His covenant with Abraham, and the sure mercies of David.

Meanwhile, the wrath of God is revealed against *sin*. But the Jew sins through the evil heart of unbelief. And thus, forsaking the promises of God, or rather, departing in heart from the God of his life, whose *mercy* is his salvation, and trusting to the sacrifices of vanity, he looks vainly for acceptance with the Righteous Judge. For God will be justified in His sayings. The word of the Law will justify Him in the case of the man who puts his trust in the Law, when such an one finds in the day of judgment that the letter killeth. The word of sure promise will have its blessed vindication, and God be justified therein, in the day when the towers of human confidence are laid low, and the mystery of Divine love and saving power in Christ is made known by the manifestation in glory of the sons of God.

But if (verse 5) human sin serves only to bring out into clearer light God's righteousness,[6] is it righteous in God to punish those who have thus been instrumentally the means of His glory? In other words, must judgment proceed, untempered by mercy, on those whose very sin displays the righteousness of God? Such is the substance of the unavailing plea by which the natural mind would vainly endeavour

---

[5] Isa. xxxii.

[6] "Our unrighteousness," ($\dot{\eta}$ $\dot{a}\delta\iota\kappa\iota\alpha$ $\dot{\eta}\mu\tilde{\omega}\nu$) I understand to refer especially to the sin of the Jew. The apostle seems here to identify himself with the nation for the purposes of his argument.

to arrest the course of Divine holiness and truth. The apostle speaks "as a man,"[7] and in the structure both of the question and reply shows both the readiness of man to criticise, rather than obey, the word of truth; and also the mode in which the Spirit of God, by an appeal to acknowledged principles of eternal validity, silences the objections of men, while the question, as to its terms, is left unanswered. God does not enter into discussion with man as to the *rationale* of His way, but confronts his conscience with evidences both of His truth and of His power, which leave the gainsayer without excuse. He claims to be the *Holy One*, and will glorify that name in act when the hour of decision comes. Accordingly, to the point of the question whether judgment must proceed, the answer is simple and positive. Assuredly it must. God, as Judge of the world, must and will judge it in *righteousness*. Now righteous judgment cannot but award wrath to sin; God can deal with sin only in the way of condemnation, otherwise He abets and allows evil, and thus denies Himself in His holiness. Circumcision, therefore, as a *legal* distinction, instead of conferring upon the Jew a blessing, brings him irrecoverably under a curse, so long as his personal fulfilment of the Law continues to be the reason of his hope.

Verses 7, 8, conclude this part of the argument, by showing that either good must be the result of evil, or that God must judge sin *absolutely*. The fallacy stated in verse 7 is just this: the lie of man, instead of obscuring God's truth, is found to illus-

[7] Κατὰ ἄνθρωπον λέγω. The presumed objector is, of course, a Jew.

trate it. God is, then, glorified by means of my lie. But is God a debtor to my wickedness for His glory? Impossible; such a notion is too grossly foolish to be entertained. Then the objection ceases to act in bar of Divine judgment on the evil-doer, whom God will recompense according to his deeds.

Verses 9–20. The apostle has shown that there is an excellency which attaches to the Jew when measured comparatively with the Gentile. There is a national distinction of Divine favour secured for Israel in the unchangeable God. He returns now to the question of our personal standing in His sight. And here, as has been already intimated, the Jew's preëminence is found to avail him nothing. Before God, both Jew and Gentile are judged as *sinners*. The standing witness of this, as it respects the Jew,[8] is the Law. Such is the general term used in verse 19 to express the Jewish Scriptures as a whole; although, in point of fact, the quotations are made exclusively from the Psalms and the Prophets. The passages which are here presented are brought together by the Spirit of God, in order to confirm the previous argument in proof of the condition of man as simply and radically corrupt. "There is none righteous, no, not one." But by the previous testimony of the Spirit, this brings him under the immediate judgment of that wrath, which is revealed from heaven against *all* human unrighteousness.

[8] Indirectly, the Gentile also. For the Law is the test of *human* condition and conduct, though ministered directly only to a particular branch of the human family. A Gentile's conscience, brought within the hearing of the Law, is immediately placed under its moral obligations. He knows *thus* the will of God. Hence the general application by the apostle, in 1 Tim. i., of the Law as made for a *sinner*, and therefore of fit application to all consciences alike, when the object is to awaken men to a sense of their need of a Saviour.

The whole passage is a solemn picture of what the human condition really is, as seen of God. Man, when searched by the God who made him, and whom he had voluntarily undertaken to serve and obey,[9] is found to be both negatively and positively *bad*. There is the absence of all good—the presence of all evil. He is pronounced therefore utterly *unprofitable*. He is profitless to God who made him, for he only lives to His dishonour. He can profit neither his neighbour nor himself; for all the works of his hands are evil, and the purposes of his heart are very vanity. Wisdom and understanding are found to be as far from the natural heart as godliness, because the fear of God, which is the beginning of all wisdom, dwells not there.

The results are then stated, and are found to be destruction and misery; inward and outward sorrow and death here, coupled with an unsatisfied responsibility toward the one Lawgiver, who has power to cast both soul and body into hell. The Law, then, though of God, is but a cruel messenger—necessarily so from the nature of sinful man. But by the previous reasoning this includes *all* flesh; and so every mouth is stopped, and the whole world becomes guilty before God.

Verse 20 sums up the matter. "Therefore by the deeds of the Law shall *no flesh* be justified *in His sight*," &c. The deeds of the Law may justify flesh before flesh—man in the eyes of his fellow-sinner, who can see no lower than the surface. But the solemn word pronounced by Divine wisdom is, "That which is highly esteemed among men, is abomination

[9] Exod. xix. 8.

in the sight of God."¹ *Dead works* must ever be such in the sight of the living God who trieth the hearts. But where the Law does not justify, it condemns. By the Law, then, sin is both discovered and condemned. But the condemnation involves man *as* man, and thus shuts up the whole world as under sin. Hope, then, is extinguished, as it respects the creature and his strength. Divine holiness, when discovering itself in the Law, proves and declares the *total* ruin of man. He is thus left at the absolute mercy of the God who has judged him. Any blessing which may reach him must henceforth, therefore, be purely of grace.

Verses 21–31. Human pretensions having been thus solemnly weighed and disallowed, the ground is already prepared for the manifestation of the Divine character, as its essential glory is unfolded, in the Gospel of free grace, in relation to man as thus judged. "But now the righteousness of *God* without the Law is manifested." The heart of man, which should be the proper fountain of human righteousness, having been proved to be unsound and corrupt, a new source must be opened, from whence, for man's sake and for his everlasting benefit, a righteousness might flow forth in a stream of might and depth enough both to obliterate all former trace of sin, and to fill with the fulness of life and blessing the vessels of mercy prepared for its reception. What had been sought for, but not found, was *human* righteousness; what is now gratuitously revealed is the righteousness of *God*. The former was demanded by the Law, the latter is revealed "*apart* from Law."²

[1] Luke xvi. 15. [2] χωρὶς νόμου.

The Law was just, and by its promulgation glorified its Giver, but the Law was not the righteousness of God. Christ is so, inasmuch as He is the active perfection of the will of God. The Word was made flesh; and having honoured by a perfect obedience the Law under which He was made,[3] He has become also, in His blessed person, the true Lamb of propitiation for believing sinners. God only can either exhibit or declare the righteousness of God; and it was that the just God might also make himself known as a Saviour, that the Father sent the Son to be the propitiation for our sins.[4] It is, therefore, in the *forgiveness of sins* that God's character as the righteous God is now discovered to the believer. But this is "apart from Law," because the Law is not of grace. Both the Law, however, and the prophets attest this righteousness, inasmuch as Christ, in His person and His work, fulfils all righteousness and verified all promise.[5] That which, by proving Israel's sin, filled up the sum of human condemnation, has been abolished in His flesh.[6] Himself the true end of the Law, though hidden from the veiled heart of Israel, He has removed, by a just fulfilment, all that was contrary to His people's hope.[7] The commandments upon which both Law and prophets hang,[8] He only either understood or kept. But Law-keeping was not the measure of His goodness. He had come into the world, not to do men's business only, but the *Father's*. He could lawfully take man's place, but according to the

[3] Gal. iv. 4.   [4] 1 John ii. 2.
[5] See further, as to the meritorious obedience of Christ, the remarks on chap. v. 19.   [6] Eph. ii. 15.
[7] Col. ii. 14; 2 Cor. iii. 13, 14.   [8] Matt. xxii. 37–40.

excellency of His own person, as the only begotten of the Father. He *is* the Truth. But grace as well as truth came by Jesus Christ. He stands before God as the fulfiller of all righteousness. He stands revealed to man as the manifested mercy-seat of God[9]—the propitiation set forth by God—set forth thus for the justification of himself, as the God of *all grace,* in the free forgiveness of sins.

The power of discerning this righteousness is faith, which is itself the gift of God. It is revealed as a testimony, without difference of person, to Jew and Gentile, because all alike "have sinned, and come short of the glory of God"[1] (verses 22, 23). But not only are believing sinners *forgiven*—they are also *justified* (verse 24). For it is not pardon only that is proclaimed to us in Christ. Divine righteousness has become to us, in His Person, both the ground of our acceptance, and a title of glory and eternal blessing from God. Faith thus invests a believer with a perfect and entire righteousness, after first absolving him from all sin. He is found in Christ, having *God's* righteousness,[2] and consequently made meet for God's joy—able to endure and to enjoy the perfect, holy Light which God himself is.[3]

But the all-important point to be regarded here is,

---

[9] Ἱλαστήριον, the term here used, and in our version rendered "propitiation," is, in Heb. ix. 5, translated "mercy-seat." Christ is surely both these. On the cross He is the propitiation in fact. As alive from the dead and received into glory, He is revealed by the Holy Ghost as the eternal rest of Divine holiness, whence the true Light of God shines forth in perfect grace and glory. *God* preaches peace by Jesus Christ.

[1] Have failed, that is, to be His praise. Man, in a state of obedience, is the glory of His maker; as a sinner, he is His reproach in the lips of the adversary. (Compare Job ii. 5.)

[2] Phil. iii.   [3] 1 John i.

the complete setting aside of all natural claims and pretensions. Man, as severally responsible, is dismissed and forgotten. The Spirit of truth, having weighed him in the balance of the sanctuary, and found him utterly wanting, takes no more account of him, except to attest his utter condemnation on his own account, and to warn him to flee for refuge to the hope set before him in Christ. Faith, therefore, by which alone Divine truth can now be recognized and obeyed, disowns man, and confesses God—God in Christ; for Christ, the true "image and glory of God," has taken personally the place of human responsibility, and has accomplished *all* righteousness. Moreover, the blood-shedding of Jesus is the release[4] of the believer from every claim. The completeness of his bankruptcy and personal forfeiture has become the reason of his total absolution. For the debt has been acknowledged, and the utmost measure of all possible demand been met, in the cross of the dying Son of God. Justice thus becomes the handmaid of pure mercy. "Being justified freely by His grace, *through the redemption* which is in Christ Jesus."

To know God *now*, therefore, is to know a Saviour —a Justifier. He reveals His righteousness by the present testimony of His gospel in no other way. He is the God of Jesus Christ. Christ is himself the propitiation set forth by God—the mercy-seat brought forth from the secret of His own eternal counsel, and now openly set up as a sanctuary of refuge for the believing sinner—the vail being rent, and grace and truth, in their ever-blessed and harmonious union, displayed in the person of the Lamb once slain.

[4] ἀπολύτρωσις.

But (verse 25) this setting up of the cross is also a declaration[5] of the Divine righteousness, on account of the passing by of *former* transgressions; of those, that is, which had place previously to the ascension of the Lord Jesus. For it was only in view of a propitiation yet to come, that patriarchal faith could feed upon the promises of truth. God has ever delighted in mercy, and to the faith of His elect, He has been known from the beginning as a Saviour. But the "good things,"[6] which cheered in hope the hearts of them who of old trusted God as the God of promise, were seen from afar, not actually possessed.[7] The Holy Ghost, as the witness of accomplished redemption, was not known in the hearts of God's saints until Jesus had risen from His finished work.[8] Yet were their sins forgiven. The cross thus clears the Holy One from inconsistency in forgiving sins, by condemning sin in the flesh—by condemning the guiltless guilty-One (for such, by imputation, was the Lamb when made in very deed a curse for us), once for all. "He hath laid on Him the iniquity of us all."[9] "He hath made Him to be sin for us, who knew no sin," &c.[1]

The cross is, further (verse 26), to all who accept the testimony of God, a *present* and *positive* manifestation of the same righteousness. "To declare *at this time* His righteousness, that He might be just and the justifier of him which believeth in Jesus." It is the standing witness of God's truth and righteousness. A witness, to the believer, of atonement and justification—the precious blood of Christ being the

[5] ἔνδειξις. [6] Heb. x. 1. [7] Heb. xi. 13.
[8] John vii. 39. [9] Isa. liii. [1] 2 Cor. v. 21.

atonement for his soul; a witness, to the unbeliever, of judgment to come, seeing that the shedding of that blood is the capital charge of the Holy Ghost against an unrepentant world.[2] God's eternal character is that of a judge of evil. He is the God of judgment. If, therefore, Christ is despised, God alters not at all. He adds no circumstance to the eternal condition of His own will. But in due time He will *show* himself as the Judge, and will then mock at the fear of sinners, who would none of His mercy in the day of mercy. If He be not now confessed in the name of the exalted Jesus as a *Saviour*, He must be known hereafter in the same Christ as a *Judge*.

Boasting (verse 27) is thus excluded, because righteousness is not by human works. The ground of natural boasting is therefore taken away, while the pardoned sinner boasts himself in God, rejoicing in His work, glorifying Him for His mercy, and making mention only of His righteousness. He glories in the *Lord*. But justification, being thus of God, respects, as its object, *man* as naturally under sin. The Jew then, if saved, (verse 29) is, equally with the Gentile, a debtor to grace.[3] His circumcision goes for nothing as a title to Divine favour. But (verse 31) does this positive assertion of faith, as the alone means of human justification, make

---

[2] John xvi. 8.

[3] God will justify both the circumcision and the uncircumcision. Flesh, whether circumcised or not, is incapable of justification in itself. If a Jew, then, is justified, it must be "in the way of faith" (ἐκ πίστεως). For the same reason, it is "through the same faith" (διὰ τῆς πίστεως) that the Gentile also can be freely justified. This appears to be the force of the article in the second clause of the sentence.

void the Law, or render it of none effect? Nay, the Law, all-righteous and holy as it is, is a consenting witness to that righteousness by which the only Lawgiver now reveals himself as the God of all *grace.* Perfect in itself,[4] it has become an ornament of praise to the Just One who fulfilled it. It has effected its mission as the discoverer of sin: it has received its accomplishment as the vindicator of holiness. It now remains, in Christ Jesus, as the eternal witness of the perfection of that blessed will[5] which, being the will of LOVE, has found its end in the free salvation of lost sinners; to the praise of the glory of that grace which has abounded *through righteousness,* over human sin. Thus, it is added, "we establish the Law."[6]

[4] Ps. xix. 7.   [5] Heb. x.
[6] In the thirteenth chapter we have a practical exemplification of the way in which grace establishes the Law as that expression of the Divine will, which the new-born child of Love can alone run forth to meet. Compare also 1 John v. 2, 3.

CHAPTER IV.

It has been shewn in the course of the preceding chapter that human justification comes by faith alone —that by the deeds of the Law no flesh can be justified—that in the sight of God no difference is admitted between Jew and Gentile,—all having sinned and come short of His glory, and all being equally addressed in the Gospel of free grace. Boasting has thus been silenced, that Jew and Gentile might unite, as partakers of a common faith, in giving glory to the only God. Thus the Jew's preeminence, so strongly asserted at the opening of the chapter, is found no longer attaching to him as a man in Christ. Lastly, the Law has been cited as the double witness, both of the condemnation of the natural man, and of the completeness of the believer as a partaker of the righteousness of God.

But such doctrine, though marrow and fatness to the established saint, had, in a Jewish mind at least, a serious obstacle to its hearty reception. Accustomed to glory in their distinctive national claim to be the seed of Abraham, and yet shrouded from their infancy in a mist of legal ordinances and traditions, which shut out from their view the true nature and meaning of Abraham's calling and title as the friend of God, some further teaching of a more special kind was needful in order to settle firmly the soul of a circumcised believer upon the true foundation of his faith.

A mighty revolution of thought was indeed needful before a mind held fast in legal bondage, and trained to regard the teaching of Moses as the substance rather than the shadow, could come to see that *all* the Scripture was, when properly interpreted, the word of *grace*.[1] The apostle knew this, and as one who had familiar knowledge both of Pharisaic bigotry and of the wisdom of the just, he now proceeds, under the sure guidance of the Spirit of truth, to expound the general statement of doctrine already given, by reverting, in the opening of the present chapter, to the acknowledged father of the Jewish race; in order that by demonstrating, through his example, the doctrine of justification by faith only as the true foundation of the national hope, he might be enabled to deprive the Law of its false pretensions as a *final* doctrine, and, by a right division of the word of truth, to free the minds of God's elect from the oppressive yoke of legal bondage, and settle them abidingly in the perfect liberty of Christ.

Accordingly, this chapter, the main object of which is to expound the doctrine of imputed righteousness, or the righteousness of faith, opens with the leading question, "What shall we then say that Abraham our father, as pertaining to the flesh, hath found?"[2]

---

[1] Acts xx. 32.

[2] The readings of this question in the original are various. The recently published and highly valuable *Codex Sinaiticus* gives— τί οὖν ἐροῦμεν εὑρηκέναι Ἀβραὰμ τὸν προπάτορα ἡμῶν κατὰ σάρκα. The position of the words is of little consequence in any

Abraham had been blessed of God. This blessing came upon him before the revelation of Jesus Christ. How, then, did he obtain it? Seeing that the seed of Abraham after the flesh were circumcised and kept the Law, had it not ever been God's way to justify and to bless His people on the ground of personal righteousness? Abraham clearly had found something—he had found favour and acceptance with God.

Was, then, this blessing to be referred to himself, as its meritorious cause, or to the sovereign grace of God? For the decision of this question, an immediate appeal is made to Scripture. "Abraham believed God."[3] The testimony of the Scripture glorifies God, while pronouncing the Divine blessing upon Abraham as the chosen vessel of promise. The beginning and perfection of Abraham's justification was, that he *believed*. God spoke to Abraham. He spoke to him *of Himself*, as the Giver of blessing— as the God of grace, meeting the ungodly in pure and absolute promise—a promise which, being without any qualification in its terms, was conditional, as to its effect, only on the faith of him to whom the word was spoken. But Abraham believed God, and so his faith was counted[4] to him for righteousness.

case, as it is evident, from the tenor of the apostle's argument, that not natural relationship, but fleshly pretension in the sight of God, is the point of the present question.   [3] Gen. xv. 6.

[4] Ἐλογίσθη. The English reader should be reminded that the three nearly synonymous terms found in this chapter—"count," "reckon," and "impute"—are but varied representations of a single Greek word. In Mark xv. 28, where it also occurs, the Lord is said to have been "numbered" with transgressors. In each of these instances its force is the same, *i.e.*, it expresses a character or state exactly opposite to *natural* truth. The Lord was no transgressor, but was counted among such. The believer is by nature "ungodly," but is counted righteous for his faith.

Abraham's reception of the promise is, then, the eternal change of his condition from sin to righteousness. *God's* righteousness becomes by this means *Abraham's* righteousness. For the word of promise which He spake contained in it the Christ of God's salvation, to be manifested in due time.[5] Receiving the word of grace, he received, as his soul's true portion, Him whose word it was. Thus faith became the parent of right knowledge. The father of the faithful *understood* the God with whom he had to do, according to the revelation of His own most blessed grace. Thus he rested, in the confidence of faith, upon the Almighty as the lot of his inheritance; finding by this means the perfect place of creature-blessing—dependence, namely, upon God as the sole Author of his wellbeing, and the Source and Sustainer of his joy.

Abraham, then, in one sense, has whereof to glory: not before God, but in the presence of the world. Before God, he is but dust and ashes—fleshly glory turning only to confessed corruption in that light; but to the world, he is the witness of God as a justified heir of grace unto glory. He makes his boast of God *before men;* and God can glory in him as the righteous man of His own creation, the justified vessel of His praise. He is not ashamed to be called his God.[6]

[5] The quotation of the apostle is from Gen. xv., because it is in that chapter that the specialty of the seed (compare Gal. iii.) as the object of Divine promise is declared. The astonishing depth and richness of that chapter in displaying Christ as himself at once the Promiser and the Promise, the Blesser and the Blessing, disclosing also to the believer the nature and security of his own standing as a partaker of the everlasting covenant, are joyfully appreciated by the soul that seeks its consolation in the word of God.

[6] Heb. xi. 16.

Verses 4, 5, are especially directed against the deeply-rooted and altogether natural association, which exists in every mind, of reward with work—with debt. The Law had distinctly enounced and enforced this principle. But Abraham, the man of blessing, did no work. "To him that *worketh not*" God reckons a reward. No work, indeed, is done by Abraham; but an especial emphasis is here given to the doctrine of justification by faith, by a reference to Abraham's original condition. He is described as believing "in Him that justifieth the ungodly." Jehovah's friend had been the slave of other gods.[7] He was ungodly in his ignorance of God. But "the God of glory" had dispelled, by the revelation of Himself, the natural darkness of his soul, and now, as the willing servant of free grace, he looks for his reward. And what a reward! "*I* am thy shield, and thine *exceeding great reward.*" To the believer, God reveals HIMSELF as the crowning recompence of that faith and patience which abides the issue of the work of God. He works in grace the sinner's salvation, and places the crown of that work, in Christ Jesus, upon the head of the saved! even as the alone Worthy One has said, when reporting to the Father the results of His finished work of love: "The glory which Thou gavest me I have given them."[8] Such is grace. Such is God—the blessed God. Blest in the blessings wherewith He fills to overflowing the called vessels of His mercy—the freely chosen objects of His love.

But to proceed. Verses 6–8 cite another witness for the yet further establishment and illustration of

[7] Josh. xxiv. 2. [8] John xvii. 22.

this subject. The special value of the testimony now to be adduced, in its bearing upon the apostle's general argument, is, that while Abraham exemplifies the doctrine of Divine justification by faith *before* the Law, the witness of David, who was personally under Law, is found to concur in the assertion of this cardinal principle of God's dealing with His saints. "David describeth[9] the blessedness of the man to whom God imputeth righteousness without works." *The man*, be he who he may. The qualification for the blessedness here described is not hereditary or other privilege, but the capacity of a sinner to receive Divine mercy.

The quotation here made from Psalm xxxii. is very remarkable, as showing how completely identical, in the mind of the Spirit of God, are the two ideas of "forgiveness" and "justification." Assuredly they are distinct things in themselves, and may be sometimes contemplated advantageously in their separateness. The negative blessedness of a gracious acquittal from guilt, and a consequent exemption and deliverance from deserved wrath, is a very different thing from the positive acquisition and possession of a perfect title in *righteousness* to Divine favour. But here, where the subject-matter of the apostle's argument is justification, as the work of God in Christ, the statement of a part involves the whole; seeing that the effect of a Divine redemption is not only to spare the guilty, but to *justify* the ungodly. To confer upon His own a perfect fitness for the Divine presence, was the aim of Him who gave Himself for our sins. "He died, the Just for the unjust, *to bring*

---

[9] Rather "declareth"—λέγει, not γράφει, as in x. 5.

us to God,[1] says another apostle. Accordingly, the language of the Spirit of prophecy, while confined in its terms to the first great article of human blessedness, viz., the forgiveness of sins, is capable of an expansion of meaning commensurate with the fulness of Him in whom that forgiveness is found. The result, then, of this appeal to the oracles of God is, that God is found to be exalted in the gracious blessing of the man of faith. Meanwhile, the blessedness of the believer is perfect and entire, positive and negative. God imputes righteousness—He will *not* impute sin. Forgiveness takes the place of judgment, and everlasting righteousness has covered the believer's iniquity—hiding it alike from the eyes of the Divine glory, and from the conscience of the justified vessel of His grace.

Verses 9–22. Human blessedness has thus been shown to be the effect *solely* of Divine grace. But the subject of circumcision, as a distinctive sign of Abraham and his natural seed, remains to be examined. This point is now discussed in the following verses.

It had been shown that Abraham was justified by faith; but he was also circumcised. Was, then, circumcision in any way necessary as a precedent condition to Abraham's blessing? The answer is clearly expressed (verse 10) in the negative. It was while yet uncircumcised that Abraham's faith was counted to him for righteousness. The word of God revealed the promise of blessing to Abraham while as yet ungodly. Grace wrought *on* him, through faith, what grace had provided *for* him according to

[1] 1 Pet. iii. 18.

the good pleasure of Divine mercy and love. Circumcision is a *work* of Abraham's faith; but justification is God's work *for* Abraham.

Circumcision was, however, of God. It was the outward token of God's separating choice, which had selected Abraham and his family to be peculiarly *His own* among the nations of the earth. Nor was this its only purpose and effect. It was, *to Abraham*, the *seal* of the righteousness which he already had while yet uncircumcised (verse 11). Circumcision had thus a twofold force and meaning. First, it was, to the natural seed and household of Abraham, a distinctive token of separation from the rest of the families of the earth. It had, secondly, an additional meaning to the believer—the real seed—the children of the promise.[2] To such it was the note and mark of separation *to God*. It was, to them, the remembrancer of everlasting righteousness, as of Him. Thus it served to form and characterize the present experience of the believer. Amidst all the abundance of temporal blessings which the faithfulness of God might confer in due time upon the earthly seed, there was ever a residue of blessing yet to come. The heirship of *the world*[3] was the measure of Abraham's expectation as being blessed, in special promise, of Him who was Possessor both of heaven and of earth. But the ultimate rest of faith to him, as to all the fathers who obtained a good report by faith, was *God*, the builder of their city of foundation—the God that raiseth the dead.[4]

[2] *Infra*, chap. ix.
[3] "In thee shall all the families of the earth be blessed." (Gen. xii. 3.)
[4] Heb. xi. 10, 13.

Abraham, as the faithful receiver of justifying promise, is thus recognised by the Spirit as the father of the family of faith (verses 11, 12). Circumcised or uncircumcised, all believers are, in that sense, children of Abraham.[5] He is, moreover, (ver. 12) the father of circumcision still,[6] but it is to the circumcised *believer*, the circumcised child of promise, born, not after the flesh, but after the Spirit—the true heir of promise—that he stands in this relation.[7] Verse 13 again introduces the Law, as that which naturally was associated in the mind of the Jew with circumcision, though, indeed, it was not of Moses, but of the fathers. It is mentioned, however, only to be disallowed as the effective means of Abraham's blessing. The promise was not to him or to his seed through the Law, but through the righteousness of faith.

The Law, which only genders unto bondage, (verse 14) could never furnish a title to the inheritance. To suppose that it could do so, would be to make both the promise of God, and the faith which trusted in it, equally worthless things. For God had *given* the inheritance to Abraham by promise. The introduction, subsequently, of the Law, could not affect the previous gift of God. It might, indeed, intercept its effect, and present a positive, and when measured

---

[5] How the *church* acquires that title, is shown more especially in Gal. iii. 28, 29, where union with Christ, himself the seed, the heir, and object of all promise, (2 Cor. i. 19, 20,) because He is the Son of God, is stated as the ground of our having *inclusively* the special title and inheritance of Abraham's seed.

[6] Phil. iii. 3 opens to us a spiritual application of this expression also. For a solemn repudiation of the merely natural claim, first by the Lord's forerunner, and afterwards by the Lord himself, see Matt. iii. 9, and John viii. 39–41.   [7] Gal. iv. 28–31.

against natural strength, a hopeless barrier to the realization of the promise—a barrier surmountable only by the faith of God's elect. This it did, until Christ took it out of the way, fulfilling, and thus exhausting it; securing thus to the believer, in conjunction with yet higher blessings, that title of life which was annexed to the perfect obedience of the servant.[8] But this, while it frees the conscience eternally from the Law, and brings it into the enjoyment of life because of righteousness, does not change the former ground of blessing, namely, the promise of God. Jesus suffered in obedience unto death, in order to take away the obstacle to human blessing according to the promise of God. Thus the heirs of promise, whose generation is of God, according to the quickening power of His word,[9] being emancipated from the yoke of bondage, which, while it remained, both questioned and obscured their native title as God's children, now assume, by faith in Jesus, their true and rightful standing.[1] Christ was himself the seed to whom the promises were made. But He was born under the Law. The Law, therefore, must be fulfilled; and so it was *by Him*. Thus Jesus personally receives the promises, while in Him the same promises are the vested portion of the believer.[2]

The 15th verse enlarges still further the present point. "The law worketh wrath." The annexation of any condition to the pure promise of God would, as we have seen, have at once altered its character,

---

[8] On the disputed question of the vicarious law-fulfilling of Jesus, see further *infra*, chap. v. 18, 19.
[9] 1 Pet. i. 23.   [1] Gal. iii. iv.   [2] 2 Cor. i. 20–22.

and would have converted it, in its principle, into Law. But, upon the ground already stated in the foregoing chapter, the acquisition by sinful man of a blessing suspended upon a condition to be performed by him, is a perpetual impossibility. But if so, then the alternative of forfeited blessing is judgment. For the breach of condition is not only a forfeiture of the blessing attached to obedience, but it leaves the man under the full liability of that judgment which naturally is the portion of all the world as under sin.

Legal condition, in the sense of Scripture, always implies a positive alternative in the event of failure. A man is either pleasing God, or he is provoking His anger. Blessing *and* cursing are set before the soul, when obedience is made a precedent condition of blessing. In like manner also, the annexation of a condition to the continued enjoyment of a blessing already conferred, as in the case of Adam in Paradise, renders the blessing already as good as lost, since it is vested in hands too feeble to hold it fast on such a tenure. Now every condition so annexed is an expression of the will of God. To fail therefore in its fulfilment is to transgress His will. And for this reason the Law, which declared the will of God, if it operates at all upon a sinful man, must work not good, but evil. It "worketh wrath," because its effect is to define the sinner, to the eye of the Divine glory, as a positive transgressor of the commandment. For where no law is, there is sin indeed, but no *transgression;* the latter being nothing but the effect of sin, when it comes into contact with a positive command. On the other hand, the *promise of God* has no condition of fulfilment other than the ability and faithfulness of Him of whose grace the promise is the expression. To this therefore the receiver of the promise looks, finding thus by faith a sure repose in God, who has already glorified all promise, by exalting Jesus to His own right hand.[3]

The apostle now infers the general conclusion as follows: "Therefore it is of *faith*, that it might be by grace; to the end the promise might be sure to *all* the seed," &c. (verses 16, 17.) The promise has become a vested possession in the person of Christ. He *is* Lord of all. The condition of the Christian's assured participation in it is the faith which binds him to Christ. But Christ is Abraham's seed. Abraham is thus the father of all believers before God, who quickeneth the dead. *He* first believed the promise of God, in its special foreshadowing of the *gift* by grace. He saw the day of Christ, and was glad.[4] *His* faith had for its object God as the *promiser* of Christ. The Christian now believes in God as the *sender* of Jesus Christ,[5] as the God who has glorified the crucified Redeemer as His Son, by means of the resurrection from the dead.

Abraham was an elect vessel of mercy, and knew God in hope through faith; perceiving the promise from afar, and embracing it, while as yet unperformed, in the full persuasion of his trust. The believer now, whether naturally Jew or Gentile, is an elect vessel of the same mercy, who knows God as the accomplisher, in Christ, of the promises then made. Standing thus in Christ, by faith, as upon the sure foundation of God, with eternal acceptance, he re-

[3] 1 Pet. i. 21. [4] John viii. 56. [5] John xvii. 3.

ceives already the end of his faith, even the salvation of his soul.[6] God's character and power as the God of glory, the Almighty God, secured to the faith of Abraham the promises which he did not himself receive (except in type, as in Isaac). The power of the same God in its *effects*, as having raised Christ from the dead, and given Him glory, is the present assurance, through the Holy Ghost, to the believer now, of peace *made*—of blessing *conferred*—of the unspeakable gift *received*—of the fulfilment in Christ *for us* of all the counsels of Divine love and wisdom. And He who is personally His people's righteousness and life, inhabits also by the Spirit the hearts which He has purified by faith. Thus Christ *in us* becomes the hope of glory.[7] Or, as it is again written: "We through the Spirit wait for the *hope* of righteousness by faith.[8] Now the hope of righteousness is glory.[9] The promise, then, is *sure* to all the seed.[1]

Verse 18. "Who against hope believed in hope,"

---

[6] 1 Pet. i. 8, 9.   [7] Col. i. 27.   [8] Gal. v. 5.   [9] Chap. v. 2.

[1] The apostle is here speaking generally of faith as the sole condition of human blessing, and specially of the Abrahamic promise of the seed, as containing in itself the entirety of the Divine purpose of blessing, whether earthly or heavenly. The distinct subject of the heavenly calling, as the portion of the Church while confessing a rejected Christ, is not here in point. The question is confined to the one subject of *justification*. But as it is by faith alone that a sinner can stand justified before God, the Church occupies here a common ground with all who are of faith, though their calling be not primarily heavenly, but earthly. The "many nations" which will rejoice hereafter with Israel, when again owned as the people of God, occupy a place in the vast display of the results of redemption materially different from that of the *one* body formed of elect believers, drawn out of every nation into the unity of the Church. This subject will reäppear slightly in the course of these Notes, but only incidentally, as it is not in the Epistle to the Romans, but rather in those to the Ephesians and Colossians, that the full statement of the doctrine of the Church is found. See *Notes on the Ephesians, passim.*

&c. Hope is a natural quality, while justifying faith is contrary to nature. But there is another hope which is born of faith; which has its rise, not in the instinctive swellings of natural desire, but in the deep well-springs of Divine truth.

Abraham, as a man, had natural hope. As a believer in *God*, he owned a hope which survived the extinction of all natural expectation. Probabilities, as estimated by the human judgment, are the sustaining warranty of natural hope. But all these were clean gone when Abraham, in his hundredth year, stood, in his natural hopelessness of offspring, and listened, in the calm and sober confidence of faith, to the words, "So shall thy seed be." It was the word of *God;* and God cannot lie. But He could perform His word, seeing that He is the Almighty. Abraham's dead body and Sarah's barren womb, as they are made no mention of in the word of promise, are likewise overlooked[2] in the estimate of faith. Abraham believed God, and thus he *hoped*. The promise spoke of life, and he looked for its fulfilment to the living God. He grew out of natural weakness to the strength of triumphant confidence by the faith whereby he gave glory to God. And *therefore* (verse 22) it was accounted to him for righteousness.[3]

[2] If, however, with some copies (including the *Codex Sinaiticus*), we drop the negative particle, the testimony here borne to Abraham's faith will become still more emphatic—"he considered, indeed, the deadness," &c., "*but* he did not hesitate," &c.

[3] The reader will not fail to notice, that while the justifying faith of Abraham dates from his original acceptance of the promise (Gen. xv.), it is to the latter trial of the same faith, recorded in Gen. xvii., that reference is here made. The reason of this is plain. Nature could mingle its own expectations with those of faith, while any natural strength remained in the receiver of the promise. It did so, and the result was the birth of Ishmael (Gen. xvi.), as the fruit, not of Abraham's faith, but of Sarah's unbelief. It was only when, after

Verses 23–25. But the righteousness thus imputed to Abraham is described in Scripture for our sakes, and not for his alone. Righteousness was imputed to Abraham because he believed in his day in God, according to the special revelation then made. The same righteousness (verse 24) shall be imputed to us,[4] says the apostle, if we believe on Him that raised up Jesus our Lord from the dead. The word (as we have already seen) which proved the faith of Abraham, was an unfulfilled promise. The faith which now justifies believing sinners is called forth by a testimony that God has sealed to them, in raising Jesus from the dead, a covenant of endless peace.[5] In our case, no less than his, the effective work by which the promised blessing is secured can only be perceived by faith.[6] No man saw Jesus rise. To those whom He had chosen in the days of His flesh, His personal identity was demonstrated by marvellous and gracious proofs;[7] and their testimony, divinely directed and sustained,

---

thirteen years of further patience, the natural vigour of Abraham had ceased through age, that he could be said to have hoped against hope. It is then that the original testimony of the Spirit, as to the quality and effect of his faith, receives its confirmation and fulfilment. (Compare, as to this, James ii. 21–23.)

[4] Οἷς μέλλει λογίζεσθαι, "to whom it shall presently be imputed," as I would here render. The apostle appears here to be referring his doctrine to the decisive issue of the day of judgment. (Comp. 1 John ii. 28, and iv. 17.) God already asserts in His word the righteousness of Abraham. He will presently also vindicate openly the title of those who now, by faith, are enabled to count human righteousness as dross and dung for the excellency of the knowledge of Christ Jesus the Lord. (Phil. iii. 7–11.) Meanwhile, what will then be triumphantly asserted, is already possessed and fed on in the heart of faith. Already the Holy Spirit of promise is the indwelling witness of Divine acceptance—the earnest, to the expectant heir of promise, of the inheritance, until the redemption of the purchased possession. (Eph. i. 14.)

[5] Heb. xiii. 20. [6] Col. ii. 12.
[7] Luke xxiv.; John xx. xxi.

was the beginning of the gospel.[8] They were effective witnesses, not of the *act*, but the *event*. But "the last shall be first." It was upon none of these, but on the once "persecutor and injurious," whose first knowledge of his Saviour was the heavenly vision of His glory, that the honour was conferred of conducting, in the enabling sufficiency of God,[9] the triumphant argument of grace. The "chief of sinners," is the suited witness to the nations of the earth of that great act, which proves the Judge of all to be the Justifier also of all but those who neglect His salvation or refuse His grace.

It may be useful to note here also the difference in *form* between the apostle's doctrine in chap. iii., on the same subject of justification, and that which we are now considering. In the former passage, Christ is set forth to the believing sinner as a propitiatory, through faith in His blood,—God, through this manifestation of His righteousness, being declared to be "the Justifier of Him that believeth in Jesus." The person and work of the Lord are thus presented as the immediate object of a justifying faith. Here, on the other hand, it is the God who justifies in whom we are called to put our trust. To be truly justified, we must know our Justifier, and not the means only which His grace provides, though it is by His provision of the means that He declares His end. When God raised Jesus from the dead He revealed himself as our Justifier; for it was to bring believing sinners unto God that the Just one died for the unjust. But He died by permission and command. The Father did not spare His Son, and

[8] Acts i.–iv. [9] 2 Cor. iii. 5.

the just God called for an atoning sacrifice. He was *delivered* for our offences,[1] and the shedding of His blood was the finishing of sin. Remission now, in the case of the believer, succeeds to accusation by the same necessity of truth which had before condemned the world![2]

Because of our transgressions He was delivered, and because of our justification He was raised.[3] As the sin caused the sacrifice, so the resurrection of the Sin-bearer is the sequel and effect of the believing sinner's justification. The act, therefore, of God, in raising Him from the dead, becomes the definitive resting-point of the believer's conscience.[4] And thus it is that, through the mediatorial grace of the Lamb, our souls are led to the "excellent glory" as to their final and abiding rest.[5] We have the Father in the Son.[6]

It may be noticed also, that the nature of the apostle's argument leads him in this chapter (and, indeed, most usually in his epistles) to contemplate the Lord's resurrection in its relation rather to the perfect obedience of Jesus than to the essential glory of His person;[7] to speak, therefore, of His

---

[1] The offences of *believers*. It seems hardly necessary to remind the reader of this, it being so entirely evident in itself. But in these days, when one of the many wiles of the destroyer is to turn the precious word of grace to the flattery of natural wickedness, confounding saving faith with mere historical acceptance and assent, no caution is superfluous that warns against so ruinous a delusion.

[2] Chap. iii. 19; Heb. x.; 1 John i. 9.

[3] Ὅς παρεδόθη διὰ τά παραπτώματα ἡμῶν, καὶ ἠγέρθη διὰ τὴν δικαίωσιν ἡμῶν. [4] Compare 1 Pet. iii. 21.

[5] Compare with this doctrine the teaching of another witness. (1 Pet. i. 18–21.) [6] John xiv. 9.

[7] How brightly the other and diviner side of this great mystery sometimes shines, in the same apostle's testimony, may be seen by examining such passages as Eph. iv. 8–10; Heb. i. 3; Rom. i. 4, and xiv. 9; 1 Cor. xv. 4, &c.

being raised, more frequently than of His *rising*, from the dead. But although He truly suffered in the flesh, yet, because He was the Son of God, Christ still survived the life which He had thus laid down. To lay it down, and to take it again, were alike in His own power.[8] Yet, as being truly man, He received from the Father the gift of resurrection-life. "He asked life of thee, and thou gavest it Him, even length of days, for ever and ever."[9] The resurrection, viewed from this point, was the answer of God, in saving power, to the prayers of Jesus in the days of His flesh.[1]

Jesus *suffered* for our sins; He *lives*, by the power of God, because of His own perfect and eternal righteousness. He is the Just One. The following chapter will exhibit the doctrine of our justification in more immediate connection with the personal merits of our Redeemer.[2] What is here insisted on, is the necessary imputation of righteousness[3] to the believer by means of the Lord's resurrection from the dead. In His death, sin yields to righteousness; we are justified by His *blood*.[4] But the open proof of the believer's justification was in the resurrection of Him who had been smitten for the offence; and by the preaching of the Gospel, every creature under heaven is called on to attest this proof.[5] If the atoning work of Jesus had been less than perfect, the death to which He was delivered would have continued to hold Him in its bonds. But this was impossible. He who wrought and suffered was the

---

[8] John x. 17, 18. [9] Ps. xxi. 4. [1] Heb. v. 7–9.
[2] Chap. v. 14–21. [3] See the note at the end of chap. v.
[4] Chap. v. 9. [5] Col. i. 6, 23; Tit. ii. 11.

Holy One of God, and according to the glory of His Person was the completeness of His work. As to the duration of the apparent victory of death over the Lamb, it had been predetermined by the same Counsel that had ordained Him for the sacrifice. According to the Scriptures He died, and according to the Scriptures, on the third day, He arose. He lay down in the dust of death, *by the grace of God*, as the bearer of our sin. He arose to be the everlasting Light of life and joy to them that believe, because, as alive from the dead, He is the witness, in His own Person, that Divine righteousness has, for us, taken for ever the place of human sin before God.

CHAPTER V.

THERE have been already stated and discussed,

I. The case of man, whether Jew or Gentile, as under sin.

II. The impossibility of self-deliverance through the Law.

III. The saving grace of God, as the revealer of His *own* righteousness, justifying the ungodly *freely* through faith, in the propitiatory sacrifice of Christ; and, in necessary connection with this,

IV. The doctrine of Imputation or Reckoning, as opposed to natural right.

The chapter on which we are now entering contains, in its earlier and shorter half (verses 1–14), a statement of some of the blessed effects[1] which result to the believer on the ground of his imputed righteousness. Afterwards, the apostle returns to the subject of justification, which, together with the correlative doctrine of sin, is examined, in the latter part of the chapter, from a new and separate point of view; and presented in its final and conclusive aspect, through a comparison of the first and second Adam. Let us endeavour to follow him in his own order.

Verse 1. "Being justified by faith, we have peace

[1] Isaiah xxxii. 17.

with God,"² &c. The first of these declared effects of righteousness is peace with God,—peace with Him with whom the world remains at enmity.³ In the previous chapter he had affirmed the prospective imputation of righteousness to the believer: "to whom also it *shall* be imputed," &c.⁴ But Christ is a "present truth," as well as a "blessed hope," to His redeemed.⁵ All, therefore, that is declared in the word of promise in connection with the Saviour's name, is appropriated and tasted now, by simple faith, according to the grace and power of the Holy Ghost. For faith brings the believer, in spirit, to where Jesus is, and discovers Him in glory above the heavens. He is seen to be glorified with the Father —set down on the right hand of the majesty on high, having been raised up thither by the power of God as the God of *peace*.⁶ The Father, who, as the God of judgment, hid His face from Jesus when He stood, in the low abasement of His wondrous grace, under the confessed burden of our sin, has now requited His obedience to the full.⁷ The precious blood

² I retain the common reading here, although there is certainly good reason for preferring ἔχωμεν to ἔχομεν on critical grounds; the best MSS., including the *Cod. Sin.* being in its favour. If this reading be adopted, its only effect will be to change the force of the clause, from a didactic affirmation to a hortative encouragement, addressed to those who, being *already justified* by faith, are invited thus to assume, as their undoubted portion, the blessings which properly attach to those whom God counts righteous in His sight. For a parallel instance, see Heb. xii. 28. I confess, however, that the proposed change, though it leaves the doctrine of the passage unimpaired, seems less suited to the general context than the old reading. A fair discussion of this point may be seen in Alford's Greek Testament, 4th edition.

³ James iv. 4; John xv. 19; xvii. 9, 14, 15.

⁴ Compare, for this view of the doctrine of final justification, the language of the same apostle, in Phil. iii. 9.

⁵ Tit. ii. 11–14; 2 Pet. i. 12.   ⁶ Eph. i. 19, 20; Heb. xiii. 20.

⁷ Phil. ii. 9–11.

of the Cross, having clean atoned for the sins which were charged upon Jesus when standing sacrificially in the sinner's stead, has turned the hand of Divine power, in holiness, towards the once slain Lamb, for the eternal reparation, in life, of the breach which death had made as the effect of sin. He has raised Him up from the dead, and given Him glory.[7]

But it was *for us* that Jesus died. For us, therefore, He also lives. His joy, as now crowned with glory and honour, is our peace. He is Himself our peace,[8] our peace with God: "I ascend unto my Father and your Father, unto my God and your God,"[9] is the declaration of the First-born from the dead to His many brethren. God now preaches peace by Jesus Christ. "The way of peace," unknown to man, whether naturally, or as under Law, is thus opened *of God*. The saying, once so strange to the disciples' ears: "*I* am the way," &c.,[1] has received its perfect exposition in the light of the ascended Christ. The assured possession thus of peace with God is the eternal condition of the Church, as the necessary result of justification by faith.[2]

But, secondly (verse 2), "We have access by faith[3]

---

[7] 1 Pet. i. 21.   [8] Eph. ii. 14.   [9] John xx. 7.   [1] John xiv. 6.

[2] The fact that Christians individually are not always in possession of this peace, does not hinder the truth here stated. If a believer has not peace practically, it is either because he has never been brought to see fully what justification by faith really means, or it is because some veil has been allowed (through carelessness or otherwise) to come between his heart and the Lord.

To be standing, in the simplicity of faith, as a justified sinner before God, and not to have peace, is impossible.

[3] The words τῇ πίστει, omitted by some recent editors upon questionable grounds, have the sanction of the *Cod. Sin.* Expressed or not, they are of necessity implied, as it is *by Him* that we have the access.

into this grace wherein we stand." In this statement there is, first, the dispensational aspect of the believer's present position, as having, through faith in the resurrection of Jesus Christ, passed beyond the former barriers of sin and Law, and entered upon the new ground of imputed righteousness. There is, secondly, a *practical* assertion of the believer's spiritual liberty as an heir of grace. This liberty, although the birth-right of the child of God, depends, for its effective enjoyment, on his standing fast in the faith which justifies,[4] and by a continued exercise of which, as a spiritual worshipper, he draws nigh with a true heart, purged from an evil conscience, and resting in the love of God, through the abiding virtue of the *Name* under which he is now known and accepted of Him.[5]

Of this practical access, the Holy Ghost is both the power and incentive. He leads to God—to the Father through the Son,[6] leading the children into their present portion as saved by hope; and so it is added, "and rejoice (or make our boast) in hope of the glory of God." While natural boasting is excluded, the Lord is the glory of His saints. Genuine righteousness must have its suited honour, and for that righteousness which is of God, His glory is the fitting crown. Standing, by faith, in Christ, the justified believer finds all his springs to be in God. The revelation therefore of that glory which is the terror of a sinner's conscience, has become the joyful end of his desires as a saint.[7] His expectations are from Him. But the measure and quality of those

[4] Col. i. 23; Heb. iii.
[5] 1 Cor. vi. 11; Heb. x. 22.
[6] Eph. ii. 18.
[7] Isa. xxxiii. 14; 2 Thess. i. 8–10.

expectations are alike ascertained by the testimony of the Spirit, as the Spirit of truth, and it is by that Spirit that Christ is revealed as the forerunner of His saints. He is the pattern to which they are in due time to be conformed, according to the almighty power which already has been displayed in raising Him from the dead.[8] Meanwhile the brightness of Divine glory is displayed to the eye of faith in the person of Christ, by the same Spirit who glorifies Him by declaring who and what He is.[9] Thus He sustains the hearts and directs the desires of the saints, while walking humbly in the Lord.[1] Marvellous, indeed, is the thought that the glory of God should be the object of hope to one who knows *himself* to be but filthiness and corruption. But it is Jesus whom God thus delights to honour. Our souls, all helpless and unworthy as they are, find their unspeakable portion of grace and glory in Him —as being *His*.[2]

Nor is this all. "We rejoice[3] (verse 3) in tribulations also." The prospect of the saint, is glory. His appointed condition in the world, is tribulation. "Through much tribulation we must enter the kingdom of God."[4] "In the world ye shall have tribulation," &c.[5] But inasmuch as all those trials into and

---

[8] Eph. i. 19-29.   [9] 2 Cor. iii. 18, iv. 6; John xvi. 14.
[1] Col. ii. 6, 7.   [2] 1 Cor. iii. 21, 23.
[3] καυχώμεθα. This word, thrice repeated (in verses 1, 2, and 11), is differently rendered in each place. Nor is there much to blame in this, as the translators have observed, on the whole, a just discrimination in their varied use of the English equivalents, "rejoice," "glory," and "joy." It would, however, have been better had they avoided any change in the present verse, or, at least, had selected a different word for "glory," which so immediately precedes it in quite another sense. Perhaps, "We rejoice also even in our tribulations," would be a truer rendering of the words in the text.
[4] Acts xiv. 22.   [5] John xvi. 33.

through which the Spirit of grace conducts the children of God, are connected immediately with the hope set before them,—constituting, as they do, the appointed furnace through which the faith of God's elect must needs be passed to prove its quality,[6]— such tribulations are for them occasions, not of fainting, but of joy.[7] In some shape, tribulation must be felt and known by the believer whilst in, and *because* he is in, the world. But no present sorrow can reach so deep as to touch with defilement or with bitterness the springs of God's love in Christ. Heaviness may be a portion of Christian experience here, but the power of the Holy Ghost, as the Comforter, is shown in raising the inner man above the stress of present trial by the revelation of the love of Christ. He is the Spirit of truth; and therefore He feeds the soul, not on evanescent fancies, but on the sincere milk of the word. But that word is the revelation of God in His ways. Thus the heart of faith, when nourished by the word of grace, is taught the manner of the God who is its trust, and is enabled to pass joyfully through the "light afflictions" of the present life, by the sustaining power of a knowledge which makes every special circumstance of trial turn to the furtherance of the soul's blessing, in the remembrance of the end to which all these things are conducing: "*Knowing* that tribulation worketh patience; and patience, experience; and experience, hope."[8]

Patience is an effect, not a cause; though producing, in its turn, its own results. It is wrought out through suffering. Tribulation of some kind

[6] 1 Pet. i. 6.   [7] Eph. iii. 13; James i. 2.
[8] Compare Col. i. 11; 2 Cor. iv. 17, 18.

must be passed through, for the soul to know its dependence on God as the God of patience and of hope. The wise believer is aware of this, and, while resting in fullest confidence upon the love of Him who giveth all things richly to enjoy, will endeavour to maintain a state of watchful preparation for any special visitations of affliction which may meet him in his way; nor will he fail, if duly observant of his own condition, to be sometimes conscious, in the absence of trial, of a spiritual lassitude, which real tribulation seldom fails to remove, by throwing the soul more immediately and with more sensible effect upon God. It is written of the Holy One himself, whose meat and whose drink it was to do the will of the Father, that "He learned obedience by the things which He suffered,[9] and it is in this path also that the justified believer is invited now to walk.[1] A great fight of afflictions may be joyfully endured by souls which are warm with the constraining love of Christ.[2] Afflictions of some kind are, in fact, a necessary part of that spiritual discipline upon which the true enjoyment of our filial happiness depends.[3] What Jesus learned in the way of perfect devotedness to the Father's will, we have too often to learn in the way of chastisement, because of the waywardness of our path. But the effect of the lesson of patience, however learnt, is experience, or "proof,"[4] and that in a double sense. It proves both the Workman and His work. The patient waiting of the tried spirit upon God, brings into the soul a richer experience of what God really is, as the fountain of living

[9] Heb. v. 8. [1] 1 Pet. ii. 21. [2] Heb. x. 32; Col. i. 11.
[3] Heb. xii. 8. [4] δοκιμη.

NOTES ON THE ROMANS. 83

waters—the eternal refreshment of the wearied soul, while it is by means of the trial of our faith that its genuine quality is finally evinced.[5] Especially there is made a practical discovery of the sufficiency of the grace of Christ,[6] through the process of soul-trial and exercise of spirit effected by the endurance of tribulation. There is, moreover, a ripening of the mind in the wisdom of the Lord's ways.[7] Where tribulation is borne with God, all turns to blessing. The grace of Jesus is proved as the stay of our souls, and His joy becomes our strength.

Hence *hope* ensues. The power of Christian hope is the Holy Ghost. But His blessed energy is ever hindered by the flesh. It is only, therefore, as a believer is kept, by prayerful watching, in a state of simple dependence upon God, that the hope here spoken of is really understood. If we are pleasing ourselves, Christ, as the river of God's pleasure, will not be enjoyed. The Spirit, when grieved by our carelessness, will not reveal to the soul that which, if revealed, would not be appreciated. Hope, then, is the result of the saint's experience of what God is. The sifting process, which bruises down, in the wisdom of the Father of spirits, the strength and elasticity of the natural heart and temper, leaves the chastened but confiding soul as a burden upon the arm of Jesus—upon God's sustaining love.[8]

The practical trials of life are but an extended lesson of dependence upon the God of hope. The experience of God as the deliverer must vary according to the specialty of the Christian's circumstances,

[5] 1 Pet. i. 7.   [6] 2 Cor. xii. 9; Phil. iv. 3.
[7] Prov. viii. 34; Psalm cxix. *passim*.   [8] Ps. lxxiii. 25, 26.

as they are moulded for him by the only wise God. But it is the privilege of *every* saint to know that the Lord God *is* his sun and his shield. "Thou hast enlarged me when I was in distress," is the retrospective celebration of a believer's grateful experience of the God who has saved him by His grace. "The Lord *is* my helper, I will not fear what man shall do unto me," is again an expression of that confiding boldness which belongs to those who, having come to the knowledge, through faith, of Him who justifieth the ungodly, cast the burden of all care upon God, who tells them that "He careth for them." "He *hath* delivered, He *doth* deliver, He *will* deliver," is the apostle's own pregnant summary of this kind of Christian experience.[9]

Moreover, the experience, by the tried believer, of Christ's faithfulness and sufficiency, quickens the flow of hope in the soul; and hope, thus quickened, reäcts again for the renewing of patience; as it is said,[1] "If we hope for that we see not, then do we with patience wait for it." So that these three— Patience, Experience, and Hope, each producing or sustaining the other, are, as it were, concurrent in their operation, and jointly confirm the confidence and rejoicing of the child of God. And so it is added (verse 5), "Hope maketh not ashamed, because the love of God is shed abroad in our hearts by the Holy Ghost which has been given unto us."[2]

"Confidence and joyful hope,"[3] rooted in and sustained by the known love of God, are the portion of

---

[9] 2 Cor. i. 10; 2 Tim. iv. 18.　　[1] Chap. viii. 25.
[2] τοῦ δοθέντος ἡμῖν, *i. e.*, to the Church definitively, as the seal of God. The doctrine of the Spirit, in His relation to the believer, is treated more fully in chap. viii.　　[3] Heb. iii. 6.

every child of God, who has and *uses* the access which the death and resurrection of Christ have opened to him by the Spirit. The Holy Ghost is *given* to the believer. Being thus given, He speaks of the Giver, of the person and the place from whence He comes—of God—of Christ—the Father and the Son;—of glory, for He is the Spirit of glory and of God[4]—of heaven—of love—for God is love. He is the unfolder, to the heart's affections, of Christ as the truth of God's eternal love. He is the revealer of the Divine *nature*, as it is made manifest in the light which Christ is, and through faith participated in by those who themselves love truth, because born of God.[5]

Accordingly, the following verses (6–11 inclusive) are devoted to the demonstration of Divine love and its effects, as they are now declared in the cross of the Son of God.

And first (verses 6–8), we have the proof of God's love in the death of Christ,[6] while the quality of that love is determined by the condition and character of those who are its objects. "Christ died for the *ungodly*." Such are, descriptively, the subjects of gospel grace; when viewed in comparison with the intrinsic nature and holiness of God. The hopeless condition of man as under sin (*without strength* as well as ungodly), has brought out into view the full character of God as Love. Sovereign power produced Creation. Perfect love has both willed and accomplished Redemption.

[4] 1 Pet. iv. 14.   [5] 1 John iv. 7, 8.
[6] Note herein the evidence, equally distinct and affecting, though incidental, of the blessed Lord's Divinity. Christ's death is the expression of *God's* love towards us. God was in Christ. The fulness of the Godhead was there, bodily contained. (Col. ii. 9.)

But it was "in due time"[7] that Christ died. Redemption, though early in God's counsel,[8] was late in its effective operation. Trial had first to be made, and was made, by the patient wisdom of God, of the natural man, whether circumcised or uncircumcised. The result of this trial has been to prove him to be essentially ungodly.[9] *Perfect* love could not be demonstrated by dealing with anything not in its nature *completely* alien, and in its condition altogether *lost*. There was nothing to excite this love. There was everything to dissuade it. Yet it came forth, fresh and pure from its eternal fountain, which is God, and by its own Divine energy it quickens the vessel which it is to fill.[1] Where, therefore, this love is known in the heart by faith, it supplants all other feelings, and settles itself, by its Divine and intrinsic weight, in the deepest recesses of the soul. Its effect is to humble, and it alone *thoroughly* humbles the heart; because it is, as it were, the pressure of God himself upon the soul. Not of something *from* God simply—His word, His holiness, or the like,—but of God himself—God in Christ arriving in the heart, and, by the indwelling Spirit, taking up His abode in the poor saved and cleansed and justified "ungodly one;" the God of peace, now known as the possessor and the ruler in that heart wherein the presence of a guilty conscience had before debarred the sinner from all knowledge of the way of peace. Christ died for the *ungodly*. This is the answer of the Spirit to the anxious inquiry of the awakened soul as to the dis-

---

[7] κατὰ καιρόν. [8] Tit. i. 2; 1 Pet. i. 20.
[9] ἀσεβής. For a synoptic view of this progressive trial of the natural man, the reader is referred to the introduction to my *Notes on the Hebrews*. [1] Eph. ii. 4, 5.

position of God towards sinners. Can God love sin? No. Can He love the sinner? "Christ died for the ungodly." "The just for the unjust, to bring *us* to *God*."[2] This is the proof on which the Holy Ghost relies, in demonstrating that God is Love—in affirming, as the Spirit of *truth*, the glory of Jesus as the *Son of God*.

In verses 7, 8, we have forcibly contrasted the grandest effort of merely human heroism with the perfection of Divine grace. To rescue suffering *goodness* from an unmerited death is considered the noblest motive of self-sacrifice among men. To establish by the sacrificial death of His very Son, an eternal claim upon the love of justified *sinners*, is the glory of Him who desires to be known and worshipped among men as "the God of all grace."[3] If we love Him, it is because He first loved us.[4]

Verse 9. "Much more, then, being now justified," &c. The death of Christ forms the ground of the *à fortiori* reasoning with which the Holy Ghost, in this and the two following verses, labours to build up the soul of the believer in grace. Wrath is revealed from heaven against all unrighteousness of men.[5] But the blood of Jesus has already justified the believer. He is justified, first, in the way of *atonement*, sacrificial blood being the discharge of sin's claim—its expiation—the purgation, consequently, of the sinner's conscience—judgment having thereby been satisfied, and sin destroyed. He is justified, secondly, by way of *gift*. The risen Jesus is the righteousness of the believer before God. As alive from the dead,

[2] 1 Pet. iii. 18.   [3] 1 Pet. v. 10.
[4] 1 John iv. 19.   [5] Chap. i.

He is the asserter, on behalf of those for whom He suffered, of His own positive and unimpeachable righteousness. He thus makes good, to those whom He confesses as His sheep, that gift of life eternal which can be possessed on no other title than that of perfect righteousness.[6] We are therefore already justified by the faith which owns Him as the Lamb; but if so, much more shall we be saved, in the coming day of wrath, by Him who will come to be glorified in His saints, and admired in all them that believe.

We must remember that it is *God's* righteousness which is in question here. *Man's* has been weighed, and found to be but sin. God's righteousness has been tried in Christ, and has come forth from the trial into the appointed glory of the Son of man. Jesus lives as the glorified expression of Divine righteousness. He *is* intrinsically the righteousness of God, while, as man, he receives, as an appointed portion, the heirship of all things. Being eternally one with the Father, as the "only begotten," He is, moreover, for ever one with the redeemed as the "*first* begotten from the dead."[7] He is, as such, *their life*. The saint, as a man, comes to his end in the cross. As it is elsewhere written, "Ye are dead, and your life is hid with Christ in God. When Christ, *who is our life*, shall appear, then shall ye also appear with Him in glory."[8] The life of the believer thus being Christ, the certainty of his salvation from wrath is of necessity established. His exemption from wrath is found in his mystic identification with Him who is to administer the judgments of God.

[6] John x. 28.   [7] Col. i. 18.   [8] Col. iii. 3, 4.

"For the Father judgeth no man, but hath committed all judgment unto the Son."[9]

But there is yet another point. Although the person of Christ, considered objectively by faith, is the real security of the Church, yet the Holy Ghost brings upon the heart of the believer, the full blessing which arises from the consciousness of his being individually capable of the love of God. *We* are *reconciled* to God. The cross has effected this. We learn from the blessed Gospel the marvellous truth and meaning of Divine mercy. In that discovery we find that what needed change was not God, but ourselves—our *will*. Naturally enemies, we have become *reconciled* to God—to Him whose nature is *love*. The discernment of the cross disposes the heart's affections towards God. The discovery of the unspeakable riches of Divine mercy subdues the hardness and impenitency of the heart. This effect is wrought, not by changing the will of the flesh— *that* knows no change. It is the especial gift of faith on God's part, whereby the once blinded slave of sin and Satan is enabled to behold the light of the Divine glory in the face of Jesus Christ. Being, then, thus reconciled to God, by the *death* of His Son, *much more* shall we be saved in the *life* of Him in whom we live before God.[1]

---

[9] John v. 22; 1 Cor. vi. 2.

[1] ΔIA τοῦ θανάτου,....'EN τῇ ζωῇ αὐτοῦ. The proper force of these two prepositions should not be overlooked. We were reconciled to God by the death of His Son. In accepting the place of our substitute, Jesus attracted to Himself, and made expiation for, all that could create enmity between the living God and sinners dead in trespasses and sins. But when the resulting effect of that expiation is declared, the salvation which is thus assured to the believer is said to be not by, but *in* the Saviour's life. Not only is it eternally true, as the Scripture plainly teaches, that Christ *is* our life, by virtue of

"And not only so (verse 11), but we also joy or make our boast[2] *in God*," &c. The believer's fellowship is not only with Jesus as the Son, but with God as the Father, seeing that he is, by grace, himself become a son. The point, however, here treated, is the bringing of the creature, by virtue of completed reconciliation, into conscious and delighted reünion with God. The power of this is the mediatorial position of the Lord Jesus Christ. It is *through* Him that we joy in God; through Him by whom we have *now received* the reconciliation.[3] The power of this reception, on our parts, is the Holy Ghost; which is sent, as the Spirit of adoption, into the believer's heart, as he shows more fully in the eighth chapter. God is already become the joyful boast of the believer, because He is thus *known*. The thought of the man of the world is, "There is no God,"[4] that thought being the creature of his own depraved will. The believer, on the other hand, says, "The Lord

His being the sole possessor and bestower of life; but his life *as man*, now manifested and glorified, after its transient obscuration and dishonour as the victim of judicial death, is the triumphant security, to the believer, of a perpetual exemption from the wrath to come.

The apostle's language expresses union here, instead of substitution, in order to enforce more distinctly the great truth, so frequently reiterated in the Spirit's testimony, that man being by nature dead in sins, and Christ, who was the sole exception to this rule, having tasted death for us by the grace of God—there remains nothing whatever of the *original Adamic life* of which God can take account, when writing up the people that are His. (Ps. lxxxvii. 6.) United to the risen man, the second Adam, we now live by faith; and because of this, we shall be surely saved from that wrath, of which Jesus never could be the object naturally, although He bore it all, in grace, for our sakes. [2] καυχώμενοι.

[3] That the marginal reading at verse 11 is the correct one, I suppose no one acquainted with the original would question. It may, I think, be safely affirmed that καταλλαγή never means "atonement" in the usual acceptation of that word, though, perhaps, in the earlier usage of the language, the two expressions might have been almost identical. [4] Psalms xiv. and liii.

liveth; and blessed be *my* Rock: and exalted be the God of the Rock of *my* salvation."[5] He knows the God of peace as *his* God, and his joy is therefore full.

Verses 12–21. The general questions of sin and justification having been discussed and settled, the apostle now presents the subject in a new light, by reviewing it, not in its detailed results, but with reference to its source and principle. The remaining verses, therefore, of this chapter, while they sum up the preceding argument, open also, in addition, the special doctrine of representative identity, as displayed in the contrasted Headships of Adam and of Christ—of the first Adam and the second.

The case of the sinner is here stated (verse 12), not on the moral evidence of personal evil, but on the decisive testimony of *death*. What men call "natural death," is God's pervading and irrefragable witness of the presence, in and throughout the world, of that which produced it, even sin. "Sin entered into the world, and death by sin." But the means of this entrance of sin are immediately stated. It was "by one man." Adam died, by the direct sentence of God pronounced upon his transgression. *Mankind* die, because born of one who was himself mortal as thus judged. Death thus passed mediately,[6] through him, to all who sprang from him. But death is not derived to the posterity of Adam merely as an effect of his mortal *condition*, but as a consequence of his sinful *nature*. Sin, having taken hold on Adam, vitiated utterly the nature in which it lodged. And so it is said, that death passed upon all men, for

[5] 2 Sam. xxii. 47.   [6] διῆλθεν.

that *all have sinned.*[7] Death is never separable from sin. The participation, therefore, of a sinful nature produces death as its necessary effect.[8] Sin, having found entrance by the one man's disobedience, corrupted utterly his being. The spoil which it had won by subtlety, it kept by its own intrinsic force; not vacating the world at the death of the first transgressor, but remaining in the nature which reproduced itself in Adam's seed. It was *in the world* (verse 13) antecedently to the Law.

But it might be alleged that sin is not imputed where there is no Law.[9] Such an objection would

---

[7] 'Εφ' ᾧπάντες ἥμαρτον. "Because all sinned." It has been noticed by others, that the use of the aorist here gives emphasis to the fact, that in the one transgression of Adam all his posterity are concerned. The principle of representative implication is, as I have elsewhere pointed out, clearly recognized also by the apostle in Heb. vii. 9, 10, where Levi, the descendant of Abraham, is included in his father's act.

It may be well, also, to notice in this place the indistinctness with which the doctrine of original sin is sometimes regarded, even by believers. Adamic imputation is often spoken of as if an act exclusively *his own* were ascribed hypothetically to us his natural offspring; whereas the testimony of Scripture is, that *we* sinned in Adam, because, as the seed of that one parent, we are not separable from the source of our being.

The doctrine of *imputation* therefore is, in this sense, quite superfluous when applied to *sin;* while, for the opposite reason, it is, when applied to *righteousness*, exactly true; because He, for whose sake righteousness is imputed to the believer, is alone, and without any natural heirs. Grace, therefore, can and does impute to its chosen objects that which naturally is none of theirs. The instinctive wilfulness of fallen nature *proves* morally the identity of the original transgressor and ourselves his natural seed. Born in his likeness as a sinner, we are but a continuous repetition of himself. (Comp. Psalms li. 5, and lviii. 3.)

[8] The act of God may, of course, intercept (as in the case of Enoch) what has thus become the course of fallen nature.

[9] The view of the apostle's reasoning, given in the text, is grounded on the ordinary reading ἐλλογεῖται. If, with *Cod. Sin.*, we read 'ἐνελογεῖτο, the expression would seem rather to refer to the imposition of the Law as an historical fact, and to be declaratory of its moral relation to its subjects. For a Law is, even before its breach, a presumptive imputation of sin. A Lawgiver forbids, not what is

be to confound *sin* with *transgression*. The apostle has already stated,[1] that "where no Law is, there is no transgression." For transgression[2] is the breaking through, or passing over, an assigned limit, a declared rule. The rule, therefore, must exist, or it cannot be transgressed. Sin, on the other hand, is the principle of an alien *will*, which may produce, and ever does produce, transgression as its result, when brought into contact with Divine command, but is clearly distinguishable from it, since a cause should not be confounded with its effect. Instead, therefore, of refuting in a direct manner the objection here implied, the apostle continues his general argument, the effect of which is to silence this and every similar plea, of a special and limited character, by such a demonstration of acknowledged facts as must constrain every man to acquiesce in the general position stated above, viz., that sin is in the world.

Accordingly, the decisive fact of universal mortality is immediately cited (v. 14), in proof of the universal presence and prevalence of sin. "Death *reigned* from Adam to Moses, even over them that had not sinned after the similitude of Adam's transgression." To the wise man and the fool, there had happened the same end. The parties here more especially contemplated are, I think, first, the Gentiles generally, who, though wrapt in guilty ignorance as the effect of their apostasy from God, were not in strictness

---

imaginary, but what exists and is to be restrained, while conditional promises imply, in their very nature, a doubt of personal worthiness in those to whom they are addressed. The Law regards man as a sinner until he justifies himself (or is justified in the way of grace) through its fulfilment. It was not made, as the same apostle elsewhere teaches, "for a righteous man." (1 Tim. i. 9.)

[1] Chap. iv. 15.   [2] $\pi\alpha\rho\acute{\alpha}\beta\alpha\sigma\iota\varsigma$.

under Law,[3] while Adam was expressly under Law;[4] and, secondly, infant children, who constantly are found to die, though by their age incapable of actual offence. For they, too, are sinners, though they have not sinned, time and opportunity being alone wanting for the active demonstration of the evil of their flesh.[5]

Death is thus accounted for independently of positive transgression. Personal unrighteousness, as expressed by acts of iniquity, has already been treated; and has been shown to form a separate and special ground of Divine judgment. Both Jew and Gentile have been alike convinced of evil in their ways.[6] The truth here stated is, that because sprung from the first Adam, the head and fount of *all* flesh, *all* are reckoned sinners from the very necessity of their birth. They are sinners, because *born* in sin. For the procreation of children, according to the will of the flesh, is but the multiplication of that which had been already condemned of God as sinful, and expelled by His sentence from the Eden of His presence: as it is written, "He drove out the man."[7]

But Adam is a figure of Him that was to come.[8] The headship of the one is to be compared with the headship of the other. In verse 15 we have contrasted the *offence*[9] and its results, with the *free gift* and its effects.[1] Man's offence is met by God's free gift of grace. As to the effect of the first, it was by

[3] They sinned without Law (*ante*, chap. ii. 12).
[4] "Ye shall not eat of it, neither shall ye touch it, lest ye die." (Gen. iii. 3.)
[5] Ps. lviii. 3.   [6] *Ante*, chaps. i. and ii.   [7] Gen. iii. 24.
[1] A figure in a double sense. First, as the natural head of the human species, and secondly, as the possessor of Eve and the lord of creation. The latter subject does not properly enter the field of view in the present chapter.

τὸ παράπτωμα.   [1] τὸ χάρισμα.

the offence of one that "the many" died. The representative sinner is also the representative *mortal*. As, therefore, all participated in his act, so all died when the first transgressor died.[2] But if so, then much more did the grace of God, and the gift by grace, abound unto "the many."[3]

Two things are here to be considered. First, the grace of God—its aspect and effects; and, secondly, the medium of its display. First, it is pure and unqualified; and, as to its aspect and its measure, it utterly excels the original cause which called it into operation, seeing that it deals with its subjects as not only mortal, through the effect of the *one* transgression, but as being also severally sinners on their own account. But, secondly, it is by *one man*, Jesus Christ. Human sin having ruined the species, human obedience also must be found to balance and set it aside, or blessing cannot come from Him who is the Righteous God. But where was the man? Divine grace might be ready to flow from its eternal fountain, but a channel of righteousness must first be provided through which it might reach effectually its objects. The work of grace, then, must begin, and did begin, in the amazing process of self-humiliation on the part of Him who thought it not robbery to be equal with God,[4] yet was found in fashion as a *man*.[5] That was the first gigantic step which grace took for the effectual accomplishment of the Divine counsels of love. But this step from heaven to earth, from

---

[2] ἀπέθανον. *Ante*, page 92. Note 7.
[3] The force of this term is more fully noticed at the close of the remarks on *v.* 19.   [4] Phil. ii. 5–8.
[5] "Ye know the grace of our Lord Jesus Christ, that, though He was rich, yet for our sakes He became poor," &c. (1 Cor. viii. 9.)

the majesty of His eternal Sonship to the similitude of sinful flesh, was but preliminary to the work of perfect obedience, which, as man, He rendered unto God, until He reached its final consummation on the cross. The death of Jesus, followed by His resurrection, has opened the hands of Divine grace to dispense the gift of righteousness to all who will receive. It is to every creature under heaven that the Gospel of the grace of God is now preached. Such is its universal aspect.[6]

Verses 16, 17, continue the argument, while gradually narrowing its scope to the specialty of the believer's *reception* of grace. The *gift*,[7] as a thing

---

[6] The authorized translation of ver. 15, though substantially correct, does not give full expression to the force of the original, especially in the latter clause, which stands thus: πολλῷ μᾶλλον ἡ χάρις τοῦ Θεοῦ καὶ ἡ δωρεὰ ἐν χάριτι τῇ τοῦ ἑνὸς ἀνθρώπου, Ι. Χ. "Much more the grace of God, and the gift which is by (or in) the *grace of the one man*, Jesus Christ," &c.; *i. e.*, while demonstrating the strictly human character of the chosen medium of mercy, the apostle takes care to keep clearly in view the *personal* glory of Him who thus mediates. When Jesus acts as the willing and effective channel of the grace of God to sinners, He is bestowing, though in the form of an obedient servant, that which is essentially His *own*. Divine grace is inseparably His, who is Divine. (Comp. John iv. 10, and x. 28.)

[7] δώρημα. The words χάρισμα and δώρημα are not to be regarded as identical in their meaning. In verse 15, the former term is opposed to παράπτωμα, and is, in the remainder of that verse, explained to mean both "favour" and that which favour gives (χάρις and δωρεά). It is, consequently, a more comprehensive term than δώρημα· and is accordingly employed in this passage to describe the scope or aspect of the Divine mercy through Christ, in contradistinction to the offence which gave occasion to its manifestation. Δώρημα, on the other hand, expresses the positive *application* of this grace. Hence it is contrasted not with the offence, but the offender: "not as by one that *sinned*, so is the gift." The reasoning of these verses is close, and much attention must be paid by those who would appreciate the apostle's argument. "The judgment," he says, "is ἐξ ἑνὸς εἰς κατάκριμα," alluding, as I believe he does, to the one transgression. "But the free gift (χάρισμα) is ἐκ πολλῶν παραπτωμάτων εἰς δικαίωμα." And then, in the next verse, following up the subject to its practical result, he shows the more abundant fulness and energy of the grace by its effect, in individual application, on the many who

effectually imputed, is here viewed and contrasted with the judgment unto condemnation, which, in the case of the believer, is thus met and set aside.

The gift of God finds the receiver of it, not merely under the inherited effects of Adam's fall, but in the midst of his own ungodliness and personal defilement. The transmitted corruption of his nature has become, in every man, the fruitful source of numberless transgressions. Grace, therefore, in Jesus, not only cures effectually the radical evil of the first man's sin; it also meets and abounds over the "many offences" which are found in each believer, as the special object of Divine mercy. It is not of offences simply, but of *many* offences, that forgiveness is declared. Deep and full will be the grateful joy of the believer, while pondering the force of this significant expression, when used by the Holy Ghost to indicate the measure of positive human transgression. "Having forgiven you *all* trespasses,"[8] is the language of the same Spirit, when elsewhere recounting to the ear of faith the manner of the grace of God in Christ. *All* are forgiven: but how multitudinous is the number of that sum! Let the weak-hearted Christian, who may read these Notes, remember that in considering the question of atonement, the Spirit of God deals with the subject of sin in its *fullest, widest* sense. To suppose that some sins are forgiven, while others yet remain, is to drink damage into the soul through a thought that entirely dishonours alike the God of all grace, who spared not His own Son,

---

receive it. That which in its nature and design is $\chi \acute{a} \rho \iota \sigma \mu a$, becomes $\delta \acute{\omega} \rho \eta \mu a$ when mixed with faith, and so vested in the believer as his own sure portion in Christ. [8] Col. ii. 13.

and that blessed One who "Himself *bare our sins* in His own body on the tree." The reach and efficacy of Divine atonement is commensurate, and more than commensurate, with the extent of human sin.

Moreover, it is not the acquittal simply of sin previously charged, and with it a restitution of forfeited privilege. It is *Divine justification.*[9] Grace never restores that which sin has spoiled and ruined, to its pristine state.[1] It is not a restorative remedy in any sense. It is an independent act of God. It supersedes therefore the former constitution of things, which He had suffered in His wisdom to be vitiated and destroyed, and supplants the very remembrance of it by a new, and altogether transcendent revelation, of Himself. Thus he who, in his place and kind, was perfect originally, but allowed to fall, remains but as a feeble type of that more excellent reality which is already disclosed to the view of faith in the glorified Person of the Christ, and is hereafter to be acknowledged, by every creature, as the true image and glory of the only wise God. Sin in Adam is the root of death—death reigns by one. Righteousness in Christ is the root of eternal life. He *is* the eternal life. But what He personally is, becomes, by imputation, the portion also of His saints; and so the justified objects of God's saving mercy, are anointed as the royal companions of the Prince of life. "They that

---

[9] Δικαίωμα. Christ is, distinctly, the "Just One" (ὁ δίκαιος), and this term in verse 16 seems to express the judicial estimate of His merit, as that merit is, by faith, now reckoned to the believer. See further the remarks on *v.* 19, and the note at the end of the present chapter.

[1] I speak of the ultimate results of grace. In the millennium there will be a restitution of all things of which the prophets have spoken. (Acts iii. 21.) But the millennium is not the ultimate goal of Divine promise.

receive abundance of grace, and of the gift of righteousness, shall *reign* in life by one, Jesus Christ;" the Spirit of promise being already the attesting seal and earnest of this hope.[2] It is not merely a renewal of untainted human existence, that is here assured to the children of promise; it is the paramount and more abundant gift of endless life from God. The believing sinner is thus changed from being the *subject* of death, because of sin, into a kingly inheritor of life, according to the title of the Worthy One in whom he trusts.

Verses 18, 19, sum up the argument in the way of general recapitulation: the one transgression of the first man[3] infects, to their ruin, all who by natural generation come of the transgressor; on the other hand, one righteousness becomes the fountain of life to all who are children of the second Adam in the way of grace.[4]

The doctrine, however, of these verses should be separately considered. In the first, there are set in

[2] 2 Cor. v. 5; Eph. i. 13, 14.
[3] By the reading, δι' ἑνὸς ἀνθρώπου ἁμ. the *Cod. Sin.* favours the text rather than the margin of the E. V.
[4] If it be thought by some that this *résumé* points rather to the aspect of the truth than to its application and effect,—a view of the subject which Universalists wrest to the destruction of the Gospel,— my objection is, that such a view is *incomplete*, though right enough as far as it extends. In summing up an argument, we ought not, surely, to omit any of its leading members: but the special application (in its ever-blessed abundance) of the grace proclaimed in the Gospel, is one of these. "They that *receive* abundance of grace," &c. Moreover it should be observed, that they who would (by a somewhat shallow criticism) insist on rendering εἰς by "towards" in verse 18, do not seem conscious that such a view is destructive of the apostle's previous argument. Adam's offence was not only *towards* all men, but attached *to* them, bringing with it its fatal results. That εἰς, the proper force of which is progress, often extends that force to attainment or completion, and so is rightly rendered "in" or "on," does not require demonstration.

contrast the specific *act* of Adam and the definitive *work* of Christ. Ruined by the offence of the one, we are established by the dying obedience of the other,[5]—we are justified by His *blood*. In the second, we are taught to compare the moral opposites of *character* presented, respectively, by the first and second man. The single offence of Adam, proved that the principle of disobedience was established in his heart, from the moment that a choice was offered to his will. The offering of Christ for our sins, was at the end of a course of absolute obedience, which had proved the Lamb of God to be "holy, harmless, undefiled, and separate from sinners." While, therefore, the former verse speaks of "justification unto life" as the proper sequel and effect of the judicial act of sacrifice[6]—agreeing in this with the doctrine already stated at the close of chap. iv.—the latter deals rather with the personal worthiness of Him who thus crowned[7] the work of righteousness by Himself, in His own body, bearing our sins upon the tree.[8]

This latter point, involving as it does the doctrine of the merits of Christ, deserves some further attention. The "Just One" has a righteousness which is *His own*, and which has shaped itself for Divine acceptance in the form of perfected obedience. It is according to the Father's estimate of Jesus and His work,[9] that believing sinners are now valued in His

---

[5] Such I believe to be the moral force of $\delta\iota\kappa\alpha\acute{\iota}\omega\mu\alpha$ in this verse. The finishing or sin was the justification also, both of the Sin-bearer and of those for whom He died; the official witness of His death being also the first among men to vindicate His *righteousness*. (Luke xxiii. 47.)

[6] Compare 2 Cor. v. 21 with Heb. ix. 14.

[7] Matt. iii. 15; Luke xxii. 37; Phil. ii. 8.

[8] 1 Pet. ii. 22-24. [9] John xvii. Comp. Isaiah xlix. 4.

sight, His Spirit being the attesting seal of this.[1] The first man's disobedience not only brought mortality, as its result, upon the entire human family, but by means of it, all men were constituted[2] *sinners*, through their necessary participation in a corrupted nature. The obedience of the second man is, on the other hand, communicated by a gracious imputation to all who, by virtue of their second birth, are enabled to receive Jesus as the Son of God.[3] Of His fulness do all such receive, and grace for grace.[4] And thus "the many," who form the spiritual progeny of the second Adam, shall be constituted[5] righteous by the obedience of the Just One, in the day when all who now are severally apprehended of God in Christ shall have attained, unitedly, their blessed hope, and are together found "in Him."[6] It is "in the Beloved" that God now accepts His saints.[7]

With respect to the form and quality of this obedience, it was threefold. The "Only-begotten" was obedient to the Father, finding meat and drink in the doing of works not written upon tables,[8] while the "Son of Man" fulfilled the double charge implied in the declaration, elsewhere made,[9] that He was "made of a woman, and made under Law." As the woman's seed, He was morally his Maker's image and glory, in all natural perfectness; He was also, as the child of Israel, the exact fulfiller of the Law.

---

[1] 1 John iv. 17; Eph. i. 13.   [2] κατεστάθησαν.
[3] The doctrine of regeneration, although it does not form a part of the apostle's argument, when treating the question of justification, is necessarily involved in it.
[4] John i. 12, 13, 16.
[5] κατασταθήσονται.   *Ante*, page 71, note 4.
[6] Phil. iii.   [7] Eph. i. 6.
[8] John iv. 34, v. 17, 36.   [9] Gal. iv. 4.

That He came to fulfil both the Law and the prophets is His own declaration.[1] "Thy Law is within my heart,"[2] are the words by which the Doer of the will of God accepted, specifically, this part of His responsibility as the "minister of the circumcision."[3] The "man" Jesus was "approved of God,"[4] and is the abiding realization of the Law's ideal of perfection.[5] Absolute love to God and to His neighbour, was the very nature of the Son of Man; while subjection to the written word, was both His chosen weapon of defence against the Tempter,[6] and the effective means of his destruction at the cross.[7] It was "according to the Scriptures"[8] that Immanuel both lived and died.

Now what Jesus was and is *to* God, He was and is *for* us.[9] His delights were ever with the sons of men. But, as already stated, this obedience found its end in *death*. For otherwise the Just One must abide alone.[1] And in the solemn act which closed it, the threefold excellency of the Lamb's obedience is not less conspicuous than in its course. It was at the Father's bidding that the Son laid down His life. By submitting to the stroke of death, the woman's seed effectually bruised the serpent's head; while the rejected "stone of Israel" was laid, by the same act,

---

[1] Matt. v. 17, 18. [2] Ps. xl. 8.
[3] Chap. xv. 8. [4] Acts ii. 22.
[5] Pss. xv. and xxiv.; Isa. xlii. 13-21.
[6] Matt. iv. [7] Heb. ii. 14.
[8] John xix. 28; 1 Cor. xv. 3.

[9] They, therefore, who would represent the Lord as vicariously fulfilling the Law, are not to be blamed for their *expression*, though too often it has attached to it a most faulty sense, as when it is affirmed that such Law-keeping, on Christ's part, is the true measure of a believer's righteousness before God. It is the Lord *Himself*, and not His work (still less a part of it), who is of God made righteousness unto us.   [1] John xii. 24.

NOTES ON THE ROMANS. 103

as the sure foundation of the covenant.[2] It was HIMSELF, in all the proved perfections of His Person, that "the Man Christ Jesus" gave as a ransom for all, when He died to give lasting efficacy to His own mediatorial grace.[3]

While, therefore, the justification of the believer is absolutely "apart from Law,"—God bestowing on Him freely His own righteousness, through the faith of Christ,[4]—yet when that righteousness is presented to us in the Person of the Just One, by the Spirit who reveals His glory, its brightness shines upon us from the face of One who, in His highest place, still wears the form and holds the names in which He once obeyed on earth. The Law and the prophets, to which He appealed as His witnesses in the days of His flesh, now bear Him everlasting testimony as the fulfiller of the words of God.[5] The head of Christ is God.[6] As the second Adam, He is the true image and glory of God.[7] And according to His meritorious perfections, as they are partly now revealed to us, and hereafter to be fully known,[8] are His brethren now presented in His person before God.[9]

Before proceeding, it may be well to notice the expression "many," or "the many,"[1] found both in this passage and in verse 15. First, it is a relative term, and therefore to be referred to that other

---

[2] Ps. cxviii. 22; Isaiah xxviii. 16; 2 Sam. xxiii. 5. The particular aspect of redemption which illustrates specifically the love of Jesus to the Church, is not here noticed, but has been treated in *Notes on the Ephesians*, chap. v.
[3] 1 Tim. ii. 5, 6.   [4] Phil. iii. 9.
[5] John v. 37–39; Acts xxvi. 22; Rev. xi. 19, xix. 10.
[6] 1 Cor. xi. 3.   [7] 2 Cor. iv. 4.
[8] 1 Cor. xiii. 9–12.   [9] Heb. ii. 10, 11.   [1] οἱ πολλοί.

term to which it stands related. This is readily perceived, on an attentive consideration of the structure of the apostle's argument. The one man sins—the many die, because of their inheritance of this one sin and its effects. Again, the one Man obeys—the many are justified in life, through the gracious imputation to them of this obedience. But in addition to this, the expression is to be controlled by what has been said (verse 17) as to the *receivers* of the abundance of grace being the objects of blessing. The apostle's reasoning evidently is, that justification of life stands not less absolutely as the derived effect of another's work, than did, and does, the condemnation which is referred to the one transgression. But as, in the latter case, the process of derivation is in the way of natural descent, and thus the entire race of mankind have been constituted sinners; so, on the other hand, the seed of the second Adam consists of those, only, who have been brought under the *effectual* operation of that grace of God, which acts contrary to nature, and by faith alone.[1]

Verses 20, 21. Having firmly established the doctrine of righteousness upon its new and everlasting foundation, the apostle takes now a retrospective view of the Law, in order to assign to it its proper place in the believer's mind. It came in by the way,[2] and was offered, not to *save* the people, but to *prove* them.[3] Grace was God's counsel, but Law must be first declared, that the excellency of mercy might be more abundantly glorified. The effect of the Law

---

[1] *Natural* headship is the relation of the first Adam to all flesh. *Federal* headship is the relation of the second Adam to such as are brought by grace, within the covenant of life and peace.
[2] παρεισῆλθεν.
[3] Exod. xix.

was to bring out the abundance of sin. It served to display man in the varied fulness of his misery, that God might, in Christ, reveal Himself, according to the surpassing richness of His own entire love. Grace superlatively exceeds in measure the sin which called it forth. It is the work of God, setting aside the work of Satan—delivering man, as Satan's captive, by the complete annihilation of that which had constituted and confirmed the destroyer's power over his victim. For the strength of sin is the Law. Sin has reigned *unto*, or rather *in, death*.[4] But to the believer, as alive in the risen Christ, this reign has come to a perpetual end. The song of victory is his.[5] The reign of grace remains. Grace shall reign, *through righteousness*, unto eternal life, by Jesus Christ our Lord. Already the Holy Ghost is the earnest of this reign, who reveals to us Jesus, crowned with glory and with honour. We see HIM.[6] We are already, if believers, translated into the kingdom of the Son of God's love. But what is thus realized by faith, remains to be displayed openly in due time. We *shall reign* in life by Him. He shall *come;* to be glorified in His saints, and to be admired in all them that believe.[7]

God has thus prepared, for the believing partakers of His grace, a change from sin to righteousness, and from death to endless life. Glory, and honour, and immortality, are become the righteous expectation of their faith. By bringing into view the glory of the second Adam, the Spirit opens to our weary souls another and eternal rest—a new and imperish-

---

[4] ἐν τῷ θανάτῳ.
[5] 1 Cor. xv. 56, 57.
[6] Heb. ii. 9.
[7] 2 Thess. i. 10.

able blessedness and joy. The old man is seen to be forgotten before God, in the presence of Him who is the *beginning*, the first-born from the dead,[8] the head of the new creation,—the Lord of all, as being appointed Heir of all things, but specially, OUR *Lord*. The confessed Lord of those who find in that confession, by the grace of God, the eternal assurance of acceptance in Him.[9]

[8] Col. i. 18.

[9] As the doctrine of justification has now been completely stated, a brief recapitulation of the distinctive terms employed by the apostle, in the course of his argument, may be fitly appended to this chapter. They are three. 1. *Righteousness* ($δικαιοσύνη$), which is natural to God only, is His gift by grace to the believer (i. 17, and v. 17). 2. *Justification*, as an *act* ($δικαίωσις$), is limited to God, but attaches in its effect to the believer (iv. 25, and v. 18). 3. Justification, as a *state* ($δικαίωμα$), is predicated, first, of Christ, as the judicial estimate of His work (v. 18); and, secondly, of the believer, as the possessor, by imputation, of a personal interest in his Redeemer (v. 16).

CHAPTER VI.

THE preceding chapter has determined the character of God as a Saviour; has demonstrated the victory of grace over sin; and, in revealing Christ as the anti-type and eternal contrast to the first Adam, has disclosed to the believer the security of his own interest, in righteousness, in the unfading blessing of the God of peace.

The question put at the opening of the present chapter, prepares the way for the *subjective* application of the doctrine of grace to the believer, as a vessel of holiness. The faith which justifies us must also be the manner of our walk. There is a "path of the just," in which none walk but they whose feet are shod with the preparation of the gospel of peace. It is the object of this chapter rather to indicate that path, and to incite the Christian to pursue it, than to explain the secret power of the just man's walk. The true energy of godliness in every believer is the *Spirit*, who reveals to him the finished love of God;[1] and in a later chapter we shall find this doctrine very fully stated.[2]

But the indwelling of the Spirit neither destroys our personal identity, nor supersedes our individual responsibility. Pardoned and forgotten, as *sinners*,

[1] Chap. v. 5.   [2] Chap. viii.

we are charged and reckoned with as *saints*. Hence, as a natural sequel to the emphatic declaration of the believer's justification, there follows this earnest exhortation to a worthy walk. But He who is our Righteousness must also be our Way. The same Christ, whom we have seen to be our living and abiding warranty of peace with God, and of a hope which maketh not ashamed, is now presented to us as the motive, also, and the measure, of our life and conduct in this present world.

It is therefore eminently a practical chapter. But the claim which it makes upon the *conscience* arises, as we shall presently see, from the clearness and precision with which the great doctrines of truth, as they are expounded in the Person and the work of Christ, are brought to bear upon the *faith* of the believer. This will ever be found to characterize the teaching of the Holy Ghost. His *end* is holiness; His *means* is truth. The new man, which is the believer's clothing, is created in righteousness and true holiness; or, as the margin more justly renders, the holiness of truth.[8]

Accordingly (verse 2), the question, "Shall we continue in sin," &c., brings forth, first, the peremptory disclaimer, "God forbid!" and thereupon follows immediately the demonstrative reasoning of the Spirit of God, in proof of the foolishness of the question, as well as of its pravity. We are *dead* to sin. How, then, shall we live therein? Such is the thesis of which this very important chapter is the amplification and development. But this truth, flowing as it does so necessarily from the doctrine of the cross,

[8] Eph. iy. 24; ἐν δικαιοσύνῃ καὶ ὁσιότητι τῆς ἀληθείας.

ought to have been *known* by those to whom it is addressed. Nay, the very outward act by which the new-born believer testified his passage, in Christ, from death into life, was a type and memorial of this most solemn and most blessed truth (verses 3, 4). Thus the fuller statement of the doctrine of substitution, which forms the main subject of the chapter, is introduced by the half-reproachful question, " Know ye not?" And thenceforward, to verse 14 inclusive, we have the general argument of Christian liberty, and its effects as they flow from the twofold doctrine of, first, the substitution in death of Christ *for* the believer; and, secondly, the union of the believer *with* Christ as alive from the dead.

The grand *moral* truth of this chapter is, that Christians are, by virtue of redemption, not only freed from sin, but brought also, as prepared vessels of holiness, *to God*. The substitution of Jesus for the believing sinner on the cross, has blotted out from before God, not only the guilt of his soul, but also the very remembrance of his *person*, as a man naturally alive—a fleshly man. Death and burial, which the Just One underwent according to the Scriptures, are the realities of God, wherein the eye of faith beholds its emancipation from the yoke of sin. " He that is dead (or rather, who *died*) is freed (or, justified) from sin"[4] (verse 7). The image

---

[4] Ὁ γὰρ ἀ π ο θ α ν ὼ ν δεδικαίωται ἀπὸ τῆς ἁμαρτίας. On this verse (here quoted in anticipation of its order in the chapter), I would say that it appears to contemplate, first and principally, Christ Himself as our atoning sacrifice; and secondly the believer, for whose sake He died. That we must have died to sin in order to live to God, is evidently the main drift of the Apostle's teaching in this chapter. But "a dead man," simply considered, is *not* freed, or justified, from sin. For after death comes judgment, for the natural

of this reality is the act of baptism. "We were baptized into His death." "We were *buried* with Him," he continues, "by this baptism into death." And then follows a statement of the proper result of this doctrine: "That like as Christ was raised from the dead by the glory of the Father, even so we also should walk in *newness* of life."

"In newness of life." This is not a figure of speech. It is a Divine reality. Faith, receiving its instruction, not from internal suggestions, but from the true sayings of God, finds the term and cessation of natural life, in the cross of the Son of God. Henceforth, therefore, the believer, taught by the Spirit to avert his eye from self, as from a dead and forgotten thing, looks forth to seek for and to find his *present* life, as well as his future hope, in Jesus. He has been already planted, by an outward expression in baptism, in the likeness of Christ's death. He *will* be, in due time, revealed in the likeness of his resurrection.

The language of verse 5 is worthy of all attention, inasmuch as it shows, very strikingly, the necessary relation which subsists between genuine faith and holiness of walk. "If we have been *planted*," &c. The force of such an expression is much impaired, if we fail to see in it a figure of the just effect of faith upon its subject. If the cross of Jesus really be, to our faith, the termination of our natural responsibili-

---

man. (Heb. ix. 27.) It is only as having died *judicially* with Christ, that freedom from sin can be predicated of any man. Moreover, had the Apostle desired to state merely, as a link in his argument, that "a dead man is released from sin," he would, I believe, rather have said, ὁ τεθνηκώς, or, perhaps, νεκρός. For a further elucidation of the doctrine, in its application to the believer, see 1 Pet. iv. 1.

ties by means of judicial death, we surely shall no longer act as other men; we shall be planted in the likeness of His resurrection also; *i.e.* our walk will be in the power of the latter truth, even as our peace and confidence are drawn solely from the former. The apostle was himself the living pattern of this, as he abundantly declares elsewhere.[5]

Such, then, is the nature of the appeal which He, who is the Spirit of *holiness* as well as grace, thus makes to our consciences in this verse, which may, indeed, be expounded also with reference to the ulterior hope expressed in 1 John iii. 2, but which more properly relates, as the sequel of this chapter shows, to the present manifestation of the life of Christ in us; just as, in the verse which follows, the foundations of our confidence are further strengthened, and the work of faith encouraged, by a distinct reference to the counsel of Him who fulfils the good pleasure of His goodness in His saints. "*Knowing* this," &c. It is given to the believer to know, not only the assured reality of the crucifixion, in Christ, of the old man, but also the present end and purpose of this, "that the body of sin might be destroyed, that henceforth we should not *serve* sin." That is, he is solemnly conscious of the judicial setting aside of the body of sin in the way of death, in order that God's claims upon his obedience might supplant, in the power of the risen life in Jesus, the former bondage of sin. The saint, thus crucified *with* Christ, is known of God *in* Christ, as alive from the dead. Christ, Himself the resurrection and the life, lives as the survivor of sin and death. He has put away

[5] Gal. ii. 20; Phil. iii. 10.

the first,[6] He has abolished the second, in the death of the cross.[7] He lives unto God, as alive from that death. Faith knows Him *thus;* no longer knowing Him after the flesh, but as the beginning, the first-born from the dead. To continue, then, in sin, is to deny the truth.[8] Hence, in proportion to the direct simplicity of our faith in seeing Jesus, will ever be our available power against sin, our *practical* victory over the world, even as we are in *Him*, already, more than conquerors.[9]

The power of Satan, as the adversary of Christians, consists mainly in his command over the feelings

---

[6] Heb. ix. 26.   [7] 2 Tim. i. 10.

[8] The believer is born of God. In the present chapter, the objective truth of the Christian's union with the risen Christ is mainly dwelt on, and is kept steadily before the eye of faith, with a view to its practical results in the believer's way. In the Epistle of John (1 John iii. 9), we have the distinct enunciation of the new birth and its results, as an ascertained reality, to which the Spirit of truth bears this witness, in declaring the nature and extent of the work of God. He begets, by the word of His truth, children who resemble Himself. This act of Divine power is absolute, and, from its very nature, subject to no change. The unalterable qualities of a nature, which is Divine in its source, and imparted by immediate communication from the Father (1 John iv. 13), remain independent of all circumstances which may bear externally upon the believer, for good or for evil. The new nature of a child of God is essentially holy. As man, in his natural state, runs instinctively into sin in his desire to please himself, so the spiritual man obeys an instinct of holiness which is inseparable from his nature as born of God. And so it is said, "He *cannot* sin, *because* he is born of God." Here, then, is an answer at once to the question with which the present chapter opens. Conversion to God is not a change of *opinion* merely; it is a renewal of *nature*. But because the flesh lusts still against the spirit, and active conflict is the result, we need a weapon of stronger temper than a doctrine whose appeal may seem in part addressed to the subjective consciousness of the believer. While, therefore, the Spirit of God affirms, as just now stated, the proper characteristics of the new man, His means of practically exemplifying in the Christian this participation in the Divine nature (2 Pet. i. 4), is by keeping ever before his mind the person of *Christ*, as the sole ground and pattern of his hope. It is *in Him* that the believer finds and maintains his standing as a child of God.

[9] 1 Cor. xv. 57; 1 John v. 4.

and sympathies of our natural hearts and minds. He plies, and that most skilfully, the various motives which act upon a heart whose *permanent* condition is alienation from God—the evil heart of unbelief. Reasonings, thoughts, conjectures, probabilities, fallacious suggestions of a conscience not yet fully purged and brightened by the light of God, as well as actual sensation, are abundantly used by him, in order to keep the soul within the small and dark circle of its own experiences, instead of rejoicing in the perfect liberty of Christ. He knows that nothing so hinders the work of Christian obedience, in its full acceptation, as a defective perception of divine truth. Hence his desire to limit, by all means, the growth of God's saints in the knowledge of *God*—to make self, in some way, the secret centre of the believer's thoughts. The effectual security against this danger is the Word, when fed upon by faith. Faith thus exercised produces knowledge, and *that* knowledge is indeed power. A Christ-fed believer *understands* the nature of his calling, and in the calm assurance that the God who alone has any right to judge him, has become, in Christ, his Saviour and his Rest, he can boldly look his adversary in the face. For he has to do with One who can neither lie nor be deceived. And so faith corrects and overawes mere natural sensation by the shadow of the Almighty, abiding there in fullest confidence and joy, a stranger to all fear, but that which is never separable from a true enjoyment of the grace of God.[1]

To resume the thread of our chapter. We have, in verse 7, the conclusive answer to any plea which

[1] Heb. xii. 28, 29; Acts ix. 31; Ps. xci. 1.

a carnal or careless believer might set up on the ground of *weakness,* as well as a solid resting-place for a soul sincerely seeking God's true peace. "For He who has died is freed from sin." The finishing of sin[2] is, for the believer, the beginning of an everlasting righteousness. For we are justified *by His blood.* Death is the sole emancipation from the body of sin, and we have died with Christ. Satan often endeavours to persuade the soul that it is *not* entirely free, and supports his insinuation by an appeal to inward experiences. But God has made the cross of His Son to be the standard of Christian liberty. The Spirit is the witness of this, who reveals the Lord Jesus as the risen *Man* to our faith. The impotency of the saint is in himself. That is indeed a weakness unto death. But in the knowledge that Christ who died unto sin once, now lives for ever unto God, faith finds and puts on the strength of God.

Verses 8–10 are strikingly emphatic in the clearness with which they shew how completely the objective view of what Christ has been and is—both as to His past sufferings, and His eternal condition as the now reässerted heir of life and glory, according to the power of the resurrection—is substituted by the Spirit of God for the natural ideas and surmisings of the mind. "We *believe* that *we* shall live with Him, *knowing* that *He* dieth no more," &c. Especially should the language of verse 10 be noted, as it contains the hinge upon which the entire doctrine of this chapter turns; the death of Christ once for all unto *sin,* or, in other words, complete sacrifi-

---

[2] Jas. i. 15. As to the specific force of the apostle's language in verse 7, see the note at page 109.

cial atonement, being the immoveable centre of all that the Holy Spirit, as the Comforter, teaches in the Church. Let us also mark carefully the completeness of Christ's personal identity, both before and after death. *He* died—*He* lives—dying once unto sin, when in gracious obedience to the Father's commandment, He laid down His life for His own; living now unto God, the same³ as He once died—having resumed, according to His word, the life which He had thus laid down. No *new* or *other* life, than that in which He glorified the Father in the days of His flesh—His state is different, but His life the same. "Newness of life" is fitly predicated, in verse 4, of His people, who by faith are joined to Him; even as "newness of the Spirit," is, in the following chapter,⁴ a characteristic description of His people's service. But neither to the Person nor the life of Christ, have such distinctive terms as old or new any proper application. Whether in humiliation or in glory, He is "Jesus Christ, the *same* yesterday, to-day, and for ever." And as having thus abolished death, and brought both life and incorruptibility to light, He is presented to His people's faith, as both the substance and the measure of their hope. The entire ground of confidence is thus transferred from self to Christ.

Accordingly, we have the application of this principle in the verses immediately following. "Likewise *reckon* ye also yourselves to be dead indeed unto sin," &c. It is not a mere sentient impression of the mind, while undisturbed by any active temptation. Nor is it that happy but temporary frame of spirit,

³ John ii. 19, x. 17, 18.   ⁴ Chap. vii. 6.

which, like a special visitation of gracious refreshment from the Divine presence, may now and then come within the sphere of a believer's actual experiences. Nor yet is it the self-flattering consciousness of a mind engrossed, and, for the time, upheld above itself, by an unreflecting diligence in outward works of godliness. It is from none of these things that the believer is to infer his practical deliverance from sin. He is to *reckon*, in the soberness of faith, that as Christ is, so is he; for it is "in Christ Jesus"[5] that he is now alive to God. Feeling may inwardly contradict the revelation of God, and *natural* feeling ever does so, because it *is* natural, and does not flow from truth—from God. Conflict of this kind must be the result of our being yet experimentally in the flesh. "The flesh lusteth against the Spirit" in every sense. But the divine power of God hath given unto us all things that pertain unto life and godliness.[6] The Spirit also lusts against the flesh, and is the stronger of the two. Hence there is assumed for the believer (verses 12, 13), a power and capacity to contradict and overrule the natural will of the flesh. He who is addressed is distinguished from that in which he dwells, and which he is thus exhorted to use to the glory of God. The complete identification of the believer with the Christ who is his life, invests him with a stewardship of trust, as it respects the control and management of his members here. For he is not his own, but His who has bought him with His own blood; and the faith that discerns this, *works* by the love which it begets.[7]

[5] ἐν Χριστῷ Ἰησοῦ. *Ante*, p. 89, note 1.
[6] 2 Peter i. 3.   [7] Gal. v. 6.

This severance of a man from himself is not mysticism. It is the soul-delivering, heart-assuring truth of God. Yet how solemn is it in its blessedness! The practical responsibilities of the saint are ever commensurate with his glorious privileges. If he is able to joy in God through Jesus Christ, in the unspeakable assurance of perfected reconciliation, he has to remember, and is here reminded, that the life which he has thus begun to taste is "unto God." He is expected, *as a man*, in this present world, to yield *himself* unto God by faith, as alive from the dead, and his *members* as instruments of righteousness unto God.[8] The Spirit of God, knowing what is in man, has seen fit to address the children of God not only in the way of comfort, but also of exhortation, and, if need be, of rebuke. Nothing is more certain than that Christians will fall into a lax and lean condition of soul (and that as the very consequence of their *doctrinal* establishment in grace), if there be not a daily living, by faith, unto God. The will of God takes the place, in the believer's conscience, of the lusts of men; and He who wills must also work. It is *to God* that we must yield our members, as instruments of righteousness. He compasses His will in us by the devoted obedience of our faith. Our members are *His* instruments,[9] to whom pertain the battle and the victory. That victory is surely ours in every struggle, so long as our eye is singly resting upon Jesus. But where the will of God is practically disregarded, the believer's ability to conquer sin, and to wield his own members

---

[8] Titus ii. 12.   [9] Or weapons, ὅπλα.

as effective instruments of righteousness, must be diminished in a corresponding ratio.

But more than this. If sin is not overcome, it overcomes. Measures and degrees are not here the question, but the moral certainty that the flesh will prevail, in its conflict with the Spirit, whenever the soul is not kept abidingly in the presence of God. There is nothing of which our wretched nature is capable (short of the deliberate renunciation of Christ), which may not be exemplified in the experience of a believer who is not watchfully abiding in Christ. The will of God is our sanctification, body, soul, and spirit. We are called to be holy, as He is holy.[1] Further, "Without holiness no man shall see the Lord."[2] And, lastly, the very seal of Divine election bears on its reverse: "Let every one that nameth the name of Christ, depart from iniquity."[3] The commandments, then, of God are clear and express, and we are sanctified unto *obedience.*"[4]

But what if, after all this, the professed subjection of the heart to Christ give place to the natural bias of the soul to sin? Does the sin of a believer frustrate his hope as a Christian? The reässuring answer of comfort to this question, so full of anxiety to an unestablished Christian, may be collected at large from Scripture;[5] but the apostle here states doctrinally (verse 14) the firm and sustaining ground of still unbroken confidence to the tried spirit. "Sin shall not have dominion over you; for ye are not under Law,

---

[1] 1 Pet. i. 16.   [2] Heb. xii. 14.
[3] 2 Tim. ii. 19.   [4] 1 Pet. i. 2.
[5] Compare 1 John i. 8, 9; ii. 1; Heb. iii. 15, 16; vii. 25, &c.

but under *grace.*" The soul that has owned in faith the Lordship of Christ, is no more under the dominion of sin. The strength of sin is the Law, because the Law looks for righteousness in the creature. But the Law has already become, to the believer, the consenting witness of his justification in the way of grace. He is *under grace.* The temporary prevalence of sin in conflict cannot vitiate his title of acceptance, which is founded, not on works, but on grace—on righteousness as found, not in the sinner, but in the Saviour. It is indeed a heavy and a saddening thought, that a believer should fail in conflict, or fall into sin. Nothing can excuse it. Grace can meet us with restoring mercy, upon the confession of our sins; but no plea of any kind can be set up in justification of failure. Blessed beyond expression indeed is the thought, that the throne of grace is abidingly the place of refuge to the discomfited and self-condemned believer. The everlasting compassions of the Father of mercies can flow, with unfailing fulness, into our souls, through Him who is, in His own blessed Person, our Advocate in righteousness with God.[6]

The presence of God is the dwelling-place of the believer. The moment he forgets that presence he becomes careless. Sin is the atmosphere of the world. It is only in the presence of God that holiness is either understood or enjoyed. But the renewed mind desires holiness, because it loves God. These desires are all the stronger by reason of the keener perception which the lively Christian has of the contrariety of everything here, whether in the world or in his own flesh, to God. The proper hatefulness of sin is never

[6] 1 John ii. 1.

rightly estimated, except in communion with the grace which has delivered from it. Alas! that the blessed Spirit, who seals in Christ unto the day of redemption the ransomed souls of His saints, should so often be grieved by the amazing discovery in them of preference for that (in some shape or other) which caused the Lamb of God to die! Still, grace abounds, and truth, though tried to the uttermost, will prevail. Satan's power to distress the tried soul consists in his counsels of doubt and mistrust as to the continuance of the love of God, when the conscience may be deeply groaning under a sense of its abuse. At such a time, a recurrence to this blessed word will, if there be simplicity of faith on our parts, suffice to turn the enemy's power to weakness, and to restore the comfort of God to the afflicted soul. May His people know the Shepherd's voice!

Verses 15–18. The positive assertion of the inviolability of the believer's title as under grace, and not under Law, provokes now a repetition of the original question, "Shall we sin?" And this leads to a further development of the doctrine of *obedience* as the rule and measure of Christian liberty. We are not under Law. Are we then at our own disposal? Are we free from responsibility to God, because exempted from the curse of the Law? Have we no master, because we have ceased to be the bondmen of sin and death? The answer is again, "God forbid!" The believer is called unto liberty.[7] But the power of that liberty is the presence of the Spirit of the Lord.[8] He is brought, by redemption, to God; where the flesh never comes. Hence the unceasing

[7] Gal. v. 13.   [8] 2 Cor. ii. 17.

conflict of Christian experience. But now the question, as to the free-born children of God, is whether they will walk so as to *please God*. The object sought, is now no longer self-justification by the deeds of the Law, but the obedience of *love* to God. A believer, who has felt the horror of bondage to sin and of distance from God, finds in the cross the end of his misery and the beginning of his hope. He is *safe* in Christ for ever. But he is not yet in heaven. Between himself and his desire, there is placed an interval of earthly life. How then shall he employ that interval? What is to be the rule, and what the objects of his walk? The apostle shows here that practically he must, in his daily life, be serving either God or sin, either righteousness or iniquity.

An independent condition can in no wise be the true place of the creature, and the common assertion of such a claim among men only proves what an ascendency Satan, as a deceiver, exercises over the natural mind. Man must be a servant of good or of evil. But his natural condition was that of bondage to sin. Grace, in the believer's case, has delivered him from that. He has gone forth from the house of bondage; but it is to meet and to serve the God of his salvation.[9] Redemption has made him *His*.

Nature is ever ready to turn the grace of God to lasciviousness. Hence the apostle's language in this passage contains in it something more than a needful and wholesome admonition to the real child of God, in whom the motions of sin are involuntary, and are deplored whenever felt. It is also a prophetic testimony against that which, while bearing the out-

[9] Exod. iii. 12.

ward form of faith, should hide an unchanged heart of wickedness under the external profession of the name of Christ. But as to those whom he addressed, he is able to thank God that they had not only heard, but had *obeyed* the doctrine. The words are remarkable: "Ye have obeyed from the *heart* that *form* of doctrine whereunto ye were delivered"[1] [margin]. Now the form of Divine doctrine, is the Person of the Son of God; and it is with the heart that man believeth unto righteousness. The "obedience of faith,"[2] which joins the believer to the Lord, has thus reversed his natural condition. He has passed into other hands; and, still a slave, not now of sin, his natural master, but of obedience (*i.e.* of Christ), he serves the Lord who has redeemed him.[3] The same God who had delivered the Gentiles over to a reprobate mind, now, in the power of elective mercy, delivers whom He will into glad and welcome subjection to the word of righteousness. Thus the mind of the believer becomes formed and fashioned by the truth which it obeys. Christian character is the proper result of a perception and enjoyment of the grace of God,[4] and amounts to this: Let us live according to the truth of our new nature and position in Christ.

The practical force of the remaining verses is sufficiently clear. It may be well, however, to note the

---

[1] εἰς ὃν παρεδόθητε τύπον διδαχῆς.   [2] Chap. i. 5.

[3] The believer is a servant of God and of the Lord Jesus Christ. The former he obeys, not as a creature only, but as a child. The latter, he is bound to serve and honour as his Lord. Yet it is our Brother whom we serve. And so the word here used by the apostle to express the believer's liberty in relation to his walk (ἐλευθερωθέντες), is not that which he has already employed, in verse 7, when asserting the doctrine of judicial emancipation, but the same which Jesus uses, when declaring the abiding liberty of those whom He has once made free. (John viii. 36.)   [4] Tit. ii. 10–14.

relation in which, as the work of faith, righteousness stands to holiness in verse 19. Holiness,[5] or sanctification, is regarded as the end, and righteousness as the means. Holiness, again (verse 22), is called the *fruit* or result of their service to God.

Sanctification, in this sense,[6] is a progressive work: it is a growth and result dependent, as to its measure, upon the degree of watchful and implicit devotedness with which the soul follows the Lord, as He leads in the paths of righteousness. Such sanctification is therefore attainable only by the absolute subjection of our members to righteousness.[7] As a double-minded man is unstable in all his ways, so the ripe fruit of sanctification cannot result from a partial obedience to the will of God. As we *are* separate in *truth* from the world, by virtue of our union with the risen and glorified Jesus, so are we called to be separate in *fact*, as those who are called, not by their own names any longer, but by His. His word, then, is, "If ye abide in me, and my words abide in you, ye shall ask what ye will, and it shall be done unto you."[8] A rich and fruitful promise to those who, in willing subjection to the Father, are sanctified by the power of His word.[9] Thus the measure of positive

---

[5] ἁγιασμός.
[6] It may not be superfluous to remind the reader, that in another and yet more important sense, sanctification is not a thing of progressive growth, but a permanent, unalterable truth—a finished and abiding result to the Christian of that which Christ Himself is. Sanctification, in this higher sense, is the effect of the one sacrifice by which Christ has perfected for ever them that are sanctified. He is Himself, of God, made sanctification unto them that are called. It is, moreover, "through sanctification of the Spirit" (in His primary act of regeneration), that the soul is alone enabled to render to its Lord and Saviour the obedience of faith. (2 Thess. ii. 13; 1 Pet. i. 2.)
[7] Παραστήσατε τὰ μέλη ὑμῶν δοῦλα τῇ δικαιοσύνῃ εἰς ἁγιασμόν.
[8] John xv. 7.   [9] John xvii. 17.

communion, and with it of conscious happiness, will ever be commensurate with the degree of watchful diligence which is manifested in the way of obedience.

The shades of difference in the actual condition of believers are many and various. Hence, while the Spirit of God seeks constantly to act on and call into exercise the finer sensibilities of the renewed affections, and thus to make the enjoyed love and grace of Jesus the meat to strengthen for the journey of the day; yet He so divides His word, as to meet the conscience with a strong appeal, where, for lack of use, the spiritual senses have been dulled, and the affections have become faint.

But now these once reckless and ungodly Gentiles were ashamed of the former fruitless works, and had already begun to taste, in their own happy experience, the pleasantness of the way of God.[1] Let us observe how wide the language is in this chapter. There is no specification. The contrast lies between nature and grace—God's glory and man's will. Anything (though, perhaps, in the abstract not evil) which does not make for holiness, which is not compatible with the liberty of an obedient servant of God, is declared to be *fruitless*. A recollection, in self-judgment, of wasted hours, misspent in frivolous pursuits, will call up a blush of shame to the face of a spiritual man, though the things themselves in which he had been engaged might be quite harmless in the eyes of men. Happy is that Christian who, in the faithful and stedfast assertion of his liberty in Christ, so walks in the spirit of obedience, as to enjoy an uninterrupted

[1] Prov. iii. 13–18.

fellowship with God, neglecting the ordinary objects of human ambition, that he may lay a firmer hold² on that eternal life unto which he has been called. "For the wages of sin is death; but the gift of God is life eternal in Jesus Christ our Lord."³

² 1 Tim. vi. 12, 19.
³ ἐν Χ. Ι. τῷ Κ. ἡμῶν. (Comp. 1 John v. 11.)

CHAPTER VII.

In the course of his last argument the apostle has affirmed, as a fundamental position, that believers are not under Law, but under grace. For those whom he addressed generally, as Gentile converts to the faith, such a statement was enough, confirming, as it does, the doctrine of imputed righteousness and of the believer's absolute acceptance in Christ, contained in the earlier chapters. But there were, among the saints at Rome, those who *knew* the Law—who had borne its yoke as Jews, and whose deliverance from it, though complete in Christ, was yet imperfectly *understood* in their souls. Again, we have here to adore the prescient wisdom and provident mercy of the Father of lights, who has made the actual condition of a few Jewish converts the occasion, not only of supplying the deficiency which then existed in their faith and knowledge, but also of exhaustively handling the subject of the Law, so as to place it permanently, and for our sakes, in its true light, and to confine it within its proper limits. The apostle, as taught of God, well knew that nothing would more effectually hinder the establishment of souls in the faith than erroneous or indistinct views of the Law. So long as it was allowed to stand before the conscience, as a monitor of Christian responsibility, there was a danger of confounding in the soul the *principles*, respectively, of Law and grace; a confusion which, wherever it exists, tends invariably to prevent that full establishment of *heart*, which it is the chief aim of the Spirit, as the Comforter, to effect.[1]

The object, therefore, of the present chapter is, first, to reässert and prove the believer's complete emancipation from the Law; and, secondly, to define and illustrate, in the way of personal example, both the nature and just effects of the Law as the probe and discoverer of human motive and conduct before God, and also the limits within which alone it can thus act.

With respect to the former of these points, the first six verses of the chapter present the case of the Jewish believer, both as to his privileges and his responsibilities, under the special image of the marriage tie. But there is a twofold application of this figure. First, the natural condition of the Jew, as in covenant subjection to the Law; and, secondly, his condition as having passed, by faith, into a new and altogether distinct relation, as the married wife of another. Further, the expiry of the former state of subjection, by the fulfilment of the terms of contract, *precedes* the establishment of the new relation.[2]

Verse 1 states the position, that "the Law hath dominion over a man as long as he liveth;" a position both enforced and illustrated in the next two verses. As to the illustration, it is necessary only

[1] Heb. xiii. 9; 1 Pet. v. 10.
[2] I will notice, presently, the wider application of this principle. At present, I confine myself strictly to the special and proper case of the Jewish convert.

to remark, that the dissolution of the marriage-bond is here contemplated under one only of its possible aspects, namely, the death of the husband.[s] The result, however, of such dissolution is the perfect freedom of the survivor from all remembrance of the former state of obligation and subjection. The dominion of the Law over its subject being thus established, it is clear that, so long as it lasts, no other state than that of legal bondage can be the portion of one under Law. The Law can only *lawfully* be set aside. But this may happen in two ways. First, by an exact fulfilment of the commandment, and the acquisition of life as the reward of obedience: and, secondly, in the way of judgment; the Law exhausting itself, and its claims, by the infliction of its last penalties upon its subject. In both these senses, the dominion of the Law has ceased in the case of the believer. In the present chapter, however, it is the latter instance which is chiefly in point, the former coming under special notice in the next.

Accordingly, in the following verse he proceeds to apply this doctrine practically. "*Ye* also are become dead to the Law *by the body of Christ.*" Now we have here, first, the condition of emancipation declared in verse 1, found attaching to the believer—he no longer *liveth:* "Ye are become dead." Secondly, there is the manner of this emancipation. It is "by the body of Christ." The Law's dominion has ceased with the life of its subject. Christ, who was made under the Law for our sakes, has, by submitting to its penalty, redeemed us from the Law. As it is

[s] The reason of this remark will appear presently.

said in the foregoing chapter: He died unto sin once for all.[4] He died under the Law's curse. He was "made a curse for us."[5] The Law, then, has done its utmost. As God's instrument of wrath against sin, it has been *used*, and used effectually, in making an end of transgression by the death of Him, who, though Himself without spot, took the place of the unjust—who, *by the grace of God*, was numbered with the transgressors, that the Scripture might be fulfilled. The sacrificial death of Christ thus becomes to the believer a definitive cessation of all legal claim. He has, "through the Law, become dead to the Law."[6] The cross of Jesus is his emancipation from the ancient yoke of bondage.

We have seen, then, how the imputed death of the believer, according to the doctrine of the cross, places him beyond the limit of the Law's dominion. But the same event, which thus terminates the epoch of legal government, by the death of its subject, has also vacated, by fulfilment, the Law itself. The shedding of the precious blood of Christ was the blotting out and removal of the handwriting of ordinances which was against us.[7] The Law which stood, as the holy expression of God's will, in perpetual contrariety to man as a sinner,—and thus opposed itself as a barrier, not to be removed by human strength, in the way of human liberty and blessing,—is now nailed to the cross of God's Son. He has abolished in *His flesh* the law of commandments contained in ordinances.[8] The first husband,

[4] ἐφάπαξ, chap. vi. 10.
[5] Gal. iii. 13.
[6] Gal. ii. 19.
[7] Col. ii. 14.
[8] Eph. ii. 15.

then, is dead; and the wife, now loosed from that tie, may marry whom she will.

We now begin to see the special application of the illustration stated in verse 3, in its reference to the case of the believing Jew. The apostle, accordingly, proceeds so to apply it (verse 4); "That ye should be married to another, even to Him who is raised from the dead, that we should bring forth fruit unto God." Here, then, is a new tie, another bond. As the entrance into the former contract was by the self-confident energy of the natural will,[9] which hastened into the covenant of works only to find the terror of the Lord as its portion, because the impotency of the sinful creature was thus brought into contact with the searching presence of Divine holiness; so, on the other hand, the soul, set free by the cross of Jesus from that reign of dread, moves swiftly, because drawn by cords of love, into the new and lasting covenant of peace. The believer thus, instead of being the Law's victim, becomes the possession, in love, of Him who has acquired the Law's right over his person, by having taken it out of the way, and Himself become, on God's behalf, the living and eternal Covenant of righteousness and truth. Being freed from the Law, he is bound to Christ—to God in Christ. Married to Him in righteousness and in judgment, and in loving-kindness and in mercies, he now *knows* the *Lord*.[1] While under Law, he had known Him in a portion of His way. He knew the Law, and by the Law he knew (in measure) Himself. But such a knowledge gave no joy to its possessor. Instead of gladness, it wrought fear; a fear that (for

[9] Exod. xix. 8.   [1] Hosea ii. 19, 20.

one who really felt its power) cast out hope, and made love's joy a thing impossible, because the clouded majesty of the God of judgment evermore presented itself to the conscience as the certain Avenger, in righteousness, of the unfulfilled requirements of the Law.[2] Love is the child of liberty. We love because first loved.[3] But the Law gendered to bondage.[4] It was a yoke which Divine holiness placed upon the neck of a nature altogether alien from God.

We shall return to this subject presently. Meanwhile let us contemplate a little further the condition, the privileges and the responsibilities, of the believer, as the wedded wife of the Lord. And now, having arrived at this point, I no longer treat the subject as especially bearing on the Jew. Having gotten beyond death into the resurrection, all such distinction ceases. The Jew has died. The *new man* in Christ alone survives.[5]

---

[2] Both love and hope were in the hearts of God's elect while under Law; but these were the effect, not of an unsullied legal conscience, but of a faith which clave to God and to His promises, in the patient expectation of good things to come. In their pleadings with Jehovah, they appeal from Law to grace: "Enter *not* into judgment," &c. (Ps. cxliii. 2.) Loving the Law and aiming at obedience, they felt still that they were as lost sheep, who needed to be sought and found by the Divine Redeemer of their souls. (Comp. Ps. cxix. 176.)

[3] 1 John iv. 19.   [4] Gal. iv. 24.

[5] A word of explanation is here offered, which some readers may find necessary. In treating the doctrine of this chapter, thus far, as properly and exclusively respecting the *Jewish* believer, I by no means lose sight of the far wider range and bearing of the subject, when considered in its practical relation to the conscience as having been under Law. In dispensational strictness, the Law is not addressed to us Gentiles. Christ is preached to us on another ground than that of legal forfeiture. The earlier chapters of this Epistle show this. But, in point of *fact*, it generally happens that the conscience is brought specifically under legal bondage. Where this is the case, what was addressed originally to the Jewish believer applies,

The Spouse of the believer is the risen Lord of glory. Christ, while known after the flesh, was no husband to the Church in *fact*, though in the eternal purpose of God He ever was; for until His death and resurrection, Jesus was characteristically a *Jewish* Christ. True, indeed, it is that He was far more. He was, in His holy and ever blessed Person, the unity of all truth. God was in Christ. But what He was in Himself as the Son, and what God who sent Him was, in the fulness of His divine character as *Love*, could not be fully known while Jesus remained on nature's side of death. He tarried there awhile, a Stranger in a strange place, until the hour having arrived for which He had come into the world, He made His passage into the joy that was set before Him, through the death of the cross.[6] But while alive in the flesh, He had declared to His disciples the consequences of His death. The Holy Ghost was to be given, when Jesus should have been glorified.[7] The effect of the presence of the Comforter was to be the assured knowledge, to those in whose hearts that Spirit was to dwell, of the Son of God—of the Father in the Son. But this knowledge was to be held and enjoyed in *love*. It is this subjective consciousness of being beloved of God in Christ, that renders the believer capable of divine communion. There is no fear in love. Entire deliverance from all dread or suspicion as to what the thoughts or intents of God may be, as possibly against us, must be attained, before this fearless love can be

as fully and immediately, to the exercised conscience of the Gentile. (See further, as to the general application of Law to the human conscience, the note at page 48.)

[6] Heb. xii. 2.   [7] John vii. 38, 39.

enjoyed. It is this liberty that we have in Christ. In Him we have seen, and in Him we *know*, the love which God has towards us.⁸ In Him we find that God *is* love. Herein, then, is love made perfect with God's believing children. That perfect love, where welcomed by a simple faith, has cast out fear; for fear hath torment. But the blessed Lord, who died to win His chosen for Himself in love, has no will that they who trust Him should be tortured still. Nay, the very price of our heart's affection for the Saviour, is the blood which has redeemed us from all that whence fear and torment can alone arise. To know Him in the faith of His Gospel, is to be joined to Him in the unity of the Spirit,⁹—to know Him as a Divine husband in love, as the satisfying rest of our souls.

But this realization of union with the risen Christ is further regarded in its present and practical results. We are married to Him "that we should bring forth fruit unto God." This forms the subject of verses 5 and 6. "For when ye were in the flesh," &c. The believer is thus invited to contemplate *retrospectively* his condition as a natural man. The former marriage had its appointed duration, and produced its fruits. Those fruits abounded while the husband lived; the Law entered that the *offence* might abound. The evil qualities of nature were brought into plenteous and varied manifestation by its contact with the Law. Fruit unto death! Such is man under a covenant of works—utterly barren of all true holiness, but fruitful in sin unto death. The rooted tree, in its own soil, can bring forth nothing but offence to God.¹

⁸ 1 John iv. 16–19. ⁹ 1 Cor. vi. 17.
¹ Isaiah v. 4; Matt. xv. 11; Luke xvi. 15.

The second marriage has likewise its duration and its fruits. As to the first, it is as long as He liveth who Himself is Life. The wedded soul is bound, for eternity, in the bundle of divine life with the Lord. The fruits of this marriage are the fruits of the Spirit, not those of the flesh. The root being changed, the fruit is likewise changed—the once empty vessel is now "filled with the fruits of *righteousness,* which are by Jesus Christ to the glory and praise of God,"[2] redounding thus to the glory of Him who *worketh in* us that which is well pleasing in His sight.[3] Christ is become the measure of the believer's responsibilities, as well as the possessor of his affections, and the security of his hope. Obedience is the law of marriage to the wife. We are servants of One who commands our service, not with the threatenings of vengeance, but by the constraint of His own unmeasured love.[4] The notion, therefore, of attempted *legal* obedience on the part of Christians, of taking the Law as the rule of conduct, &c., is a thought altogether faulty in principle. "The *end* of the commandment is *love* out of a pure heart, and of a good conscience, and of faith unfeigned."[5] The desires of the renewed mind for the attainment of this end can only be realized in Christ, who is become already, to the believer, the end of the Law for righteousness.[6] Legal teaching,. therefore, when admitted into the Church, is a practical disruption of the new marriage

---

[2] Phil. i. 11.
[3] Heb. xiii. 21. Would that it were so universally in fact! I speak here, however, not of the practical condition of the Church as it is, but of the just effects of the grace and truth which are in Christ, when, in the energy of the Spirit, they are duly realized by faith in the soul.   [4] 2 Cor. v. 14–17.
[5] 1 Tim. i. 5.   [6] Chap. x. 4.

NOTES ON THE ROMANS. 135

bond. The Law, being only addressed to man on the presumption of his *sinful* condition, has no application to those whose condition is that of *righteousness*, as being justified of God in Christ. Hence the apostle, in that same passage, speaks of those who desired to be teachers of the Law to Christians, as understanding neither what they said, nor whereof they affirmed. It was a perverse substitution of the oldness of the letter for the newness of the Spirit.

The believer's calling is to endeavour to walk so as to please God. Now the extent of this rule is measurable only by the perfect obedience of Christ. To follow Him, then, is the saint's responsibility. To be *yoked* with Him, in patient subjection to the teaching of His Spirit, is to find rest to our souls.[7] The commandments of love are not grievous. But, until the believer is able, through grace, to see the true nature of his present standing, as "rooted and grounded in love,"[8] as loved and blessed *in* Christ, as well as forgiven for Christ's sake, there will ever be the vain endeavour to satisfy conscience in a legal way. But solid peace can never result from this, because perfect peace can only be the effect of *righteousness;* and it is Christ alone, as known and enjoyed by faith, who is our righteousness with God.

The description of the incarnate Son of God, when sent by the Father's grace into the world, is that He was "born of a woman, born under law."[9] The believer, on the other hand, is said to be "born of the Spirit,"[1] and subjected to Christ.[2] Moses the

[7] Matt. xi. 29, 30.   [8] Eph. iii. 17.
[9] Gal. iv. 4.   [1] John iii.   [2] 1 Cor. xi. 3.

servant is dead, but Jesus, the beloved Son, both lives and speaks; and to Him as "the beginning, the first-born from the dead,"[3] the Church is now subject as to her anointed Head.[4] Liberty of conscience is thus the very law of the believer's being, as a new and risen man in Christ. What Jesus promised,[5] ere His dying love had ratified His words, is now, in the light of His ascended glory, a settled and eternal truth, and they who by faith abide in Him are "free indeed." The old liabilities are dissolved with the old *man* wherein they lay. Henceforth, as *new creatures*, as born children of God in Christ, we are called to be imitators of God—to walk worthy of Him—to be perfect, as He is perfect.[6] Thus, in the place of the former debt of unfulfilled legal obedience, an obligation which redemption has perfectly discharged, there is substituted the new and never-to-be-satisfied claim of that love which passeth knowledge. Gladly, indeed, may we own this claim, whilst yet we may have ever to mourn the faultiness of our endeavour to meet it in the way of practical devotedness. Blessed love, that at once stimulates the heart and conscience to abound in the work of the Lord, and withal meets, in the unupbraiding fulness of *grace*, the constant failure of its objects to walk worthy of the vocation with which they are called!

Let us turn now to a separate consideration of the remainder of this chapter. It has already been shown that by the Law is the knowledge of sin;[7] that the

[3] Col. i. 18. [4] Eph. v. 25.
[5] ὄντως ἐλεύθεροι ἔσεσθε, John viii. 36.
[6] Eph. v. 1; Matt. v. 48. [7] Chap. iii. 20.

Law worketh wrath;[8] that the abundance of sin was by the Law;[9] and lastly, in verse 5 of the present chapter, that the motions of sins which wrought in the members to bring forth, in the natural man, fruit unto death, were likewise by the Law. Since, then, sin and its effects are thus referred to the Law, the question suggested and answered in the seventh verse, seems to furnish the natural mind with its last weapon of conflict against the truth of God, so far as the Law is concerned, Is the Law sin? Such a question might be sincerely asked by an inquiring mind, but half delivered yet from the mists of its own ignorance. It might, on the other hand, be insinuated by the unbelieving heart of natural wickedness, still seeking means of self-justification by charging God foolishly. To meet the just demand of an inquiring conscience, and at the same time to deprive the perverse will of man of its last plea of excuse, by turning such plea into a decisive evidence of guilt, is the twofold object of the apostle in what follows.

The Law is not sin, but holiness. Being such, it is the detector of sin. And now, before proceeding with the apostle's argument, I would remark, that the process of illustration here employed pre-supposes the presence of renewed life in the subject, who is here contemplated as experimentally proving what the Law really is. The apostle, as is usual with him, when stating emphatically any point of directly personal application, speaks here in the first person. Whether, however, the experience which he here details be an exact reflection of what had at

[8] Chap. iv. 15.   [9] Chap. v. 20.

one time passed in his own soul, or whether he has chosen this form of statement, simply as being more distinct and vivid, is quite immaterial. The point of real moment is to remember that, while he is thus reviewing, for our profit and instruction, the fearful realities of sinful experience, as they are necessarily found in the case of a soul made capable of self-judgment by the Law; yet he is addressing himself to those whom he has already conducted into the cloudless peace and blessedness of the risen life in Christ.

Resuming now the apostle's argument, we find (verses 7–11) a general statement of the power and effect of the Law, as the discoverer and stimulant of sin, and the minister, because of sin, of death also to the soul. The Law is not sin; "nevertheless,"[1] says the apostle, "I had not known sin but by the Law." The Law is the revelation of the Divine will, as the measure and rule of human obedience. It not only therefore prescribes and forbids actions, according to their qualities of good or evil, but applies itself also to the motive springs of action in the heart. But in so doing, it necessarily, because it is the expression of *God's* will, denies and disallows the will of *man* as something independent of God. It claims for God the undisputed right of governing His creature as He will. The condition of the man previously to the arrival of the Law, was that of self-guidance. He lived, and thought, and acted according to the light of his own judgment, and the suggestions of his own desire. "I was alive without the Law once."

---

[1] ἀλλά. As has been justly remarked, the characteristic point of the reasoning in this verse is obscured by the A. V.

But the Law came, bringing with it all the weight and sanction of Divine command. The smooth current of the hitherto unchecked human will, became thus suddenly arrested in its course by the peremptory opposition of the will of God. The effect of this was not to change the native disposition of the human will, but, by shedding in the light of Divine truth upon the conscience, to disclose to the soul, thus awakened to the fear of God, the real character of that will, in its effective contrast to the holy will of God. Old things now receive new names. That which had before been followed as the bent of nature, unreproved by conscience, because not yet referred to God as the standard of its quality, becomes now a lust forbidden by the Law of God. "For I had not known lust, exeept the Law had said, 'Thou shalt not covet.'" There is no mention made, in the apostle's argument, of *acts* of transgression. The question of sin is argued, not in the open court of man's judgment, but in the secret chambers of the heart. The fact that the Law contains in its expression anything repugnant to the will of man, proves conclusively the natural alienation of his heart from God. Man thinks, and feels, and wills, and acts, not to God-ward as his object and his end, but self-ward. He is the centre of his own thoughts, and the end of his own desires. He acts, naturally, as if he were independent of Him who created him. This is SIN. Sin is the name given by the Spirit of God to the course of the human will, when its measure and direction are guaged by the Law of Divine commandment. The single prohibition in the garden of Eden acted thus, when the lie of the tempter had aroused the independent action of the human will. Adam's inclination, coming into contact with the expressed command of God, revealed sin in the form of transgression. Let us remember that it is the secret conscience (and not external acts) that is in question in the present argument. "I had not known sin but by the Law," is a general expression of the judgment formed in the inner man, respecting the effect of Divine truth upon the conscience, when it acts as a discoverer of sin. Desires which had slumbered undisturbed by temptation, and which lay forgotten or unknown upon the low ground of the heart, suddenly awoke, and moved, when the voice of God, as of a stranger, was heard saying in the Law, "Thou shalt not covet." The very utterance of the will of God, is the suggestion of sin to the heart of fallen man!

But the spark thus kindled in the soul, grows quickly to a raging and consuming flame. "Sin, taking occasion by the commandment, wrought in me *all manner of concupiscence.*" "For," it is added, "without the Law sin was dead." As the pressure of a heavy weight on some elastic substance, calls into positive effect a native power of repulsion, untried and latent until then; so the restraint of Divine commandment, serves but to develope and call into exercise the resisting forces of the natural will. But the discovery of indwelling sin, thus effected by the application of the Law to the conscience, brings to the awakened mind a fatal conviction of its hopeless condition, as already judged, and under the declared condemnation of the Law. The conscious revival of sin is the utter extinction of the sinner's hope. The commandment which was ordained unto life is found (verse 10) to be unto death.

This result, however, must be referred to its true cause. If the Law works death, it does so, not as being in itself a destroyer, but as instrumentally furthering the completion of sin. It is sin alone that produces death. "Sin, when it is finished, bringeth forth death."[1] Accordingly, we have a striking expression of the same solemn reality in the eleventh verse: "For sin, taking occasion by the commandment, deceived me, and by it slew me." Sin first deceives, and then destroys. But the Law is here its instrument of deception. The meaning of this must be familiar experimentally to every Christian, who has, in any measure, known the deceitful workings of his naturally self-righteous heart. "All that the Lord hath spoken we will do,"[2] was the unhesitating reply of the natural heart, when first the covenant of works was offered for its acceptance. The same people, whose way had been but a continuous repetition of failure and unbelief, from the time that God had brought them out of Egypt, now find it in their heart to close thus eagerly with a proposal, which made their inheritance of blessing to depend no longer upon grace, but works—not on God, as their Saviour for His name's sake, but on themselves, as the self-justified fulfillers of the Law. Sin thus deceived them. The specious self-flattery of momentary zeal, rivetted upon the neck of the nation a yoke which no merely human strength could bear, and which nothing but the Samson-might of

[1] James i. 15.   [2] Exod. xix. 8.

the Captain of Salvation could break. And as it was with the nation, so is it with the individual heart of any one who has been awakened by the Spirit's voice, to find himself entangled in the evil net of destruction, through the lying seduction of a self-righteous heart.

The principle of duty is so inherent in every conscience, that the idea of legal obedience is of all things the most natural. But the purposes and resolves of an awakened conscience, so long as they are taken in ignorance of redemption, are but the evidences of a mind deceived by the dream of its own sufficiency, and unconsciously hardening itself in sin. Again let me repeat that it is the *renewed* mind alone, which can experience the consciousness of what the apostle is here describing. The carnal, unawakened heart can boast itself in the Law; and, far from doubting its own safety, can despise others from the ideal vantage ground of its own self-imputed righteousness. It is only where the Law is *known*, as nature never knows it, that this boasting is turned to mourning and complaint.

Verse 12 pronounces the deliberate estimate of the renewed conscience as to the quality of the Law and the commandment.[3] It is "holy, and just, and good." But, from this confession arises the further question (verse 13): "Was then that which is good made death unto me?" Nay; it was not the goodness of the commandment, but the opposing power of sin, that wrought this death. The absolute evil of sin, its exceeding sinfulness, is made apparent through

[3] That is, the specific prohibition "Thou shalt not covet," on which the whole reasoning of the apostle practically turns. (Comp. John ii. 10.)

the effect thus produced upon the sinner by the ministration of holiness and righteousness and goodness. These things are in the Law, but their very presence serves only to bring out into active contrast what is in me, to discover the sin which *dwells* within me. But if so, holiness, which can never tolerate sin, finding sin in me, as the answer on my part to the righteousness which is in God, pronounces on me the necessary judgment of death. Thus sin works death in me by that which is good.

Verse 14 declares the solution of the whole difficulty, by stating the eternal contrariety of the Law as spiritual, to fallen nature as carnal. " I am carnal, sold under sin." Nature, once vitiated by the entrance of sin, remains in perpetual subjection to the power which has subdued it.

We come now to another and a most important, as well as interesting, feature in this case.

In the verses which follow, presenting as they do a picture of the ceaseless conflict of a pure mind[4] against indwelling sin and corruption, we find the sufferer distinguishing *himself* from that which he hates, though it be the tabernacle of his very life. The body of sin and death is one thing—the renewed soul, groaning under the weight of that body, and calling aloud for deliverance, is another and entirely different thing. The great discovery, that in the flesh "dwelleth no good thing," is never made by the natural mind. Nature can never reveal to itself the secret of its own disgrace and ruin. Nor does it heed the revelation which God makes of these things.

---

[4] That is, a *renewed* mind, which none but a quickened soul can have. (Comp. 2 Pet. iii. 1.)

Light and truth are of that *good*[5] which is not found indwelling in the flesh. Hence, it is not until the soul has been quickened by the Holy Ghost, and is thus alive to God, that this holy judgment of the true nature of sin, and the proper work of the Law, can take place. But the renewed mind not only knows the holiness of the Divine character, and recognises the Law as the expression of the will of God: there is also, in every regenerated soul, an instinctive desire after holiness, and a corresponding hatred of sin. As the natural heart turns willingly aside from God, to seek its pleasure in the ways of sin, so the desires of the new man ever turn toward God, and away from the objects of men's natural lusts.

But while enabled thus to detach *himself*, as alive to God, from the sin which dwells within him, and while fully conscious of desires of good, of a will quite opposite to the lusts of nature, yet the spirit of the godly man, so long as he remains in ignorance of the liberty of redemption, is in bondage still. He finds himself utterly powerless of escape from that which he loathes. True it is that he may justly say, "It is no more *I* that do it, but *sin* that dwelleth in me" (verse 20). He may, moreover, "consent to the Law that it is good" (verse 16). Nay, he may "delight in the Law of God after the inward man" (verse 22). All this may be, and *will* be, in the case of one alive to God, and practised in the ways of holiness. But the very presence of these convictions and desires only renders the awakened lover of holiness more acutely sensible of the pressure of that

[5] ἀγαθόν.

other thing—that opposing and ever-dominant principle of sin in his members. He sees (verse 23) another law in his members, not only warring against the law of his mind, but *bringing him into captivity* to the law of sin which is in his members. He is a poor slave still. The glimpses of liberty which open on him in his meditations on the Law, do but enhance the bitterness of that hopeless bondage under which he lies. This is the perfection of human misery— the being endued with desires of holiness and life, but experimentally proving the mastery, in the members, of sin (whose only fruit is death) as a dominant, compelling principle, a Law with strength to enforce its rule. The very Law of God, in which the inward man delights, becomes thus the weapon of utter destruction against the self-judged, yet self-acquitted sinner—sinning not willingly, yet sinning unto death. "O wretched man that I am! who shall deliver me from the body of this death?" (ver. 24.) Such is, at once, the heart-broken confession of human extremity when brought, by means of the spiritual Law of God, into a right appreciation of the weakness and wretchedness of the flesh; and, at the same time, the utterance of a vague but genuine invocation of Divine compassion, which fails not to reach the ears of Him whose end is not Law, but Grace. Everything is now given up. The conflict is at an end; and the cry of the captive is gone up to the heaven which seems to be closed against him by the sentence of the Law. Sin's victory is complete. The lawful captive may mourn, but his captivity is lawful still.

Such then is the end of the Spirit's comment upon the work of the Law, as that which brings out, in their full completeness, the nature and effects of sin. It is found to work death, and not life. The vain attempt to keep the commandment, ends but in augmented wretchedness and disappointed hope. The child of bondage[6] lies fast held in the fetters of sin and death. But it is here that God, in Christ, can meet him, and can set him free. Accordingly, in the verse which closes the chapter, we have the solemn thanksgiving of the delivered soul. His cry of despair is turned into the note of praise at the revelation of the name of Jesus Christ the Lord.

No mention has been made of that blessed Name during the previous description of the soul's exercise while consciously under Law; the object of the apostle there being, not to speak of the conflict of flesh against Spirit in one already established in the grace of the gospel, but to shew forth, clearly and vividly, the inevitable effect of the Law in its operation on the conscience of an awakened sinner, so long as he remains in ignorance of Christ. But when that knowledge is attained by faith, then "Not *I*, but *Christ*," becomes the believer's motto; and though he has his conflicts still, they are of another kind entirely, while the strength of his resistance to the enemy is the faith which sees the Captain of his salvation, already "for him" on the throne of God.

In concluding this subject, I will remark on the closing words of verse 25, that, while the deliverance of the Gospel sets the conscience perfectly free into the liberty of Christ, it alters nothing with respect either to the intrinsic holiness of the renewed mind, on the one hand, or to the characteristic evil of the

[6] Gal. iv. 24.

flesh on the other. Moreover, the believer, though no longer under Law, because no longer under sin, does not cease to serve the Law of God in another sense.[7] The characteristics of the Law of God are holiness, and righteousness, and goodness; and these things the spiritual man pursues, running, as a child of liberty, along the pure way of holiness and peace in which the blessed Spirit of Christ alone can lead. Meanwhile, the flesh remains, as ever, the servant of sin.

[7] 1 John v. 3.

CHAPTER VIII.

THE last chapter has closed up the case of man, as under Law, in helplessness and death; and has shown that power of deliverance belongeth only to God. "I thank *God*." The entire question of legal responsibility has now, for the believer, been set finally at rest. What man is, as *carnal*, or in his natural state, has been thoroughly sifted and passed in review. His entire world of experiences, his capabilities, his prospects, his hopes and his fears, have been brought by the Spirit into the light of Divine holiness, and have there been found to be intrinsically worthless and vain. The solemn verdict of the true and faithful Witness,[1] when, in the days of His humiliation as the rejected Truth of God, He pronounced the flesh to be utterly unprofitable,[2] has been thus amplified and confirmed, by the extended proof which the Holy Ghost has now set in order, for the decisive refutation and effectual silencing of every natural plea.

Man, moreover, in his awakened state, has been cited as a witness in his own case, and has condemned himself. He is a *wretched man* by his own confession. And now that the creature has delivered himself of this confession of his wretchedness, the blessed God, who made him, and whose

[1] Rev. iii. 14.   [2] John vi. 63.

counsel of redemption³ was of earlier date than the first work of creation, finds fit occasion to reply. The precious chapter we are now about to open contains the declaratory testimony of the Holy Ghost with respect to the condition of the believer, now viewed no longer in his own person, but *in Christ Jesus*. It is the contrasted statement of the privileges, the capacities, the security, and the prospects of the *Christian*, or man in Christ, as having the Spirit, that is here presented as the divinely-wrought counterpart of the preceding description of the *natural* man, as " carnal, sold under sin." The proof and witness of human wretchedness, is the Law. The title and the measure of Christian blessedness, is Christ. As alive in Christ, the believer has therefore to estimate himself no longer by the variable standard of his own emotions and experiences, but according to the eternal fixedness of Divine truth, which his faith discovers in the person of the exalted Saviour, now seen in triumphant victory and honour before the face of God.⁴

The chapter accordingly opens (verse 1) with the blessed and decisive declaration, that there is now *no condemnation* to them which are in Christ Jesus.⁵

³ 1 Peter i. 20. ⁴ Heb. ii. 9.

⁵ The remainder of this verse, as it stands in the English Version, is now generally rejected by the best and most recent critical editors of the original; a decision fully sustained by the testimony of the *Codex Sinaiticus*. It probably was repeated from the fourth verse by some transcriber, who might have found the words placed, as a marginal gloss, against the present passage. As the passage stands in our Bibles, the reference to the walk, preceding as it does the statement, in verse 2, of the liberty on which that walk is founded, is apt to suggest an obstructive doubt to a weak believer as to whether his walk be really thus, and so to keep him back from the proper enjoyment of his position as unconditionally free in Christ. It may not be superfluous however to add, that, whether in or out of place, the clause in question expresses, in its present connection, a very im-

Wrath is revealed against human sin, but in Christ Jesus, God takes no further knowledge of the believing sinner as a man in the flesh. He deals with him henceforward as a new and other man. He regards him, and thinks of him, and loves him, in His own beloved Son. The regulating spring of all His dealings with His saints, is His confessed relation to them as the Father of their spirits. For He has given them of *His own* Spirit, whereby they know that they dwell in Him, and He in them.[6] Simple boldness of faith is needed here, in order to overrule and silence the risings of natural unbelief, and the constitutional proneness of every mind to doubt the possibility of absolute and unconditional grace. But the blessed Spirit of God, in declaring categorically the believer's freedom from all condemnation, does not conceal from our view the solid basis of this liberty. It is "the law of the Spirit of life in Christ Jesus" (verse 2), which has thus released him from the law of sin and death.[7]

Divine love has broken for us, through the dying of the Lamb, the chain of an otherwise hopeless liability to the just claims of our Maker; by consummating, in that death, an absolute obedience to His will.[8] But, death having been thus sacrificially endured, life takes its place—the Life Eternal

portant moral principle. For if we are not walking in the Spirit, we cannot be really enjoying the liberty of Christ, but are condemned by our own hearts. (See 1 John iii. 18–20.)

[6] 1 John iv. 13.

[7] It is an interesting fact, that the best MSS. (including *Cod. Sin.*) give σε, instead of με, in this verse: *i. e.*, while the apostle in the foregoing chapter uses the first person, in giving subjective expression to the effect of Law upon the conscience, he *preaches* the triumphant results of redemption, and thus declares to every believing heart its full participation in the liberty of Christ. [8] Phil. ii. 8, 9.

of Him who, by dying, has abolished death, and is now openly revealed as the Resurrection and the Life. He liveth unto God. Now death is the seal and first effect of condemnation. Condemnation, therefore, can take no effect on those who by faith are *in* Christ, and thus already are alive to God. Further, it is a *law*.[9] It is a permanent, eternal principle of life, taking the place *for* us, in Christ, of that which, *in* us, had had its contrary effects of sin and death. The believer now lives according to the power and the title of Him who is the quickening Spirit—quickening His people, at His will, from death in themselves to life in Him.[1] He is possessed therefore of a principle of life which begins in God and endures *with* God, who hath given us of His own Spirit, and therefore endowed us with *eternal* life. The believer then is free, and the law of his liberty is the life of Christ. Let the reader remark here again the essential difference between the subjective experience of his own feelings, and the simple reception, by pure unquestioning faith, of these most astonishing yet faithful sayings of the blessed God. Conscience, when freshly apprized of the indwelling sin of nature, which knows no change, is ready to deny this liberty. But faith, bringing in upon that conscience the pure light of Christ, sets up again the throne of God, *in grace*, above the erring imaginations of the heart and the contradictions of the devil, and turns the feebleness of the believing soul to strength, by putting it in mind that, though *itself* be free, its liberty is *Christ*.

Verses 3, 4, follow in explanation of the general

[9] νόμος. [1] John v. 21; 1 Cor. xv. 45.

statements already made. The former chapter has exhibited the struggling of an awakened sinner in the impotency of his endeavours to fulfil the righteousness of the Law. The Law proposed life as the result of natural obedience. But the Law could not justify man, because its very effect was to discover sin as dwelling in and ruling him. "The impossibility of the Law"[2] was human justification; for it could work for this end only through the flesh, and the flesh being what it is, instead of justification of life, there resulted *universally* condemnation unto death. The Law, therefore, was too weak an instrument to work the will of God; for God's pleasure is not in the sinner's death, but rather that he might be justified and live. To effect this He must *act* as well as speak. The counsel of His mercy could be accomplished in no other strength than His. The work, therefore, of human justification must be done by Him alone. But in going about to justify the ungodly, God could not disregard the witness of the Law, nor qualify its claims, which did but represent to man the demands of His own holiness. It was, therefore, in the likeness of sinful flesh, that God sent forth His Son; for the Law which was imposed on man must also be fulfilled by man. The righteousness which the Law contained in itself must be fulfilled, not only *for* us, but also *in* us. The first of these things has been accomplished in the life and death of Jesus in our stead; the second has its realization in the resurrection.[3] God's purpose towards His people was their justification unto life. With this view He dealt with sin, absolutely, and entirely apart from those

[2] τὸ ἀδύνατον τοῦ νόμου.   [3] *Ante*, page 99, *seq.*

who naturally were transgressors. The Cross of Christ is the revelation of God as the judicial destroyer of sin. Making Him to be sin for us, who knew no sin, He visited sin, for its destruction, in the flesh of His own Son, on whom He had laid "the iniquity of us all." By the grace of God, Christ tasted the reality of death *for us*. He suffered in the flesh. It was "on account of sin"[4] that the Son of God had come into the world. God sent Him thus, as His own fore-ordained Lamb; and in giving the incarnate Holy One to death for sin, condemned sin in the flesh.

Sin, being thus condemned and silenced in judicial death, remains no longer (as it respects the believer) as a bar to human justification. *God*, who alone is Judge, has Himself abolished it and done it quite away. But this was done in order (verse 4) "that the righteousness[5] of the Law might be fulfilled in us, who walk not after the flesh, but after the Spirit." God sees the righteousness of the Law fulfilled in the Church, in which His Spirit dwells, as alive in Him who, after having suffered in the flesh, was quickened in the Spirit. The "spiritual Law," therefore,[6] instead of being opposed to the Christian as a damnatory witness of his sin, is become, through its complete fulfilment by the Saviour, a muniment and voucher of his perfect peace. The voice of the Law

[4] περὶ ἁμαρτίας.
[5] τὸ δικαίωμα, τ. ν. This expression appears to signify, first, the complete verdict of acquittal, which the obedience of Jesus draws from the Law on the believing sinner's behalf; and secondly, the positive title of praise and honour, which a really righteous man would win from the tribunal of impartial truth. Perhaps the "justification of the Law" might better express the meaning of the text.
[6] Chap. vii. 14.

speaks now in simple approbation of the way of faith. For not only is the total sum of legal righteousness laid, inclusively, to the account of those who stand possessed, through faith, of the *Divine* righteousness in Christ, but, because their walk is in the Spirit, they are experimentally fulfilling (though by the operation of an entirely new and different principle of action) what the Law proposed. Obedience was the Law's demand, and the Christian is characteristically a child of obedience. By *faith* he yields obedience unto God. Christ having become the end of the Law for righteousness to the believer, the Law has now for him no separate existence. It is absorbed into Christ. It can, therefore, never be rightly brought to bear upon a Christian's conscience, because he is not under Law. The Giver of the Law has Himself become, in love, the Law and Standard of His people's walk. *Christ* is the ground, and Christ is the measure, of proper Christian responsibility. Christ takes the Law's place *wholly*. And so the believer is said to be under Law to Christ.[7] His responsibilities are those of grace; of holiness, as known in love. "We love Him, because He first loved us."[8] Liberty, therefore, is the spring and power of a Christian's obedience; seeing that he has not to toil in chains *for* his life, but rather his obedience is "the work of faith and labour of love," itself the active energy of a life already possessed and enjoyed in God.

[7] 1 Cor. ix. 21. μὴ ὢν ἄνομος Θεῷ, ἀλλ' ἔννομος Χριστῷ. "Not lawless to Godward, but in immediate subjection to Christ." It is worth remarking that, in the verse preceding, the best editions of the Greek Testament agree in inserting the words μὴ ὢν αὐτὸς ὑπὸ νόμον, after τοῖς ὑπὸ νόμον ὡς ὑπὸ νόμον. With this also *Cod. Sin.* agrees. [8] 1 John iv. 19.

The believer, then, as thus alive, is characteristically *spiritual*. His habits, therefore, and his ways, his *walk* (in a word) is expected to be consistent with his nature; his new nature, as being no longer after the flesh, but after the Spirit (verse 5). It is to be carefully remarked, that what is stated in the sequel (verses 5–8), where spiritual conduct is insisted on, as distinguishing practically the spiritual man from him who is carnal, is stated by way of corollary to that which has already been laid down as the demonstrative testimony of the Spirit to the *standing* of the justified believer as "in Christ." It is not in the language of exhortation that the apostle here speaks; *that* is introduced further on; but it is a wider and more complete unfolding to the Christian's view of what he *is*, as spiritual, in comparison and contrast with what he *was*, as natural.[9]

The spiritual man[1] is, as such, a totally distinct person from the natural man. This truth has been viewed under one of its aspects in the preceding chapter, where, while under Law, the result of conflict was ever to the discomfiture of that which was

---

[9] It is important to observe carefully the wide scope of the expression "things of the flesh," as contrasted, in verse 5, with the things of the Spirit. If we turn to Phil. iii. we shall find the same apostle distinctly specifying among the fleshly things, in which he once had made his boast while ignorant of Christ, an exact outward compliance with the letter of the commandment: "touching the righteousness which is in the law, blameless." It cannot be sufficiently insisted on, that the utmost conceivable amount of individual "religiousness" is in itself nothing but a thing of the flesh. Nothing is really "of the Spirit" which does not flow from a deep and thorough conviction of the sinfulness in quality, and therefore *nullity* in point of value, of all that proceeds from the natural man.

[1] It should be noticed, that although this description belongs, in one sense, to all who at any time have been "of God," it applies more strictly to the believer in this dispensation, as having received the indwelling Spirit of God. (See below.)

spiritual, because the law of liberty was not known in the conscience. The converse of what is there exhibited is presented in this chapter. Power is found now to be on the side of the spiritual man. Because he is in Christ, he is no longer under Law. He has become the subject, not of that which was against him, but of Him who has broken the hard fetters of his bondage. He is free in Christ. The sinew of his strength is the *grace* that is in *Him*.[2] He has not only the *desires* of holiness, and life, and peace, but he has also, in Christ, the assured *possession* of what is thus desired; for he is sanctified no less than justified in Him. Hence, to be spiritually-minded, or, rather, "the mind of the Spirit,"[3] is life and peace; not only in eventual result, but in actual enjoyment. The bitterness of death being passed already, in the cross of Jesus, the knowledge of the perfect truth in Him confers on the believer a victorious energy, in every conflict in which he finds himself confronted by the enemy of his soul.[4] "The

---

[2] 2 Tim. ii. 1.   [3] Τὸ φρόνημα τοῦ πνεύματος.

[4] *Infra*, verse 37; 1 John v. 4, 5. Such is the true and proper result. In point of fact, it is often otherwise. Christians, through deficiency of faith, or from having failed to add knowledge to their faith, are too often found by the enemy in a state but ill prepared to meet him. The *whole* armour of God is needed in order to stand fast. Divine truth, as God alone teaches it, is the only girdle of strength wherewith the soul can stand in collected readiness to contend with Satan, who endeavours to dispute, in the heart of the believer, the title of life and peace which he has in Christ. Again, positive sin may arise. The Christian may find bitterness of heart within, because of some allowed evil, having to judge himself for things which, instead of being of the Spirit, are wholly of the flesh. Still, the very capacity of self-judgment which he has, and thus exercises, is, in itself, an effect of his being not carnal but spiritual. The precious word of grace has a ready balm at hand for the bruised and wounded spirit; but where, as in the text, conduct is described as an effect of life, it is exhibited as the *perfect*, and not the imperfect, expression of that from whence it springs.

mind of the flesh is death." Such is the concise summary of mortality and its perishable energies, by which the Spirit of truth declares the alienation of nature from the life of God. The Lord knoweth the thoughts of man, that they are vanity.[5] But as He thinks He acts. The works, therefore, of nature are uniformly *dead* works. They savour of death and not of life, because they are the product of that which is, in its nature, enmity against God. Moral philosophy may separate, in its analysis of human motive and conduct, things amiable from things hateful, things lovely from things repulsive, and things noble from things base. The Spirit of God, viewing the varied phases of human character in the clear light of His own holiness, and testing, at their common source, the intrinsic qualities of human thought and action, pronounces a judgment in which all those things which men distinguish are indiscriminately united, and the common fountain of all is declared to be "*enmity* against God." The proof and evidence upon which this solemn judgment is pronounced immediately follows: "For it is not subject to the law of God." This has already been shown at length, and need not now be further insisted on. But if human obedience is withheld from the Law of God, it is because of the condition of that will which directs and governs the ways of men. Now the very existence of an active will, independent of that of God, is the necessity of insubjection to that which is the expression of His will; and therefore it is added, "neither indeed *can* be." The inevitable conclusion

[5] Psalm xciv. 11.

is then stated: "So then they that are in the flesh⁶ cannot please God."

With respect to the descriptive expression, "they that are in the flesh," its meaning and limitation are to be found in what is said, in verse 7, respecting those who stand in the opposite category, as being *not* in the flesh, but in the Spirit. Now, as to this, the word is, "Ye are not in the flesh, but in the Spirit, if so be that the *Spirit of God* dwell in you." Presently it is added, "If any man have not the Spirit of *Christ*, he is none of His." The grand distinctive truth which separates a Christian, as a vessel of Divine mercy, from the world which knows not God, is the indwelling presence of the Spirit of God. I would remark on this, first of all, that this *presence* of the Spirit, as indwelling, is not to be confounded with the regenerative *operation* of the same blessed Spirit in originally quickening dead souls, and bringing them, by faith, to the cross of Christ. What the apostle is here considering is the state and standing of the believer, as having been so quickened. The indwelling, therefore, of the Holy Ghost is the result of the Christian's being already alive in Christ. This subject will further unfold itself presently. Meanwhile let it be further borne in mind, that the indwelling presence of the Spirit of God is something quite distinct from those resulting influences and energies which more or less distinguish those in whom He dwells.⁷

---

⁶ οἱ ἐν σαρκὶ ὄντες.

⁷ The bad results which have arisen from the constant use of the unscriptural expression, "influences of the Holy Spirit," it is easier to feel and to lament than to estimate. The Spirit of God does assuredly influence and govern (where not grieved) that wherein He

We have, then, here the distinct statement, that those in whom the Spirit of God does *not* dwell—those who have *not* the Spirit of Christ—are in the flesh; and if so, that they are in a state of enmity against God, are incapable of pleasing God.

The expression, "Spirit of Christ," must not be misunderstood. The same Spirit who is, when declared under a single and absolute title, the Spirit of *God*, is the Spirit of the Son, even as He is also the Spirit of the Father. Moreover, "the Lord is that Spirit."[8] The Spirit of Christ, therefore, is a far other thing than what is often spoken of as "a Christian spirit," where the amiable conduct of some professing Christian is meant to be commended. The Spirit of Christ is a living power, which produces its own effects. That Spirit is a Person, not a thing. He dwells, for Christ, within the hearts of those who are sanctified by faith in Him. He is the Divine tenant of the temple which the blood of Christ has purged. Residing thus within the children of God, He indicates the secret of His dwelling-place by the energy whereby He acts upon the soul. His operation produces, both outwardly and inwardly, its own characteristic results in those in whom He dwells.

The Spirit of Christ, wherever present, confesses the *name* and only Lordship of the Christ, according to the revelation of the Gospel. That name is JESUS.[9] The Spirit of Christ manifests His presence in the saints by the distinct and total denial, on their part,

---

dwells, as the Lord in His own house; but what is commonly implied, in the expression here objected to, is some occasional impression from without upon a man, instead of the gracious energy of One who is in us abidingly, as the Witness of acceptance and the Hope of glory.

[8] 2 Cor. iii. 17. [9] Acts x. 36; 1 Cor. xii. 3; 1 John iv. 2.

of all hope, or joy, or confidence,—of all worthiness, or righteousness, or goodness,—as by any possibility to be found elsewhere than in Christ. The Spirit of Christ glorifies Christ, by filling the heart in which He dwells with joy and peace in believing. The Spirit of Christ, again, in confessing, through the lips of faith, the name of Jesus as the only Lord, confesses Him to be in very deed the Son of God.[1] Lastly, the Spirit of Christ is, in the believer, not only the seal and earnest of his personal acceptance in the Beloved, and the source and fountain of all fruitful obedience in his way, but He is also the Spirit of judgment in holiness; whereby not only are the contrarieties of flesh to Spirit, of self to God, inwardly detected and condemned, but also the world, which neither seeth nor knoweth the Holy One, is understood and shunned, as that which in heart denieth both the Father and the Son.

The difference, then, between being in the flesh and being in the Spirit, is nothing less than the difference between death and life; between the condition of one who stands, as a child of wrath, exposed to the recorded judgment of God, and that of a pardoned, and accepted, and justified man; the seal of whose acceptance and the witness of whose purity, as sanctified in Christ, is the indwelling presence of God Himself. And so it is elsewhere written: "Whosoever shall confess that Jesus is the Son of God, God dwelleth in him, and he in God."[2]

Verses 10, 11, recite some further consequences and effects of this indwelling of the Spirit. And, first, let us notice, in verse 10, the identification of

[1] Acts ix. 17–20; 1 John v. 9, 10.   [2] 1 John iv. 15.

Christ with the Spirit of Christ. In the unity of Divine nature they are one. The Lord is that Spirit. "If Christ be in you," &c. We have already seen that the ground and title of the believer's blessedness is his being in Christ.[3] We have here the counterpart of that truth. A Christian is not simply a man who has Christian ideas and notions, as men speak, but one in whom *Christ is;* who lives, yet not he, but Christ liveth in him.[4] The results of this are now stated. First, "the body is dead because of sin;" and, secondly, "the Spirit is life because of righteousness." The body is *dead*. It is plain that such language, since it flatly contradicts our natural experience, is appreciable only by our faith. The doctrine of this verse is briefly a re-statement of what has already been exhibited at large in chapter vi. What Christ is, what He has suffered, the vicissitudes through which He has passed, &c., are true, by imputation, of the believer, for whose sake all has been and is. Now Christ was put to death in the flesh, but quickened by the Spirit, and, *because of this*, both death unto sin and resurrection unto life eternal, are declared to be the truth of God in reference to the sinner who has, once for all, been justified by faith.[5]

The moral effect of this doctrine has also to be noticed, as it is produced by the effectual working of

[3] John xiv. 20, xvii. 23.   [4] Gal. ii. 20.
[5] Let the reader who may need further establishment in this truth refer to 1 Pet. iv. 1, 2, where the same doctrine is stated in conjunction with an exhortation to the saint to "*arm* himself with the same mind;" *i. e.* to stay his soul upon the full persuasion of the great *fact* of substitutional atonement, in order that upon the faith of that completed work he may ground his present estimate of his own standing in the sight of God, and so become practically ready to obey the will of God, instead of walking in the former lusts.

the word within us. The Christian, though an heir of immortality, is mortal still, while in the unchanged body of his flesh. Though Christ, the Lord of life, be in him, he differs as yet from other men, only in the possession of a knowledge and a hope which make death but a stingless sleep, until the awakening trump of God be heard. Meanwhile, the continued presence of the ransomed soul in a body which has, in every fibre of its structure, the earnest of mortality and dissolution, is felt to be burdensome exactly in proportion to the liveliness of our faith. We that are in this tabernacle do groan, being burdened, as the same apostle says elsewhere.[6] Thus, while freed from the fear of that judgment which is after death, because already freed from sin through the death of Jesus, we have still to bear, each his own burden, for the trial of our faith; sustained meanwhile by the gracious energy of that Spirit, which is the earnest of our inheritance and the present comforter of our hearts. The body then is dead. To be treated therefore as such, not indeed to be tormented by factitious discipline, but to be exercised and regulated by the Spirit of a sound mind. To be moderated in its appetites, and restrained in its desires. To be used, and not served: to be governed, not obeyed. To be brought into subjection, and yielded, as we have seen,[7] to *God*. Meanwhile, the Spirit is life; living in us, because of righteousness imputed to us: Christ in us, the hope of glory. But though the body be dead, because of sin, yet "if the Spirit of Him that raised up Jesus from the dead dwell in you, He that raised up Christ from the dead shall also quicken

[6] 2 Cor. v. 4.   [7] Chap. vi.

your mortal bodies by (or, because of) His Spirit that dwelleth in you."[8]

The Spirit of the Father, who has glorified the exceeding greatness of His power in the resurrection of Jesus from the dead, now dwells in them that believe. Solemn, wondrous, and most blessed truth! The mighty energy which is presently to reveal the Divine glory in the children of the resurrection, by the turning of corruption into incorruption, of dishonour and decay into glory and enduring strength, is already hidden (though it slumber till the time be come) in these bodies of humiliation;[9] which are thus to be made, in due time, vessels of eternal honour to the praise of His glory, who, as the Father of glory, has already raised up the First-born from the dead.[1] Resurrection thus becomes the familiar thought, the near and constant desire of the saint. Already he is sealed for *that*. The power which is to raise or change[2] his mortal body is in him now. The glory, in the hope of which he is called to rejoice, instead of being enveloped in the indistinctness which, to the natural eye, invests all objects which are "very far off," is presented clearly to his view. He sees, in Jesus risen,[3] the goodly heritage which is his portion, and by faith has access into the light wherein He dwells. The hand which is to open to him *visibly* the gates of glory, to lead him in, and present him faultless before the majesty of the heavens with exceeding joy, is upon him even now.

---

[8] The precise reading here is not easily determined. Διὰ τὸ ἐνοικοῦν αὐτοῦ πνεῦμα seemed on the whole to be favoured by the best authorities, until the recent discovery of *Cod. Sin.*, which gives διὰ τοῦ ἐνοικ. αὐτ. πνεύματος.

[9] τῆς ταπεινώσεως. Phil. iii. 21.   [1] Eph. i. 17–21; Col. i. 18.
[2] 1 Cor. xv. 51.   [3] Eph. i. 11.

Verses 12, 13. Resurrection having been declared to be the destiny of the believer,—his near and proper expectation as a spiritual man,—the flesh, as a thing already dead, has no longer any claim upon him. The two verses now under examination are worthy of all attention, because they furnish to the Christian conscience a test of its practical condition, while confirming, to the full, the precious doctrine of spiritual liberty already laid down. Liberty is, indeed, the very emphasis of the passage. "We are debtors, *not* to the flesh, to live after the flesh." As freed in Christ from the law of sin and death, the believer is no longer a debtor to the flesh, even in this present life. He lives to God, in the liberty of redemption. This assertion of liberty is to the Spirit life and joy, while to that which is Christian only in name, and not in power, it is the searching edge of the word of holiness discerning the thoughts and intents of the heart. Practical holiness is here insisted on, as the necessary effect of living faith. It is a question, not of degree, but of principle. A Christian may abound much in the fruits of righteousness, or he may be in a very feeble and defective state in this respect. But he cannot, if alive to God at all, be at the same time alive in the flesh. Life in the flesh is death to God.

And so he proceeds: "If ye live after the flesh," &c. The standing principle, already laid down in verse 6, is here expanded in the way of practical application. The apostle's words express both a testimony and a promise. We are reminded, by an explicit declaration, of the certain issue of the way of nature, while the believer is incited, as a man no longer in the flesh, but in the Spirit, to lay firm and positive hold upon the true hope of his calling.[4] Nor let it seem strange to any that death and life should thus be offered to the choice of those who, unless they have believed in vain,[5] are already, by the foregoing testimony of the apostle, completely justified in Christ. For it is by *warning* not less than teaching, that God's people are preserved of Him.[6] But God's warnings are addressed to us according to the truth of our present condition—as alive, that is, to God by faith, but entirely *unchanged*, as it respects the quality and tendencies of our old nature.

The aim of all hortative teaching is to evoke and exercise the *power of godliness*, and therefore is such teaching ever welcome to all who in honesty of heart are holding faith and a good conscience.[7] For in the heart of the exercised believer, the eternal contrariety of flesh to Spirit is not only acknowledged as a doctrine, but practically *understood*. He is (in virtue of his birth to God), by choice and in desire, a lover of God's way. "Thy will be done" is the very life-breath of the new man, which is renewed in knowledge after the image of Him that created him.[8] What is born of God is incapable of sin,[9] and the believer, as a child of God, although Divinely preserved, is said to "keep *himself*."[1] The working out of their own salvation, is committed to the trust of those who are to reap eventually its perfect fruits. But although the personal responsibility of God's

---

[4] Phil. iii. 17–21; 1 Tim. vi. 11, 12. [5] 1 Cor. xv. 1, 2.
[6] Col. i. 28.   [7] 1 Tim. i. 19; Acts xxiv. 16; Heb. xiii. 18.
[8] Col. iii. 10.   [9] 1 John iv. 9. *Ante*, note at page 112.
[1] 1 John v. 18; 1 Pet. i. 5; Jude 1.

saints, whose sanctification is "unto obedience,"[2] is everywhere insisted on, the Scripture is equally explicit as to the means by which alone God's children can fulfil His will. It is *Himself* that worketh in them both to will and to do, of His good pleasure;[3] or, as it is expressed in the verse now before us: "If ye *through the Spirit* do mortify," &c. The mortification (or practical putting to death) of the deeds of the body, is the result of the energy of that Spirit which is already *Life* to the man in whom He dwells, because of imputed righteousness in Christ. Thus the very terms of the injunction contain, for the willing ear of the believer, a ratification of his personal safety and acceptance in the Beloved. For the Holy Spirit of God is the seal of our adoption until the day when grace shall end in glory.[4] It is thus that conditional warnings act directly as a stimulus to the new man (for they that are of the Spirit do mind the things of the Spirit), while they condemn, by anticipation, the careless professor in the presumptuous folly of his way.[5] Faith is not staggered by such sayings, because they only echo what is already settled as a rudimental sentiment in the heart of the believer, where both sin and grace are experimentally known. Conflict is not compromise; but while the former is a necessary experience in the hearts of all who are "of God," the latter is instinctively abhorred.[6] Self-judgment throws the penitent believer into the arms of never-failing mercy; but systematic and impenitent abuse of grace marks out for sure destruction

---

[2] 1 Pet. i. 2. [3] Phil. ii. 13. [4] Eph. iv. 30.
[5] Tit. i. 16; Jude, *passim*. [6] Ps. cxix., *passim*.

those who, while professing to know God, have no true relish for His way.[7]

There is, therefore, nothing in this verse that need chill, in the least, the confidence of the poor weak-spirited, self-judging Christian. Nay, those who are most addicted to self-judgment, are they to whom the warning here expressed has the least application.[8] Nor should the mortification of the deeds of the body, of which the apostle here speaks, be confounded with what men naturally mean by such an expression, with that asceticism of which the same apostle elsewhere speaks in such condemnatory terms, as a mere deceptive counterfeit of the wisdom which is of God.[9] The power of fleshly mortification in a believer, is the enjoyed consciousness, through faith, of the abundance of life in Christ. It is the known and appreciated grace of God, as that which has brought salvation to the soul, which alone *teaches* those who by faith have received that grace, to deny ungodliness and worldly lusts.[1]

The world, then, has no longer any claim upon the saint. He is not a debtor to it in any shape. He is

---

[7] 2 Thess. i. 8, ii. 10. On the kindred subjects of conflict and comfort, see further, *Notes on the Hebrews*, passim.

[8] One word more on this point. It is quite possible for a real believer to be living in a certain measure as a man, to be walking carnally in many ways; to be sowing, in his vanity, to the flesh instead of to the Spirit. Now the end of all this is death. Corruption is the harvest of the flesh in all its ways. There is a day coming when the fire will try every one's work, and what is not of God will go up as dust and smoke before the presence of Divine holiness. Yet is the life of the believer safe still, for his life is Christ. In that life are bound up hopes of glory, honour, and immortality. These hopes shall never fail, for they are pledged in Christ by the Spirit to the Christian. Nevertheless, the difference between a faithful and devoted servant, and one less careful of his Master's Name, is a real difference, and will be so found in that day. (Comp. 1 Cor. iii. 13–15.)

[9] Col. ii. 20–23.   [1] Tit. ii. 11, 12.

Christ's. He is God's, as redeemed in Christ unto Himself—as bought with a price. He is therefore exempt from all that which the world lays down, either as the condition of its favour or as the price of its goods.[2] He is independent of the world—independent of man, because upheld of God. The galling trammels of the prince of this world have been broken, and their place supplied by the cords of Divine love and power in Christ. The believer is *led* by the Spirit of God. He is not dragged as a captive, but guided as a son.

In what follows we have a further enunciation of those positive privileges and blessings which constitute the portion of the spiritual man. But first, the characteristic name and operation of the Spirit which dwells in the believer are declared and explained (verse 15). "Ye received[3] not the spirit of *bondage* again to fear; but ye received the spirit of *adoption*,[4] whereby we cry, Abba, Father." We have already seen, in chapter vii., what were the effects of the full realization, in a renewed mind, of the Law, as spiritual. The Spirit of truth, when acting upon an awakened conscience through Law, can produce no other effect

---

[2] He is to walk by faith, not by sight. He is to labour willingly and patiently, that he may provide things honest in the sight of all men. But in the practical transactions of life he is the Lord's servant still. What he does, he is to do to *Him*, and not to men. A Christian is never rightly out of the place of testimony. He is called to glorify God in his ways. He is in all things to walk worthy of the vocation wherewith he is called. He is a pilgrim and a stranger, not by the force of circumstances, but in the power of Divine truth. His calling is to walk in a dead world as himself alive, in the present power of the resurrection of Christ. (Phil. iii.; Col. iii.)

[3] οὐ γὰρ ἐλάβετε κ. λ. *i. e.*, at the time of their conversion, just as in chap. v. 5, the Holy Ghost is spoken of as having been given absolutely to the saints as such.

[4] Of sonship, πνεῦμα υἱοθεσίας.

than bondage and fear, because the legal standing was that of a servant, *not* of a son. The Holy Ghost, therefore, as the Spirit of adoption, could never rest upon such. Moreover, although the Spirit filled and used holy men of old, making them thus the fitting witnesses and messengers of Divine truth; yet was this a wholly different thing from what is now the portion of a saint. They were moved[5] by the Holy Ghost, who came upon them at His will, and bore them often far beyond the feeble scope of their then spiritual understanding. He could and did reveal to them, in part, the mystery of the ways of God; not only quieting their hearts, by unfolding to their view the covenanted certainties of Messianic promise, but acquainting them also, in their appointed measure, with the ordered sequence of yet undiscovered truth.[6] But their personal standing was not that of sons. Like their forefathers, they waited still for Israel's Hope.

The spirit of bondage unto fear, then, had had its sphere of operation, and had wrought its work.[7] But now, having been made free by the Son, these once alien Gentiles had received another Spirit. Entrance into the house, with the abiding title of sonship, was thenceforth their indisputable right. The Spirit of the Son of God is sent into the heart of the believer, not to confer, but to *attest*, his filial standing.[8] As

[5] $\phi\epsilon\rho\acute{o}\mu\epsilon\nu\omicron\iota$.   [6] 1 Pet. i. 11, 12.
[7] I do not mean by this that experience of this kind is not, as I have before noticed, often felt by Christians: but if it be felt, it is not a feeling according to the full truth of the Gospel. Again, the same spirit of bondage will operate according to the truth of their actual position *hereafter* upon the godly among the nation of Israel, when waiting, as prisoners of hope, for the Deliverer to appear. Our present question is with the believer as standing in the full light of accomplished redemption.   [8] Gal. iv. 6; 1 John v. 10.

thus sent forth He is *received* by us; unawares it may be at first, until His blessed presence is disclosed by the utterance which He alone can truly bring forth from *the heart*. The cry, "Abba, Father," is our own; but it is by the Spirit of the Son that it is produced. *We* cry Abba, because we know Him thus; but the power of that knowledge is the indwelling presence of the Son. "The Spirit itself beareth witness with our spirit that we are children of God." There is a concurrent testimony of the Spirit of the Son, and of the quickened spirit of the new-born child of God, whose heart that Spirit fills. Both speak, and speak to God. The Spirit cries Abba, because it is the Spirit of the Son,—our hearts repeat that cry, because we know, by the same Spirit, that the living Christ is *our* life to God.

It is thus that they who once were aliens, are become, through faith, the children of the living God. They have therefore a Father whose name stands eternally betwixt them and all fear. But a child, because he is a child, has expectations from his parent; and so it is with us. The all-gracious name with which the God of glory has now clothed Himself for our sakes, is not an empty sound. If children, we are also *heirs*—"heirs of God, and joint-heirs with Christ" (verse 17). Now, "the Father loveth the Son, and hath given *all things* into His hand."[9] He has appointed Him, as alive from the dead, heir of all things.[1] He was from the beginning, by virtue of His eternal Sonship, in full participation of Divine glory.[2] As the Creator moreover of all things, He stood possessed, from the

[9] John iii. 35.   [1] Heb. i. 2.   [2] John xvii. 5.

moment of their creation, of the perfect right of universal propriety; for all things were created *by* Him and *for* Him.³ He is now revealed upon the Father's throne as the vested Possessor of the inheritance of God, after having made Himself capable of such investment by becoming flesh, and tasting death for everything⁴ by the grace of God. And this inheritance He shares with us! As He has said elsewhere, "The glory which thou gavest me I have given them."⁵ All that the created capacity of the children of God can receive from Himself, is the portion of their inheritance as heirs of God. All that the blessed Lord can share with and impart to, the objects of His unmeasured love, is the portion of the brethren as joint-heirs with Christ. As eternally Divine,—in the distinctness of His Sonship, as the Only-begotten, as well as in the unity of the Godhead with the Father and the Spirit,—He will be for ever the object of His creatures' worship, and they will see a glory,⁶ and delight in its effulgence, which yet they will not share, because it is essentially Divine. But there is a glory which they are called to share. And who shall tell the amount of that weight of glory, or sum the measure of that perfect blessedness, which the Father has counted Jesus worthy to receive, and which Jesus in love has made us worthy to enjoy?

A goodly view of this glory and blessedness, in some of their most striking features, is opened to us

---

³ Col. i. 16.
⁴ ὑπὲρ παντός. Heb. ii. 9. A comparison of this passage with Col. i. 20, seems to justify the rendering of these words given above; but I do not insist upon it as unquestionable. See *Notes on the Hebrews*, in loc. ⁵ John xvii. 22. ⁶ John xvii. 24.

in the verses which follow. But before advancing further, let us for a moment recapitulate the actual effects of the indwelling presence of the Spirit of adoption, so far as they have yet been stated. There is, then, first, the assured possession of the Father's love; there is the equal assurance of fellowship with the Son; there is the certainty of the life to come, with all that constitutes the peculiar privileges of the heirs of God; and there is the conscious blessedness, in Divine intelligence, of present entrance into the known love of Christ (though yet it pass all knowledge),[7] as that alone wherein and whereby the inheritance is either comprehended or desired. Thus the promised Comforter fulfils, in the saints, that unexpected saying of the Master, when about to part from His disciples: "It is expedient for you that *I* go away; for if *I* go not away, the Comforter will not come," &c.[8] Strange words doubtless to those who heard them, but now understood and rejoiced in, though not less wondrous still, by those in whom the blessed Spirit has become the full river of God, as the revealer of the unclouded light of life and joy in the glory of the ascended Christ.

Think, then, poor sorrowing Christian who may haply be seeking comfort in these pages, think no longer of the indwelling sin of nature which torments you, but of the indwelling Spirit of Christ, who thus seeks to cheer and reässure your heart by putting into your mouth the children's bread. You are not what you think yourself to be. You think yourself a sinner. Such, indeed, you were, and such (as in yourself) you are and must be still. But, as a

[7] Eph. iii. 17–19.   [8] John xvi. 7.

sinner, you are *dead*. The living Spirit of the Son of God is given now to reveal to you what you are as alive in *Jesus;* as estimated of God according to the priceless value of that which has been expended on your redemption; as a branch therefore of acceptance, of enduring fragrance and richness, upborne for ever upon the living stem of Christ. You cannot learn these things from men, least of all from yourself. But God reveals them in His precious word. Let not the misgivings of your heart withstand any longer the pure testimony of Christ's own free and boundless love. To listen to these misgivings, is to listen rather to the whisperings of God's enemy than to God himself. It is unbelief, and therefore sin; and darkness and leanness can alone result from that. *God has spoken* in His holiness. Let it be yours, therefore, to rejoice in that which He has said;[9] offering continual praise from a heart fixedly established in His grace,[1] and silencing the opposition of an evil heart of unbelief, by the living voice of Him who cannot lie.[2]

To proceed now with our chapter. The latter part of verse 17 makes mention of fellowship with the sufferings of Christ, as the precedent condition of our being glorified together. Suffering of the sort here mentioned is the portion, more or less, of every believer in Jesus. As a man, he has his share of all those ills which sinful flesh is heir to; but in addition to that, he is the subject of a class of sufferings which can attach to none but those in whom the Spirit of Christ dwells. Remaining in a world from

[9] Ps. lx. 6.   [1] Ps. lvii. 7; Heb. xiii. 9–15.
[2] Heb. iii. 12; 1 John v. 9; Tit. i. 2.

which he has been already separated in heart, he cannot but find suffering, by reason of the contrariety of everything here to that for which he is apprehended of Christ Jesus.[3] He groans, moreover, as being in the body of sin and death, though rejoicing, with a joy which is unspeakable and full of glory, in the certainty of speedy release. But more especially, it is as a servant and witness of the truth of God that he is called to suffer. Jesus suffered thus, and thus too have they to suffer in their measure, who are called to follow in His steps.[4]

Christian sufferings may be great. Not unfrequently they are so. Nor could any one speak more experimentally of such things than the blessed servant of Christ whose epistle is now in our hands.[5] Yet how does he here estimate them, when weighed, in the sober balances of truth, against the glory which is soon to be revealed! The comparison is of present sufferings against eternal glory. Thus weighed, the momentary trial of faith and patience is found to be as *nothing*, to be unworthy of all comparison with that which is to be revealed *in us*.[6]

---

[3] Phil. iii. 12.   [4] 1 Pet. ii. 21–23.
[5] 1 Cor. iv. 9–13; 2 Cor. xi. 21–33.
[6] εἰς ἡμᾶς. The E. V. has, I think, correctly represented the force of the preposition in this place. For it is not only *to* the saints that the glory of Christ is to be revealed, but He will also be glorified *in* them, and admired in all who now believe, in the day of His epiphany. (2 Thess. i. 10.) The leading idea, however, in the present verse is, no doubt, the compensatory view of that glory which they who now suffer with Christ shall enjoy when the requests of Jesus on their behalf shall receive their completed fulfilment. (John xvii. 24.) The eye which now sorrowfully affects the heart, because of vanity and weariness, will then affect it with ineffable delight, because of the eternal manifestation of glory and perfection in the person of the Lamb. The verses which follow treat more directly of the display of the same glory and its effects *in* those who now suffer for His sake, as they will hereafter appear in relation to others.

This he *reckons* (verse 18). There is no sort of doubt in his mind: it is a deliberate measurement of truth with truth, of real suffering with most real and most certain and eternal glory. The believer, when thus sustained by the hope of glory, is able to endure the afflictions of the Gospel according to the *power of God*.[7]

The blessed position and characteristic hope of the Christian, as an heir of Divine glory, having been thus stated, the apostle now proceeds to discover more distinctly and definitely to our view, a portion of the prospect which is opened to the faith of the Church, as having the mind of Christ.[8] And first, it is not personal deliverance merely for which the believer is waiting. He looks, indeed, with much desire to be "clothed upon," that mortality may be swallowed up of life;[9] but, because he has received the Spirit of the Son, there is in him a capacity, even now, of entering by anticipation into that joy which, being originally the portion of the Blessed One Himself, for the sake of which He endured the cross,[1] is communicable, and is in measure imparted, to those in whose hearts His Spirit dwells.

The Spirit of God, in unfolding to the saints the hope of their calling, addresses Himself to that inner man, in the believer, which, because it is born of God, is capable of thinking and desiring according to the sympathies of Christ. Accordingly, we have opened in the following verses of this chapter a wide view of creation in its actual condition, as subject to vanity. This is done in order that a juster estimate

[7] 2 Tim. i. 8.   [8] 1 Cor. ii. 9–16.
[9] 2 Cor. v. 4.   [1] Heb. xii. 2.

may be formed, in the hearts of God's children, both of the manner and the measure of that glory for which they wait, by a description of its distinct effect upon the now groaning creation, which awaits the hour of their complete adoption as the expected moment of its own release. "For the earnest expectation of the creature waiteth for the manifestation of the sons of God. For the creature was made subject to vanity, not willingly, but by reason of him who hath subjected the same, in hope; because the creature itself also shall be delivered from the bondage of corruption into the glorious liberty of the children of God. For we know that the whole creation groaneth and travaileth in pain together until now" (verses 19–22).

We have, in this remarkable passage, the emancipation of the groaning creation made immediately dependent upon the manifestation of the sons of God. The Church, that is, not only shares, as a part of the creation, in the deliverance which is the effect of redemption, but it is itself, as a chosen medium of display for the fulness of the Divine glory which is in Christ, the very light which shall dissolve, at its revelation, the thick darkness of vanity which as yet holds the creature in the bonds of travail and of pain. Creation is represented as still lying under a ceaseless and painful oppression from its universal subjection to vanity, but in immediate and earnest expectation[2] of deliverance. But the appointed moment of this deliverance is declared to be the revelation of the sons of God. It is not said, of the Son of God, but of the *sons* of God. Doubtless, it is with His glory

[2] ἀποκαραδοκία.

that they will shine; but the point kept before our view here, is the place which the children (already sealed for the inheritance by the Spirit of adoption) are manifestly to hold in that day.

Creation³ has been subjected to vanity. The cause of this subjection is to be found, not in that which now suffers, but in him under whose dominion all earthly things had been originally placed. The sin of Adam was the ruin of creation. But this ruin, though complete and irremediable, as it respected any inherent power of self-adjustment or redress, was not without all hope. Glory, and rest, and blessing were in the view of that Divine counsel in virtue of which the worlds were framed by the Word of God. If the first man's sin has wrapped the creature in the shroud of vanity and death, the power of redemption, in the person of the second Man, shall, in due time, turn the shadows of death into the morning of a cloudless day of blessing and of joy.⁴ The title of dominion, which fell from the death-stricken hand of the first Adam because of sin, is now held fast in the firm and worthy grasp of Him who, while known for ever as the Son of Man, is King of righteousness and King of peace; to be manifested and to reign as such over

---

³ It is, I think, plain that κτίσις has here no wider meaning than terrestrial creation. That the effects of redemption are felt, and will be manifestly displayed, not only in the earthly creature, but also in the heavenly, is clear from Col. i. 20. In the unity of creation, as the work of God, the presence of sin in one part defiles the whole. All things, therefore, whether earthly or heavenly, which are comprised within the kingdom of the Son, when God will be glorified in the consummated glory of His Christ, will stand in blessing through the blood of reconciliation. I do not think, however, that in the present passage our view is extended beyond the earthly sphere of creation—a view which brings the doctrine of this passage into harmony with the prophetic witnesses of the Old Testament, as to which more hereafter. ⁴ 2 Sam. xxiii. 3, 4.

this now-groaning creation, when the times of refreshing shall have come, and He, who alone is the mourning creature's hope, shall come forth from the presence of the Father of lights, to gladden and revive that which as yet groans on while waiting for that day. Solemn and terrific things are, indeed, connected with these promises of joy. Judgment will, as a mighty stream, sweep clean away the refuge of lies, and cleanse the stage on which the fair scene of creature blessedness shall be displayed. These things will be found more fully treated in the sequel of this Epistle. Our present subject is the joy, and not the terror, of the Lord.

Jesus, then, will thus come forth. But will He come alone? Nay. "He will come," as the same witness elsewhere testifies, "to be glorified in His saints, and to be admired in all them that believe (because our testimony among you was believed) in that day."[5] The light of that day of brightness shall shine forth upon the delivered creature from the manifested glory of the children of God.[6] The First-

[5] 2 Thess. i. 10.

[6] With respect to the declaration that the creature is to be delivered into the glorious liberty of the *children* of God, some help may be gained perhaps by a comparison of Eph. iii. 15 with Gen. ii. 4. In the former of these, "every family" in heaven and earth is said to be named from the Father of our Lord Jesus Christ. (*Notes on Ephesians*, in loc.) In the latter we read: "These are the *generations* (תוֹלְדוֹת) of the heavens and the earth," &c. (Compare also Job xxxviii. 4–7.) In the work of creation God rejoiced in the goodness of His handiwork; but in the regeneration, or second Genesis (παλιγγενεσία, Matt. xix. 28), when the once crucified Redeemer will be revealed upon His throne, and both heaven and earth be brought under the acknowledged headship of Christ—all things which were created, both by and for the Son (Col. i. 17), being then as it were baptized in the light of His glory, whose essential name as the *Son* will be honoured throughout all creation—each creature which has groaned beneath the heavy yoke of vanity will witness, in its joy, to the general paternity of God.

born will be there; and the brethren, whom He is not ashamed to call His own,[7] will be there also. The world shall then know the truth and power of that saying, now unheeded by it in its day of pride, that they whom the Father's will hath given to Jesus are fellows with their Saviour in His joy.[8] God will reveal in glory, unto His own praise as the Father of glory, the many sons whom already He has brought to glory in Him in whom the full numbers of salvation are completed, according to the perfect counsels of His will.[9] Meanwhile, creation groans. Nor is this groaning heard with indifference in the ears of the blessed God. He knows the thoughts that He thinks as to this, and by His own Spirit He reveals them to His saints. The Holy Ghost, as the teacher of God's children, teaches them *according to God*. Searching all things, even the deep things of God, He draws aside the thick veil of natural appearances, and discloses all things to the heart of the believer as they are seen and known of God.

It is a characteristic of the spiritual man that he judges all things, while he is himself judged of none.[1] The passage before us affords an illustration of this principle. Creation groans. The natural man enters, experimentally and with reluctance, into this truth, in so far as he is himself involuntarily the subject of time and change. Observation and sensation alike concur to press upon him, as a practical conviction, a truth which, while he is in this sense ever learning, yet he never really understands. He feels it, indeed; and, making a merit of necessity, he acquiesces in a

[7] Heb. ii. 11. [8] John xvii. 22, 23.
[9] Heb. ii. 10. [1] 1 Cor. ii. 15.

state of bondage and corruption which is altogether beyond his own control or cure. The believer, on the other hand, knows these things (verse 22), because himself standing in the light which makes everything manifest. Moreover, he sympathizes with the groaning of creation, as being himself a part of it. He is not emancipated, by virtue of redemption, from the travail and pain which are the portion of fallen man. Things which befall other men befall the Christian also; though, in his happy case, the bitterness of natural grief is made to turn to the furtherance of his spiritual blessing; to fill yet fuller the cup of Divine joy, with which the Father of spirits knows how to comfort and revive them that are under the gracious discipline of His love.[2]

The Christian, then, has his part in the groaning of the creature. But there is another groaning which belongs to the hearts of God's children, of a kind peculiar to themselves, and in which the natural creation has no share. Of this groaning the apostle now proceeds to speak. "And not only they, but ourselves also, which have the first fruits of the Spirit,[3] even we ourselves groan within ourselves, waiting for the adoption, to wit, the redemption, of our body" (verse 23). The groaning here spoken of is one of the direct effects of the indwelling of the Holy Ghost as the Spirit of adoption. We have

[2] Heb. xii. 7-9.

[3] "Ἀπαρχὴ τοῦ πνεύματος. This expression appears to relate to the Church generally, and not to apostolic gift. As Christ is Himself the "First-fruits" of the resurrection (1 Cor. xv. 23), so is the Church described by the same title in James i. 15, and, as I believe, also in Rev. xiv. 4. The gift of the Holy Ghost therefore (v. 5), bestowed first on those who are, as fellows of the now exalted Christ, described elsewhere as the "First-born" (Heb. xii. 23), may appropriately bear this name.

already seen how that gracious presence produces in the child of God the delighted assurance of the Father's love, and the blessed anticipation of glory as the children's inheritance. Closely connected with these results, we have described to us, in this and the next two verses, the further operation of the same Spirit, as the power of active yearning and desire in the soul, and the producer of a sorrow which has its rise in the contrariety of all actual things to that Divine principle which lives and thinks, and loves and desires, within the poor tabernacle of clay, wherein, as yet, while hoping for release, it is constrained to dwell.

The presence of the mortal body, with its manifold infirmities, and all that accompanies a state of humiliation and corruptibility, maintains in God's saints a perpetual sense of being burdened. The body is, indeed, redeemed; for the price of its redemption has been paid in the precious blood of Christ. But the Redeemer has not yet appeared to claim His right. The *power*, therefore, of redemption has not yet been applied to these bodies of humiliation, as He will apply it at His glorious appearing. The earnest of its being so applied, in due time, is the indwelling Spirit of Him who raised up Jesus from the dead. We wait, then, for this; for the completion, in open and undeniable fact, of that adoption in which the believer already rejoices, as alive in Christ.

We are saved, but it is by *hope*.[4] As yet we see

---

[4] τῇ γὰρ ἐλπίδι ἐσώθημεν. "For it is for (or, in) this hope that we were saved," viz., the completed redemption spoken of in the preceding verse.

not that for which we hope. If it were visible, then hope should have no place. The eternal things for which we wait can only be discerned by faith, until our mortality has been swallowed up of life. We hope, then, for what we cannot see. But though we see it not, yet *knowledge* is the ground of our hope. The certified assurance of the God who cannot lie, is the living fountain of a Christian's hope. But a hope, thus born, creates desire; and growing desire brings a sickness to the heart, whose quickened consciousness of prospective liberty lays the more forcibly and sensibly upon the spirit, which delights in God,[5] the weariness of still-protracted bondage. A free spirit, in a bound and vile body, must needs groan. Thus the operation of the Comforter, in stimulating the desires of the believer's heart for the promised glory, makes room for the proper knowledge and enjoyment of God, as the God of patience:[6] "If we hope for that we see not, then do we *with patience* wait for it."

Nor is this all. The believer, by having the Spirit of the Son, is capable of entering, in his measure, into practical communion with the thoughts of Christ; not only concerning the future results of redemption, but also as to that which now occupies the sympathies of His heart. The power of contrasting the existing condition of the Church here below, with the Divine realities of its calling and its hopes, is in itself a fruitful source of groaning to the exercised spirit of one who has the mind of Christ. Personal circumstances, though they rightly, as well as of necessity, occupy much of the believer's thoughts,

[5] Pss. xlii. 1, 2, and lxxxiv. 2.   [6] *Infra*, chap. xv. 5.

and furnish special grounds of communion with God in prayer, are surely not the limit of that Spirit's sympathies who dwells within the saints. "*The things of Christ*,"[7] are ever the true subject of the Spirit's interest. To mind those things, to the neglect of other things which only promise personal advantage, is the true glory of a risen man.[8] The eye, also, of a saint affects his heart, and the spectacle of a sin-corrupted world makes him, of necessity, a man of sorrows, in proportion to the intimacy of his fellowship with Him who sighed deeply in His Spirit, as He wrought, as if in vain, His works of light amidst the night of unbelief.[9] Christ's fellow-sufferers must needs be sad, until He come to raise them to His throne.[1] When, too, as not seldom happens, the believer finds himself shut up and silent, in the midst of those towards whom all the natural affections of his heart would fain flow forth, yet to whom the very possession of his hope in Christ has rendered him a stranger—such experience is again a further occasion of groaning. But, blessed be God, these groanings are not without relief. The groaning of a Christian, which results from his having the Spirit, is a groaning *toward God*. It is an emotion of the new nature, and is produced by the consciousness of a pressure which nothing can perfectly remove but the presence of Christ in power. It is upon this condition of soul that the blessed God can act, as the God of comfort, of patience, and of hope. Meanwhile, the door of present relief is found in prayer.

But while prayer is among the dearest privileges

[7] Phil. ii. 21.   [8] Col. iii. 1.   [9] Lam. iii. 51.
[1] Mark viii. 12; Isaiah xlix. 4; 2 Tim. ii. 12.

of the saint, it is at the same time the witness of our infirmities. We pray indeed because we trust, and freely may we make known what is in our hearts to God, casting all care on Him who careth for us in His love.[2] But a *perfect* knowledge of our need belongs to God alone. This is at all times true, as the apostle elsewhere acknowledges specially in his own case.[3] But if this is so when men are in their happiest and most collected frames, how much more in seasons of heaviness, and amid the manifold distractions of this present life! The burdened heart may often find itself too full for speech; too much perplexed, perhaps too wearied, for the ordering of its thoughts. But there is an utterance of supplication that makes no sound. There is a mute expression of right though undefined desire, which is cognizable only by Him who searches the hearts. It is the *Spirit*, as the helper of our infirmities, that makes these desires known to the Father of mercies. Groaning in sympathy with the tried and longing heart, He makes His intercession for the saints according to the God whose messenger He is (verse 27).[4] Thus the mind of the Spirit in us is known of God. "*We* know not," indeed, "what we should pray for as we ought;" but this very ignorance, the very imperfection and smallness of our intelligence of divine things, is made to turn to the nourishment of our faith. The special subject of a believer's prayer may not be brought distinctly, and to its full extent, before the consciousness of his own soul, yet he is not the less confident. We can ask and think, at the best, within but narrow limits, compared with the

[2] Phil. iv. 6, 7; 1 Pet. v. 7. [3] Phil. i. 22, 23. [4] κατὰ Θεόν.

ability of God to purpose and to act. But *God* is Himself the object of the prayer of faith; and if the flight of the poor straitened thought toward its aim be weak, yet that very weakness leaves the wider interval for the special operation of the Spirit, as the Spirit of love and sympathy, in His intercession for the saints.[5]

Hence quietness and contentment take, in the hearts of those who are truly spiritual, the place of fretfulness and impatience. For though we know not what to pray for as we ought, yet we *do know* "that all things work together for good to them that love God." And the believer loves God. The very occasion of all his groanings, is the presence of the Spirit, crying, Abba, Father. The soul, then, whilst in heaviness because of temptation, of weakness, and of unsatisfied desire, is yet kept in joy. The power of God to work good, is the practical solace of the heart that knows Him as its eternal portion in Christ. Thus godliness with contentment becomes great gain.[6] The Blessed One Himself, amid the sore amazement of His matchless sorrow, could utter His request, in the fulness of filial trust, as to the God of His life, "Father, if thou be willing, remove this cup from me;" yet He straightway adds, "Not my will, but thine, be done."[7] So is it with the soul that, as led of the Spirit, is walking in His steps. The will of God is, to such, the measure of obedience and the rule of patience. Faith reposes in God,

---

[5] It is most needful to distinguish between the intercession of the Spirit which is here spoken of, and the heavenly intercession of Christ at the right hand of God. This latter subject is mentioned in verse 34.
[6] 1 Tim. vi. 6.   [7] Luke xxii. 42.

committing all to Him; knowing that He is not overcome of evil, but that His end is glory and rest. Joy thus fills the sufferer's prospect. Happiness is the settled condition of the inner man, under the quiet assurance, that all that is suffered is but a process whereby Almighty power is working out, in *grace*, the counsels of the will of Love.

The verses immediately following have the effect of still further enlarging and confirming the "strong consolation" of the believer, by their direct and emphatic assertion of the glory of God, as the alone founder and completer of His own eternal purpose in the work of redemption. The descriptive title of the saints is that they are "called" of God. But this calling is "according to His purpose" (verse 28). The origin, then, of the believer is the *purpose* of God. Again, the entire results of this calling are according to the *power* of God. The praise of His glory, is the end which is to be reached by the establishment of the Church before Himself, according to the good pleasure of His will. The several branches of the Divine glory, as displayed in the production and perfecting of the vessel of His own pleasure, are now opened in succession to our view.

We have, first, "foreknowledge" mentioned as that which precedes and is to be distinguished from "predestination" (verse 29).[8] The Church as a whole, and the individual saints which are its members, were eternally present in Christ before the mind

---

[8] Foreknowledge expresses the original operation of the Divine mind, considered with reference to the pure and unapproachable majesty of the blessed and only Potentate. Predestination respects rather the condition of that which is thus foreknown, objectively regarded as a creature of His will.

of God. His purpose was to multiply the vessels of His glory. He intended the impartation of His own blessed nature and happiness (so far as either can be communicated to the creature) to those whose everlasting habitation should be His own rest. He foreknew, in that love which is His nature, the several objects of His gracious purpose. The same will, which, in producing the material and natural creation, wrought not at hazard, but according to the knowledge of what was willed, works likewise now in redemption. God knew beforehand what worlds He would create. Even so has He foreknown the fashion and the stature of each several child of His love, for whom an inheritance has been prepared in Christ. But those whom He thus foreknew, in the absoluteness of sovereign purpose, He also predestinated to their appointed blessing. Conformity to the image of His own Son, is the ultimate endowment which God has in His grace provided for the foreknown objects of His purpose. It is not glory simply, but the exact similitude of Christ, which is the destiny, and as it were the definition, of each individual saint. The pattern of this similitude was eternally present with the Father in the light of the Divine counsel, but the displayed realization of it by the principalities and powers in heavenly places, was not until the ascension of Jesus, as the first-born from the dead.[9]

The eternal Son of God first takes, in grace, the form of man, in order that believing men may be conformed to Him who is the true image and glory of God.[1] The grace of Divine mercy, which in its

[9] Eph. iii. 10. [1] Chap. v. 14; 2 Cor. iv. 4, 6; 1 Cor. xi. 7.

manifestation has produced the Church, was received and holden for us of Christ before the worlds. It was "given to *us* in *Him*." It was *promised* before the world began.[2] The receiver of the promise was Christ, while the gift itself was nothing less than the fulness of life and blessedness in Him. The life of the believer is Christ. The hope of the believer is likewise Christ. The destination of the believer is to be the reflected image of Christ. The Church, then, is Christ's, according to the eternal promise and gift of the Father. It is Christ's, moreover, from the day of His resurrection,[3] as His acknowledged possession; kept now by the Father *for* Him, even as it is preserved *in* Him and by Him for the Father's presence and glory, when the hour of that joy shall have arrived. He will be known in that day (even as He now is by the faith of His saints) to the entire creation of His power, both in heaven and on earth, as the First-born of many brethren. Yet never will the First-born be *confounded* with His brethren. The grace which has made Him capable of human fellowship, will only enhance, to the delighted yet adoring hearts of His brethren, the ineffable glory of His Person as the eternal Son of God— the Only-begotten of the Father.

Thus predestinated of God, the Christian is also *called* of God (verse 30),—called with an effectual calling,—spoken to by a voice which quickens the dead. The believer is called in a double sense. As

---

[2] 2 Tim. i. 9; Tit. i. 2.

[3] More strictly I should say His *ascension*, as it was from the right hand of the Father that the Spirit, as sent of the glorified Jesus, came forth to witness in the saints, (and through them to the world,) the perfect truth, as it is objectively revealed in Him. (Eph. iv. 21.)

a quickened sinner, he is called from darkness to light, from death into life. Again, regarding him as the foreknown vessel of God's pleasure, he is called forth from the secret of the Divine purpose into the manifested light of His glory, as revealed in the face of Jesus Christ. The foreknown and predestinated believer answers to the word which testifies, to all alike, repentance towards God, and faith towards our Lord Jesus Christ.[4] Listening in the Gospel to the living truth of God, he does not disobey that call, because himself awakened and regenerated by its power.[5] For a contrary reason, the natural man, though freely addressed in the Gospel of God's grace, does not respond to the call. But our business now is with the proper workmanship of God. The calling of the Gospel is to believe in Jesus. The quickened soul hears and obeys. But the effect of this faith is justification, as we have seen. Now justification is an act, not of him who is justified, but of Him who justifies. The called believer, then, is justified of God: "whom *He* called *He* justified." And here we might not unnaturally expect the apostle to pause in his description of the work of sovereign grace; for, as already said, we are saved as yet only "by hope." But inasmuch as his present subject is the glory of God, as the fulfiller of His own purposes in Christ, the *end*, no less than the beginning, of His perfect work must be declared. Viewing the consummation of all the Divine counsel in the person of Christ alone, the Spirit of God beholds in Jesus glorified the security of all those exceeding great and precious promises which nourish and sustain the

[4] Acts xx. 21.   [5] 1 Pet. i. 23–25.

hope of God's elect; and so it is added, "whom He justified, them He also *glorified*."

Such is the work of God. He has called His foreknown vessel of mercy, first, by creation, from nothing, into natural and mortal life; next, in redemption, from the ruin of nature into the newness of the Spirit, and the hope and promise of *eternal* life. He has justified one for whom none on earth or in heaven, and least of all the sinner himself, could, *in His* sight, truly plead a favourable word; beautifying with salvation those whom He had sought for and found in the filth of their native iniquity and ruin. He has placed such in Christ, opening their eyes to look upon Him as the Lord their Righteousness, and giving them to know that they are justified in Him. Last of all, He has glorified them. As we are justified in Christ, so are we glorified in Him. Presently we shall be glorified *with* Him, wearing those crowns which shall surely rest, in brightness of eternal joy, on each several head of the brethren of the Lord. But already the same blessed God, who of old made promise of life in Christ to His children yet unborn, now sees His purpose effected and complete in the presence of the One in whom that promise was made, now crowned, after the suffering of death, with glory and honour at His own right hand.

Thus has God attained, in Christ, the end of His eternal purpose. Glory was His purpose, who is the God of glory. To bring many sons unto glory, is His own most blessed work. *He* brings the children into glory, even as the children are begotten of Himself.[6]

[6] Heb. ii. 10.

And already in Christ Jesus they sit, complete in number and in blessing, in heavenly places before Him.[7] God can thus rest in Jesus, as in the accomplishment of His desire. The *power* of God is now the sweet and triumphant theme of Christian praise.[8] True worship dates from hence; for spiritual worship is the grateful celebration of Divine glory, in an intelligent perception of the perfect truth. The Father seeks such worship, and finds it in the lips of those whom He has thus taught to know Him in the confession of His Son. We bless God, who has blessed us with all spiritual blessings in heavenly places in Christ. We cease from man, and find our rest and our joy in God.

"What shall we then say to these things?" (verse 31.) Shall we question them, or shall we affirm them? Shall we deny them, or shall we joyfully confess their truth? And if so, what room is there for human utterance in the presence of this glory, save in ceaseless and full-hearted praise of the God of all grace? Can any part of the believer's full title of blessing be now impeached or called in question? Falsely and vainly it may, but not in truth, for God is on our side. It is God who has wrought for us. He has done for us great things, and therefore we are glad.[9] But "if God be for us, who is against us?"[1] The world, the flesh, and the devil, are against us. Principalities and powers are against us. The rulers of the darkness of this world, the power of spiritual wickedness in heavenly places[2]

---

[7] Eph. i. 3, and ii. 6. [8] Ps. xxi. 13.
[9] Compare, as to the principle of the believer's joy, Psalm cxxvi.
[1] τίς καθ' ἡμῶν. [2] Eph. vi. 12.

are against us.[3] There is nothing that is capable of exciting or influencing the natural man, which is not hostile to the spiritual man. The food of one is the bane of the other. All these things, then, can be and are against us. But God is above these things, and He is for us.

All is thus made to hang henceforth evidently upon *God;* and the security of the believer arises, simply and entirely, from the assurance he feels that the God with whom he has to do will neither repent of His own calling, nor dishonour His own righteousness, nor turn the glory of His Christ to shame. That he is himself elect of God, foreknown and predestinated individually in Christ, is a matter of certainty to the soundly-taught Christian, because he is forbidden by this passage (not to speak now of others)[4] to refer his own conscious and thankful acceptance of the free message of salvation to any other cause than the decisive act of God, who, when He justifies the ungodly in the way of faith, is but bringing to a riper stage of completion the work which He had always had in view. The disputer of this world may indeed have much to say to each and all of "these things," but such disputations never can result in either happiness or hope. Beginning in presumptuous ignorance, they lose themselves, and soon expire, among the mists of death. Life, and joy, and peace, are in the knowledge only of Him who cannot be found out by intellectual search, but whose gracious love is tasted to perfection by the heart that takes Him at His word. His faithful sayings are a clue placed by

---

[3] τὰ πνευματικὰ τῆς πονηρίας ἐν τοῖς ἐπουρανίοις.
[4] Comp. 1 Pet. i. 2; 2 Tim. i. 9 &c. &c.

the Spirit in the hands of the believing pilgrim, whereby he may safely thread his way through the tangled maze of all present experiences. He is girt for his journey by the hand of God. The strength of his way is truth, and that truth is Christ.

Verse 32 contains an unfailing talisman of reassurance to the drooping spirit of the saint, when harassed by the working of an evil heart of unbelief. In truth, it is a sorrowful and evil thing, that the thought of *deficiency* should ever arise in the heart of one who already is complete in Christ,[5] and who sets out on his course as a saved sinner, under the assurance of his being, in Christ, the object of God's unutterable love. Yet so it is. And since, by reason of our weakness, we are ever more ready to think of what we have not than of what we have, the Spirit of God, in order to still all restless self-communings in our hearts, and to quiet the cravings of ignorance with the satisfying knowledge of truth, leads forth our souls here again to view the palpable evidences, not only of the reality of our interest in the love of God, but also of the completeness, in point of measure, of the blessing with which we are blessed. "He that spared not His own Son . . . . how shall He not with Him also freely give us all things?" Can there be a question in the heart of faith as to this? The gift which God gave to the ruined creature, ruined by *sin*, was Christ. Are then lesser gifts to be withheld? Having delivered His own Son to redeem sinners, is the Father going to deal out grudgingly the present supply of His children's need? Having reconciled His enemies by the death

[5] Col. ii. 10.

of His Son, is He likely to shut up His bowels of compassion from His friends? Or rather, is there any true blessing to be enjoyed which is not comprised in that which has already been bestowed?

Now, with respect to things spiritual and things eternal, no question *does* arise in the heart of a well-taught Christian. It is in the actual path of faith and patience here below, and by means of those trials which are common to us as men, that such exercises of heart arise as are met in this precious verse. How many a soul has had its desires or its affections severely tried in the disappointment of some cherished hope, or the withdrawal of some familiar and heart-prized blessing! Yet God is not less rich, and it is according to the riches of His glory that He prepares, with an abundance far exceeding all we can ask or think, for the unfading joy of the children of His love. The lesson (and it is found in practice a hard one to acquire) which we have to learn *here*, is the lesson of dependence upon God. A heart thoroughly disciplined of God possesses the secret of unfailing contentment and joy, because it knows that, though the desirableness of the object which frustrated natural desire has vainly sought to reach be never so great in appearance, it is in reality *nothing*, if withheld of God. As it is a characteristic of Omnipotent Divinity to call that which is not as though it were, so is it a prerogative of faith to deny all semblance through the knowledge of what is real; to call that *nothing* which is something, to say, "It is well," amidst nature's sorest anguish,[6] by means of its ability to claim the Father of Lights, from whom

[6] 2 Kings iv. 26.

NOTES ON THE ROMANS. 195

descendeth *every* good and perfect gift, as its own everlasting Habitation and Reward. God withholds nothing but evil from them that love Him, or, rather, whom He loves. To trust God *now*, in the varying circumstances of natural life, and to trust Him, not as men often speak, under the name of Providence, but in the clear-minded and strong-hearted confidence of *filial knowledge*—such trust, while it honours, and because it honours God, becomes to the believer an unfailing source of peace. The natural Israel fell in the wilderness because they erred in heart, not knowing the ways of God who had redeemed them out of Egypt. It was not that they doubted the reality of Canaan as a prospect, but that they could not trust God as the conductor of their way. They could not wait on God. Nature never can. And so they deemed it a worthy thought to think of Him, who for their sakes had cut Rahab and smitten the dragon, that He would starve them in the wilderness, instead of bringing them in safety to His land!

A Christian has to watch incessantly this evil heart of unbelief. The most thorough mental knowledge of the most precious truth, the largest appreciation, in the spiritual judgment, of the blessedness of that standing which grace has given him in Christ, will not avail to keep the believer from murmuring and fretting in the time of trial, unless he is habitually sunning his heart's affections in the light of God's first, His *unspeakable* gift.[7] Hence the paramount importance of evermore recurring to the Cross in order to have our thoughts of God, as it were, *adjusted* continually. It is there alone that we truly

[7] 2 Cor. ix. 15.

learn ourselves; and there, too, it is that what God is as *our* God is most searchingly known and felt. If the appreciation of *grace* be strong and simple in the heart of a believer, his soul is humbled, while blessed. His estimate of present circumstances becomes corrected and settled, because he can then view them in the presence of God; and, viewing them there, he can rate them at their true value in comparison with that which he finds, and has even now begun to taste, as his eternal portion in Christ. "I *have* a goodly heritage" becomes thus the expression of faith, while thinking of the possessed gift of God. And so it is elsewhere written: "All things are yours; whether Paul, or Apollos, or Cephas, or the world, or life, or death, or things present, or things to come; all are yours, and ye are Christ's, and Christ is God's.[8] The giving God is thus the light and solace of the children of His love.

But God gives not foolishly, though the blessed Gospel of His grace may be esteemed foolishness by the world. He does not pamper wickedness by His favour, for He is of purer eyes than to regard iniquity. But do not Christians fail and sin? First, we have the positive statement, "In many things we offend all."[9] Again it is said, "If we say that we have no sin, we deceive ourselves, and the truth is not in us."[1] A Christian, then, may sin. Though called to walk worthy of God, he may so far fall short as to be practically carnal, and walking as a man.[2] Is he, then, chargeable on this account with blame before God? (verse 33.) He may be charged,

[8] 1 Cor. iii. 21–23.　　[9] James iii. 2.
[1] 1 John i. 8.　　[2] 1 Cor. iii. 3.

for there is one whose name is the accuser of the brethren, who, until finally cast forth from the heaven which he as yet pollutes with his presence,[3] will not cease to bring his accusations against the saints of God. But how do his accusations sound in the ears of God? They whom he charges are *God's elect;* appointed, not unto wrath, but unto salvation.[4] The ultimate mark, therefore, of the accuser's aim is not the receiver, but the Almighty *Giver* of this grace. And He is justified in His sayings, and clear when He is judged. The advocacy of the Righteous One[5] is already present to turn to falsehood every charge of blame which Satan may make concerning those for whom He pleads. The Hater of sin is the righteous Justifier of the believer in Jesus. An evil and a bitter thing, indeed, it is when children of God turn in anywise to folly. The Lord is not mocked. He will judge us if we judge not ourselves; but if He do so, it is that we may *not* be condemned with the world.[6] Although, then, the believer may be charged, yet there is none to condemn. For God, who should do it, as the only Judge, is already the Justifier of the accused. Condemnation is not for them for whom Christ died (verse 34), for whom He rose, and for whom, as now alive unto God, He makes unceasingly pure intercession unto Him.

We have seen how the intercession of the Spirit is described in the former part of this chapter. We

[3] Rev. xii. 9-11. [4] 1 Thess. v. 9, 10. [5] 1 John ii. 2.
[6] 1 Cor. xi. 31, 32. This passage is only one of many in which the distinction between the chastisement of God, in mercy to them who are really His, and the *wrath* which is coming upon the children of disobedience, is clearly stated. (Heb. xii. 5-7; 1 Cor. v. 5; 1 Tim. i. 20, &c.)

have here the intercession of Christ, not as living *in* us, but as living and appearing *for* us before God. Christ, thus regarded, is the immediate object of our practical, daily faith, as worshippers of God. Nothing but the discernment of this truth suffices to keep the soul in its just position before Him. The Epistle to the Hebrews[7] treats in full the subject to which I can only here refer. The value of this doctrine will be felt by the believer, in proportion to the measure in which godly self-judgment is habitually exercised, and to the earnestness of our endeavour to walk worthy of the vocation wherewith we are called. Especially is it precious as the divinely enabling power, which meets and counteracts the striving of Satan against the soul's peace, while toiling in the weary passages of its pilgrim way.[8]

The active sympathy of Jesus, as now seen at the right hand of God, is that in which the soldier of faith finds the secret of sustaining strength in conflict. Christ's occupation in the midst of Divine glory, is the condition of His struggling brethren here. Condemnation, then, is no longer for the believer. Instead of condemnation on account of sin, he looks for glory as the hope of righteousness. Nay, because his calling is to be glorified with Jesus, he will in that day be himself a judge: "Know ye not that the saints shall judge the world?" And presently again, "Know ye not that we shall judge angels?"[9] Thus is it written in the record of God's word, concerning them whose present calling is to suffer; and who groan amidst a careless world's

---

[7] *Notes on the Epistle to the Hebrews*, passim.
[8] Heb. vii. 25; Exod. xvii. 11–16.   [9] 1 Cor. vi. 2, 3.

delight, because of the still endured burden of the unchanged body of humiliation and of sin.

The remaining verses of this wondrous chapter stand little in need of comment in this place. To one who has entered at all into the general doctrine of the apostle in that which precedes, they must come with a power of self-commending truth and blessing, which may more easily be marred than helped by methodical exposition. One or two remarks will suffice. The question, "Who shall separate us from the love of Christ?" provoking, as it does here, the triumphant answer of the Spirit, implies clearly that such separation, though impossible,— because it is not our love that is in question, but the love of Christ,—would yet be attempted. Satan made the attempt when, in the days of the Lord's flesh, he withstood Him in the path of His devoted obedience unto death. The same adversary renews the trial now, when, by all the varied means with which he plies the hearts of God's saints, he endeavours to alienate the mind, or to deter the hearts of believers from the right ways of the Lord, and thus to force them, as he thinks, beyond the limits of Divine mercy.

But it is not so. Mercy is a covenanted portion to God's saints.[1] The sheep of Christ are safely kept of Him. Hard and strenuous efforts may be made by the destroyer, to drag the saved from the hands of the Saviour; but He holds them still. There is not a thing here mentioned as striving thus to sunder us from Christ, which is not in itself above the strength of nature![2] But the faith which sees Jesus glorified

[1] Ps. lxxxix. 28–33.   [2] Mark xiv. 38.

in heaven is the victory which overcomes the world. The Divine energy of that Spirit, who sheds abroad the love of God in our hearts, is mighty to sustain in every conflict; leading as in a perpetual triumph those who, like the apostle, are enabled to commit themselves unreservedly to Him.[3]

We may remark here the extended scope of verse 36, characteristically describing, as it does, the condition and prospects of the believer here below, as the consequence of his being so entirely severed from the world, because possessed (as we have seen) of the Spirit of adoption. There is not even an especial, certainly no *exclusive* reference here, to apostolic experiences as matters of fact. The question is about those who are the objects of God's love in Christ; that is, about *all* Christians who are really such. It is desirable to keep this in view, lest our souls should haply count it a strange thing if, at any time, the sharp afflictions of the Gospel were again to return upon us. The world has undergone no intrinsic change (except, indeed, that it has in one sense become worse) since these words were written. Flesh is still flesh, and lusts as ever against the Spirit. They that are born of the flesh have still the hearts of persecutors towards the children of promise.[4]

It is the realization, through faith, of the present effects of redemption, as they are detailed in this chapter, which makes the probability of persecution a familiar thought to the believer's mind, because of the distinctness with which the contrariety of the world to the Father is then seen and felt. That the world knoweth not Christians, is because it knew not

[3] 2 Cor. ii. 14, xii. 9, 10; 2 Tim. iv. 7, 8. [4] Gal. iv. 29.

Christ.⁵ But there is in the world an active *power*, which is that of Satan and of darkness; and from that power the children of light must expect to suffer, if they walk in the manifestation of that which has produced them.⁶ Hence the general warning uttered by this same apostle when, in writing expressly on the subject of the last times of Christian defection and corruption, he says, "*All* who are willing to live godly in Christ Jesus shall suffer persecution."⁷ Lastly, in connection with this subject, I would remind the reader that in the final Revelation of the Lord to the beloved disciple, we find persecution unto death a familiar thought in relation to the Church, not only in the epistles to the Churches, but in the sequel of the book, until the place of the destroyer is no more found in heaven, because the time is come for the celebration of their triumph who loved not their lives to the death.⁸ It is well to recall these things to our minds in the present day, though, as I have remarked above, it is hard to understand their being long absent from the thoughts of any who know their calling by the teaching of the Holy Ghost.

Nothing, then, can separate us from the love of Christ. For of all that is against us, there is nothing which is not His creature, and as such, the *servant* of His love to us-ward who believe. All thus work for good, and not for evil, though the intent of the enemy who uses creature-power against the truth be not so. No attribute of God can cross this love; for already He has glorified all His attributes in

---

⁵ 1 John iii. 1. ⁶ Eph. v. 8.
⁷ οἱ θέλοντες ζῆν εὐσεβῶς, 2 Tim. iii. 12. ⁸ Rev. xii. 10, 11.

binding us to Himself in Christ. From such a love no species of trial can separate us; for it is God who in the trial proves His own work, that it may be for praise, and honour, and glory, in the day of salvation and of rest.[9] Life may not do this; for, in the higher acceptation of the word, the Love which has begotten us and the Life which we are everlastingly to enjoy, are one and the same; while as to this mortal life we are already dead with Christ. Death cannot do it; for by faith we have already been quickened with Christ, and raised up with Him from the dead.[1] Neither angels, nor principalities, nor powers, can reach for harm those who are even now complete in Him, who is the Head of all principality and power,[2] and who are already made to sit with Christ above the heavens. Present things may not separate, though fear may be on every side; for the power of God is already known in victory, and His sustaining presence, as the God of all comfort, is sweetly witnessed by His Spirit in the heart; while the retrieving mercy of Him who is both the Shepherd and the Bishop of our souls, is our effectual preservative from the ruinous corruptions of the world.[3] Things to come, instead of separating, shall by their advent bring yet nearer the end of our hope; for the day of nature's dread, the day of judgment, has no fear for those whose boldness in that day is, that they are already one with Him who is the Judge.[4] Height or depth are equally vain to obstruct the energy of a love which has already measured all

[9] 1 Pet. i. 7.   [1] Eph. ii.   [2] Col. ii.
[3] Ps. xxiii. 3, xxxvii. 24; 1 Pet. ii. 25; 1 Cor. xv. 57; and 2 Cor. i. 3, 4.   [4] 1 John iv. 17.

heights and sounded all depths, in the effectual operation of redeeming grace.[5] And is there any other creature which might lift itself in anger against the peace of God's beloved? The Spirit of God finds none. Having filled the blessed vessel of God's choice with the pure knowledge of Divine love, as witnessed in the Father's unspeakable gift, persuasion of eternal exemption from all ill becomes the necessary effect of our being thus beloved.

This chapter has opened to us, in part, the love of God: of the *Father*, in delivering His Son; of the *Son*, in the perfection of His grace; and of the *Spirit*, as the indwelling revealer of all truth; the minister of our joy, the groaning intercessor of our grief, and the effectual helper of our infirmity.

May the hearts of those who read these things so enter, as led of that Spirit, into the gracious realities of the Gospel, that, as they stand, if believers, eternally held in the unchanging love of God in Christ, so they may hold fast, on their part, a worthy and constant remembrance of Him. The danger ever is that something (and, alas! how light a thing will often suffice for this!) should separate Him practically from *our love*. Yet does He love us still.[6]

[5] Eph. iv. 8–10.   [6] Rev. ii. 4, and iii. 19.

CHAPTER IX.

THE termination of the chapter we have just quitted is also the close of one great division of this Epistle. The foregoing chapters have displayed the perfection of the Divine glory in unfolding the character of the God of all grace. They have shewn us how holiness and truth shine cloudlessly, in Christ, upon the justified believers in His love. God has been seen dealing, in the cross of His own Son, with sin, as the God of *judgment;* with the sinner, as the God of *peace.* The eighth chapter, in conducting the believer to the summit of all blessedness, as an anointed heir of glory, has summed up the recital of his privileges and his hopes by the discovery of the deep foundations of his rest, as laid fast from eternity in the changeless purpose of God. The strong reason of the Christian's hope is no other than the God in whom he trusts.[1] The blessed and only Potentate has been seen to be the effectuator of His own counsel in Christ, even as He is the all-wise purposer of that good pleasure in which alone the salvation and the glory of His many sons are made to stand.

A fair and wondrous page of living truth has thus been opened to our view. But much more yet remains to be perused, if we would acquire the wis-

[1] 1 Pet. iii. 15.

dom of God-taught *men*,² while still delighting and adoring in the liberty of God-begotten children. Infinitely precious as the Church is in the sight of the Father who gave it to Jesus, the doctrine of the Church is not the entire truth of God.³ The Church is, indeed, a comely object in the Father's eyes. She has been predestinated by His love, and is being made ready by the word of His grace to be in due time revealed in glory, as the bride, the Lamb's wife.⁴ She is a chaste virgin espoused to Christ;⁵ the beautiful perfection of His own eternal thoughts of love. But the Church is not Israel. Her birthright is not the inheritance of Israel's earthly hope,⁶ nor does she enter into her true position by virtue of an earlier prophetic promise (for the grace wherein she stands was bestowed on her in Christ before the world was),⁷ but as the work and product of Divine creative power, acting effectually in the Gospel of the grace of God for the accomplishment of a purpose which, until its appointed season came, remained an undisclosed mystery in the mind of God.⁸ The time and opportunity for the revelation and effecting of this purpose was the apparent frustration of the written promises through the rejection, by the natural heirs of promise, of Him in whom alone those promises were secured and could be enjoyed.

² 2 Tim. iii. 15–17.
³ Nor, as has been already stated, is it completely presented in this Epistle. This will be noticed more fully as we proceed.
⁴ Rev. xix. 7.   ⁵ 2 Cor. xi. 2.
⁶ Inclusively it is so, of course; *all* the promises being in Christ yea and Amen, to the glory of God *by us*. I speak here of her distinctive calling and hopes as standing apart from Jew and Gentile alike. For a fuller view of the true doctrine of the Church and its calling, I must refer the reader to my *Notes on the Epistle to the Ephesians*.   ⁷ 2 Tim. i. 9; Tit. i. 2.   ⁸ Eph. iii. 9.

To clear up all doubts as to the true and ultimate aim of prophetic promise in the Old Testament; to place the question of Israel's national prospects in its just light; and to prevent by these means the dangerous though easy error of substituting the Church in the stead of Israel, as the true and proper object of the promises made to the fathers, may be said, in general terms, to be the intention of the Spirit of God in the present and two following chapters. In treating these subjects, the apostle is enabled to disclose to us a far and deep view of the otherwise inscrutable mystery of Divine government. The solemn and pride-quelling truth of the resistless supremacy of the will of God, is the ground upon which are traced the varied events of human vicissitude which severally invite our attention. The same mighty truth is afresh disclosed to the eye of faith as the exhaustless well of its own sure blessedness, as having all its springs in God. The unity also of God's way, and His consistency with Himself, in the exhibition both of His goodness and His severity, are strikingly displayed. In connection with the subject of the administrative power and wisdom of God, the Church also is contemplated from a *dispensational* point of view. Solemnly and most practically interesting is the instruction contained in the eleventh chapter with respect to this. But I will not extend these preliminary remarks. May the Spirit of wisdom and of revelation guide both myself and the reader of these Notes into a deeper and richer knowledge of the only wise God, the Saviour.

Let us now turn to the chapter immediately before us. The first three verses are full of meaning, as well as of most deep and tender feeling. The apostle knew well that Jehovah had permanently connected His own name with that of Israel; that the very title which the nation bore, was the token of their supremacy among the nations of the earth. He knew also that the God of glory who had revealed His promise to Abraham, and sworn His oath unto Isaac,[9] had confirmed the same unto Israel for an *everlasting* covenant.

It was the knowledge of this which had enabled him to affirm, in the earlier part of this Epistle,[1] the preëminence of the natural seed of Abraham, in comparison with the Gentiles who knew not the covenants of promise. The statement which was then made of the still existing excellency of the Jew, was substantiated by an appeal to the indestructibility of Divine promise, as secured in the name and eternal character of the God of truth. As a vessel of Divine power, filled with the Holy Ghost, the apostle could only write in the order of Divine inspiration. Accordingly, after having, as we have seen, affirmed the Jew's hereditary title of superiority, when contrasted with the Gentile, he does not immediately proceed to develope fully the history of the nation, either prophetically or retrospectively (except so far as sufficed to the necessary conviction of the Jew as under sin), but rather to bring into clear and full distinctness the especial glory of the grace of God, as it finds its expression in the calling of the Church from Jew and Gentile alike.[2]

Having done this, he now returns by an abrupt transition to the subject of Israel. How near that

[9] Ps. cv. 8, 9.   [1] Chapter iii.   [2] Chaps. iv.–viii.

subject was to his heart may be understood from the striking and emphatic expressions with which he gives utterance to his desire at the commencement of the present chapter.

Now it was not the strength of natural feeling merely which governed the emotions of the apostle's mind. He was indeed, as touching the flesh, a Hebrew of the Hebrews. He had been, in conversation, a more than Jew in the consistent energy of his zealous devotedness to the religion of his fathers.[3] But he had, since then, learned and felt the power of a truth, which had rendered the loftiest advantage which flesh can compass no better than dross and dung, in the estimation of one who reckoned and valued according to the realities of the heavenly calling, as they are now revealed by the Spirit.[4] The very keenness, however, of this perception and enjoyment of his blessedness as a Christian, reacts upon the deep-seated love of his heart toward his brethren, his kinsmen after the flesh. His feeling was not patriotism, in the ordinary acceptation of the term. He regarded the natural seed of Israel, not according to the instincts merely of blood, and soil, and language, but as the Divinely chosen nation to whom the promises of God were made. With an eye like that of Moses when he looked upon the burdens of his brethren in Egypt,[5] he now beheld them as they lay hard bound in the fetters of judicial blindness and unbelief. He knew that already one national distinction of the Jew was to be a denier that Jesus was the Christ; and because, by the grace of God, the chief of those recusants had been, in his own

[3] Gal. i. 13. [4] Phil. iii. [5] Exod. ii. 11.

person, transformed from the madness of self-righteous opposition to the glad and heartfelt acknowledgment of the truth as it is in Jesus, he felt but the more acutely the wretchedness of his brethren after the flesh, while still remaining in their unbelief.

Nor was it only the gracious sympathy of a loving heart which thus yearned to impart a portion of its own blessing to the objects of its love. The Divine sanction of the name of God was upon these strong emotions of His servant's heart. His conscience bore Him witness in the *Holy Ghost*, while uttering a desire which has but one parallel[6] in the Word of God.[7] Paul, the apostle of the Gentiles, was nevertheless an Israelite; and although, in Christ, he knew no man after the flesh, and gloried in that cross which had abolished utterly the personal claims and pretensions of Jew and Gentile alike, yet, because Christ died *for that nation*,[8] there was a clear warrant of Divine truth which justified the ardent yearnings of his desire towards the natural children of the covenant.

God had of old made promise to the *fathers*, speaking good things for the people which He called His own. Had, then, the calling of the Church in

---

[6] Exod. xxxii. 32.

[7] I believe the words ηὐχόμην γὰρ αὐτὸς ἐγὼ ἀνάθεμα εἶναι ἀπὸ τοῦ Χριστοῦ to be exactly rendered in the English Version. Compare, for the construction, Acts xxv. 22. It is interesting to observe, in the case both of Moses and of Paul, how a right and holy sentiment may, through the weakness of the flesh, degenerate into an expression of merely natural vehemence. The same spirit which produced the emotions of grief and disappointment would, if unresisted by the flesh, have brought the soul of God's servant into ready and perfect submission to His will. How different is the expression of the same apostle's personal longings, when raised above the level of all natural or earthly associations, to behold truth in its everlasting perfections in Christ! Comp. Phil. iii. 8, 9. [8] John xi. 51.

anywise set Israel aside? Had the promises become void because of their unbelief; or had the mind of God altered, with respect to the original object of His choice? The apostle knew that this was impossible. The name of Jehovah, as the God of *Israel*, was the eternal pledge of the accomplishment eventually of the nation's blessing. While, therefore, the heart of this devoted servant of Christ might be wrung by the proofs, so constantly before his eyes, of the fatal stiff-heartedness of the Jews in his own day, he finds in the revelation of the ways of God, which it was given him first to perceive and then to minister to the Church, a solace and compensation of his grief. Rising by the power of faith above the actual sphere of things, and quieting the turbulence of natural sorrow by a recollection of the steadfast continuance of the nation's hope in God Himself, he presently enters into the general question of the faithfulness of Jehovah, as the sovereign dispenser of blessing according to His own promise. Drinking, as he runs, from the deep springs of Divine joy in the gradual unfolding of the perfect way of God, he finds his heart strengthened to utter, at the close of this inquiry,[9] the memory of the Lord's great goodness,[1] and to sing of the righteous mercy of His faithfulness while discovering the unsearchable greatness of His way. Let us now follow him as he opens to us some of the secrets of this way.

Verses 4–6. We have, first, in these verses, a recital of Israel's national and distinctive prerogatives. These are here reviewed not only as things which once had been, but as enduring realities of national

[9] Chap. xi. 26–36.   [1] Ps. cxlv. 7.

preëminence. I will notice them very briefly. First, we have emphatic mention made of the national name, "who are *Israelites.*" We have already seen, in part, the peculiar force and meaning of this name. As we advance in our present subject, we shall find a fuller explanation of the emphasis which it here receives. The national privileges then follow—"to whom pertaineth the adoption or sonship."[2] The peremptory message of Jehovah to the king of Egypt was: "Israel is my son, even my first-born; and I say unto thee, Let my son go," &c.[3] He was the Rock that begat them, their Father that had bought them.[4] This was the gracious name which the Holy One assumed when He essayed to go and take a nation from the midst of another nation, that they might be His people, and that He might be their God. But the nation had meanwhile corrupted itself, and the spot of His children was no longer their spot. Nevertheless, the same mouth that bore this testimony to their self-corruption, and spoke words of fierce rebuke against their sin, maintains their cause, and asserts their eventual security and blessing as a people whom the Lord will save.[5] The prophets abundantly testify to the time when Israel, brought back from their own ways and established in the new covenant, shall be known and glorified as the nation of Divine adoption.[6]

[2] υιοθεσία.   [3] Exod. iv. 22, 23.
[4] Deut. xxxii. 6, 18.   [5] Deut. xxxii. 15–26, xxxiii. 26–29.
[6] Jer. xxxi. 9. "I am a Father to Israel, and Ephraim is my first-born." It is necessary to remember that it is *national* adoption, and not that of individuals, which is here in point. It is written, indeed, concerning the earthly Jerusalem, "Thy people shall be *all* righteous," (Isa. lx. 21,) but the adoption as here mentioned is regarded as a national prerogative, to be vindicated in due time. (Jer. iii. 19.)

212   NOTES ON THE ROMANS.

The next mentioned of the national distinctions is "the glory." Much need not be said on this point. How the Divine glory filled the tabernacle of witness in the wilderness; how the temple of Solomon was afterwards filled with the same glory; and how that glory was seen by the prophet Ezekiel to withdraw from the place of Jehovah's name, because of the exceeding abundance of the national sin, are things which are, probably, sufficiently known to all who will read this book. But it is not, there is reason to suppose, so generally recognised that the glory which withdrew from Jerusalem because of Israel's sin, is eventually to return thither, when the Lord shall have Himself returned to the long forsaken place of His earthly rest. Yet are the voices of the prophets equally distinct in affirming this. The very prophet who describes so fully and circumstantially the departure of the glory, is the one whose vision comprises within its scope the return *to the same place* of that which he had seen depart.[7]

The building up of Zion from the waste of her ruin, will be at the appearing in glory of the Lord Himself.[8] There is a day coming when He will reign in Mount Zion and in Jerusalem, and before His *ancients gloriously*.[9] It has, moreover, been expressly promised that the latter glory of the house of Jehovah shall be greater than the former.[1] The house of

---

[7] Ezek. xliii.   [8] Ps. cii. 16.
[9] Isa. xxiv. 23.   נֶגֶד זְקֵנָיו כָּבוֹד   "*Vor seinen Aeltesten ist Herrlichkeit.*"—DE WETTE.

[1] Haggai ii. 9. גָּדוֹל יִהְיֶה כְּבוֹד הַבַּיִת הַזֶּה הָאַחֲרוֹן מִן־הָרִאשׁוֹן μεγάλη ἔσται ἡ δόξα τοῦ οἴκου τούτου, ἡ ἐσχάτη ὑπὲρ τὴν πρώτην. LXX. "*Grösser soll dieses Hauses letzte Herrlichkeit denn die erste seyn.*"—DE WETTE. I have no doubt that the translations here given are right. They who look on the first advent of Christ

God is one, and not many. It may be overthrown and trampled on, but when the time of restitution comes, it is the same house still. The longing wish of David was fulfilled by his successor, and the presence of Jehovah had filled with glory the house which Solomon had built.[2] Again, the glory had departed, and the house been broken down. To the remnant employed, under Haggai and Zerobabel, in rebuilding the house in the midst of weakness and conflict, the promise of abiding restitution was prophetically addressed. But, like every other Jewish promise, it bears on the glory of the Messianic reign. Intermediate events are scarcely touched on, but a contrast is made of the former glory of the house with its latter glory, when, the promised Redeemer having come to Zion, the glory of Jehovah shall have again arisen upon her, and He will "glorify the house of His glory."[3] To enter further into this subject now is incompatible with the object of this work. I content myself, therefore, with repeating the apostle's assertion, that to the Israelites pertains not only the adoption, but the glory also.[4]

Moreover "the covenants" are theirs. The first covenant and the second alike pertain to Israel. The Church finds her place within the second covenant, because, as it is the covenant of saving grace in the

---

as the fulfilment of this prophecy, are principally induced to do so from the tenor of our English translation. But it is well to remember that, in point of fact, *that* house had virtually ceased to exist when our Lord first came, the repairs under Herod amounting to an almost entire rebuilding. (Compare John ii. 20.)

[2] Ps. cxxxii.; 1 Kings viii. 10, 11.

[3] Isa. lix. 20, lx. 7.

[4] I need hardly pause to remind the reader that in all these considerations the glory of the Church is quite out of view. The subject before us is Israel, and their national prerogatives.

blood of Jesus, the justified sinner, whether Jew or Gentile, whether partaking dispensationally of a heavenly or an earthly calling, can alone find his security *there*. But though this be so, and therefore the fullest application of the second covenant is everywhere in the New Testament made to the Church,[5] yet this does not in any way impair the force of what the apostle here affirms. It is "with the house of Israel and the house of Judah," that the new covenant is to be made (and already is made in Christ, though as yet they know it not), and its rich and triumphant effects will hereafter be seen when, under its gracious power, Israel will blossom and bud, and fill the face of the world with fruit.[6]

"The giving of the Law"[7] is next mentioned. With respect to this expression, some hesitation may be felt in fixing its positive meaning; in determining, that is, whether it should be taken with reference to their own condition as receiving the Law from the only Lawgiver, or whether it relates to their standing as the "head" and not the "tail" of the nations— their being the destined lawgivers to those who, in the day of the Lord, shall own Immanuel's land to be the glory of all lands, and shall render homage, in humble guise, to those whom once the nations had despised. I shall not delay the reader by any further discussion of this point, but remark merely that both things are true of Israel, and of Israel *alone*. They only received statutes and ordinances immediately from God, and of Jerusalem alone it is said, that the nation and kingdom that will not serve her shall

---

[5] See further, as to this, *Notes on the Hebrews*, chap. viii. *ad fin*.
[6] Isa. xxvii. 6.   [7] ἡ νομοθεσία.

perish.⁸ For out of Zion shall go forth the law, and the word of the Lord from Jerusalem⁹ in that day.¹

"The service of God"² next follows in the catalogue of national distinctions. I think I need not do more than remind the reader of what has already been said about the temple, to make it appear that one perpetual characteristic of the nation, when contemplated in its state of blessing, is that of worship toward God. "A kingdom of priests" is the descriptive title of conditional promise addressed to Israel when about to receive the old covenant. This title will be realized when, under the covenant of grace, the seed of Israel will be named afresh the priests of the Lord, and called, by the nations who will drink of the overflowings of their cup, "the ministers of their God."³

"The promises" come next; for these too are theirs,⁴ and shall be fulfilled in their appointed time, as the sequel will further show.

"The fathers," too, are theirs. They are the lineal seed, the natural successors of them to whom the promises were made. Last of all, it was "from them that Christ came, as concerning the flesh, who is over all God blessed for ever."⁵

---

⁸ Isa. lx. 12.   ⁹ Isa. ii. 2; Micah iv. 1, 2.

¹ My own judgment decidedly inclines to the latter of these views. $Nομοθεσία$ means legislation. It thus describes the act or conduct of a $νομοθέτης$, or lawgiver. That it may mean a code of laws is true; for the word is found (not in Scripture, where it occurs once only) in this sense. In the LXX. it is used where $νόμος$ might have been expected. I only add that, as to the former of the meanings mentioned in the text, it is involved in what is said respecting the covenants.   ² $ἡ λατρεία$.   ³ Isa. lxi. 6.

⁴ That they pertain also to the Church, in a yet higher and fuller sense, by virtue of her union with Him in whom they all are found, is of course no less true (*ante*, p. 205, note).

⁵ This clear and careful enunciation of the mystery of the Incarnation has a forcible significance in this place; since it was their

Thus to the nation of Israel are assigned and secured all the special dispensations of Jehovah's goodness, so far as they are the subject of revelation in the Old Testament. God promised nothing apart from Abraham and his seed, and Christ, as the true seed of Abraham, becomes the root on which, in due time, the nation of God's choice is to grow and have its increase. But the apostle had already spoken of Israel as having rejected Christ, and he was himself the apostle of the *Gentiles*. Had then a change taken place in the purposes of God? If Christ was "of Israel," how came it that, as a nation, Israel alone seemed excluded from its own proper portion as having the word of Divine promise? The reply to these questions will be found in verses 6–13.

And first, the word of God had not failed of its effect. The statements which follow in proof of this position unfold the principal truth of all Divine teaching; namely, that human blessing is the result of elective mercy alone; that God, that is, confers nothing upon flesh for its own sake, or on its own merits; and that consequently all title to Divine blessing must be "of faith," and not in the way of natural right. Thus Israel, when as a nation it enters into the blessings promised, must previously have been brought nationally within the covenant of that electing mercy of which Christ crucified is the secu-

blind rejection of the Lord of Glory that both degraded Israel from their natural supremacy, and prepared the way for the present manifestation of Divine wisdom and power in the calling of the Church, the very foundation of which is that rejected but now glorified Name. Hereafter, when the eyes of blinded Israel look forth upon the Light of God, they will sing with understanding the now oft perverted strain, "Unto *us* a Child is born," &c. Meanwhile to the Christian, "it is evident that our Lord sprang out of Judah." (Isaiah ix. 6; Heb. vii. 14.)

NOTES ON THE ROMANS. 217

rity, and Christ risen and glorified the abiding pledge. It is in Him alone that *all* the promises of God are yea and Amen.[6] Until, therefore, the time be come for the fulfilment of the promise of national regeneration,[7] Israel, as a nation, is shut up in unbelief, and hence, incapable of attaining what it seeks. Meanwhile, though the covenanted blessing be deferred, because of the unprepared state of the nation to receive it, both the name and the hope of Israel are preserved. The unity of the nation, as the foreknown vessel of election, was not impaired by the defection of nature from the truth of God. "For they are not all Israel which are of Israel."

The specialty of Divine election, as the necessary origin of all enduring favour, is now illustrated by examples. Abraham had many children; but among them all, one only was born according to promise. The successor, therefore, to the title and expectations which pertained to Abraham, as the holder of Divine promise, was not Ishmael but Isaac. Ishmael was no true heir of promise, for his birth was at the will and in the power of the flesh; while in the order of nature he was Abraham's heir. But natural inheritance can never comprise within itself the promises of God. God's children only can possess His goods. The *word* of promise must create effectively the predestined heir of blessing. And so Isaac's generation

[6] 2 Cor. i. 20. The verse thus concludes: "To the glory of God *by us.*" This expression is important, not only as pouring into the lap of Christian faith now the fulness of all blessing, but also because it indicates the mediate position of the Church of God, as having *first* trusted in Christ, when the day shall have arrived for the vindication of the promises in their direct application to their proper and original object, which we have already seen to be the *nation* for which Christ died. See *Notes on the Ephesians*, chap. i. and iii.

[7] Ezek. xxxvi. 25-28; Acts iii. 19-21.

was postponed to the extinction of the force of nature, that his birth might be of God. The child of Sarah, as the fruit of promise, is thus a type also of the nation's birth,[8] when, in the latter day of regeneration, Jehovah will be known as their Father, though Abraham be ignorant of them, and Israel acknowledge them not.[9] That is, when the expectation of nature, on the ground of the Abrahamic name and title, shall have been found to end only in the last affliction of Jacob's trouble, and the hard bondage of the oppressor has all but extinguished the common and hereditary hope of all the tribes,[1] then it is that the set time of promised mercy will have come, and God will bring up again the broken and dishonoured house of Israel from its grave, and the nation shall be born at once to its inheritance of promise.[2]

The general assertion of Divine election as the ground of blessing having been sustained by reference to the birth of Isaac, the case of *Jacob* is next introduced, in order to narrow the principle in its application, and thus to place the doctrine in a yet more striking light. Rebecca was the wife of Isaac the heir of promise. She had, moreover, been appointed for him of God, who guided the messenger of Abraham when on his way.[3] God, then, was in the birth of Isaac and the choice of Rebecca. Further, the conception of Rebecca was in answer

---

[8] Let not the reader suppose that I am here diverting this type from its object, as elsewhere expressed in Scripture. Isaac, as the heir of promise, is a threefold type. First, of Christ, as the true Heir. Secondly, of the Christian, as individually quickened according to the calling of God. And, lastly, of the nation, when brought into its blessing, as the chosen object of grace and promise, under the new covenant.

[9] Isa. lxiii. 16.
[2] Ezek. xxxvii.; Isa. lxvi. 8.
[1] Acts xxvi. 7.
[3] Gen. xxiv.

to the prayer of Isaac's faith. He prayed for seed, and a double answer came; twins were in the womb of Rebecca. While, however, the children were as yet unborn, their appointed destiny was revealed to their mother. "The elder shall serve the younger,"[4] was the expression of His will, who is not only absolute in the original choice of His vessel of promise, but who likewise directs the course of the blessing once conferred.

The promises of God do not perpetuate themselves and flow to their fulfilment through a natural channel. Esau had nature's right of inheritance, for he was the first-born; but the thing to be inherited being Divine promise, it can attach only to the object contemplated in the purpose of the Promiser, and by Him prepared to receive it. The calling of God is thus made to anticipate the course of nature, and to contradict it. Blessing is kept in God, and visits only where He wills. Abraham could confer on Isaac the wealth which God had given him, when God had first created Isaac to be the receiver and holder of the blessing. In the case of Jacob, God in like manner directs positively the course of His own blessing, according to the immediate choice of His own will. Now all this was done, as the apostle here tells us, "that the purpose of God according to election might stand, not of works, but of Him that calleth." God loved Jacob, and hated Esau. But why was this? Had Jacob earned His love? Nay, he was loved while as yet unborn. Had Esau by evil works incurred His hate? As Jacob's twin, he too was yet within his mother's' womb, and so had done no evil.

[4] Gen. xxv.

Jacob and Esau were alike incapable of blessing, as the natural seed of Rebecca. For nature, as we have seen, cannot enter into the promises of God. Jacob's blessing came by love: "Jacob have I loved." But the love of God is not constrained, any more than it is purchasable with a price. It is the good pleasure of the Divine will that is pleased to call the elect vessel of His love. Now Jacob is here considered not only personally, as contrasted with Esau, but *nationally,* as the quotation from Malachi is sufficient to prove.[5] The love, then, which chose the younger twin while yet unborn, and pronounced a promise of supremacy on one whom nature would have condemned to serve, will in due time exalt its object to the appointed sphere of blessing which, as the holder of the promises, it is surely destined to attain.[6]

The liberty of God to purpose and to act without let or hindrance, according to the pleasure of His own will, has thus been asserted as a doctrine, and vindicated by historical fact. Keeping in mind the specialty of the apostle's aim, as it respects the elucidation of the Divine dealings with Israel, let us now pursue the further development of this all-important principle.

Verse 14. "What shall we say, then?" &c. We have here, as in former instances, an expression of human feeling and judgment on the ways of God. The mind of man, reasoning upon the strange facts above quoted by the apostle in illustration of the dealings of God, finds its ideas of right and propriety entirely traversed. The *natural* ground of all dis-

[5] Mal. i. 1–5.   [6] Isa. lviii. 14.

tinction is merit in the object of honour. And because fallen humanity is alienated from the way of God, no less in thought and judgment than in affection, men are continually striving to establish a claim upon God; of whom, if they remember Him at all, they think only as a Judge. The plain, direct statement, consequently, of elective grace, as the Divine witness of God's sovereignty in mercy, only provokes the natural heart to a resentful insinuation of unfairness in the Divine character. Yet man, in thus forsaking his own mercies, is a witness against himself. For all the reasonings of men as to the duty of obedience, and the equity of the legal condition of acquiring blessing, are grounded on nothing else than the experienced fact of personal imperfection, which suggests *amendment* as the practical law of man's life. Nature never penetrates the mystery of her own corruption. For neither sin nor holiness are clearly visible without the light of God. "*Deteriora sequor*," is the reluctant admission of weakness and conscious imperfection, in an honest mind yet ignorant of God. It is the Holy Ghost alone who, as the Spirit of truth, reveals the secret of human *ruin*. He makes manifest the helplessness as well as depravity of the natural man, in order that the rest which unfallen nature refused to find in the *goodness* of God, as a Creator, might be discovered and enjoyed by those who taste, in Christ, His *mercy* as a Saviour.

The suggestion, therefore, as to the possibility of there being unrighteousness with God, after calling forth from the apostle his usual exclamation of indignant repudiation, becomes an occasion for the more distinct and emphatic enunciation of the doctrine of mercy as a particular aspect of the electing will of God: "For he saith unto *Moses*, I will have mercy on whom I will have mercy," &c. (verse 15.) It was to the lawgiver of Israel that Jehovah revealed the secret of His way, in sovereign elective grace, after the nation had for ever forfeited all claim of *legal* blessing, by their breach of the covenant of works.[7] After having been for a moment admitted to a higher moral elevation than other men, by virtue of their promised obedience to the Law, they are precipitated, by their sin, to the ordinary level of an ungodly world.[8] But the common guilt and consequent ruin of the creature having been once proved, the question of *justice* is necessarily excluded from any display of Divine favour towards such. That is, considered in themselves and with reference to their own works, the entrance of God into judgment with men must destroy all hope. For vengeance against sin is the natural march of Divine justice. But this would involve the destruction of *all*, for all have sinned. Power belongs to God, and the natural condition of man, as a sinner, provokes the exercise of that power in wrathful indignation. But *mercy* also belongeth unto Him. Now this must, in its very nature, of necessity be controlled and directed by the *will* of Him who shows mercy. It is drawn by no attraction of desert. Moreover, human wretchedness, being in

[7] Exod. xxxii., xxxiii., *passim*, and Acts vii. 42. The force of this allusion to so important a crisis in the national history is obvious. The Jewish mind, in order to be delivered from the inveterate notion of self-righteousness, needed to be taught or reminded, by such references, that the principle to which it clung with such infatuate tenacity had been disallowed from the very first. Long-suffering, mercy, and faithfulness had been the security of a stiff-necked people, whom righteous judgment, untempered by mercy, must have blotted from the earth. [8] Amos ix. 7, 8.

itself the natural effect of Divine judgment against sin, is no compelling cause of mercy. Its deep and blessed spring is to be sought for and found (if, indeed, that depth be searchable), in the mystery of the love of God—in God himself, whose name is Love.

Nor is this all. The objective display of mercy, when revealed in its full brightness in the person of Jesus, is not enough to secure the blessing of God's elect. Nature never can believe the truth of God, whether for good or for evil. "*Because* I tell you the truth, ye believe me not,"[9] is the expostulation of Truth itself, when dishonoured and withstood by those who, as touching the flesh, nevertheless stood near to God. The vessels, therefore, of Divine mercy must be *fitted* to receive mercy. Truth must act subjectively on the heart and conscience, by the power of the Holy Ghost, or all promise and testimony alike will fail of their effect. And so he adds, "It is not of him that willeth, nor of him that runneth, but of *God* that showeth mercy."[1]

Now it was to Moses, the man of God, that the secret of electing mercy was declared.[2] Its grand exemplification to Israel will be in the day when, having wearied itself in the greatness of its way,[3] the scattered and dispersed nation shall again be brought into its own land. For the mercy which their sin under the old covenant had caused to depart, will yet again revive when the time of promise shall have come. "I will have mercy on her that

[9] John viii. 45.
[1] The probable allusion here to the fleshly preference of Isaac for Esau, and the going of the latter in quest of the venison, will easily suggest itself to the reader.
[2] Ps. xc. will be read with special interest (reference being had to its title) in connection with this subject. [3] Isa. lvii. 10.

had not obtained mercy,"[4] is the word spoken concerning her who had first been repudiated for her sins. Moreover, the Lord will yet return with mercies to *Jerusalem*. His house shall be built in it, and a line stretched forth upon Jerusalem.[5] For a small moment He has forsaken Zion, but with great mercies He will gather her.[6] Thus we find, first, the solemn assertion of the will of Divine mercy in its sovereignty, as the alone condition of blessing; and, secondly, the distinct assurance that the good pleasure of that will is to show mercy unto Israel in the latter day.[7]

Verses 17, 18. It is in close connection with what goes immediately before, and in further illustration of the doctrine of Divine *mercy*,[8] that the manifestation of righteous power in the way of judgment is next exemplified:—"*For* the Scripture saith unto Pharaoh," &c., &c. The same Holy One, who reserves to Himself the sovereign prerogative of mercy, is equally God, in the just infliction of His vengeance upon rebellious sinners. The question, "Who is the Lord?" which was asked by Pharaoh in his pride of heart,—a question which, whether audibly expressed

---

[4] Hos. ii. 23.   [5] Zech. i. 16.
[6] Isaiah liv. *passim*.
[7] As I am not writing a treatise on the nation and its hopes, but merely noting in succession what I find in this Epistle, I here and elsewhere assume many things which some would no doubt question. The application of Jewish promise to Israel in its restored unity, I hold as a fundamental maxim of prophetic interpretation. As the apostle's subject here is Israel nationally, I have quoted prophecies which refer severally to Israel and to Judah, though they are not to be confounded by any means. The reader who is desirous of pursuing this subject further, may perhaps find some help in what has been said in my *Notes on the Psalms*.
[8] Compare Psalm cxxxvi. 10–21, where Jehovah's mercy to His chosen is declared to be the motive and measure of His righteous acts of judgment, whether upon the Egyptian or the Amorite.

or not, lurks always in the depths of unregenerate nature,—must one day receive its decisive answer. As it has happened to Pharaoh and his host, the fame of whose catastrophe has filled all lands, in lasting testimony both to the power and the faithfulness of God, so will it again be done when the "sudden destruction," which has so long impended over an unrepentant world, shall be at last permitted to descend.[9] Our present concern, however, is rather with the clear establishment of the *principles* both of mercy and judgment, as already exemplified in the dispensational government of God.

The apostle's summary, in verse 18, while it affords to the spiritual mind a quiet resting-place and a grateful refuge from all fruitless questionings of heart,[1] presents also, to the unbroken pride of nature, a barrier against which it frets itself in vain. The *will* of God is affirmed to be the ultimate and sufficient *reason* of the opposite conditions of good and evil, as they are exemplified among men: "Therefore hath He mercy on whom He will have mercy, and whom He will He hardeneth." After what has been already written, it will not be needful to dwell further on the former clause of this verse. With respect to the latter, we have only to recall to our minds the earlier teaching of the apostle, as to the intrinsic qualities of corrupted nature, in order to see clearly that, independently of positive judicial blindness,—itself the beginning of that everlasting punishment which is awarded to obdurate sinners,—whenever God refrains from *softening* the heart, He *hardens*

---

[9] 1 Thess. v. 3; 2 Thess. ii. 8–12.   [1] Ps. cxxxi.

it:[2] *i.e.* if left to its natural tendencies, the various dealings of God, whether in goodness or in judgment, serve only to evince more decidedly the native contrariety of the unregenerate will to that of God. For, as has been shown already, the natural mind can never be subject to the Law of God.[3]

Accordingly, this mode of expression is continually employed by the Spirit of God, when describing the way of evil men, whether Jew or Gentile.[4] So long as Israel remains under the old covenant, the heart of the nation is declared to be a *stony* heart, to exchange which for a heart of flesh is the promised effort of regenerative grace.[5] While the special visitation of judicial blindness is announced in such words as these: "He hath blinded their eyes, and hardened their heart," &c.,[6] the cause of their infatuation is by the same Spirit referred solely to themselves: "They refused to hearken, and pulled away the shoulder, and stopped their ears, that they should not hear. Yea, *they made their* hearts as an adamant stone, lest they should hear the law and the words."[7] For it is a fearful truth, that the more plainly and directly the voice of God addresses itself to the natural heart, the more decided and manifest will be the evidences of intentional resistance to His will. And so it is

---

[2] If He leaves it to itself, He suffers it to harden, and is so said by His own act to harden it. In chaps. i. and ii. of this Epistle, the same point is clearly illustrated. In chap. i. it is God who gave up the Gentiles to a reprobate mind; but it was through their own lusts that their dishonour came. And so in chap. ii. 5, the hardness and impenitency of men are charged entirely upon themselves.

[3] Chap. viii. 7.

[4] Though more frequently of the Jews, as might be expected; inasmuch as it was the position of the latter, as standing in a covenant relation to God, that gave such occasion for the manifestation of this hardness.   [5] Ezek. xxxvi. 26.

[6] John xii. 40.   [7] Zech. vii. 11, 12.

that we find the same repentant people, who, when their eyes are opened to behold the Light of Israel, make such confessions as these:—" All we like sheep have gone astray; *we have turned* every one to his own way," &c.; expostulating with Jehovah when first awakened to a sense of their ruin and distance from Him in the following strain:—" O Lord, why *hast thou made* us to err from thy ways, and hardened our hearts from thy fear?" &c.[8]

So true is it, that when that "strong delusion" comes, which is to seal up for judgment those who have so long trifled with the overtures of grace, the depraved will of man will be the ready medium through which the art of the deceiver will effect his aim. If men are led to destruction, it is by the cords of their own unhallowed lusts.

We have seen thus how the sovereign attributes of elective purpose, of absolute mercy, and of judicial power, not only appertain to God, but are severally associated with His name as the God of *Israel*, the pledged fulfiller of the mercy promised to the fathers. The verses immediately following have a more direct application to the special calling of the Christian now, and therefore demand our close attention.

Verses 19–24. The assertion of Divine sovereignty, in power as well as mercy, provokes a reply against God. " Why doth He yet find fault?" is the utterance of the natural heart, which, while quailing helplessly before the Omnipotence of God, still avoids the confession of its own condition as ruined *by sin*. God, though dreaded, is not feared. The attempt is made to charge the weight of human misery upon

[8] Isa. liii. 5, 6, and lxiii. 17; compare also lxiv. 6.

the name of the blessed God, as if He were the author of evil and not of good; while the excellency of His grace in the display of His glory, as the Saviour of the vessels of mercy, is ignored and dishonoured by the unbelieving heart of nature, which reasons darkly on the ways of the only wise God, and scruples not to impute respect of persons to Him who is alone the righteous Judge.

The world ever rebels in heart against that which, from its habit of measuring God by its own faulty standard of perfection, it regards as iniquitous in the declaration of His will. Just as Pharaoh was strengthened in his resistance to Jehovah by the evil arts of the magicians of Egypt, so the devil now, as the spirit of error, stirs up men to resist indirectly the truth of God, as it is revealed in the Gospel of His grace. He does so by insinuating to the self-flattered heart of nature, that that is attainable by the will and power of man, which it belongs to God alone to dispense and confer, according to the abundance of His grace through Jesus Christ. Hence the fatally delusive dream of self-righteousness on the part of those who, while professing holiness and zeal for God, are really denying Him in the very works to which they attach the most value, and on which they vainly rely.

But even true-hearted believers are not unfrequently staggered and alarmed by the broad statement of the doctrine of election. Satan is often busy with this truth in the hearts of God's children. By a sort of argument "*ad verecundiam,*" the poor faint-hearted Christian, more versed in the sad experience of personal unworthiness than accustomed to the clear shining of the Sun of righteousness, is pricked and startled by an appeal to his own conscience, as to whether such an one as he is can safely deem himself the object of God's special choice. Now, let a soul, harassed by temptation through an indistinct apprehension of the doctrine of election, question itself simply thus: Do I believe that I can save myself? but if not, do I believe that salvation is solely of God? And if so, does the doctrine of free mercy and declared grace, through the blood of Jesus, meet the conscious need of my soul, as under sin? If there be life in the soul from God, the answer to the last two of those questions will be as certainly in the affirmative, as that to the first will be in the negative. But, if able thus far to confess the truth of God, the believer may rest safely assured that he is, in very deed, elect of God. For it is not in nature either to confess its own completed ruin, or to welcome God in Christ as a Saviour. Repentance and faith are alike gifts of God, and what He gives, He gives not at random, but according to the perfect election of His will.

The universality of the testimony to grace in the Gospel, becomes thus the instrument of God's will in separating the chaff from the wheat. Nature never lays hold of any Divine truth, except to adorn itself. Faith, on the other hand, awakens out of sleep at the hearing of the report, and hastens from the leprous house of natural experience into the prepared ark of God's deliverance. Faith thus honours God. The day of the Lord's appearing will be the moment of God's justification against the hard speeches[9] of those

[9] Jude 15.

who, with present impunity, lift their heads, and bend their tongues as a bow, against the eternal Truth which is enthroned in heaven.[1] At present the short and sufficient question to be addressed to an objector is: Are you then unwilling to receive the mercy of God? His will is to glorify His mercy in the persons of saved sinners, through Jesus Christ. Do *you* then refuse to bow to this will of God, to worship Him, whom you profess to acknowledge as the living and righteous God, as the God of *grace*, according to the riches of His glory now revealed in the Gospel of His Son? It is in the *will* of man that the fatal disease of unbelief has always had its seat. And so the apostle, when replying to the infidel's complaint, contents himself with reminding him of the difference between the creature and the Creator. The former could never attempt to dispute with the latter, if he had not first abandoned, in the spirit of his mind, the only place which he can rightly fill. The hypocrisy also of the heart is shown by the very form of the objector's question: "Who hath resisted His will?" Why Pharaoh did, when he refused to let Israel go, and in like manner *you* are now doing so, in rejecting the witness of God against yourself. When man can willingly submit to God, His ways are found to be the ways of peace; but in any and in every case, His absolute sovereignty must be maintained.[2]

Man then is but the clay, while God is the potter,

---
[1] Ps. cxix. 89.

[2] Jer. xviii. 1–12, is a passage to be studied in connection with this subject, putting, as it does, both the absolute sovereignty of God, and the perfectly equitable and gracious principle on which He exerts the power which belongs to Him, as the God of the spirits of all flesh, in a clear and striking light.

to do at His pleasure with His own (ver. 21). A few remarks seem desirable on the next two verses. The vessels of wrath are said to be "fitted to destruction."[3] The force of this expression appears to lie in the fact of man's natural condition as a sinner placing him, from his birth, under the eye of Divine holiness, as obnoxious to judgment. God destroys nothing but sin. As His nature is holiness, so His pleasure is not death, but life. Hence it is said, that He is not willing that any should perish.[4] That is, God is not the deviser of destruction as the good pleasure of His will. He is the Author of life and blessing. Hell and destruction are indeed before Him as the instruments of His will, when that will is contradicted by the madness of sinners; but His delight is in mercy. The fitness, then, of man for destruction is his being a sinner before God. The will of the first Adam wrought death by defying God. He tried the rash venture of an attempt to live without God. Mankind, as Adam's seed, inherit both his condition as a condemned sinner, and the intrinsic pravity which made him such. Considered, therefore, apart from the specialty of Divine election, man's nature and position are such as to invite and attract the wrath of God as his portion. Hence we are said to be *by nature* children of wrath.[5] Nothing in man can remedy his natural condition. He is a *born* rebel. The blood of corruption is in his veins because of inherited sin.

[3] Κατηρτισμένα εἰς ἀπώλειαν. Their *state* is described, not the means by which this state was produced. "Thoroughly ready for destruction" just expresses the meaning.

[4] 2 Pet. iii. 9. Μὴ βουλόμενός τινας ἀπολέσθαι.

[5] Eph. ii. 3.

Viewed in this light, the world's continuance, in its present state, is a marvellous proof of Divine patience and long-suffering. God endures with *much* long-suffering the vessels of wrath. Destruction, however, is the end of such; for there is a judgment of evil-doers, according to truth and according to righteousness, as we have already seen.[6] Men know this. But alas! the heart of man, though faithfully admonished by his conscience of the truth of all God's sayings, may still proudly refuse to humble itself beneath His mighty hand, though it be with perfect mercy that that hand is filled. Thus it is not an active and irresistible decree of God, but the strong hand of human perverseness, that binds the seal of destruction to the self-ruined vessels of wrath.

But there are vessels of another preparation, and for another end. It is not the power of Divine anger that is alone to be revealed in the day of the Lord's arising. He will also "make known the riches of His glory on the vessels of mercy, which He had afore prepared unto glory" (verse 23). The foundation of all glory that can be revealed in men is *mercy*. The Church (verse 24), as the destined vessel of glory, is founded upon mercy, upon God as showing mercy. It is built upon Christ, as the manifestation and eternal security of this mercy. The believer, then, is a vessel of mercy. But if so, it is because God prepares him as such.[7] Naturally a child of wrath, he becomes, when taken into the

---

[6] *Ante*, chap. ii.

[7] Compare 2 Cor. v. 5, "He that hath wrought us for the self-same thing is God," &c.

plastic hand of Divine grace, transformed into an heir of glory. The potter sees fit to form, at his will, a vessel for beauty and for praise. Even so does the blessed God exert the power of His good pleasure in preparing His vessels of mercy. The expression, "He prepared before,"[8] is full of meaning. As a vessel of elect mercy, the believer is God's workmanship from the first. Dating His choice in Christ before He created the first Adam in His own image, the after-history of man is but a stage in the progressive preparation of the work of God. Sin itself becomes thus capable of being regarded as a means to the end of Divine glory. God suffered man to fall. The effect of this fall, bringing man, as it did, under sin and death, made way for the operation of *grace*. Although sin was the work of the destroyer, and though it cast down from his former excellency the first man, made as he was in the image of God, yet it becomes, in the wisdom of God, a preparatory means for the accomplishment of His eternal counsels of mercy and of glory. Glory was God's end. This glory was to appear and be displayed in man as His image. Christ, the second Adam, is the absolute fulfilment of this, according to the accomplishment of the mystery of redemption. Believers, whether Jew or Gentile, who, when called of God, partake consciously of His grace, as vessels of mercy, are fitted for glory; they will shine, to the praise of His glory whose workmanship they are, in His light who

---

[8] .... προητοίμασεν εἰς δόξαν. The use of the active verb here, as contrasted with the passive participle in the former verse, is expressive of the difference between the negative fitness of the vessel of wrath, and the positive preparation, as an act of God, of the vessel of mercy. The change of words still further conveys this difference of meaning.

is already in them the Hope of glory.[9] The Holy
Ghost thus turns everything into an argument for
the praise of God, as the only wise God, the Saviour.
Satan has himself been made to contribute indirectly
to the furtherance of the work of God, that power
and dominion, salvation and praise, might belong
alone to Him.

Verses 25–29. The quotations which are now
made by the apostle, in support and corroboration of
what he has stated, are remarkable in two ways.
First, they confirm in a striking manner the general
doctrine of this chapter, and bring the prophets who
spake to the fathers distinctly forward, to witness to
the unity and perfection of God's way. Secondly,
and more especially, they afford an instructive instance of the manner in which the Spirit of truth
often adapts a portion of His own former testimony,
given primarily for another purpose, to the illustration of a general principle in the dealings of God,
within which, in its effective operation, both the present and the original objects of testimony are found
equally to fall. An attentive reader of the prophet
Hosea must, I think, conclude that the proper subject
of what is there written is the nation of Israel. Yet
the apostle evidently quotes from this prophet in support of the extension of the calling of grace to the
Gentiles. The reason is plain. Israel, as the object
of prophetic promise, must be brought first into the
condition of mere repudiation[1] as now, and thus occupy
the same level, morally, as the sinner of the Gentiles.
This must needs be, that *grace* alone may reign.
Hence we see at once how the passage *applies* to the

[9] Col. i. 27.   [1] Compare Amos ix. 7.

Gentile election, while its full force as a national *prophecy* still remains.[2]

The quotations from Isaiah respect the nation more immediately. A remnant, according to Divine election, is shown thus to have been ever the order of God's dealings with Israel. I need not point out the bearing of these last quotations upon the leading argument of this chapter. It may, however, be remarked, that in the use here made of these passages the apostle comprises in the alternative of condemnation, not only the unbelieving seed of Abraham, but in an equal measure *every one* who, while professing to recognise the truth of Scripture, withholds the obedience of faith from the saving doctrine of gracious election.[3] We have already seen that grace and election are almost convertible terms—that grace effectually received into the heart of a believing sinner, is the resulting proof of his election of God. The Scripture reveals but one alternative. Sodom and Gomorrah are the standing types of the progress and result of natural iniquity. They are the especial exemplars of a self-guided and self-governed world. Whether under Law or Gospel, they are of equal force, as descriptive and prophetic warnings to the natural man. The reasonings of an alienated mind

[2] Perhaps, even, it would be a sound distinction, if, as has been suggested by another, the latter part of Hosea i. 10 were appropriated exclusively to the Gentile election. In favour of this view, it has been pointed out by the same writer that Peter, whose Epistle is addressed, in the first instance, solely to converted Jews, neglects this passage, while he quotes Hosea ii. 23. (See 1 Pet. ii. 10.)

[3] Full well I know that no one who calls upon the name of the Lord in the day of grace shall perish. But never was there one really born of God who, when giving a reason of the hope that was in him with meekness and fear, according to the Gospel of the grace of God, referred his justification to aught else but sovereign mercy. Such has ever been the faith of God's elect.

concur with the wilful impulse of his lusts to estrange him from the faith of God's elect. He is, while unreclaimed by sovereign grace, a hopeless wanderer in the streets of the city of Destruction.

We come now to the conclusion of this branch of the general argument (verses 30–33). The apostle had delivered the doctrine of Divine election: first, absolutely; secondly, in its relation to Israel; and lastly, in its application to the Church. The result is found to be, that Gentiles,[4] who followed not after righteousness, have obtained that which they did not seek, while Israel's fleshly hope, founded upon pretended legal obedience, has altogether failed. They are an unrighteous nation still. The Gentiles, naturally aliens from the commonwealth of Israel, and strangers from the covenants of promise, were without hope and without God in the world; yet justification and acceptance were now known by many such, through faith in the Son of God. The nation of God's election, having the promises, *surnamed* for blessing and supremacy by Jehovah, had nevertheless missed their blessing, and lay broken on the stumbling-stone of Christ. They sought for righteousness but found it not, because they sought it "not by faith, but as it were by the works of the Law." But this their stumbling had been foreknown of God, and was in itself among the intended means of compassing His eternal purpose with respect to the Church. We shall see in the sequel whether the breach of Israel shall be again repaired.

[4] Ἔθνη, not τὰ ἔθνη. Meaning, of course, elect Gentiles, as distinguished from the nation which had not attained to righteousness, though individually many had.

Meanwhile, the practical application of the doctrine of this chapter to the Christian is as solemn as it is precious. The sifting of the creature already effected in the earlier chapters is here renewed. Man is found to be naturally incapable of attaining any prize, as the reward of his endeavour, but death. He runs his course as a sinner, and meets the Judge at the goal. Righteousness may be sought for, but cannot be found, save in the revelation of the grace of God. But that blessed grace is now revealed. God has laid in Zion His chosen stone. We must not allow the force of the last verse to escape our observation. It is *in Zion* that the stone is laid.[5] It is Christ crucified that is the foundation upon which all the glory of the Divine counsels rests. Christ in the flesh was, as we have seen, a Jewish Christ. Christ crucified is the foundation of peace to the believing sinner, whether Jew or Gentile. Christ glorified, after having been raised from the dead, is the eternal and (to faith) manifested security of all the fruits of Divine counsel and promise, whether relating to the nation or the Church. The risen Jesus is thus the living stone, the Rock of Ages, under whose shadow the weary may find rest. God stands upon that Rock to cause His voice of mercy to be heard by any wandering sheep of His numbered flock that He may espy still erring in the wilds of a condemned world. God rests in Christ. The believing sinner rests there too, finding confusion and shame turned to light and glory, in the knowledge of righteousness and life in Him. Such shall never be ashamed; they have boldness, both now and in the

[5] Compare Heb. xii. 22, &c.

day of judgment; while He, who now feeds them with His own flesh and blood, shall not cease to be known even in heaven as the Lamb. He shall there lead His chosen flock for ever to the fountains of living waters, while His God and theirs shall wipe away all tears from their eyes.[6]

[6] John vi. 54, 55; Rev. vii. 17.

CHAPTER X.

THE calling of the elect Church of God, although it glorifies the riches of Divine grace, does not meet the desire of the apostle's heart with respect to Israel. He knew that the nation was the object of Divine promise, as well as the chosen depository of the oracles of God. He had, indeed, already shown that the word of God had not failed of effect, while justifying, in the preceding chapter, the ways of God; who, in the sovereignty of His wisdom and power, is pleased to fulfil His word in the manner and at the season which are good in His sight. Still, though his heart rejoices perfectly in that which God is working by His Gospel, the condition of the nation, as self-excluded from the hope of their fathers, oppresses him with the burden of a lasting sorrow. The opening of the present chapter accordingly gives expression to this feeling. But it is most interesting to observe how the tranquillizing effect of the Divine communion, with which the writing of the last chapter had filled his spirit, shows itself in the softened expression of the same desires, as he utters now his wishes in the sight of God.

Ver. 1. "Brethren, my heart's desire and prayer to God for them,[1] is for their salvation," &c. It is

[1] The best MSS., including *Cod. Sin.*, give αὐτῶν instead of τοῦ 'Ισραηλ in this verse.

thus that he testifies the fixed affection of his soul, when pleading as an intercessor on behalf of his own flesh. He prays in the Spirit for that which he well knew to be the final purpose of God towards His people; urging for them his desire with the more intense earnestness, because of his ability to bear witness to their zeal for God. (Verse 2.)

And surely none could speak with a more perfect appreciation of what he said on such a subject, than the writer of this Epistle.[2] He could thoroughly sympathize, in every *natural* feeling of his heart, with a zeal which had once been the distinctive honour of his own name as a child of tradition, while exposing, as an apostle of *truth*, the futility and total unprofitableness of such zeal. Thus, while he could find it in his heart to make their zeal for God a ground of advocacy for that nation, as distinguished from other nations, who neither knew nor cared to know Him; he has to pronounce, as from God, the entire rejection of that which, unless produced and directed by the Spirit of truth, is but a dead work of the flesh. Zeal, not according to knowledge, ever turns in its result to envy, and hatred of that which truly is of God. "He has spoken blasphemy," was the decision which led to the cry, "Away with Him, away with Him, crucify Him." "Why persecutest thou me?" was the question which awakened the most zealous of those who thought to do God service by shedding the blood of His saints, to the fearful discovery that that which his self-satisfied heart most gloried in, was the direst of all transgressions against God.

[2] Acts xxii. 3.

Verse 3 declares the nature of the controversy which God had with the nation. They were going about to establish their own righteousness. But God had in Christ revealed *His* perfect righteousness, to which He required the obedience of faith. Israel, then, so long as he thinks of legal righteousness as an object of personal attainment, remains in a state of disobedience. The *ignorance* of God's righteousness which is here imputed to them, was from no defect of knowledge, for the open declaration of the gospel did but confirm and verify the earlier prophetic witness;[3] but, blinded judicially through their self-reliant pride of heart,[4] they refused submission to a doctrine which testified the emptiness of all natural pretensions, by setting forth Christ crucified as the righteousness of God. Rejecting, therefore, the word of eternal life, they clave more tenaciously than ever to the obsolete and unfruitful rudiments of the world. But ordinances and traditions can neither enlighten the heart, nor quicken a soul dead in trespasses and sins. There was, then, a reason for the apostle's grief. And would God that the natural Israel were alone in this controversy with Him! How many in the present day, while adopting with all confidence the Christian name, and persuading both themselves and others that they are truly zealous for the cause of God, are in reality opposing themselves to the righteousness of God! Self-righteousness, inherent as it is in the natural heart at all times, is the bitterest mockery with which the father of lies can bewitch and stultify the human soul. "There is more hope of the fool than of the man wise in his

[3] Isaiah xlv. 25.   [4] 1 Pet. ii. 8.

own conceit," says the true proverb:[5] and it is even so with the man who, in self-complacent reliance upon Christian "ordinances," deems himself secure, while his heart, perhaps, has never truly learnt one syllable of saving grace, nor ever really felt his need, as a self-condemned and truth-convicted sinner, of the atoning blood of Christ. There are such as I have described; and should the eye of any such light on this page, may the God of all grace arrest him in his way, and awaken him from his dream of self-confidence to find the saving truth of life! It is more probable, however, that the reader of this book will be himself, if not already established in the faith, at least seeking, with a right desire, an experimental knowledge of the peace of God. To such an one I would earnestly commend the apostle's argument of Divine righteousness in the verses of this chapter which remain to be considered.

Verse 4 dissolves and sets aside for ever all ground of reference, on the part of the believer, to the Law as the measure of human justification, by showing its perfect accomplishment in Christ. "For Christ is the end of the Law for righteousness to every one that believeth." We should be careful to distinguish between the "end of the Law" and "the curse of the Law." The end of the Law was justification of life, if attainable. Its curse was uttered at its very promulgation, and so was its *beginning* rather than its end.[6] Now this end of the Law, so hopeless of attainment to the natural man, has been reached and

---

[5] Prov. xxvi. 12.

[6] And so the apostle predicates universally of the natural man, that as many as are of the works of the Law are under the curse, &c. (Gal. iii. 10.)

far exceeded by the "man approved of God."⁷ And having proved Himself to be the Just One, by personally fulfilling all righteousness, He has become, in His most blessed Person, not only the realized desire of those who vainly toiled in honesty of heart beneath the legal yoke,⁸ but far more than this. For the fulfiller of the Law is also the eternal righteous- of God. The *name* of Christ thus supersedes, to the believer, the claims of the Law. Christ stands for such in the Law's place. Both could not stand together. Human righteousness and Divine righteousness cannot harmonize; for one is a lie, and the other is the truth of God. The first was proposed by the Law, but it proved, as we have seen, "the Law's impossibility,"⁹ and by the Law came only the knowledge of sin. Yet it continues, as a deceitful phantom, to delude the souls of all who still desire to be under the Law.¹ The second having come in the person of the incarnate word, and having perfected its work by an effectual atonement for sin, the false pretensions of the first are supplanted in the triumphant power of both truth and love. Life and incorruptibility because of righteousness have now, in Christ, taken the place of the death and judgment which were ministered by the Law because of sin.²

We have next (verses 5–9) a comparison of the conditions of human blessing, as they are expressed by the language respectively of Law and of grace. The quotations which are made by the apostle are drawn, the first from Leviticus,³ and the second from

---

⁷ Acts ii. 22. *Ante*, p. 101, *seq.* ⁸ Ps. cxix. *passim.* ⁹ Chap. viii.
¹ Compare the apostle's argument in Gal. iv. and v.
² 2 Cor. iii. 6–18.   ³ Levit. xviii. 5.

Deuteronomy.[4] If we examine these quotations, we shall find that they respect the nation of Israel under widely-differing circumstances. In the first they are addressed as under the responsibility of obedience to the Law as yet untried, themselves undertaking the charge of the Lord's commandments as the condition of their blessing.[5] In the second passage they are regarded as broken and dispersed through the countries, because of national disobedience and admitted breach of covenant. Instead, therefore, of the confidence of unbroken strength, we see the expression of fruitful repentance towards God, in the confession of their failure, and a turning to Him who had smitten them as to the one who alone could heal. Their remedy was not in seeking *back* to the Law, as if it yet remained as an available means of blessing through their obedience, but in remembering the word which, while it condemned their ways, yet led their hearts to God as the God of promise and of grace. They would seek Him, indeed, in the light of the Law, and that would be the rule of their practical obedience until taken out of the way;[6] but God would meet their return of heart to Him in the riches of His grace in Christ, binding up the breach of His people according to the truth and mercy which had been declared of old.

[4] Deut. xxx. 12–14.

[5] In reality the covenant had been both tried and broken, and the Levitical ordinances of priesthood and sacrifice which had been prescribed to Moses in anticipation of the national apostasy, were already become the alone effective means and sustaining power of Israel's acceptance. But the covenant continued still in its full force, and as a yoke had been but newly imposed upon the people's neck, where it was destined to remain, until by its intolerable pressure it had brought them to the dust in an unfeigned confession of their inability to stand in their own strength. [6] Mal. iv. 4.

Now that which Moses spake in prophecy to the nation, the apostle here applies in the widest manner, as a preacher of the Gospel of the grace of God to man. The fitness of this application becomes immediately apparent when the true nature of the principle thus illustrated is perceived. God dates the commencement of the believer's blessing from the moment when he confesses, unreservedly, his helpless ruin on account of sin. He must, in order to act effectually in grace, first bring man into practical acquaintance with the secret of his own wretchedness. What Israel have to learn nationally through the chastisements of Jehovah, in order that in the latter day they may seek Him and His goodness,[7] every individual vessel of Divine mercy has to learn, in measure, by the convincing power of the word of truth, as applied by the Spirit of God to the conscience.

Verse 6. "But the righteousness," &c. It is interesting to note the change here in the apostle's language. Legal righteousness may be *described* by Moses, but has no verified existence except in Christ. But the righteousness which is of faith *speaketh*. The Spirit of grace addresses himself immediately to the heart of man, as the Divine revealer of Jesus. The Law never got beyond an ideal description of the righteous man, but that ideal having been realized by the advent and obedience of the Just One, the discovery of righteousness is announced by Divine proclamation to the willing ear. What is here called "the righteousness of faith,"[8] is, in verse 3 and else-

[7] Hosea iii. 5.

[8] ἐκ πίστεως descriptive, that is, of the manner of its administration and reception on our parts, as distinguished from its intrinsic quality and source.

where, called "the righteousness of God."[9] That righteousness bestows itself in speech on the believer, for the Gospel is the ministration of righteousness—not a statement of God's claims on man, but a declaration of the sovereign bounty of His grace.

In the passage before us, the voice of Divine righteousness is heard addressing itself to the already quickened and enquiring soul, whose communings of heart, though active and sincere, are found to be inadequate to the discovery of the way of peace. The wisdom of the just is the object of desire; but its attainment is found to be beyond the utmost effort of the toiling spirit; neither height nor depth give answer to its call.[1] To man in this state, the voice of truth comes first in the form of a dissuasive from self-communing: "Say not in thine heart," &c.; and secondly, invites the listener to a simple and unreserved acceptance of the grace of God (verses 8, 9). Communing of heart is, in its right place, not only a natural, but a necessary thing;[2] but the heart of man is incapable of conceiving *truth* until it has been brought by the power of God to turn to Him in the way of faith—hearkening to His voice to whom alone it belongs to reveal truth as the blessed expression of His own thoughts of peace. By shedding, therefore, into the heart of the believer, the knowledge of Jesus, as the manifested righteousness of God, the Spirit of truth puts an end of all such heart-communings and self-counsel. *God* speaks in the Gospel of His truth, and declares the secret of His will as the God of grace. But the word of God is *final;* and, therefore, when He speaks, delibera-

[9] *Ante*, p. 50, *seq*.   [1] Job xxviii.   [2] Ps. iv. 4.

tions, which were seasonable only while His will remained unknown, give place to faith and obedience in every one whose heart is taught of Him. Those communings of heart, which, while carried on in ignorance of Christ, end only in deepened perplexity and despair, must now be replaced by the precious verities of God's ripened counsel, as they stand revealed in Jesus. Blessed thought! A helpless and self-condemned sinner has now but to countersign, by his own amen, the charter of his everlasting liberty and peace,[3] which God presents for his acceptance in the name of His own Son. Such is now the condition of salvation. The Law tries to make something of man, and fails, turning conditional blessing into hopeless condemnation. Grace, finding man lost beyond all hope in himself, lifts him into Christ, and in Him presents him without spot to God.

It is instructive to remark that the communings of a man's heart with itself result naturally in an expression of unbelief. A *sign* is desired (verses 6, 7), wherever God is not already in full possession of the heart's confidence through faith. In noticing the different form of the questions (similar in motive and tendency) put in Moses and in Paul, we have to remember the difference of dispensation. In every case, the doing of the will of God must be the aim of a genuine worshipper. Ignorance of that will is accordingly the plea most commonly alleged by the natural man in excuse of his disobedience. In Deut. xxx. it is the "commandment" that is represented as the object of longing to those whose hearts should turn to the Lord in the latter day;[4] for true faith in

[3] John iii. 33. [4] Comp. Isaiah xxvi. 18.

God must, until the full discovery of Christ and the doing away of the veil,[5] so express itself in the heart of an Israelite after the flesh. But Paul, as an apostle of Christ, putting in the place of the commandment Him whom he had just before declared to be the end of the Law for righteousness to every believer, shapes his questions according to the quality of His doctrine.[6] His words are then equivalent to this: There is no need either of a further work or of a new revelation. What you ask has been already done. Christ, the alone true hope of the human soul, has both descended and ascended; and, from the throne of the majesty in the heavens, His name is now published for salvation among men. Your part, therefore, is no longer to inquire, but to believe; not to feel after a Saviour whose name and disposition are alike unknown, but to *receive* Him whose gracious love and power have already been convincingly displayed in the Gospel.

The only barrier now to a sinner's salvation is his own will. Power is not demanded. Work is not required. "*Wilt* thou be made whole?" is now the gracious question addressed in the Gospel to every one who hath an ear to hear. But (verse 8) there is such a thing as having the word of life in the heart, and as it were upon the lips, while yet the confession of the name of Jesus is never heard. Conscience, that is, may and often does inwardly corroborate the record of God's truth, although the heart refuses Christ its love. And even where the work of God

---

[5] 2 Cor. iii. *ad. fin.*
[6] This is also a sufficient explanation of the change of expression in verse 7, as compared with Deut. xxx. 13.

has had a real beginning in the soul, and the possession of His peace is become the chief desire of the awakened heart, yet the misdirected search of the believer may have failed as yet to obtain a clear and satisfying view of the great Rock of his salvation. Haply, some reader of these Notes may find his own heart painfully familiar with those care-trodden ways, in which the tired spirit vainly searches for that rest which can be entered only by the foot of faith.[7] If such an one has found the name of Christ as yet insufficient to dispel his fears, and to pour the full joy of salvation into his bosom, let him be assured that the cause of his distress is not only within his view, if he will turn his eyes towards it by the light of the apostle's testimony in the present passage, but also that it is within the power of his own removal; if he be only willing to put more honour upon the word of the living and eternal God, than upon the mutable counsels and most fallacious suggestions of his own weak and deceitful heart.

The terms and substance of the "word of faith" are now given in verse 9, wherein we find a clear and express statement of the conditions of Christian salvation. Two things are here affirmed to be necessary to this salvation. First, confession; and, secondly, faith. I quote the words: "If thou shalt confess with thy mouth the Lord Jesus, and shalt believe in thine heart that God hath raised Him from the dead, *thou shalt be saved.*" The person of Jesus, now exalted above the heavens and made both Lord and Christ,[8] is the saving truth to be confessed. The crucified and dishonoured Man is thus acknowledged,

[7] Heb. iv. 3.   [8] Acts ii. 36.

with Divine worship and honour, to be the only Lord. This confession at once separates the believer from the world, on which the guilt of rejecting Christ lies, and places him under the eternal sanction of the Father's acceptance, who has willed the Son's honour as His own.[9]

Confession of the name of the Lord is first stated, because it is that which forms the decisive token of distinction between the living Christian and the dead world. As it is presently after added, "with the mouth confession is made unto salvation." Confession, then, seems placed here first in order, lest Satan, whose lie deceives the whole world, should seek occasion from such a passage to persuade men that a mere belief of the resurrection as a matter of fact, or even as a proof of Divine power, could suffice to save the soul. The credibility of Gospel testimony may be admitted, upon grounds satisfactory to the merely natural understanding, while the heart is still a stranger to the true knowledge of Christ; but the source of this acceptable confession is a heart which, by faith, not only perceives the reality of Divine truth, as declared in Scripture, but believes in *God* who raised Jesus from the dead. He who has thus been raised is recognised by the believer according to the witness of the Spirit, and therefore openly declared by the lips to be the only Lord. This subject will presently enlarge itself more fully. Meanwhile, let us remember that the object presented to faith in the preaching of the Gospel is Jesus the Lord.[1] Through Him, as raised from the dead, we are called

---

[9] John v. 23.   [1] Phil. ii. 11.

on to believe in God, who raised Him up and gave Him glory.[2]

To the inquirer after salvation, the Spirit of God can make no other reply than this. He may amplify it in His mercy, in order to win our slow hearts to a more ready acquiescence in such strange terms of salvation; but the essential truth which brings deliverance to the soul, is the Name and glory of the exalted Lamb of God. Amplify it He does, as we shall, I trust, presently see: let us only first remark the pointed individuality of the language in the present passage. "If *thou* shalt confess," &c. The professing world admits the truth of the resurrection.[3] It is, as a generally received scriptural fact, allowed a place in the memories of men, lying there side by side with other great facts of Divine witness, which men are not yet bold enough to disallow.

But God's question, as the revealer of Jesus, is with *me*. He finds me wretched, and professes to bring me health and cure. He speaks to me, in His blessed Gospel, of *Jesus*, affirming Him to have been given to death by the counsel of His own free grace. The word of God, then, addresses my heart, where all the fruitless and disquieting thoughts of nature have hitherto had their birth and exercise. "What thinkest thou of Jesus?" is the simple question which the Spirit of truth propounds to me. If, by the grace of God, I think Him indeed such a Saviour as I need, such, that is, as God reveals Him, then I must needs

---

[2] 1 Pet. i. 21. *Ante*, p. 72, *seq.*
[3] Speaking, that is, generally. There are, indeed, some who flatly deny it, endeavouring, by the sound of their own denial, to silence in their consciences the voice of a truth which speaks no joy to them. But there *is* a resurrection, both of the just and also of the unjust.

confess this truth. But to confess it in the sight of God is to become for ever safe, by returning an answer of acceptance to His offer of salvation; for His witness of Jesus is, that by Him all that believe are justified from all things.[4] And this first, this secret confession that Jesus is indeed the Lord, uttered as yet in no ears save those which had been first filled with the echo of the heart's self communings in its own secret bitterness,[5] is the prelude to another confession which the now truth-liberated soul is not ashamed to make before the world. "I am not ashamed of the Gospel of Christ; for it is the power of God unto salvation," is the language, not of apostolic boldness only, but of simple-hearted faith, which can find no cause of shame in the acknowledgment of a truth that has filled with the Lord's joy the once empty vessel of vanity and despair.

Let us now pass on to the consideration of the four following verses (10-13), the connected sequence of which, in their order, is remarkable, as well as the united bearing of them all upon the statement in the ninth verse which we have just been examining. These verses are a series of demonstrative assertions made by the Spirit of truth, in order yet more surely to establish the weak-hearted believer in Jesus on the firm foundation which has been already laid.

First, we have a re-statement in general language of the doctrine of the preceding verse, in which the

---

[4] Acts xiii. 39. Compare Exod. xix. 8. God takes His people at their word. By accepting the first covenant Israel abandoned mercy to confide in Law. By accepting the Gospel men renounce their own works to confide in sovereign grace. Justification results as certainly in the latter case as condemnation in the former.

[5] Prov. xiv. 10, and xviii. 14.

order previously observed is now reversed. "For with the heart man believeth unto righteousness," &c. It is the justified who are saved, but it is by faith that justification comes. Justification is firmly bound by the Spirit of truth to faith alone. Nothing is said here about degrees of knowledge. Still less is anything mentioned respecting the world of the saved sinner's inward experiences. *I* am not *Christ:* but it is of Christ that the Gospel speaks, that I may *believe*. Nor is anything which Satan can help my naturally unbelieving heart to set in order, as a reason for hesitating to appropriate the freely proffered grace of God, an argument of delay; but rather, when rightly judged, a motive to a more earnest and decided faith.

It is often hard for the tried soul of a believer, when in conflict, to keep steadily and simply in view the Object which the Gospel sets before his faith. A sense of personal unworthiness, how deep soever it may be, is intended by the Spirit (whose searching power as the Witness of truth produces it within us) to render us more susceptible of the infinite preciousness of Christ—to compel our souls more forcibly to the cross. But it often has an effect widely different from this. Satan, whose aim is directed to the dishonour of God in the frustration of His purposes of grace, knows well how to use truth itself as a means of obstructing truth. The sense of sin, and consequently of distance from God, is a gracious result of the operation of the Spirit as the awakener of souls. But it is something very different from the effect produced by a disclosure to the sinner, thus awakened, of truth as it stands revealed in the person of *Jesus*, and *not* in himself. The truth of God with respect to man's condition is, that he is ruined in sin.

Now, when this truth, which we can read calmly enough as a mere doctrine, fastens on the heart and conscience in direct personal application, the effect is always painful; sometimes it is utterly withering to the soul. It is, moreover, Satan's interest to magnify by all means the effect of Divine truth upon the receiver of it, so far as it tends to depress and intimidate his spirit by alarming his conscience. The adversary's object is to deter, by an overwhelming sense of personal depravity and wretchedness, the advances of the heart towards God; to make, that is, *sin*, and not *Christ*, the immediate object of its contemplation. So long as God can be kept before the eye of an awakened soul through the medium of an evil conscience, the knowledge of peace is impossible.

But it is well for us to remember, that the purpose of God in preaching the Gospel is not only to acquaint us with ourselves, but, especially and finally, with *Him*. He is not inviting us to a renewed scrutiny of our own hearts, if haply some lurking principle of good may yet live, unextinguished though sore oppressed, amid the sea of evil that is there. The record which God has given in the Gospel is concerning *His Son*. The ministry which He has committed to the servants of His truth, is the ministry of *reconciliation*. It is as a Saviour, not as a Judge, that He is pleased to reveal himself in Christ.

Now the case of a man, as reported by his conscience, may be very desperate. He may be cognizant in his own polluted soul of every imaginable form of evil. His ways may even have been strange, and but little known to the common herd of sinners. He may have been saturated with iniquity to such a degree, and may have been so deep in the mire of corruption, that, in the ears of ordinary men, the recital of his acts might easier provoke disgust than obtain belief as credible, experimental facts. Add to this the indescribable maze of unfulfilled desires, whether of flesh or of mind, the summing up of which would baffle the most tenacious memory of the most alarmed conscience. A man may be such as I have described. All that he is may be forcibly brought to his remembrance, by the power of truth, and bound, as with an iron shackle, to his conscience.

And now, if this be so, what is it that is described, when language has been exhausted in the effort to portray the hideous features of human sin? *It is God's ruined and degraded creature.* No amount of aggravating circumstance can place the case beyond the limits of that Divine testimony which, while it affirms that *all* have sinned, and come short of the glory of God, makes the condition of man, as under sin, the occasion of manifesting the righteousness of God. What God meets in the blood of Jesus is human sin. The most polluted of evil-doers is but a sinner; a great one, doubtless; but the magnitude of his offence is not the question. The Spirit of God does not use Divine truth as a measure of number or quantity in searching a man's heart. What He does is to convict of *sin*. "More in number than the hairs of my head," may and will be the confession of the exercised conscience, when vainly seeking, in the spirit of godly sorrow and self-judgment, to number that which God alone can tell. Yet the proclamation of grace is not to great or to small sinners as such, but to sinners as *lost* in the ruin of their sin—as *dead* in trespasses and sins. A man may have to speak of himself as the "chief of sinners," when, in the sober judgment of his way, he finds no parallel in the world without him to that which, in all the nearness and distinctness of self-consciousness as in the Divine presence, he discovers with dismay to be in himself. Still, when the varied measures and phases of sinful experience are gone over and weighed, the result is in principle the same. Sin is ascertained to be the *intrinsic condition* of fallen nature.

But God meets sin in Christ. "The blood of Jesus Christ His Son cleanseth us from *all* sin," is the affirmative assurance to the believer, that, let the multitude of his transgressions be what it may, the yet richer abundance of Divine mercy is sufficient to remove them all. God opposes the redemption-price of Christ's blood to the accumulated debt of our sins. Moreover, sin has its limits, be they never so wide. But the love which God commends to us in Christ has no limits. It is the sovereignty of *perfect* love, accommodating itself, in grace, to the known condition of the object beloved, of which the Gospel speaks. Now, holiness and love being alike in God, until one is satisfied the other cannot act upon its objects so as to be felt and understood. But it is this that has been fully done in the cross of God's Son.

God, then, has in Christ accomplished a work which enables Him to make the confession of a sinner's misery a reason of forgiveness, and not of wrath. While, therefore, the measures and degrees of positive transgression in man are almost infinitely various, and while the profoundness of the heart's self-acquaintance as a sinner before God may vary, and certainly does vary, even in the same individual, according to the paucity or abundance of his real knowledge of God, the standard and condition of acceptance with Him remain perpetually the same. God accepts *nothing* intrinsically but *Christ*. The heart of a believer, perceiving the love of God in the sending of His Son into the world, trusts God as a Saviour. For faith judges of God by His declared ways; and when it sees the precious blood of Christ flow under the stroke of Divine judgment, finds no solution of this strangest wonder but that which is furnished by the written word. God, then, has acted in the matter of our sin. He has given His own Son to die, the Just for the unjust. Now this act of God in grace meets, in the mind of simple faith, all possible questionings about sin. Let its indwelling presence be ever so much felt and hated, it is a thing both condemned and destroyed in Christ crucified. It is a *forgotten* thing with God. The Holy Ghost bears this express witness, when reasoning on the value of the sacrifice of Christ. "Their sins and their iniquities will I remember no more,"[6] is the word of promise to Israel in the New Covenant, which is already fulfilled to us, the moment we have come in faith to the blood of the cross.

It will be remarked, perhaps, in reading this chapter, that, in enumerating the conditions of salvation, no mention is made of repentance. The reason is doubtless this. It does not fall specifically within

[6] Heb. x.

the line of the apostle's present argument. The controversy lay between human righteousness, as dreamed of by the Jew, and the righteousness of God, as perceptible and to be enjoyed by faith alone. Moreover, it may be remarked, that repentance towards God must ever precede faith towards the Lord Jesus Christ, and is therefore presumed to have place in every heart in which true faith is found.[7] Repentance[8] means a turning to God on the part of one whose mind had been previously alienated, and is the first instinctive movement of life in a soul which God has quickened by His word. That this must be a precedent thing to the decisive exercise of the will in the way of faith is clear. We are not, therefore, called on here to ask ourselves whether we have repented, but to believe on the Lord. If faith responds to the call, it is because the heart *has* already repented towards God. Looking into oneself, in any way, is not looking at Christ—is not faith. But we are commanded to look at Him—to believe. Now it is with the heart that man believes unto righteousness. With the heart also, if not established with grace, he doubts and distrusts. But the reason of such misgiving is suspicion of God; a disbelief of His goodness in our own particular case; a hateful evil, truly, for our hearts to harbour respecting One who has demonstrated His love toward us in the cross of His own Son!

Of all sins this is the worst. For it makes God a liar, if we believe Him not.[9] Unbelief is the only sin which, if persisted in, is unto eternal death. The difference between a real Christian and an unreal

---

[7] Acts xx. 21.   [8] μετάνοια.   [9] 1 John v. 10.

one is, that the former does not draw back *unto perdition*, but believes to the saving of the soul.¹ Have I then a will for Christ? And if so, can I trust the word of God, who cannot lie, more implicitly than I can rely on my own heart, which is deceitful above all things? Can you *not* do this, reader? Let not the word, which may be trembling to escape your lips, be still repressed because you yet feel the sense of personal vileness. God is not addressing you because you are not unworthy, but because you are so. He preaches peace to them who in themselves can have no real peace. He bestows on you His own righteousness in Christ, in the same word which pronounces the full forgiveness of your sins, if you believe in Jesus. The depth of our feelings in regard to sin is, in one sense, immaterial.² It is not by experimental inferences that we are justified, but by faith. Conclusions inferred from within are exactly opposite to the venture of faith, that casts all on Jesus at the bidding of God's word.

I may seem, to some readers, to have lingered

¹ Heb. x. 39.
² Experimental convictions of sin are unquestionably felt in every instance of genuine conversion. But these are not always so deep at the beginning of the soul's acquaintance with God as afterwards; when, in a riper knowledge of His grace, the intrinsic qualities of nature are better understood. All are not criminals, though all are sinners; and according to the life led previously to conversion, will the measure of personal distress about sin frequently be found. Yet this is far from an invariable rule, those who have been least obnoxious to moral censure having sometimes the acutest sufferings of conscience.

The one point to keep steadily before our view is this: that all that is involved in the word "salvation" hangs, absolutely and exclusively, upon such a believing confession of the Lord Jesus as is described in the text. Salvation is obtained by our coming, through faith in His *name*, to Jesus; it is "wrought out" experimentally unto perfection, by our *abiding* in that faith. (Phil. ii. 12, 13; John xv. 4; Col. i. 23.)

already too long over this part of our chapter; yet I add one word further on the subject of confession, for the sake of any weak or tried conscience to which it may be found to apply.

Satan has power to turn the most precious truths into weapons of offence against the soul, where the heart is not simply discerning and resting in *grace*. Thus a question might suggest itself to the mind of one who desired to find rest in the large and free expressions of this passage, of this sort:—salvation is made dependent on confession, and not on faith alone. "Now, I believe," the heart might say, "but how far may I be said to have *confessed* the Lord? Has my confession been sufficiently ample and clear? But are not my life and walk, as a consistent Christian, the sort of confession on which alone I can safely rely?" To such an inquirer, I would reply that the word is, "With the *mouth* confession is made unto salvation." As to relying upon any length of consistent conduct, it would not be relying on Christ; it would not be faith at all, and would have nothing whatever to do with salvation, except in so far as it would hinder your true perception of it, in hiding Christ from your view by the intervention of your own shadow. What you acknowledge, in confessing Jesus as the Lord, is the power and glory of the blessed God as a Saviour. Moreover, you thereby confess that God is *true*, and estimate yourself therefore according to His word. A Christian is a child of truth; he is begotten by the Word of truth, according to the will and by the power of God. The name of Christ once spoken from the heart, in obedient confession before God, establishes the lip that makes such confession *for ever* in His sight.³ The testimony of the Gospel is the record of *God*. By accepting, therefore, such testimony, and confessing to its truth, I set my seal to the witness of God.⁴ Henceforth, then, my soul remains safe kept of Him, within the shelter of that truth which is the everlasting buckler of defence to the believing children of His love.⁵

Verse 11. "For the Scripture saith," &c. We have here a corroborative appeal to the word before spoken. The unity of God's counsels, and their perfect attainment in the Person of Jesus, now demonstrated to be the Lord, are thus more clearly shown. The exclusive claim also of the Jew to the Divine favour is refuted as it were out of his own lips. It is *Jewish* Scripture that affirms, that *whosoever* believeth on Him shall not be ashamed. But more especially the citation by the Spirit of God, in the New Testament, of passages from the Old, is valuable to the believer, as distinguishing between what does and what does not directly apply to the Christian as under grace. The Holy Ghost, by thus corroborating, in evangelical testimony to the person of Jesus, the prophetic promise addressed of old to the fathers, at once reveals to the believer the point of view from which he is to regard the Old Testament. His conscience is thus freed (and this is practically an important consideration with reference to the present state experimentally of many Christians), from any and every burden which might otherwise seem to be laid upon it through the reading of such parts of the Old Testament Scripture as treat of personal respon-

³ Prov. xii. 19.   ⁴ John iii. 33; 1 John v. 9.   ⁵ Ps. xci. 1–4.

sibility; because they address themselves to those who were dispensationally under Law, although the hope of better things to come might be disclosed to those whose hearts believed the word of prophetic testimony. Ill-taught Christians are often in a legal state. It is quite natural, under such circumstances, to misapply the truth of God. But, though real believers are often experimentally short of the liberty with which Christ has made them free, they are never *rightly* thus, because such a state is plainly incongruous with a true perception of the grace of God. For a Christian is in no sense under Law. He is not lawless towards God, for he is bound in subjection to Christ;[6] but it is as the Lord's freedman that he is thus bound. He is subject to Christ, as the wife to her husband, as we have seen.[7] Moreover, "He that is joined to the Lord is one spirit."[8] The only power that rightly exercises dominion over a believer's conscience is the Lord himself. But Christ is not a minister of sin, but of grace. Hence the ability of the Spirit to bear such witness as He does here, to the eternal stability of the believer as an heir of the righteousness which is by faith. He shall *never* be ashamed. Neither in this life nor in that to come, can disappointment blight the hope of one who casts the burden of his soul upon the Lord, and reposes confidently on the faithfulness of Him who preaches peace by Jesus Christ.

Verse 12 magnifies the riches of the blessed Lord, as the lavish dispenser of the wealth of salvation to all that call upon Him. Jew or Gentile, Pharisee or Canaanite, are alike, and in precisely equal degree,

[6] *Ante*, p. 154, Note.   [7] *Ante*, p. 132.   [8] 1 Cor. vi. 17.

eligible as objects of Divine grace. "There is no difference."[9] Their personal characteristics may differ, to the widest range of possible variance; but when regarded by the Spirit of truth, they are sinners alike. Now the Lord is rich to *all* that call upon Him. As He has elsewhere said, "Him that cometh unto me, I will in no wise cast out."[1] A rich Christ, then, reader, waits still to be gracious—to prove the riches of His mercy as the unupbraiding welcomer of all who will confess His Name. "For (verse 13) whosoever shall call on the name of the Lord shall be saved."[2] This last quotation adds a final corroboration of the apostle's thesis in verse 9; and bears its witness, first, to the world-wide aspect of the Gospel, and, secondly, to the identity of the Jehovah of the Old Testament with the Jesus of the New.

I make only one further remark on this verse. The calling here spoken of is not the vague cry of an uneasy conscience, but it is the voice of *faith*. "Lord, if thou *wilt*, thou *canst*,"[3] is the language of petitioning faith; while as yet no clear indication of the mind of the Lord has been given. "Lord, I believe,"[4] is the glad expression of the same faith; when the revelation of the truth in the person of Jesus lays the believing sinner as a willing worshipper at the feet of the Son of God. Self-distrust is the counterpart of confidence in God. True faith lays hold of the person of Christ with the firm grasp of a conscious dependence upon Him alone—of utter hopelessness of help or safety, from within or from without, save only in Him. The cry, "Lord, Lord," may,

---

[9] Compare the apostle's reasoning in chap. iii. 20–24.
[1] John vi. 37. [2] Joel ii. 32. [3] Matt. viii. 2. [4] John ix. 38.

alas! as we are solemnly warned, proceed from lips whose sound never came from a believing heart. But the note of true faith is, that its aim is *God*. Its misery is distance from Him. Its joy is in the name of Jesus, because by His precious blood the believer is brought nigh in Him.⁵

Verses 14, 15, vindicate the wisdom of God in making the foolishness of preaching the instrument of His saving power.⁶ But the preacher must be sent. Divine truth can be rightly delivered only by those whom God is pleased to send. The word preached is *His*. The souls addressed are His. His messengers proclaim the Gospel of His mercy. But who are thus sent? Firstly, of course, the *Apostles*, whose very name is derived from their mission.⁷ But quite apart from this primary and especial designation of the heralds of Divine mercy to the world, it is evident, from the very nature of the believer's calling, that every Christian who has himself tasted that the Lord is gracious, has both the liberty and the responsibility of "holding forth the word of life."⁸ As possessed of the Spirit of God, the heart of a believer is fitted to impart to others a portion of the blessing with which he has himself been blessed of God in Christ.⁹ "I have sent them into the world," is the Lord's word respecting His disciples, when He was regarding them, not as office-bearing servants in the Church of God, but as the first-fruits of that Divine election of mercy which, in due time, would grow to the completion of the body of Christ. Fur-

---

⁵ Eph. ii. 13. ⁶ Comp. 1 Cor. i. 21.
⁷ πῶς δὲ κηρύξουσιν ἐὰν μὴ ἀποσταλῶσι.
⁸ Phil. ii. 16. ⁹ John vii. 38.

ther, "Let him that heareth say, Come;"[1] calling not only on the Lord to return from heaven in fulfilment of His promise,—that He may take His own to the prepared mansions of their rest,—but also upon those who may yet be within the hearing of the word of grace; to come ere the day of long-suffering patience be closed, and to take freely of the water of life. But, secondly, *evangelists* are sent. There are those whom the Spirit of God especially sets apart for the work of the Gospel. An evangelist is one of the gifts of the ascended Christ.[2] He is sent forth at the will of the Spirit, who empowers him to preach the Gospel to the world. The Church has no authority to send evangelists, because the source of evangelism is not the Church, but Christ. An evangelist is an ambassador of Christ, not of the Church. Collectively, the Church in its unity was the world's great evangelist (alas! where is it now?) as the pillar and ground of the truth. Paul and Barnabas may be separated by their brethren for an especial work,[3] but it is at the express command of the Holy Ghost; and when they go forth it is as sent by Him, and not by the Church. In a word, evangelism, like every other species of ministry, is derived to its vessel immediately from God. It is held, therefore, in responsibility to the Lord, whose servant the minister is. We shall return to the subject of ministry when examining the twelfth chapter. Meanwhile, we have in this passage another quotation from Isaiah, where, if the context be examined, the deliverance of the earthly Jerusalem will be seen, I think, to be the proper subject of the

[1] Rev. xxii. 17.   [2] Eph. iv. 11.   [3] Acts xiii. 2–4.

prophecy.[4] Accordingly, the apostle, having opened to view (as we have seen in the former part of this chapter) the wide range of Gospel grace as now preached, a range limited in its aspect only by the extent of the ruin which it is designed to meet, proceeds, in what follows, to view the especial application of this principle to the case of Israel.

Glad tidings had been brought to Zion. The lips of Truth itself had opened in Immanuel's land, to preach the acceptable year of the Lord. But they had stopped their ears against the word of the Gospel of the kingdom of God, and had refused to hearken to the voice of Divine wisdom when speaking in their streets. They had slain the Heir, and cast Him out of the vineyard. Nor was this all. The prayer of the rejected Sufferer, when upon the cross He said, "Father, forgive them; for they know not what they do,"[5] had not been in vain. The nation lives by virtue of that intercession of Jesus, echoing as it did the eternal counsel of peace, which, in the deep thoughts of God, had ever looked towards that people as a chosen means for the display of His glory. Accordingly, we find that the Spirit of Christ, when He first announced the full truth of accomplished salvation, addressed himself to the nation.[6] "Men of Israel" were the first subjects of the grace of the Gospel, which preached remission of sins in the name of Him whom they had crucified. But although the prayer of the dying Lamb of God produced a present and abundant return, in the wondrous effect of the preaching of Peter and the other apostles in Jerusalem, yet the bulk of the nation remained

[4] Isa. lii. 7.   [5] Luke xxiii. 34.   [6] Acts ii. 22.

unconvinced. The rejection, first, of the testimony of Peter and John, corroborated as it was by the miraculous and apparent energy of Divine power, and next of the direct appeal made through Stephen[7] to the conscience of the people,—as it was represented by the high priest and elders, who sat in judgment upon that first martyr, to the death, of them who were appointed as sheep to the slaughter,— proved that, though Christ died for that nation, the time for the national repentance was not then come. They were still children in whom was no faith.[8] Hence the apostle introduces here (verse 16) the quotation, "Who hath believed our report?" as applicable to the state of the people out of which, nevertheless, a present election of grace had been gathered. They had not *all* obeyed the Gospel. In the succeeding chapter we shall see the bearing of this expression more distinctly.

Verse 17 states the Divine order in which saving faith is produced. "Faith cometh by hearing, and hearing by the word of God."[9] The report may not perhaps be in all cases communicated audibly, but sometimes by other means; but the thing reported is Divine truth. *God's very word* alone has power to convey to the human soul the knowledge of himself. That oral testimony is the appointed mode of preaching is clear, though blessing may flow, and many times has flowed, from a written testimony to the same saving grace. The conclusion, whether it relate to the nation of Israel or to the world at large, is that the rejection of proffered mercy is the sole reason of a

[7] Acts vii.   [8] Deut. xxxii. 20.
[9] Ἄρα ἡ πίστις ἐξ ἀκοῆς, ἡ δὲ ἀκοὴ διὰ ῥήματος Θεοῦ.

sinner's ultimate perdition. Ruined already by sin, and that from the womb, the Gospel meets him thus as the report of completed redemption and unqualified grace. To reject this is to perish. But Israel had rejected it, as we have seen. Israel, then, as a *people*, is a lost and outcast people. Not believing on the Son of God, they could not call upon Him; and not calling upon Him, they could not be saved: seeing that no other name is given under heaven whereby men may be saved.[1]

Yet, though they had not believed, they had heard (verse 18). The quotation from the 19th Psalm is remarkable. The subject of that Psalm is the glory of God. This glory is there celebrated as pervading creation, letting fall its light upon every visible thing, and disclosing nothing that did not witness of God. Especially, it was the heavens in their silent beauty, and the alternations of day and night, that gave the most emphatic testimony to the power and Godhead of Jehovah. No speech or language could exist where their voice was not heard. If man's tongue remained dumb, and rendered no responsive praise to the Creator, it was because, in the madness of his heart, he had given himself to vanity.[2] Similarly now, the reach of the Spirit's witness as the revealer of Christ—the true light of the Divine glory—is to the creature under heaven.[3] Such is its aspect. The sunshine of the Gospel, as the witness of Divine grace, is as freely shed upon the unthankful and the evil as is the light of the revolving day. The responsibility of rejection attaches, of course, to those only who have heard the report. The apostle's matter

[1] Acts iv. 12. [2] *Ante*, chap. i. [3] Col. i. 23.

here is not a statement of *results*, but an enunciation of the *principle* of universality, as that which characteristically belongs to the existent dispensation of grace.[4]

The remaining verses, in which Israel, as the infatuated forsaker of his own mercies, becomes again the single object of our contemplation, are fraught heavily with the burden of Divine denunciation. Yet is there in the first quotation (verse 19) a ray of hope discoverable, which the coming chapter will brighten to a clearer and enduring day. In the next (verses 20, 21) an example is given, both of the energetic boldness and precision of the Spirit of prophecy, as He taught the holy men of old to speak; and of the folly and blindness of those who, with such testimonies in their hands, could fail to perceive their application to themselves. Meanwhile, the Lord is justified in His dealings with His people. He had spoken, and they had refused to hear. Again, they had heard, but they had not *known*. But all these things had happened according to the prediction of God through the prophets. Israel's condemnation was thus doubled. They not only refused, that is, the abounding grace of God in the cross of Christ, but in doing so they contradicted the very truth in which they professed to make their boast, as disciples of Moses. On the other hand, their disobedience to the truth confirmed and fulfilled the testimony of Jehovah in all these things. Not

---

[4] Divine election directing, meanwhile, and controlling the administration of this grace. The apostle and his companions in labour, for instance, were not suffered to enter Bithynia, though they essayed to go in. They were forbidden again, by the Holy Ghost, to preach the word in Asia, &c. (Acts xvi. 6, 7.)

knowing the voices of the prophets, any more than they knew the person of the Son of God, they had fulfilled them in condemning Him.[5] The spirit of slumber had settled upon the eyes of Jacob because of the judgment of the Lord. Israel had been weary of Jehovah, and He had fed them upon the bitter bread of their own delusions. Their stumbling was of Him. He was *Himself* become their rock of offence.[6]

To sum up, then, the contents of this chapter. The apostle shows us, first, that Israel, nationally regarded, is lost. Secondly, the cause of his perdition is stated.

Viewing the nation at large, he has to bring them under the condemnation of the word of God; as having forsaken their own mercies, and set up the idol of their vanity in their hearts. They had rejected God. Deliberately so, having both seen and hated the Father and the Son.[7] Moreover, this had been done in the light not only of the word of the prophets, and of the manifestation of God himself in the flesh, but also in spite of the gracious testimony of the Holy Ghost, confirming His word by signs and wonders.[8] They had resisted unto blood the ministry of grace. They were, then, without excuse. They had of old broken the Law, and despised the covenant; and now that grace had opened in the blood of the Lamb a fountain of cleansing for their sakes; and the God, whom they and their fathers had grieved from the day He knew them, was preaching peace through Jesus Christ, they were meeting

[5] Acts xiii. 27.
[6] Isaiah viii. 14.
[7] John xv. 24.
[8] Heb. ii. 2-4.

His message of mercy by a protestation of legal righteousness!

This filled up the measure of their provocations. Wrath, therefore, must come, and had already come upon them.[9] Thus the apostle's desire of heart toward his kindred is found to have no rest or relief whilst reviewing their actual condition, and what had led to that condition. The case was indeed desperate. They had counted themselves unworthy of eternal life.[1] They would none of Christ. Walking in the way of their own thoughts, they dwelt still as a rebellious people in a dry land.[2] The Rock of their strength was turned to be their enemy, and had sold them to the bondage of their own delusions.[3]

[9] 1 Thess. ii. 14–16.
[2] Ps. lxviii.
[1] Acts xiii. 46.
[3] Deut. xxxii. 30.

CHAPTER XI.

The close of the last chapter left the nation in a state of complete alienation from God. All the promises which pertained to them as the people of His choice were, so far as they depended for their fulfilment on the national obedience, entirely gone. Israel had rejected God. In denying Jesus they had cast His word away from them, and with it all their hope. The story of the nation, then, has been told. The Spirit of God has demonstrated, in the two chapters last considered, the present condition of Israel as the result of their own way, the fruit of their own will. One question, however, yet remains. Had God cast off definitively the people which He once had called His own? The present chapter contains the answer to this question. Israel has indeed destroyed himself; yet in Jehovah is his help still found.[1]

A new point of view is now taken from which we are to regard the nation. The prospects and destinies of Israel are examined in the chapter now before us in their immediate relation to the Name of Jehovah. What *He is*, in the sufficing fulness of His own grace and power, as the God of Israel, is exhibited in contrast to the foregoing picture of the provocations of

[1] Hosea xiii. 9.

the rebellious house and their effects. The patience of His grace, the faithfulness of His covenanted love, and the effectual display of His righteous power are all exemplified in His dealings with Israel. He had named them with His name because He had formed them for His praise. Accordingly, it is here shown that, though the nation had stumbled, yet its ultimate position is uprightness and glory. *God's* people are a people of blessing. The very womb and fountain of Israel is the promise made to Abraham. The fulfilment of this promise in Christ—the nation's forfeiture of its natural interest therein—the development of the hitherto secret counsel of God with reference to the Church, as the result of the national failure—the prophetic intimation of the foreknown issue of the dispensation of Gentile mercy—and the eventual fulfilment, in the restored nation, of the promises which, though long suspended in effect, remain immovably secured in the record of Divine truth— these are the topics which receive in this chapter the especial treatment of the apostle, to whose calling it pertained to feed the sheep of Christ with a knowledge which it behoved them not to be ignorant of, lest they should be wise in their own conceits (verse 25). Let us follow the chapter in its order.

First, in the opening verse, the question is asked, "Hath God, then, cast away His people?" This enquiry comprises not only Israel nationally, but individuals of Jewish blood severally considered. Seeing that the nation had so emphatically disowned the Lord, had God altogether abhorred His own, so as to leave himself no remnant? Had He, in turning to the Gentiles, shut up for the present all His mercies to the natural seed of promise? In reply to this question, the apostle refers to his own calling as a conspicuous and decisive proof that the conduct of the nation and its rulers could not frustrate the purpose of Divine mercy, so far as it respected individual election. Paul was no proselyte, but a born Jew—a Hebrew of the Hebrews. He had, moreover, by his cruel and uncompromising zeal, given active effect to the national hatred of Christ. Yet, by the grace of God, he was now the chosen messenger of the Lord to the Gentiles.

But in the direct answer to the question (verse 2), we have not only the assertion of personal election, but also the assurance that, though Israel be nationally cast off and lost, in the righteous award of Divine judgment, still the *people of God* are both foreknown and safe. The expression "people," in this verse, appears to bear a double sense. First, the election of grace draws, during the present dispensation, lost sheep of Israel to the bosom of Christ, just as it does godless and hopeless Gentiles. The Church, thus formed, is a people for His name. But, secondly, the Spirit of God would, I believe, by the use of this expression, still keep our minds fixed upon the *nation* as the object, eventually, of Divine favour, according to the truth of the mercy sworn of old. This will appear more distinctly as we proceed.

The quotation which follows is in every way remarkable. Its immediate application here is to the election of grace from among the blinded nation, of which the apostle had been a specimen; but it is cited as a solemn and most touching proof that *God* never forsakes His people who are such indeed.

The contrast between the intercession of the prophet against the nation, and the Divine response,[2] is as instructive as it is wonderful. The eye of man, dwelling upon things visible, and affecting his heart by the evidence of facts, guides his mind to a judgment which, though his heart be true and faithful, is ever found to come short of the perfect will of God. For His counsels are wider and deeper than may be expressed by human action, or understood by human thought. Accordingly, the righteous zeal of God's devoted servant leads him to make intercession *against* Israel. He had had a long and weary experience of the utter apostasy of the people from their God. He seemed to stand alone in the confession of His name. He did so in fact. That is to say, he only was *known* in Israel as a servant of Jehovah.[3] It was an effect of this experience to concentrate his thoughts and desires upon himself. His *office*, as God's witness, is above his strength. The faith which had so magnified him in the day of public controversy, does not bear him through his trial when alone. Hence, while zealous still for God, he is overlooking and despising His *people;* he forgets, in his affliction, that the name of his holy One is the God of *Israel*.

But man's intercession against his fellow brings forth the deep response of Divine power and grace: "*I* have reserved," &c. God had been acting, while He made as though He acted not. Israel was reprobate; but God remembers His own Name. Nature,

---

[2] ὁ χρηματισμός.
[3] Publicly and avowedly, that is. Though Obadiah and the hundred prophets, whom he hid from Jezebel, should have been to Elijah an assurance that the grace of God had not yet utterly forsaken Israel. (1 Kings xviii. 12, 13.)

indeed, can merit nothing but a curse instead of a blessing. God, first committing His name to a promise of blessing,[4] afterwards prepares the vessels of mercy in which the promises are to become vested, for their fulfilment in due time. The appeal of the prophet was as true as it was forcible. They *had* killed the Lord's prophets. They *had* digged down His altars. They *did* seek His poor weary servant's life. Yet God had a remnant of mercy then. A large and goodly band, when matched with the solitary unit which then occupied the prophet's view— "*I* only am left alone." Still they were but a few among the many thousands of Israel. But they were God's people, the men in whose hearts His name lived, and for whom His power was ready to be put forth.

"Even so, then," argues the apostle (verse 5), "at this present time also there is a remnant according to the election of grace." The fulfilment of all wickedness in the generation that slew the Lord of life did not impede, but furthered the sure purposes of love. The children whose fathers had slain the prophets, and had digged down the altars of Jehovah, had indeed excelled in their deeds the sin of their fathers. They had destroyed the living Temple of their God.[5] They had preferred a murderer to the Prince of life, who had healed their sick and raised their dead. They sought the life of Him who indeed was left *alone*. They sought it, and they found it in due time; for there was a hand they wist not of, that led them to that prey. The counsel of salvation was the secret truth of the only wise God, which, long withstood,

[4] Exod. iii. 14, 15.   [5] John ii. 19.

and reaching its effects by degrees imperceptible to men, who viewed the progress of events with merely natural eyes, and with a conscience wholly unawakened to a true sense of their need, rose into victory and eternal praise out of the grave of the crucified Son of man. The first-ripe fruits of God's finished mercy were tasted by an election from among the very murderers of His Son.

And here let us remark, before advancing further into the subject, that the special operation of Divine election in the days of Elijah left the *nation* unimpaired in its capacity to become the subject of future dealings on the part of God. The prophecy of Hosea, for instance,[6] pregnant as it is with national promise, was delivered after the days of Elijah. In like manner, the calling now of an election of grace out of Israel into Christ, leaves the nation itself in unimpaired completeness, as the subject of such especial promises and dealings of God as may yet remain to be fulfilled,[7] and the fulfilment of which appears, from the testimony of the Scripture, to be incompatible with the calling and standing of the Church of God. To proceed with our chapter.

Verse 6. The remnant was according to the election of grace. Works, then, were excluded. Grace and works cannot consist, but contradict each other. Both things are perfect in themselves. Salvation may be proposed as attainable by either, but cannot

---

[6] I quote this prophet because his subject is generally " Israel" as distinguished from " Judah." But, although the prophets often treat them separately, it is evident that the nation, in its undivided unity, is the object before the mind of the apostle in this chapter.

[7] Acts xxvi. 7, affords a good illustration of this: εἰς ἣν (ἐπαγγελίαν) τὸ δωδεκάφυλον ἡμῶν . . . . ἐλπίζει καταντῆσαι. Our *twelve tribes*, &c.

be by both. Fully as I have treated this point in earlier pages of these Notes, I feel desirous, on account of the importance of the subject, of yet again pressing upon my reader the antagonism of works and grace, when considered respectively, as means of human salvation. But one may say, Am I not to satisfy myself that I am in the faith, by referring to my works? The answer is, that Scripture never directs such a process. Your works may be a satisfactory indication to *others* of the faith which has produced them, but your own confidence must rest on other grounds. When the apostle elsewhere calls upon Christians to examine themselves whether they be in the faith,[8] his appeal is to the spiritual consciousness of the believers addressed; "*Know ye not your own selves, how that Jesus Christ is in you, except ye be reprobates?*" The internal testimony of a heart which, because it is possessed by the Spirit of God, believes that Jesus is the Christ, is the evidence of a man's being in the faith. Works, if good, flow from love, and love is gendered in the soul by faith. If, therefore, I want to know whether I believe, I must look at the Object of my faith, I must look at Jesus. If my heart feels comfort at the mention of the dying love of Christ, then, why is it so? And again, if, rising above the miserable feelings of my own distrustful nature, I am emboldened to claim that Christ as mine, whom God gave freely for the sinner who might feel he needed such, what is it that I find in Him? Do I find *less* than a Saviour?

But if it be a denial of all truth to detract from the

[8] 2 Cor. xiii. 5.

glory of the Lord, by diminishing the weight and measure of His perfect work, then it is a similar contradiction for me to doubt respecting the true nature of my standing as a believer in Him. A Christian's faith is, as has been shown already, an effect of his election of God. He is elect by the grace of God, through sanctification of the Spirit and belief of the truth. The sanctification of the Spirit begins its effect, according to Divine foreknowledge, from the moment that the mighty hand of God is laid upon the sinner to lead him to Christ. But the purpose and object of this choice of God is salvation.[9] Salvation, then, is an end, a result. It is so, but it is *God's* end; the result of Divine purpose, and the crowning effect of a Divinely finished work. Again, the same witness testifies that it is "*not* by works of righteousness which we have done, but according to His own mercy *He saved* us............that being justified by His grace, we should be made heirs according to the hope of eternal life."[1] The means are stated in the same passage. It is instrumentally " by the laver[2] of regeneration, and renewing of the Holy Ghost." God is thus the operator in the means as well as the deviser of the purpose. Regeneration can only be the work of the Regenerator. It is *God* who quickeneth the dead. Moreover, the renewing of the Holy Ghost is effected by the abundant shedding forth of that blessed Spirit "*through Jesus Christ, our Saviour.*" That is, the Spirit, which is the sole power of effectual work in man, acts thus only in those who already, because born of God, are regenerate; and who, as believing confessors of Jesus

[9] 2 Thess. ii. 13.   [1] Tit. iii. 5, 7.   [2] λουτρόν.

Christ, the *Lord*, already rejoice in Him as a *Saviour*. But if so, then are they safe. *Now* may they work. The fear of wrath being replaced by the peace of God, they may well bethink themselves how they shall henceforth walk so as to please Him. In a word, the *only* ground and starting-point which the word of God reveals for good works in His sight is perfected acceptance in Christ. Where grace is known, work *must* result; for faith is a living and an operative thing.[3]

I do not forget that we are exhorted to work out our own salvation with fear and trembling; but this exhortation, instead of disturbing the doctrine of the grace of God, owes its very existence to the completeness of that grace. It is the indwelling energy of God in the believer which accomplishes the doing of His pleasure in the vessels of His mercy.[4] A believer is sanctified unto obedience. Because *he is* a son, obedience as such becomes the principle of his conduct. But because his knowledge of Christ is now by faith, and in a body as yet unredeemed, his obedience is ever rendered in opposition to the will of the flesh. The life therefore of a Christian is of necessity a life of conflict. He is saved *by hope*. His progress, as a liberated captive of sin and Satan, is toward the rest that remains for the people of God. His way lies through dangers which will surely swallow up and overwhelm everything but faith.

---

[3] James ii. 26. The argument of the apostle James against the hollow pretensions of mere verbal profession turns upon the very point insisted on above. It was the presence of faith in Abraham and Rahab that produced the works whereby they obtained a good report. God bare them witness of their *faith*. (Heb. xi. 17, 31.)

[4] Phil. ii. 12, 13.

He has, then, to fear, lest by any means he depart from the living God.[5] Moreover, he has to order his conversation aright in the fear of the Lord. But he has, above all, to hold fast, without wavering, the beginning of his confidence.[6] Now the beginning of his confidence, as a believer, was God in Christ. To that he has to cleave. His first rejoicing, on emerging from the darkness and dismay of a sinful conscience, was Christ. That rejoicing he is exhorted to hold fast and firm unto the end. The hope of the Gospel is also Christ; already *in* Him as the hope of glory[7]—objectively *before* him as the end of his race.[8] He is to take heed that he be not moved away from thence.[9]

But I feel that I am carrying my patient reader further from the present matter in hand than he may consider wise or profitable. Yet for his sake it is done; and if by the grace of God his own heart, because already firmly set in Christ, needs no such aid as is here offered to the feeble-minded saint, he will not grudge the labour of perusing a page which, though it seem superfluous to himself, may prove a word in season to some whose feet are not yet firmly planted on the Rock.

Verses 7–10. These verses place the nation of Israel in direct contrast to the election. That which Israel had vainly sought for, the election had obtained. The rest were blinded, or hardened. The quotations which the apostle here makes, in proof of his doctrine, do not appear to call for any especial notice; but as the term itself is used in this passage for the

[5] Heb. iv.   [6] Heb. iii. 6–14.   [7] Col. i. 27.
[8] Phil. iii.   [9] Col. i. 23.

last time[1] in contradistinction to the national title, it is desirable to consider, for a moment, the order and manner in which this grace of election then acted.

The election of which the apostle speaks is plainly that which the grace of God drew forth from the apostate and blinded nation. Hence, the term is used in this chapter in a more restricted sense than in the ninth. Now what separated the saved remnant from the rejected nation, was the faithful confession of Christ. The election had obtained, in Him, that which the nation still groped for in the darkness of their unbelieving hearts. But the effect of this separation of the elect from the natural Israel, was to unite the Jewish believer apparently and outwardly (as well as intrinsically because of common birth, being alike begotten of the truth), to that which held and confessed the name of Christ in the world. He became, that is, a member of the *Church of God*, as the necessary consequence of his being quickened into life through the Gospel.[2] So long, then, as that Church stood in its manifested unity as the pillar and ground of the truth, salvation could reach none but those who were identified, by their confession, with the Church as Christ's sole witness in the world. To be in the visible Church may, in this sense, be said to have been a condition of salvation, so long, that is, as the one body of Christ abode in its confessed completeness, and the light of life shone forth from His virgin spouse,[3] upon the nations of the world; the Spirit of glory and of God meanwhile

---

[1] In verse 28 it is applied to the nation itself, as we shall see.

[2] Historically, and in the order of facts, the Church was itself at its commencement an election from the unbelieving nation. (Acts ii.)

[3] 2 Cor. xi. 2; Rev. xxi. 9; Matt. v. 14.

resting upon her, in her patient endurance of the afflictions of the Gospel.

But the chapter before us is written mainly to unfold and explain to us a mystery respecting the dispensational government of God, by means of which the ancient counsel of truth and promise, of which the nation of His choice is the object, is in its own appointed season to be brought to pass. The chief feature of the mystery here referred to is the order and standing of the Gentile body of nominal believers, which in our own day is but too well known as the *professing* Church, being distinguished by that title from that which really belongs to Christ as alive from the dead. The place which this body occupies in the dispensational arrangement of God, and the result of its professed acknowledgment of the faith of Christ, will appear as we approach the close of this chapter. In the meanwhile, the verses which immediately follow will show us how the wisdom of God has provided for the carrying out of His counsels respecting Israel, and for the preservation of His remnant through the long interval of their national repudiation, even when the light of Divine truth should have ceased to rest upon the shattered candlestick of the divided and corrupted Church, and when, in the total failure[4] of that which is sometimes called "the Christian dispensation," preparation should have been made for the resumption of the cast-off branches of the natural olive, and for fulfilling, in Israel's

---

[4] Failure, that is, on man's part, to glorify, by a believing obedience, the God whom he professes to know through the Gospel of His Son. Viewed, on the other hand, with reference to *God*, the present dispensation is, like those which have preceded it, the further unfolding and accomplishment of the good pleasure of His will.

redemption, the remainder of the mercy promised to the fathers from of old.

Accordingly, in the eleventh verse, the apostle, dismissing for the present the subject of the election, turns again to the consideration of the broken and rejected nation, as the yet-reserved object of Divine mercy. "I say, then, Have they stumbled that they should fall? God forbid: but rather through their miscarriage[5] salvation is come unto the Gentiles, for to provoke them to jealousy." This is a truly important passage. In order to estimate justly the force of these words, it is necessary to recall to mind the tenor of those Old Testament prophecies which bear as their burden the prospective blessing of the Gentiles. I shall quote here a few passages, and only a few, in proof of the general assertion that the prosperity of the other nations of the world, as partakers of the blessings of the Abrahamic promise, is most frequently regarded in the Old Testament as dependent on, and immediately resulting from, the establishment of Israel in the enjoyed blessings of the new covenant in their *own land*.

First, we have in the song of Moses the following words, "Rejoice, O ye nations, with His people: for He will avenge the blood of His servants, and will render vengeance to His adversaries; and will be merciful unto *His land*, and to His people."[6] The apostle's use of a part of this quotation, in the fif-

---

[5] τῷ αὐτῶν παραπτώματι. "Fall" is not a good word, as it had just been said that they have *not* stumbled to their fall. "Lapse," "transgression," or "offence," would be preferable. It is in the last two meanings that the word is everywhere rendered in the New Testament, except in this chapter. DE WETTE renders it here by "*Fehltritt*," which appears to express it very justly.

[6] Deut. xxxii. 43.

teenth chapter will be noticed when we arrive at that part of our work. I now make only two remarks: first, the joy of the Gentiles is here stated to be *with* His people, and not without them: and, secondly, that by the term "people" is meant the nation, and and not the elect remnant, is evident from the mention which is made of the *land*.

My next proof shall be from the prophet Isaiah: "And it shall come to pass in the last days, that the mountain of the Lord's house shall be established in the top of the mountains, and shall be exalted above the hills; and all nations shall flow unto it. And many peoples[7] shall go and say, Come ye, and let us go up to the mountain of the Lord, to the house of the *God of Jacob;* and He will teach us of His ways, and we will walk in His paths: for *out of Zion* shall go forth the Law, and the word of the Lord from *Jerusalem*," &c.[8] It is only necessary to remark on this passage that, after deducting for figurative language, if it be so regarded, there remain these clear facts:—first, the mountain of the house of Jehovah is recognised as the centre of the world's worship; secondly, the locality of this worship is Zion or Jerusalem; and, thirdly, the nations which set their faces toward the Lord, seek Him under the express title of the God of *Jacob*.

Further on in the same prophet, we read as follows: "And in that day shall ye say, Praise the Lord, call upon His name, declare His doings among the *peoples*, make mention that His name is exalted.

[7] עַמִּים Having quoted this one instance, I shall not feel it needful to repeat my reference to the Hebrew text, in justification of future changes of number from singular to plural.

[8] Isaiah ii. 2, 3.

Sing unto Jehovah, for He hath done excellent things: this is known in all *the earth*. Cry aloud, and shout, thou inhabitant of Zion, for great is the Holy One of Israel in the midst of thee."[9] On this it is enough for the reader to observe, first, that we have here the restored nation calling upon the name of the Lord, and therefore saved;[1] and, secondly, a proclamation of the name of Jehovah to the nations is stated as an effect of this restoration and salvation. *Earth* is the scene of this chapter, and not heaven. The God of Israel is known in the midst of Zion, as having returned thither after His anger had been turned away.[2]

The whole of the sixtieth chapter of the same prophet is devoted to the celebration of the glory and blessedness of the earthly Zion as the branch of the Lord's planting. In contrast to what she had been, when forsaken and despised among the nations, she is there presented as receiving the homage of the Gentiles, and as the acknowledged centre of blessing to the nations on every side. Again, in the following chapter, we read, "Their seed shall be known among the Gentiles, and their offspring among the peoples: all they that see them shall acknowledge them, that they are the seed which Jehovah hath blessed."[3] Independently of the strong Jewish character of the context, it is evident from its very terms that this passage does not relate to the Church;

---

[9] Isa. xii. 4–6.   [1] *Ante*, chap. x. *passim;* specially, verse 13.

[2] Compare verse 1. If the whole of this short but richly beautiful chapter be read thoughtfully, noticing its connection by the introductory words, "In that day," with what precedes, I think much light will be acquired on this subject. But, indeed, it is hard to select proofs of what is the main burden of all prophecy.

[3] Isaiah lxi. 9.

seeing that nothing can be more contradictory to the calling of those who are to count it no marvel if the world hate them—whose very calling is to suffer, who are appointed as sheep for the slaughter—than such a description as this.

The same subject is richly illustrated in the remainder of the prophecy of Isaiah; while Jeremiah recites at length the covenant which is not only to purge the people from their sins, but also to rebuild the desolations of Jerusalem.[4] In Ezekiel also the reader may peruse, at his leisure, an amplified declaration of the latter-day mercies of Jehovah to the place and people of His name.[5] Nor are the minor prophets less explicit. From these I make but two extracts:—First, in the prophet Zephaniah we find, after a recital of the Lord's purposes both of judgment and of mercy, the end of which is the restoration and blessing of Jerusalem because of the presence in the midst of her of Jehovah, her God, as King of Israel,—the following promise: "I will save her that halteth, and gather her that was driven out; and I will get them praise and fame in *every land* where they have been put to shame. At that time will I bring you again, even in the time that I gather you: for I will make you a name and a praise among all *peoples* of the earth, when I turn back your captivity before your eyes, saith the Lord."[6]

My last reference is to the prophet Zechariah, where we read in the 14th chapter, after mention has been made of preceding events, as follows: "And it shall come to pass, that every one that is left of all the nations which came against Jerusalem shall even

[4] Jer. xxx.–xxxiii. [5] Ezek. xxxvi.–xlvii. [6] Zeph. iii. 19, 20.

go up from year to year to worship the King, the Lord of hosts, and to keep the feast of tabernacles."[7] That the language here is simply literal, and not at all figurative, must, I think, be apparent to any one who reads the remainder of the chapter from whence the above extract has been made. I add no more to this series. Some additional references will be made as we proceed, but my task thus far has been to select enough to place in a clear light, and without encumbering the general argument, the point immediately under our notice. From the Psalms I here make no quotations, though they present at almost every page the completest proofs of what I have thus endeavoured to substantiate.[8]

If the above extracts and remarks have been effectual in convincing the reader's mind of the correctness of the assertion in support of which they have been used, the language of the apostle in the verse on which we are commenting will be seen to refer to a dispensation of God towards the Gentiles, differing materially, as to the instrumental means of its accomplishment, from that to which the prophecies in general relate. Instead of a reünited and prosperous nation, Israel lies manifestly before our eyes completely broken upon the stumbling-stone. But the Lord's own words assure us of a time when the self-same city which rejected Him and would none of His love, though from of old He had been to them as a hen towards her chickens in the compassionate tenderness of unwearied mercy,[9] should yet with seeing eyes behold Him, and with blessings

---

[7] Zech. xiv. 16.   [8] See *Notes on the Psalms*, passim.
[9] Matt. xxiii. 37-39.

receive Him as the One who cometh in Jehovah's name. In the Psalm from whence the Lord takes some of His words,[1] we find a full and richly triumphant strain of national thanksgiving on the part of Israel, who will celebrate the glory of Jehovah; first, as their deliverer from external oppression, and, secondly, as the opener of their eyes, once dark, to the shining of the light of life, to see and to accept with blessing the advent of His Christ. "God is the Lord who has showed us light," &c. The stone once refused by the builders is there gloried in and built upon, as the head of the corner. Another builder has taken the work in hand, even He of whom it is said, that "when the Lord shall build up Zion, He shall *appear in His glory*."[2]

The contrariety of the state of Israel, as regarded in these chapters, to what has been adduced from other parts of Scripture which relate to the restored prosperity of the nation, having now been shown, I return more immediately to the verse before us. Israel has stumbled, but not to his fall. On the contrary, the present state of that nation is a part of the dealings of Jehovah with them as *His people*. They had provoked Him to anger with that which was not God; and He would move them to jealousy with that which was not a people.[3] The dispensation of Gentile grace stands thus in a direct relation to the eventual purposes of God with respect to Israel nationally. It intervenes, as a distinct manifestation of Divine power and wisdom, between the rejection of His ancient people and their restitution in the

[1] Psalm cxviii. [2] Psalm cii. 16.
[3] Deut. xxxii. 21.

day of the Lord.[4] Nothing is more important, when considering the general subject of God's dispensational government, than to remember that no promise of God, once addressed specifically to an expressed object, can never fail of its *exact* accomplishment. We have to bear in mind that these promises proceed out of the mouth of Him, who displays the riches of His wisdom and prudence, not less than of His mercy, in the varied dispensations of His will, to the praise of His own glory as the God of *truth*.[5] Intermediate events, therefore, while they bring into fuller and more immediate view the glory of the Divine wisdom, instead of frustrating, will be found in the end to have conduced to the fulfilment of anterior promise. Now, as we have seen in the ninth chapter of this Epistle,[6] there are promises which belong to Israel. They are made to them nationally, and until the time shall arrive for the fulfilment to the nation of God's choice of the assurances expressly made to it, those promises remain securely in reserve.

It is most important to remember that God has never yet acknowledged as *His people* any nation of the Gentiles.[7] He calls, it is true, by the Gospel of witness, a people from among the nations, which people, as the united body of Christ, stands alike distinct

---

[4] I use the expression, "day of the Lord," here, as a general term by which to distinguish the millennial dispensation from that which is now drawing to its close. The latter is styled "man's day" (1 Cor. iv. 3), being the time during which the absence of the Lord from the earth leaves opportunity for faithfulness or unfaithfulness, on the part of those who bear professedly His name. He is gone to receive a kingdom, and *to return*. (Luke xix. 11, 12.)

[5] Compare Eph. i. 8.   [6] Chap. ix. 4.

[7] *Prophetically* He does so. See Isaiah xix. 25.

from Jew and Gentile. But no *nation* has ever been set in the place of Israel, so as to become the direct object of Israelitish promise. Most true it is, as we are presently taught, that the Gentiles who outwardly own Christ are regarded dispensationally as having taken, *ad interim*, the place of Israel, and are dealt with according to the responsibilities of their position, as the self-styled people of God. Nevertheless, the present mercy to the Gentiles is, in the mode of its administration, a part of the chastisement wherewith Jehovah chastens that people which alone He *knows* as such among the nations of the world.[8]

The verse which follows opens this further: "If their miscarriage[9] be the riches of the world, and the diminishing of them the riches of the Gentiles, how much more their fulness?" The transgression of Israel has opened the treasures of Divine mercy to the world. The Gentiles are enriched by the diminishing of the now disowned seed of Abraham. But if so, he argues, how much more amply will these benefits result from their restoration; from the reopening and filling with the fulness of blessing the channel through which, as we have seen above, the eventual abundance of Divine favour is to overspread the nations. The force of the apostle's *à fortiori* reasoning arises from this, that the present dispensation of Gentile grace is limited in its effects, and most precarious as to its continuance. It is the undefined duration of Divine long-suffering which alone postpones the second advent, in glory, of the Lord Jesus; whose coming will be for judgment upon that which, in His absence, has had the witness of

[8] Amos iii. 2. [9] παράπτωμα. *Ante*, p. 284, note.

His name. The fidelity of those to whom is committed the stewardship of the mysteries of God,[1] is now chiefly evinced by the earnestness with which they labour, as ambassadors of Christ, to persuade men to escape out of a world already condemned by the rejection of the Son of God, and to flee for refuge to that Name which is now preached for salvation to every creature under heaven. The descent from heaven of the Lord Jesus Christ,[2] to accomplish the salvation of His saints by the redemption, in quickening power, of their bodies of corruption, has been, from the day of His ascension, the hope and promise of them that believe.[3] While the Church stood fast in its unity, its attitude was patient looking for the Lord. To the faithful remnant, who may find themselves in the last days of apostasy and ruin, the same blessed hope and glorious appearing of the great God and Saviour is ministered by the Holy Ghost, as the sustaining power of their faith and patience.[4] They are exhorted to hold fast what they have received until He come.[5]

But the administration of Divine truth among the nations will then be in the manifested power of the kingdom of God. Instead of a testimony exposed to the derision of those who regarded the preaching of the cross as foolishness, and treated its messengers as the offscouring of all things, there will be the overspreading, in commanding power, of the knowledge of the *glory* of the Lord. The nations that have for so long toiled in vain, and laboured in the very fire,[6] shall then be brought to acknowledge that the

[1] 1 Cor. iv. 1, 2.
[2] 1 Thess. iv. 15–18.
[3] Acts i. 11.
[4] Jude 20–22; Tit. ii. 13.
[5] Rev. ii. 25; Heb. xii. 28.
[6] Habak. ii.

one God of all the earth is also the Redeemer of Zion.⁷ The throne of wickedness will then have been cast down, and the seat of righteous judgment be establi-'.ed in its place. "A king shall reign in righteousness, and princes shall rule in judgment."⁸ Christ and His fellows will administer that kingdom in power, which as yet is but a testimony to the world; the value and reality of which are felt only in those hearts which are opened of the Lord to receive it, according to the election of His grace. Satan will then be bound, and the creature set free into the glorious liberty of the children of God. The name of Jerusalem, then recognised as the joy of *the whole earth*,⁹ will be, "The Lord is there." The God of Israel will be known and acknowledged as the giver of strength and power to His people, when, because of His temple at *Jerusalem*, the kings of the Gentiles bring gifts of homage unto Him.¹ As to the endurance of this reign of blessing, it is affirmed to be coëqual in continuance with the ordinances of heaven.² Until the time arrives for the Son to render up the kingdom to the Father,³ that the ultimate accomplishment of revealed purpose may be brought to pass in the new creation where God shall be all in all,⁴ the kingdom and dominion of all which is under heaven⁵ shall prosper in the hands of the anointed King of nations.⁶

⁷ Isa. liv. 5.   ⁸ Isa. xxxii. 1.
⁹ Ps. xlviii. 2.   ¹ Ps. lxviii. 29, 34, 35.
² Ps. lxxii.   ³ 1 Cor. xv. 24.   ⁴ Rev. xxi. 1-5.
⁵ Above the heavens too, most assuredly, as no Christian, I trust, needs to be reminded.
⁶ Daniel vii. 14, 27; Psalm ii. 6-12. That $\dot{\epsilon}\theta\nu\tilde{\omega}\nu$, and not $\dot{\alpha}\gamma\dot{\iota}\omega\nu$, is the correct reading in Rev. xv. 3, is now, I believe, generally admitted by the soundest critics. *Cod. Sin.* however, gives a third reading $\beta\alpha\sigma\iota\lambda\epsilon\dot{\upsilon}\varsigma$ $\tau\tilde{\omega}\nu$ $\alpha\dot{\iota}\dot{\omega}\nu\omega\nu$, "King of the ages or worlds."

Well might the apostle, then, as a scribe well instructed unto the kingdom of heaven, while joyfully contemplating the special and limited dispensation of Divine mercy, of which he was himself a partaker, look forward with a yet fuller joy to the time of the more abundant display of the same mercy through the accomplishment of the long-deferred national promise.

Verses 13–15. The casting away of the natural Israel, is thus shewn to be the commencement also of that new and distinct dispensation of God towards the nations of the earth, exclusive of Israel (except as Israel may now take its place among other nations,[7] and be therefore comprehended in the generic appellation of *Gentile*), which forms the era of the world's mercy. It is with reference to this that he is able to speak (verse 15) of the casting away of Israel as the reconciliation of the world. The immediate object of the testimony of the Holy Ghost is now *the world*. "*Now* is the accepted time, now is the day of salvation," is a descriptive expression of the aspect of Divine grace as it is now preached through Jesus to every consenting ear.

He magnifies his office as the apostle of the Gentiles, not only on account of the glory which intrinsically attaches to it, but that he may, by so doing, "provoke to emulation them that are his flesh." His heart, ever yearning towards his own, seeks comfort thus even in the work which most emphatically witnesses of Israel's rejection. Some at least from among them might, he hoped, be saved by this very means. The testimony of the Spirit of

[7] Amos ix. 7.

God among the Gentiles, confirmed as it was by the signs and mighty wonders of apostolic energy, according to the power of God, might act upon the conscience and the heart of the individual Israelite, and stir him up to go forth without the national camp,[8] in order to meet and be owned by Him who had forsaken His former habitation. For this he hoped, though the nation as a whole had dropped, for the present, beyond the actual range and limit of Divine mercy. Meanwhile, he knew that though repudiated in fact, Israel was not forgotten in those counsels which from of old were faithfulness and truth; and which in due time were to ripen into the rich and abiding harvest of peace and glory for that broken and afflicted people, whose end was to be yet more wonderful than their beginning.[9]

The language of the fifteenth verse is remarkable. Its drift and general meaning seem to be as follows. The casting away of Israel is the reconciling of the world. The nations, that is, instead of being known afar off, are dispensationally brought near. God wills now that all men should repent and come to the knowledge of the truth. But, though general in

[8] Heb. xiii. 13.
[9] Isa. xviii. 7. The gifts and calling of God are without repentance. The promises, therefore, of which Israel is the object are the recorded pledge of the national restoration. For no dealing of God with a third party, for instance, with the Church, can ever amount to a fulfilment of promises made specifically to Israel *by name.* Peter, addressing the election then standing in Christ (1 Pet. ii. 9, 10), applies to them language which is elsewhere used of the natural Israel when brought under the new covenant. The reason is clear. They were, as an election, saved by the same grace which by and by will visit the people as such, when the nation shall itself be chosen. Thus they occupied morally, and by anticipation (in conjunction with yet higher blessings as a part of the body of Christ), a position and privileges which will nationally be enjoyed by Israel in the day when the vail is taken away.

its terms, the grace preached is partial in its effect. The *blessing* of the Divine mercy, which is proclaimed and dispensed to the Gentiles in the message of the Gospel, is confined really to the vessels of mercy chosen from among them, as we have seen.[1] If, then, this visitation of the Gentiles by the God of grace, by a means and ministry quite unexpected, and in its character altogether dissimilar to that of which the prophets speak, be the result of Israel's rejection, what shall their restoration be but the perfecting of that blessing in its fulness of effect, by the accomplishment, finally, of those promises of Gentile mercy which the word of God has for ever bound up in the name and with the blessing of Israel as His people? As it is written, "Thus saith the Lord of Hosts, It shall yet come to pass, that there shall come *peoples*, and the inhabitants of many cities: and the inhabitants of one city shall go to another, saying, Let us go speedily to pray before the Lord, and to seek the Lord of hosts. I will go also. Yea, *many peoples* and strong *nations* shall come to seek the Lord of hosts *in Jerusalem*, and to pray before the Lord. Thus saith the Lord of hosts, In those days it shall come to pass, that ten men shall take hold, out of all languages of the nations, even shall take hold of the skirt of him that is a Jew, saying, We will go with you; for we have heard that God is with you."[2] In this passage we have a most striking description of the effect to be produced by Israel's restoration on the hearts as well as consciences of the Gentiles. With respect to the expression, "life from the dead," although its exact

[1] Chapter ix. 23, 24. [2] Zech. viii. 20–23.

NOTES ON THE ROMANS. 297

meaning cannot be easily determined, I have little doubt that it is to be regarded as a strong figure, in which Jacob's leanness and judicial degradation are contrasted with his future glory and fruitfulness, when the filthy rags of his own righteousness shall have been exchanged for the garments of Divine salvation.[3] The figure of resurrection is more than once used in the prophets in order to express the revival of the nation from the death of its natural hope;[4] while in the reception of the returning prodigal we have an application of the same figure very closely approximating, in its moral force, to the passage now before us.[5]

In the sixteenth verse the unity of the nation's destiny is further exemplified. "If the first-fruit be holy, the lump is also holy; and if the root be holy, so are the branches." By the expression, "first-fruit," I understand the apostle to mean the nation of Israel in its primal calling and honour.[6] As it is written: "Israel was holiness unto Jehovah, the first-fruits of His increase."[7] The nation had been thus owned when God brought them up out of Egypt, and gave His strength to the people in whom He would not see iniquity.[8] But the blessing of the Lord had departed, and Israel had become an empty and dishonoured vine.[9] Yet the Shepherd of Israel and the Stone of their help abode still in His counsel. He had ordained blessing for the people of His calling,

[3] Isa. lxiv. 6, and lxi. 10.   [4] Ezek. xxxvii.; Isa. xxvi. 19, 20.
[5] Luke xv. 32.
[6] Although the same term ($\dot{\alpha}\pi\alpha\rho\chi\acute{\eta}$) is applied to the Church in James i. 18, I do not see that it has here any reference to it. It is not until mention is made of the branches of the olive, that the Church as a dispensation comes under review.
[7] Jer. ii. 3.   [8] Numb. xxiii. 21.   [9] Ps. lxxx.

and whose name He had joined for ever with His own.[1] The apostle's argument, accordingly, is, that the eventual destiny of the nation will be worthy of its original calling. So Balaam judged, when, in his reluctant utterance of the commanded blessing, he made mention of the latter day of glory which was to fulfil the promises of Divine faithfulness to the people of Jehovah's choice.[2] The nation is itself the creature of Divine promise. *Grace* is the true fountain of Israel. But the law had entered, and a curse came instead of a blessing. Because they had rejected the Lord, in His prophets and in His Christ, the nation was now cast off. Yet was there hope in their latter end. They will yet be an unleavened lump in the day when their iniquity is purged.[3] The Spirit of God appears to be here connecting the past display of Divine grace and power, in the Exodus from Egypt, with the future manifestation of the same mercy in yet more abundant richness of result. That mercy still holds fast, in the counsels of God, the seed of Abraham His friend. Deeply graven on the palms of His hands, there remains the recorded number of the many thousands of Israel.[4] The sanctity of the former generation, when Jehovah walked among them in the tabernacle of witness, will be yet excelled by the generation who shall date their birth not only from the natural fountain of Israel, but from the effectual power of quickening grace. The name of Jerusalem, when, as a place without walls,[5] she shall overflow with the multitude of Jehovah's increase, will be, "The Lord is there;"

---

[1] Exod. iii. 15.
[2] Numb. xxiii. 10.
[3] Isa. liv. 13, lx. 21; Ezek. xi. 19.
[4] Isa. xlix. 16.
[5] Zech. ii. 4, 5.

and upon the very bells of their horses shall be read in that day the inscription of His most holy name.[6]

With respect to the remainder of this verse, the "Root" means, I believe, originally *Christ;* the Eternal Word being the alone true fountain of life or holiness.[7] But secondly, and especially, it here signifies the promise made to Abraham. This root was, in the order of nature, the producer of the nation, while it is effectively also, through faith, the origin of God's acknowledged children.[8] Promise brought Isaac forth by preternatural birth, and in Isaac had the natural seed been called. On the other hand, the Gentiles, who are by nature "strangers from the covenants of promise,"[9] must be grafted in in order to connect them with the root. If, then, the root was holy, so were the branches, whether natural or ingrafted. The general application of this is plain. But the apostle's words, though wide enough to comprise the calling of the Gentiles, seem rather to refer (consistently with the drift of his teaching in the verses which follow), to the natural branches as they will hereafter appear, when, after having been for a time estranged from the root that bare them,[1] they will be again ingrafted into their own tree, and become fruitful in blessing to the nations of the earth.

Verses 17–21. The mention of the branches in

---

[6] Zech. xiv. 20.
[7] And thus it is that when the Lamb is seen in *heaven*, in connection either with the undeveloped mystery of God, or with the symbolical display of the end of all His counsel, it is as the *Root* of David that He appears. (Rev. v. 5, and xxii. 16.)
[8] Chap. iv.; Gal. iii.   [9] Eph. ii. 12.
[1] Isaiah i. 2; John i. 11.

the last verse brings now more immediately into our view the mystery of the Church dispensation, which occupies its own appointed place and time, according to the order of God's manifested dealings as the sovereign Governor of the world. It is this subject which will now engage our attention. Nor can we, if believers, be occupied by anything of deeper practical interest than a consideration of the Spirit's testimony with respect to the dispensation which has produced ourselves, and in which we live. May we have wisdom to perceive and accept with joy *all* that the grace of our Father has provided for the profit of our souls.

The Church of God, as the quickened and anointed vessel of Divine grace and power, has already come, in a measure, under our notice in the earlier chapters of this Epistle.[2] Viewed in its perfection as the elect body of Christ, it has no place in the apostle's present argument. What he is here contemplating is the eventual result of the dispensation of Gentile mercy, during the period of Israel's alienation.

It is a principle obvious in itself, and everywhere exemplified in the testimony of Scripture, that any especial revelation which God is pleased to make of Himself, not only confers upon the obedient receivers of it its own peculiar blessings, but places all who outwardly acknowledge it under the responsibility of endeavouring to glorify God, according to the special Name and character by which He is made known. We have had before us, in the former chapters of this Epistle, some striking examples of this. It was because men, while knowing God, refused

[2] *Ante*, pp. 69 and 205, notes.

Him His honour as the *Creator* (though in Him they lived, and moved, and had their being, and though His goodness filled their hearts with food and gladness), that God brought judgment to avenge on the abusers of His mercies the eternal holiness of His name.

The waters of the flood brought in upon the world of the ungodly, and the catastrophe of Sodom and Gomorrah, exemplify the same principle. More largely, and with a more forcible and immediate application to ourselves, we find the history of Israel under the Old Covenant to be the appointed page of instruction and of warning, prepared by the wisdom and mercy of God for the admonition of those on whom the ends of the ages are come.[3] Nor is the Church, considered dispensationally, an exception to this rule of Divine government. On the contrary, we find the New Testament full of the most varied and emphatic testimony to the general truth, that the assumption of the name of Christ renders the professor of that name responsible to the Lord, as the Judge of His own house. That we must all appear before the judgment-seat of Christ, is a certainty to all who receive the Scripture as the word of God. A believer, who has been truly established in the grace of God, finds no cause of dread in the prospect of meeting Christ as the Judge of His

[3] 1 Cor. x. 11. Τὰ τέλη τῶν αἰώνων. The force of this expression appears to be this. There has been a sequence of successive dispensations of God from the days of Eden until now. The publication, in the Gospel, of life and incorruptibility through the righteousness of Him who is both our Saviour and our God, closes the long day of Divine patience, during which the qualities of man have been in every way put to the test. Grace rejected brings on the judgment which will usher in the cloudless morning of a brighter day—the day of the Lord, and not of man.

servants. The knowledge of perfected love gives boldness in that day,[4] as has been already fully shown. A sense of his own wretched shortcoming and unfaithfulness may, it is true, cause a Christian, while engaged in judging himself, to feel something like a shrinking of shame from the ordeal of that day. This, however, is not the effect of any doubt of his own acceptance, but arises from a sentiment exactly opposite. He feels, that is, in proportion to the distinctness with which he apprehends the unqualified freeness of grace, a corresponding sense of self-reproach at having so ill requited the Lord; together with an anticipation of loss,[5] when respect is had to that recompense of reward which, by the soul that loves the Master, will be held in no light esteem.

But I may not here pursue this topic.[6] Another question than that of the adjudication of reward to the true servants of Christ is now before us. The Lord will judge His people. He does so now.[7] But there is a time at hand when He will suddenly return to that which, during His long-protracted absence, has borne His name in the world. The effect of that visitation will be according to the condition of the professing body, as it will be judged unerringly by the decision of Divine holiness. With respect to this, the Spirit of God bears ample testimony in the Scripture to the introduction, the progress, and the final result of *evil* in the professing body of Christ. The seal of the sure foundation of God is, first, "The

---

[4] 1 John iv. 17–19.   [5] 1 Cor. iii. 11–15.
[6] The reader will find some further treatment of this subject in chap. xiv. of these Notes.   [7] 1 Pet. iv. 17.

Lord knoweth them that are His;" and, secondly, "Let every one that nameth the name of Christ depart from iniquity." But the express witness of the Spirit is, that instead of departing from iniquity, many would depart from the *faith* [8]—that evil men and seducers would wax worse and worse, deceiving and being deceived [9]—that the pernicious ways [1] of such would draw many back from faith unto perdition. It is, moreover, plainly affirmed that the principle of evil had already found its lodgment in the Church, which in due time should ripen into its destined climax of impious hostility to God. [2]

The passage upon which we are now entering is fraught with instruction of the utmost practical value on the same subject, inasmuch as it defines the limits of what is called the Christian dispensation, and testifies distinctly to the causes and the manner of its coming to its end. Let us examine the verses in detail. "And if some of the branches be broken off, and thou, being a wild olive tree, wert grafted in among them, and with them partakest of the root and fatness of the olive tree, boast not against the branches. But if thou boast, thou bearest not the root, but the root thee." [3] We have the Gentile Church regarded here, dispensationally, as an adventitious graft, which finds its place on the stem of Divine promise during the absence of those branches which had been broken off to make room for it. Essentially, the Gentile is a wild olive branch. Without promise or birth-right in himself, he becomes, by grace, a partaker of the promises of God

[8] 1 Tim. iv.   [9] 2 Tim. iii.   [1] 2 Pet. ii.
[2] 2 Thess. ii.; Jude, *passim*.   [3] Verses 17, 18.

through the Gospel. A violence had been done to
the natural growth and development of the root of
promise, before the foreign branch could be received
so as to become an integral part of the tree. Through
the fall of Israel salvation is come to the Gentiles.
But being grafted in, the Gentile branch became
immediately connected with the root in all its fatness.
The danger then was, that in the consciousness of
actual favour there would be a haughtiness of place
on the part of the adopted branch, while contemplating the subversion and rejection of the Jewish
nation as a preliminary to the recognition of the
Gentile body. It is this which the apostle here
endeavours to anticipate and counteract, by reminding them that they owed their standing to no other
thing than their being upborne upon the root which
naturally was none of theirs. And if, as was too
likely, a spirit of carnal security should seek its justification in the admitted fact that it was for their
sakes that the natural branches had been broken off
(verse 19), the warning reply of the apostle is as
ready as it is decisive: "Because of *unbelief* they
were broken off; and thou standest by faith. Be
not high-minded, but fear; for if God spared not the
natural branches, neither will He spare thee" (verses
20, 21).[4]

The position of the Gentile Church as an ingrafted
branch of the olive root has been already stated.
We have now declared to us the tenure by which
alone that position is maintained. *Unbelief* had
broken off the natural branches. *Faith* was the in-

[4] All the earlier MSS. (including *Cod. Sin.*) omit μή πως, and read
οὐδέ σου φείσεται.

strumental means of ingrafting the foreign shoot. Now the very mention of faith, as the condition of their standing, should be sufficient to still the self-gratulating boast against which he had just before warned them. For since faith is the only possible means of binding the professing body to the promises, whenever that cement shall lose its proper virtue, the branch, already grown strange again by ceasing to draw its life-sustaining supply from the root, remains but a burden to the tree, and is in readiness to be again cut out. Regarded, then, as a dispensation, the Gentile Church takes the place of Israel, and holds that place just so long as it continues to stand by faith. There was, therefore, cause of fear rather than of self-confidence. The blessings in which they might boast themselves were *by the grace of God*, and could in no wise be tasted in reality, except by the faith of His elect. Yet was there a possibility that the once pure and unleavened Church might, through the subtle insinuation and stealthy growth of error, lose altogether its distinctive glory as "the household of faith." There was yet the more cause to fear, in the remembrance of the Gentile origin of that which, for the present, stood in the manifested favour of God. If once cut off, there remained no covenanted promise of restitution. There is no hope in her latter end, as is the case with the natural branch.[5] God, who did not spare the natural branches, would not spare, but cut off finally that which had taken their place, if the condition of its standing were not maintained.

The three verses which next follow (22–24) bring

[5] Jer. xxxi. 17; Hosea ii. 15.

the subject now before us into a still closer application to the conscience, as a practical warning to the Church. We are called on to behold the goodness and severity of God. The unchangeableness of His character as the God of judgment is presented to us in conjunction with the display of the riches of His kindness. It was the maintenance of the glory of God, as the righteous avenger of His own name, that caused the cutting off [6] of them that had fallen. The self-same line of righteousness, when applied to the professed people of His name who, from among the Gentiles, hold the title of Christ as their own, would condemn, in equal impartiality, whatever was found to fail of the alone condition of continuance. Meanwhile the conditional standing of the Gentile profession is the goodness of God. "Toward thee goodness, *if thou continue* in His goodness; otherwise thou also shalt be cut off" (verse 22). We have here a direct intimation that upon failure on the part of the professing Gentile Church to stand in the goodness of God, that Church will be cut off.[7]

The all-important question now is: Has the con-

[6] ἀποτομία.

[7] The reader should keep clearly before his mind the entire difference in principle between the judicial dealings of God in His righteous government of the world, and the manifestation of His faithfulness and power (still in perfect righteousness, but in the way of redeeming grace) towards His own elect people. With them the question of standing or falling can never be raised, their characteristic description being, that they " are kept *by the power of God*, through faith, unto the salvation which is ready to be revealed," &c. (1 Pet. i. 5); faultless perfection in Christ being the eternal condition of those who, as the workmanship of God, will bring glory to His name in that day, as has been abundantly shown by the apostle in the eighth and ninth chapters of this Epistle. To argue, therefore, from the conditional quality (and therefore instability), of the dispensational standing of the nominal professor, to the questionable security of the real believer, would be to confound together two things essentially different in kind.

dition here stated been kept? Has the Gentile body, as an aggregate, continued, and does it still continue, in the goodness of God? In endeavouring to meet and reply to this question, we must first recall to our minds what the foundation is upon which the Church of God was originally laid. The goodness of God now revealed in the Gospel is *Christ*, as the propitiation for human sin and the manifestation, in grace, of the righteousness of God. The goodness of God, in a word, as well as His wisdom, reveals itself in presenting Christ as made of God to the believer righteousness, and sanctification, and redemption. Continuance in the goodness of God, then, can only be affirmed of such as, having once received the knowledge of that goodness by faith, have remained unmoved away from Christ the true and only hope of the Gospel. The substitution of works for grace—the gradual corruption of the doctrine of justification by faith alone into that of self-righteousness and external forms—the retention of the name of Christ and the letter of the Gospel, while the vivifying power of the Holy Ghost is denied or unknown—these things, inasmuch as they are severally and unitedly derelictions from the goodness of God, which is expressed and imparted in Christ alone, disqualify the body to which they attach for its continuance as a branch in the tree of promise.

If, as we are bound to do, we steadily apply this principle of judgment to nominal Christianity as it has existed, and continues still upon the earth, what result shall we find? First of all, let us diligently bear in mind the testimonies of the Holy Ghost—to which I have already referred in a former page of this chapter[8]—in proof, first, of the commencement of an evil work in the Church; and, secondly, of the foreseen progress of that evil as it should conduct the self-deceived, while apostate, body towards the closing days of the dispensation. I pass by very much Scripture, both from the Gospels and the Epistles, which might be adduced in further evidence and corroboration of the general statement which I now make on the authority of the chapter before us, supported by the passages already referred to—that *from the apostolic times* the Church had become practically corrupt, and that the word of God contains *no warrant* for the expectation of any other termination or issue of the long-suffering grace of God in this dispensation, than the quickening of His elect unto eternal salvation, and the hardening of that which has a name to live, but is dead, to its ultimate destruction. As a corollary to this, it follows that that which now overspreads so large a part of the earth in the form of Christianized Gentilism, whilst to the heart and conscience of every real believer it is not the Church of the living God, is nevertheless the ripe subject of the solemn warning contained in the verse now under consideration.

And now, with respect to historical facts which might be demanded in support of this general assertion, I answer, first, that to a godly mind the declared testimony of Scripture is sufficient in itself to afford an assurance altogether infallible as to the soundness of conclusions drawn directly thence. When the Spirit of God delivers a prophecy, He foretells an

[8] Page 303.

event. The event thus foretold is, to the believer, a fact already assumed, and therefore to be used in aid of his spiritual understanding in forming a judgment on the actual circumstances in which he may find himself, and in penetrating the disguise of contradictory appearances with which the prince of this world ever seeks to mislead the minds of men. God has, in fact, written the world's history (in all its essential features) beforehand for the children's sakes. His prophetic testimonies are therefore, to the simple believer, a light of sure guidance in the darkest hour.[9] When we read, therefore, in His word, that in the last days perilous times shall come[1]—that the form of godliness shall be found lingering over the utmost excess òf all practical sin, which will then be found to hold the place of ong-departed holiness and truth, so that the foulest features of natural apostasy are reproduced under the mask of religious profession—and when, in connection with this, we are warned of a time to come, in which the pure truth of God would no longer be tolerable in the ears of those who would be nevertheless distinguished by a prurient eagerness for religious novelties—that men should turn away their ears from the truth, and should be turned unto fables[2]—in these passages of Scripture a revelation of Divine foreknowledge is plainly set before us, as to what must surely come to pass. Did, then, the outward aspect of things, at any stage of the dispensation, seem to contradict such a statement of results, we ought still to bear in mind that judgment according to the appearance is never righteous judgment,[3]

[9] Comp. 2 Pet. i. 19-21.
[2] 2 Tim. iv. 4, 5.
[1] 2 Tim. iii. 1-5.
[3] John vii. 24.

and that God alone is capable of pronouncing upon the character and progress of that which He holds Himself in readiness to judge.

Yet as appearances are most deceitful, and as occasional instances in which the saving power of the Gospel has been strikingly authenticated by very numerous conversions, are not unfrequently turned rather to the sanctioning of the existing condition of things,[4] than used as a stimulus to a nearer and fuller knowledge of God's ways; I shall here devote a few lines to the consideration of the bearing of the passage before us on the Church, under the aspects in which it is presented to us historically. Let it, then, be remembered that the question before us is, Has the Gentile branch continued in the goodness of God?

Passing by, for the present, the Book of Revelation, where the last of the seven phases in which the Church, as a local witness to the truth of God comes before our view, is pronounced by the Lord as fit only to be spued out of His mouth,[5] and in which mention is afterwards made of the mystery of abomination;[6] I would ask the Christian reader, who may be acquainted with ecclesiastical history, whether, in the extant monuments of the earliest post-apostolic times, he finds the Church of the Gentiles continuing in the goodness of God? Let him enumerate the heresies of the first and second centuries—let him compare the average standard of practical doctrine among those who are quoted as orthodox teachers

---

[4] Notable examples of this tendency may be observed in much of the "revivalist" literature of the day.
[5] Rev. iii. 16.   [6] Rev. xvii.

and fathers in the Church, with the pure word of Gospel truth as it was delivered by the apostles—let him ponder the several points of controversy which divided church from church during the interval which elapsed between the death of the last of the apostles and the accession of Constantine to the imperial sceptre; and then, when he has meditated sufficiently on the practical condition of the mass of professed worshippers, as indicated by the numerous writings in those times of a hortatory character, and has well examined the factitious sanctity of ascetic observances (so highly extolled by those who, by their office and personal influence, gave the tone to the general religious sentiment of the day), and compared them with the precious fruits of the Spirit which are borne only in hearts established with grace, and not with meats; let him say whether he finds continuance in the goodness of God to be thus far characteristic of the professing Gentile body.

It is not needful to pursue this enquiry through the following ages anterior to the Reformation. Most Christians are aware that the riper iniquity and more deeply corrupted doctrine of Rome, were but the growth and expansion of that radical subversion of the pure grace of the Gospel, which, to speak generally, prevailed in the professing Church at the time of the Council of Nicæa. I pass, therefore, at once to the Reformation. What, then, was this? Its name would imply, that from a state of declension the professing body had regained its pristine purity. But was it so in fact? First, after taking the largest estimate of the extent of the Reformation, we find at least one half of Christendom remaining as before. But, secondly, was its effect, within the sphere of its actual operation, to restore the Church to its original condition? Now whilst, in common with every one who through grace is able to value the truth of God, I bless the exceeding mercy which wrought for the recovery of sound doctrine through the instrumentality of the Reformers, I feel that it is only needful to refer any sound-minded believer to the history of that movement, whether in his own country or on the Continent, in order to convince him that no such effect was produced. Blessing to individual souls most surely abounded, through the preaching, in more or less clearness, of the word of grace: but the adoption by states and governments of a sounder form of doctrine, and the settlement, according to the will of the powers that be, of means for the diffusion of Scriptural knowledge, though in one sense ascribable to the mercy of God, is a very different thing from a return of the collective Church of God to its normal position, as the habitation of God through the Spirit —the single and undivided pillar and ground of the truth.

Without pausing to dwell on the political results immediately or indirectly flowing from the Reformation,—the wars, the intrigues, the complicated evil and wickedness which, alas! meet us as familiarly in the history of Protestantism as of its less enlightened and therefore less guilty rival; I hasten to close this digression by a momentary glance at the condition of the Christian world in this our own eventful day.[7]

---

[7] It is not, I hope, necessary to remind the reader that I am speaking of Protestantism as an aggregate system, in reference to its responsibilities as bearing the name of Christ; not overlooking,

Looking first to the Continent, we find that, after a lapse of more than three centuries, the doctrines of grace recovered at the Reformation, instead of being the universal delight of those who profess a knowledge of the truth, are in many quarters becoming daily less esteemed. Romanism, with its kindred yet rival Greek system, Socinianism, Rationalistic theories (varying indeed according to the perverse windings of the darkened mind of nature, yet all far apart from godly edifying which is in faith), Pantheistic Gnosticism, and avowed indifference to all that is called God or worshipped,—occupy, respectively, so large a space in European Christendom, that the places where even the form of godliness maintained exhibits anything like Scriptural accuracy, are by no means numerous. Efforts are, indeed, being made, with a zeal which does honour to those engaged, to circulate the Scriptures, and to turn to account the political changes which so remarkably distinguish the present age, by endeavouring to answer the craving for national freedom by a proclamation of the liberty of Christ. But although the saving mercy of God has undoubtedly attended to a certain extent these efforts, their effect is but slightly appreciated in a general estimate of the condition of modern Europe.

And is it in continental Europe alone that these things are to be found? Let us regard for a moment the most favoured of the Gentile kingdoms. After all that has been done and all that has been hoped, is the love of Christ a growing, not to say

meanwhile, the vast amount of blessing, both spiritual and temporal, of which it has instrumentally been the means.

a pervading, principle of English society? Is the dark-minded zeal for human ordinances and lifeless works on the one hand, or the more widely-prevailing liberalism which every day demands more room for the free development of what is in man's heart, and already deems professed subjection to the name of Christ a needless qualification for a British legislator, to be regarded as a symptom of continuance in the goodness of God?[8] The progress of Romanism in this island of late years, and its present accredited standing, are facts sufficiently well known. But there is an evil in England yet more deadly than Popery, difficult as it is to overrate the evil of that which speaketh lies in hypocrisy. But there is now in its early development a methodical system of anti-Christian blasphemy, which openly aims at the subversion of the faith even in name. The letter of inspired Scripture is the present object of attack. Modern science is the false light by means of which men who glory in being *Protestants* are labouring to undermine the foundation of Divine knowledge. Books in which every distinctive doctrine of Christianity is denied, and the letter of the word, both of the New and of the Old Testament, is openly blasphemed, are put forth by those who are accredited as public instructors of the youth of this country,[9] and by some even

---

[8] In America, the operation of the wilfulness of human opinion in overriding and corrupting the faith once delivered to the saints, is even more openly visible than in this country.

[9] Events move rapidly in the present day; and error, always active in its working, seems, by means of the diffusive appliances of modern civilization, to propagate its essence and multiply its forms more busily and successfully than ever. The particular reference made in the first edition of these Notes to *one* of the bolder and less scrupulous of the modern falsifiers of Divine truth is unhappily no longer needful, as he no longer is entitled to such solitary distinction; his folly

of the nominal pastors of the flock of God. And I would earnestly call on those who are fondly congratulating themselves on the various existing institutions which the zeal of modern times has created for the furtherance of evangelical blessing,[1] to remember that what the Spirit of God is contemplating in the passage before us is the *aggregate* of professing Gentilism, and not a fraction of the whole. The contrast lies between the nation of Israel now discarded, and that which, as a united testimony to the name of Christ, occupies its place dispensationally as the people of God. Few things are more injurious to the soul of a believer than a partial apprehension of a general truth. In such a case, quickness of discernment and decision of conduct will generally increase his blindness to the full revelation of the mind of God; the effect of which on the position of a Christian, as a witness for the truth, I need not stay to point out.[2]

And now I shall leave the reader to furnish such reply to the question above proposed as his conscience may suggest to him, on a thoughtful consideration of

being now emulated by a crowd of others to whom equally with himself the apostle's description in 1 Tim. vi. 5 may be applied: "men of corrupt minds, and destitute of the truth."

[1] A zeal often, I doubt not, flowing from true devotedness to Christ, and therefore worthy in itself of all praise, even where deficiency of knowledge may cause it to be misdirected. Nor should grateful mention be withheld of the amount of real blessing which in divers quarters has crowned the efforts of missionary enterprise in distant lands. God gathers, and will gather, His elect; but the nations out of which He gathers them remain the same.

[2] This remark applies with peculiar force to those Christians who, under the influence of Protestant partisanship, might be induced to limit the apostle's warning in this passage to the Church to which he is immediately addressing himself. Though it was no doubt with an especial reference to the later pretensions of the Roman system that this epistle has been chosen as the voice of general warning to the Church.

what has been said. The Gentile branch either has or has not continued in the goodness of God. But if the latter be the case, then there remains but one event which must befall it, and that at an hour whereof they who are the subjects of the judgment will be the least aware. It is when men are saying "peace and safety,"[3] that the undesired advent of the Judge will bring a destruction upon them from which there will be no escape. Let us now proceed to the following verse.

"And they also, if they abide not still in unbelief, shall be graffed in: for God is able to graff them in" (verse 23). The counterpart of the judicial excision of the reprobate branch is here stated. God is able to replace the once discarded branches, if they abide not in unbelief. They shall be graffed in again. There is much force in this last expression. Although by hereditary title they are the natural branches, they must, in order to bear fruit, be treated as if they were of alien growth. When Israel is restored, it will be from a condition similar to that from whence the grace of God took up the Gentile vessels of election. Yet will it be *their own* tree (verse 24) into which they will be again graffed; to be no more thence removed, but to flourish in everlasting righteousness as the trees of lign aloes which the Lord hath planted, and as the fragrant cedars of His choice.[4]

Verse 25. The apostle expresses directly and explicitly, in the verse at which we are now arrived, the object for which the important chapters which have so long occupied our attention were written. "I would not, brethren, that ye should be ignorant of

[3] 1 Thess. v. 2, 3.   [4] Numb. xxiv.; Hos. xiv.

this mystery, *lest ye should be wise in your own conceits:* that blindness in part hath happened to Israel, until the fulness of the Gentiles be come in." There was a necessity for his imparting to the Gentile Church so much of the determinate counsel of God as respected the dispensation under which they lived, lest in ignorance of the Divine counsel, and actuated by a spirit of natural self-complacency, they might hastily regard the calling of the Gentiles as the last of those dispensational manifestations, by means of which the wisdom and power of God have been from time to time displayed.

The natural conclusion which the minds of men would infer from the two-fold fact, first, of the rejection of Israel nationally; and, secondly, of the fusion of the elect remnant into the new and distinct body (which, under the name of the Church or assembly of the living God,[5] now took the place of the former witness of His name), was the permanent endurance of that to which the favour, which God had withdrawn from His ancient people, had now been transferred. But such an inference from facts would have led them into a similar danger to that which ruined the nation whose fall had been their rise. It was the saying, "The temple of the Lord,"[6]—in the vanity of a self-confident boasting, which mistook the possession of national privilege for the true knowledge of God, whose name they were dishonouring in the far-removal of their hearts from Him,—that provoked the fierce anger of Jehovah to lay that temple waste, and to drive His people into captivity. It was the same pride of self-deceived ignorance which led the

[5] Ἐκκλησία Θεοῦ ζῶντος (1 Tim. iii. 15). [6] Jer. vii. 4.

yet more fatally-blinded children of these fathers to stumble at the manifestation of the Hope of Israel, because they looked for one like-minded with themselves, and dreamed of peace and national triumph while as yet unwashed from their sins. They thought that the Holy One of Israel was even such an one as themselves,[7] because they believed not the words of the prophets whom He sent.

The national catastrophe of Israel owes its origin, in a word, to the folly of heart, which led them to forget that the sole condition of their being owned as God's people must ever be their subjection, wholly, to His declared will. They were a "foolish nation"[8] the moment they began to think themselves to be something, on the strength of national privilege, in such a manner as to lose sight of their immediate dependence upon God. Yet was there in their case, as compared with that of the Gentile body, a reasonable ground for this confidence. They were, as distinguished from the Gentiles, the chosen seed of Divine promise. The name of God as *their* God was published in His word, as a perpetual memorial of the preëminence of Israel among the peoples of the earth. The standing, on the other hand, of the Gentile branch is, as we have seen, solely by *faith*. Hereditary title can have no existence where the blessings to be enjoyed are ministered only by the Gospel of the *grace of God*. No privilege or hope stood in any way connected with the nations of the world apart from faith. The word preached might be known and received outwardly by those who heard it, and such reception might produce a nominal pro-

[7] Psalm l. *passim*. [8] Deut. xxxii. 6.

fession of Christ, but if unmixed with faith, it profited nothing.[9] Still they to whom it was fruitlessly addressed are judged according to the word they hear, as was the case with the people in the wilderness of old. God judges men according to the responsibilities attaching to the name which they assume.[1]

We have shown already, from other parts of God's word, what the testimony of the Spirit is to the rise and progress of evil in the Church of God. The end of this is judgment. As it was with the nation whose place the Gentile profession now holds, so will it be in due time with the grafted branch. In the case of Israel, a remnant of election was called out of the nation's ruin, and found its place in the new dispensation of Gentile mercy. The rest were blinded and dispersed in judgment. In the prophetic history of the Church dispensation, a similar result is disclosed. The continual progress of corruption would leave but a remnant of true believers at the end, who would still rejoice, in the midst of general earthly-mindedness and apostasy, in the blessed hope and glorious appearing of their God and Saviour. They would be awaiting the day of the revelation of the Lord, for the realization of their long-deferred hope of rest and glory;[2] loving and desiring that day the more earnestly, as they saw its approach indicated externally by the fulfilment, in the Church and in the world, of the several predictions which the grace of God had caused to be uttered, for the sake of those whose eyes should see the ripened evils of the last times.[3] It was the descent of the Holy Ghost from

[9] Heb. iv. 2.
[2] Jude 17–21.
[1] *Ante*, chap. ii. 17, *seq*.
[3] 2 Pet. iii. 2–4.

heaven that, in the former case, was the immediate preliminary to the change of dispensation; by the solemn renunciation of the people of Israel and their rulers, and the turning of the full stream of gracious testimony immediately towards the nations of the world. A last appeal was made to the heart of Jerusalem, by the preaching of the apostles; but the stretching out of the arms of Divine mercy was, as we know, requited by murderous and decisive proofs of unrepentant hatred and rejection on the part of the gainsaying people. God then proceeded to do His marvellous work. Severity and goodness showed themselves forth at the same time, but upon different objects. The nation was cut off, and the era of Gentile mercy began.[4]

The fruit of sovereign grace through the preaching of the Gospel, is the gathering out of the nations of the *Church of God*. Of the members of this Church the characteristic description is, that they had "turned from idols to serve the living and true God, and to wait for His Son from heaven."[5] The distinctive blessing of the Church, as well as of the individual Christian, is the indwelling Spirit of God. The substitution of form for life, and of word for power, was the natural progress of evil in corrupting the Church, if evil found its entrance there at all. The flesh having been once allowed to gain that grand victory over the Spirit, whereby nominal profession and external rites were held good as a title to Christian fellowship, the Spirit, where it moved at all in power within the professing body, would necessarily act in testimony against its position and

[4] Acts xiii.; Isa. xxix.   [5] 1 Thess. i. 9, 10.

its discerned evil. It did so. The result of this was to array a merely outward and natural "Christianity" against that which was really "*of God.*" The born-hatred of flesh against Spirit exercised its persecutive energy within the nominal fold of Christ. As it had been with the Jewish prophets, who suffered for the truth at the hands of those who yet said, "The Lord be praised!" so has it been, and still is, in the case of the professing Gentile body.

Now the judgment of God must have reference to the *aggregate body* of those who form, by their outward profession, a testimony for His name, to be approved or condemned. The dispensation of Gentile mercy, after having run its allotted time, will be terminated by that event which, from the beginning, was the distinctive hope of those who knew that mercy indeed, by the effectual grace of God. The Lord will *return.* His coming, as we have before seen, respects both the elect remnant of living believers, and the dead mass of apostate profession.[6] He will take the former to himself, transferring them to the sphere of eternal blessedness, which will be their manifested place in the dispensation yet to come.[7] He will execute the judgment written upon that which shall then be found unnumbered among the election of His love, though laden with the responsibility of having borne and dishonoured His most blessed and most holy name.

The excision thus, from the olive tree, of the reprobate Gentile branch, will be the preparation for

---

[6] Twice dead. Once by profession, to the world; and again dead to God, by apostasy from the faith. *Vide* Jude, *passim.*

[7] The dispensation of the fulness of times. Comp. *Notes on Ephesians;* i. 10.

the reïntroduction of the natural branches. That they were to be so replaced is a part of the mystery which it behoved the Church at Rome to know. The blindness which had happened to Israel was for a season only, and partial in its extent.[8] The appointed duration of this season of hardness is the incoming of the "fulness of the Gentiles." God has enclosed the Gentile dispensation within fixed limits, and has indicated those limits with a distinctness quite sufficient to guide the spiritual mind to right conclusions. Faith, rendered conversant with the mystery of the Divine dealings with Israel, by means of the sure word of truth, abides in Christ as its secure place of rest and blessing; and, while learning lessons of solemn yet fruitful instruction from the visible page of human events, as it unfolds itself in a continually increasing distinctness of approximation to the recorded testimony of the Holy Ghost, has yet no need of those events in order to form its judgment as to things to come. Led by the word of grace, it *knows* the manner of the God who suffers long, and patiently awaits the advent of its living and ever-blessed hope. Carnal self-confidence, on the other hand, mistaking a nominal profession for the true power of godliness, is nourishing itself as in a day of slaughter, and sporting itself with its own deceivings. Men are willingly ignorant of God's past ways in judgment, and utterly careless of the prophetic testimonies of His Word.[9]

Does, then, the Christian reader, who has weighed the apostle's general doctrine in these chapters, think that the Church has heeded the solemn caution here

[8] $ἀπὸ\ μέρους$.   [9] 2 Pet. iii.; James v. 5.

given? When we consider that until within the last half-century the idea of a national restoration of Israel seemed to have been almost entirely renounced: and when, even now, by far the greater measure of the real godliness of the day is devoted to objects which clearly indicate the persuasion, that it is the Gentile Church which is to be regarded as the minister of the world's millennial promise, it seems difficult to suppose an affirmative reply to such a question. The permissive settlement of a few foreign missionaries in the city of Jerusalem,[1] under the sanction of international treaty, and the erection there of a visible representation of two of the numerous and all-discordant bodies, into which the unity of the Church of God has been divided by man's sin, may be a matter of congratulation to those who look on Gentile Christianity as the means for filling the earth with blessing. It is, at least, a solemnly instructive fact, in proof of the practical neglect with which the warning of the Spirit has been received; since it plainly indicates an expectation that the restoration of Israel to its own olive-tree is to be effected mediately through the Gentile branch, instead of this being (as the apostle here declares) an act of God subsequent to the previous cutting off of the former. Misdirected though well-intentioned efforts of this kind afford but small encouragement of hope, to any who have learned, from the sure word of prophecy, that the founding of Zion shall be of the Lord, and that when He does build it up, it will be in the appearing of His glory.[2]

[1] I allude to the Anglo-Prussian Episcopal establishment, set up not many years since at Jerusalem.   [2] Ps. cii. 16.

But I will not dwell further upon this. May the Lord preserve the reader of these pages, as well as myself, from the easy snare of self-conceited wisdom. It is by the living truth of God that the simple are enlightened.[3] It is by the word of His lips alone that we can be kept from the paths of the destroyer.[4]

With regard to the expression, "fulness of the Gentiles," it stands in contrast with the diminishing of the nation.[5] It seems to be used here in reference to the advancement of the Gentile at the expense of Israel's disgrace. But it may, and probably does, refer also to the measure of Christ's harvest of Gentile election, to be reaped at His appearing; the partial blindness of Israel being compensated, more abundantly, by the ingathering of grace from every nation.[6] It is in the former sense, however, that the word seems to exert its chief force in the present verse. The world is now the object of God's testimony. The Son of God has given His flesh for the life of the world. The Spirit of grace thus declares the title of the crucified and risen Jesus as *Lord of all*.[7] The acceptance of the Gospel as the truth of God places its professors, dispensationally, under the direct government of God as His people. The professing Gentile world now holds that place.[8] It is

---

[3] Ps. cxix. 130. [4] Ps. xvii. 4.

[5] In verse 12, we have both words, πλήρωμα and ἥττημα, applied to Israel; the latter indicating its actual condition, the former expressing its prospective restoration.

[6] The Church began at Jerusalem. Israel's elect were thus, in an especial sense, the first-fruits (John i.), of which the Gentile election are the πλήρωμα, or full measure. *Historically*, therefore, the Church has a Jewish beginning, and a Gentile completion; while, mystically and essentially, it stands in *Christ*, remote alike from the old man under either of its conditions. [7] Chap. xiv. 9.

[8] Dispensationally only. For in no other sense is it true that the Gentiles are, as such, owned of God. What the Church of God is,

this which is the very ground of the judgment which is to act against that which has a name to live, but is dead.

Now the things before mentioned as consequences of the national fall of Israel are these. First, the turning of God to the Gentiles. Secondly, the dispensational establishment of a Gentile body as His people. Thirdly, the decision of God's judgment as to the substituted Gentile branch, according to the responsibilities attached to the nominal owning of Christ. But all these things have their place and their accomplishment during the period of Israel's depression, and the last of them is, as we have seen, the immediate antecedent to the return of Jehovah with everlasting kindness to His ancient people.

Accordingly the apostle proceeds (verse 26), "And *so* all Israel shall be saved,"[9] &c. The purpose of God is to save the nation—*all* Israel: the election of that day will be the entire people. But the heart of Jerusalem must be washed[1] before salvation can be placed in Zion for Israel His glory.[2] Hence the advent of Him who is to turn away ungodliness from Jacob, is the truth next stated. As Christ died for

in which there is neither Jew nor Gentile, is not now in question. But although the Gentile masses under Christian profession constitute, in this sense, the nominal people of God, it is on grounds quite distinct from the special standing which belongs to the natural seed of Israel. Never can an Englishman, for instance, simply as a member of the nation to which he belongs, apply justly to his own countrymen the words of Isaiah: "The Lord is our judge, the Lord is our lawgiver, the Lord is our King; He will save us." (Isa. xxxiii. 22.) To do so, would be to usurp the place of that nation whose truthful appeal is to be yet made in the latter day: "*We* are thine, thou never barest rule over them (the Gentiles); *they* were not called by thy name." (Isa. lxiii. 19. Compare Amos iii. 2.)

[9] $\text{Καὶ οὕτω πᾶς 'Ισραὴλ σωθήσεται, κ. τ. λ.}$
[1] Jer. iv. 14.   [2] Isa. xlvi. 13.

that nation in the day of His gracious humiliation, when His judgment was taken away, even so shall He again appear to claim Zion as His own, and to turn away iniquity from Jacob. He shall come out of Zion as the deliverer;[3] for He will be in that day the strength of the children of Israel, when the dark night of Jacob's trouble shall have come to its close, and be already dawning into the morning without clouds.[4] But in that day there shall be also a fountain opened to the house of David, and to the inhabitants of Jerusalem, for sin and for uncleanness.[5] Then will the once-rejected Jesus be known, as the Saviour of His people, both from their outward enemies and from their then acknowledged sins. For Israel shall be saved in the Lord, with an everlasting salvation, when their eyes open on the day which He hath made.[6] The verse next following claims for Israel the full blessing of the New Covenant. Already it has been shown that both the covenants are *theirs*,[7] though the Church, as foretrusting in Christ, enjoys the fatness of the blessing, while the natural object of the covenant remains as yet an outcast.

Verse 28 is important as a confirmation of the general argument. It clearly implies that Israel *cannot* be recovered by the preaching of the Gospel. "As touching the Gospel they are *enemies* for your sakes." The alienation of Jacob is of equal duration

---

[3] "Ἥξει ἐκ Σιὼν ὁ ῥυόμενος, κ. τ. λ. This is not an exact quotation from the LXX., nor, on the other hand, is it a close translation of the Hebrew of Isaiah lix. 20. It is a repetition by the Spirit of God of His former testimony, with such verbal change as might serve to render its application to the actual subject more distinct and emphatic.
[4] Joel iii. 16, 17.
[5] Zech. xiii. 1.
[6] Isa. xlv. 17; Ps. cxviii. 10–24.
[7] Chap. ix.

with the present ministry of reconciliation.[8] I do not see that the expression will bear limitation. The Gospel is to be preached as a witness of the truth of God's grace, and of the saving power and coming glory of Christ. It is to be preached thus to all nations. But the conversion of Israel will be by other means. Yet the time of their conversion will surely arrive; for, "as touching the election they are beloved for the fathers' sakes." We have here the term election directly applied to the *nation*. It is used anticipatively as to the order of fact, because, as we have already seen, he elsewhere contrasts the election as a present thing with the nation in its apostasy. But it expresses the purpose of God, according to the breadth and completeness of which the entire nation will in due time be saved. His elect, when brought into the prepared mercy of Him who has chosen them, will long enjoy the work of their hands.[9]

The grand principle on which rests all the stability of creature blessing is then stated (verse 29) in its application, not to the elect Church, but to the dishonoured nation, as still held fast in the unchanging faithfulness of the God of promise. He who has spoken good of Israel's latter days, "is not a man that He should lie, neither the Son of man that He should repent.[1]

Verses 30, 31, require the more attention from their exhibiting one of the few instances in which the usually accurate authorized version is evidently

[8] Strictly speaking, even longer, as the Book of Revelation seems to show: but the leading features of the dispensation are alone the subject in this chapter.
[9] Isa. lxv. 22.   [1] Numb. xxiii. 19.

at fault. Nor is the mistake unimportant. The verses as they stand in our English Bibles afford quite a justification (if, as is too often the case, they be read apart from their context) of the common but delusive view of Gentile continuance referred to in an earlier page of this chapter. The mistake lies in the 31st verse, which should be read thus: "Even so these also have now not believed your mercy, that they also may obtain mercy."[2] The more critical reader is referred to the note at the foot of this page. Meanwhile, I remark that with this, as I venture to say, *necessary* change, the passage is not only consistent with itself, but entirely so with the preceding argument, a continuance of which it is. As the passage is now misrepresented it quite contradicts the whole doctrine of dispensational sequence and its accompaniments, so solemnly laid down by the apostle in the verses which precede.

I can only attribute the very forced construction which our Translators furnish of verse 31 to a gener-

---

[2] I quote the whole passage. ["Ωσπερ γὰρ καὶ ὑμεῖς ποτὲ ἠπειθήσατε τῶ θεῷ νῦν δὲ ἠλεήθητε τῇ τούτων ἀπειθείᾳ,] οὕτω καὶ οὗτοι νῦν ἠπείθησαν τῷ ὑμετέρῳ ἐλέει, ἵνα καὶ αὐτοὶ ἐλεηθῶσι. I think I may venture to affirm that ordinary rules of construction demand that the words τῷ ὑμετέρῳ ἐλέει be regarded as the object of the verb immediately preceding, as in the case of τῷ Θεῷ in the verse before. This is no correction of mine. I believe the common rendering of verse 31 is generally condemned by those acquainted with the original. I add Luther's translation of that verse, as follows: "*Also auch jene haben jetzt nicht wollen glauben an die Barmherzigkeit, die euch widerfahren ist, auf dass sie auch Barmherzigkeit überkommen.*" This is further confirmed by Tyndale's version: "Even so now have they not beleved the mercy which is happened vnto you, that they also maye obtayne mercy." It is noticeable that verse 30 is entirely wanting in the *Codex Sinaiticus*, an omission which I have indicated by brackets in the above quotation. This is a fact of interest, as bearing upon the question of construction, though the presence of the bracketed words seems almost necessary for the full expression of the apostle's meaning.

ally prevailing misapprehension of the context, in their day even more than in our own. According to the verse as altered above, the argument stands thus: They had disbelieved the mercy to the Gentiles, that which should have been for their welfare becoming a trap.[3] They had utterly rejected the counsel of God against themselves.[4] The effect of this was their degradation to the level of Gentile distance from God. But this was in order to bring them, as a nation, within the effectual reach and operation of that absolute mercy which, in Christ, was the appointed means of Israel's blessing. The promises made to the fathers could be fulfilled only in the way of perfect *grace*. The promises are yea and amen *in Christ*. The Divine love, then, which chose the fathers, and contained, for their sakes, the nation in the unrepented purpose of ultimate favour, must express itself to the children in the way of pure mercy. The assertion of their right had produced their ruin. Going about to establish their own righteousness, they had stumbled and been broken upon the rock of offence. The vindication of *Immanuel's* right as the stone and shepherd of Israel, will be the visitation of the outcasts in the fulness of a mercy that never shall be taken away—the sure mercies of David.[5]

This mercy, sure and abiding in its effects, is not less comprehensive in its extent. It is elsewhere written, "In the Lord shall *all* the seed of Israel be justified, and shall glory;"[6] and similar is the language of the apostle in the verse next following, "For God hath concluded all in unbelief, that He might

[3] *Ante*, verse 9.   [4] 1 Thess. ii. 15, 16.
[5] Isa. lv. 3.   [6] Isa. xlv. 25.

have mercy upon all." I only remark on this verse, that while the common translation gives a just and consistent meaning as far as it goes, yet the needless introduction of the pronoun "them" renders the force of the words rather ambiguous.[7]

The apostle has now arrived at the close of the general argument, in which he has been unfolding the glory of Divine wisdom and power in the varied dealings of God, whether with Jew or Gentile. The present verse, being a *résumé* of the whole, expresses in a word the main principle on which all those dealings turn. To make man, whether Jew or Gentile, a debtor to *mercy*, is God's purpose. We have seen how this has been exemplified in the calling of the Church, and how it is to be fulfilled yet more abundantly in the future reëstablishing of Israel. God thus, as the fulfiller of His own purposes in the way of mercy, is discovered to be the "hope of Israel, the Saviour" still.[8] The Law had entered, destroying in its result all hope. But the hand of mercy is guided to the recovery of the nation by the counsels of eternal truth, which did not suffer the entrance of the Law until the certainty of the destined blessing had been first secured in the word of irrevocable promise.

The remaining verses of this chapter express to us the effect which his meditation of the ways of God produced on the mind of the apostle. Solemn, indeed, as well as infinitely precious, is the knowledge of those ways which, to the Christian, as having the

---

[7] Συνέκλεισε γὰρ ὁ Θεὸς τοὺς πάντας εἰς ἀπείθειαν ἵνα τοὺς πάντας ἐλεήσῃ. I cannot doubt that the reference is here to verse 30, as well as 31; that τοὺς πάντας, that is, includes Gentiles as well as Jews. [8] Jer. xv. 8, xvii. 13.

mind of Christ, are thus unfolded in the word of truth. The destined effect of such knowledge is to fill the souls of God's children with a profounder sense of the amazing riches of that grace which has deemed poor outcast sinners to be fitting objects, through the Divinely furnished atonement of the Lamb, of a mercy which not only has eternally obliterated all memory of their iniquity, and made them to shine in brightness before the face of God, but has also rendered them capable of *fellowship* with God, in the understanding of His mind. There is a knowledge, the effect of which is to puff up and deceive its possessor;[9] which, even though accurate, as it respects truth in the letter, is not the knowledge of God in the Spirit. There is another knowledge, acquired instrumentally through the same word of truth, but learned neither by intellectual diligence and acuteness of research, nor as the easily comprehended outline of the Divine dealings which may be presented to the mind in the way of human exposition. It is such knowledge as God alone can teach, and which He ever delights to communicate to the hearts and understandings of His children. It is a part of that wisdom which is found only with the lowly, but which baffles while it judges the prying inquisition of the fleshly mind.[1] Such knowledge, while it informs the mind of coming events, and acquaints it beforehand with the terrors of the God of judgment; yet, because it is an understanding of God Himself, and not merely of events ordained of Him, acts as the healthful and nourishing diet of the soul, which gives firm strength to the man of God

[9] 1 Cor. iii. 18, and viii. 2.   [1] Prov. xi. 2; Col. ii. 18; 2 Cor. x.

when, as a soldier of Christ, he is called to stand, for His name, in the evil day.

What prepares a Christian's soul for advantageous meditation on the word of God generally, is a just appreciation of the grace in which, as a blood-redeemed child of mercy, he stands already before Him. Knowledge is the portion of those who first have obtained "precious faith." It is to this faith that knowledge is to be added.[2] To be growing in the grace and knowledge of our Lord and Saviour Jesus Christ,[3] is the natural progress of Christian life, where the unhindered energy of the Spirit is doing its blessed work as the leader of the sons of God. All such knowledge, while it both interests and delights the mind of a spiritual man, still keeps it humble in the presence of that God whose loving mercy in Christ is the satisfying portion of his heart.[4] The result is to render the instructed Christian a more fervent, because a more intelligent, worshipper of the blessed God. It was the profound view vouchsafed to the apostle of the mysteries of Divine wisdom, that called forth from his heart this tribute of adoring admiration. Those ways, which are past finding out by human search, are now expounded by the all-searching Spirit of Christ; and are spread forth before the eye of faith, for the more abundant comfort and blessing of those whose perfecting in grace is with a view to their initiation into the true wisdom of God.[5] The knowledge of Him as purposing all things, as filling all things, as effecting all things, as containing all things, makes the shadow of the Almighty to be

---

[2] 2 Pet. i. 5.   [3] 2 Pet. iii. 18.
[4] Chap. v. 5.   [5] Comp. 1 Cor. ii. 7–16; Col. iii. 10.

a present and appreciated reality to the heart and conscience of the watchful saint. The remembrance that He who inhabiteth eternity, dwelling in the light which no man can approach unto,[6] is become, in the perfection of His nature and the glory of His power, the assured portion, in Christ, of the poor believing sinner; while it deepens evermore the astonishment of his joy, in proportion to his growing acquaintance with the God who has redeemed him, keeps him firm set upon the deep-laid foundation of eternal mercy, which upholds him for ever as an acceptable vessel of His praise.

[6] Isaiah lvii. 15; 1 Tim. vi. 15, 16.

CHAPTER XII.

WE enter now upon the last of the three great divisions of this wonderful Epistle. The apostle has opened to us at large, in the three chapters last examined, the mystery of the present dispensation. The subject which forms the material of those chapters is so complete in itself, that it is capable of being regarded independently both of the preceding part of the Epistle, and of the chapters which follow, and it may be sometimes profitable to consider it separately. But let it not be supposed that it is a mere parenthesis in the Epistle. If we recur to the close of the eighth chapter, we shall find that the point to which the Spirit of God had there conducted the believer, presented to him a bright and cloudless view of the glory and unalterable blessedness of his hope as an assured heir of salvation; God himself, in Christ, being the eternal portion of his inheritance.

Passing thence, to the subject of the ninth and two following chapters, the same blessed Spirit has opened to us a deep and solemn insight into the mysteries of the kingdom and glory of God, as they relate to the display whether of power or of mercy, and as they pertain to the glorifying of His name in faithfulness and wisdom, as the accomplisher of His own unrepented promise. The bright line of inextinguishable light which leads the believing soul, as a clue, through every maze of the labyrinth of human circumstance, is the enduring mercy of God. Read by that light, the mysteries of the kingdom contain no terror for the simple heart of faith. The solemn spectacle of Divine severity in the case of the natural branches, and the yet deeper woe which awaits its accomplishment in the judgment and rejection of the grafted shoot of Gentilism, although both fitted and intended to teach sobriety of mind, and to set God's children on their watch-tower,[1] can in no wise shake their trust. Receiving a kingdom which cannot be shaken, they rest securely on the faithfulness of Him whom they fear no more as strangers, but as sons.[2]

Knowledge has now been added to faith, and its effect is to enlarge the believer's comprehension of the grace in which he stands. And now, returning from what might seem to be, but is not in reality, his *digression*, the apostle proceeds, in the remainder of his work, to treat more at large the question of practical obedience in service. The manner in which exhortation is combined with, and made the vehicle of still increasing instruction, presents itself remarkably in the chapter now before us.

Verses 1, 2. "I beseech you therefore," &c. The ground on which exhortation is here addressed to the believer is his own subjective acquaintance with mercy.[3] An appeal is made to the hearts of the

---

[1] Comp. Habak. iii. 16-19.   [2] Heb. xii. 28, 29.

[3] "I beseech you διὰ τῶν οἰκτιρμῶν τοῦ Θεοῦ." There is a difference between the terms ἔλεος and οἰκτιρμός, as used in the New Testament, which it is desirable to notice. They appear to me to be distinguished thus. The former signifies "mercy" as an attribute of God simply, without any special reference to its object. The latter denotes rather "compassion," as respecting more directly the condi-

brethren as being themselves personally conversant with the mercies of God. The effect of tasted grace had been to acquaint them with God as their portion.[4] The proper aim, therefore, to which the residue of their mortal life should be directed was the glory of God. They were His. Originally such, as creatures of His power, they were now become so in a new and especial sense, as new-created in Christ to the praise of His glory. The "reasonable service," then, of a Christian is devotedness to God. It belongs to the character of all whose glory it is to confess themselves the creatures of Divine mercy, to be in unreserved subjection of His will.[5] Self-denial is to such a commanding principle of conduct. But this, which is a negative thing, is subordinate to and produced by a positive principle, anterior in its possession of the heart of the believer; love, namely, towards Him whom we desire to serve.[6] There is a *self-affliction* which is not, properly speaking, self-denial at all; because, as it proceeds upon a false estimate of the requirements of the Divine will, formed in the soul's ignorance of completed mercy and grace in Jesus, it is but one form of self suppressing and supplanting another. A legal or self-righteous heart is incapable of self-denial in the true sense of the term, because it really is self that is

---

tion of him who receives mercy. The active display of grace, while it originates in the ἔλεος of God, acts towards the poor outcast sinner as οἰκτιρμός, and is as such owned on his part. Hence the practical force of the present appeal. They had received all the rich blessings of the heavenly calling in Christ, not only through the will of the Divine mercy in giving Jesus, but also through the especial compassion of Him who had begotten them severally again, and had brought up each of their souls from destruction through the gift of saving faith.

[4] 1 Pet. ii. 3.   [5] 1 Pet. iv. 2.   [6] 1 John iv. 12; Gal. v. 6.

ultimately sought. The alabaster box of very precious ointment can be broken for the feet of Jesus, only by the hands of one whose heart is filled to overflowing with the first love of a Saviour.[7]

That the bodies of God's saints are demanded as a living sacrifice to Himself, is a consequence of their being indwelt by the Spirit of adoption. It is clear, therefore, that no hand can offer such sacrifice but that of faith. If a Christian is truly conversant with the doctrine of the cross, so as to be realizing by his faith the power of the resurrection, his standard of practical conduct will be according to the declared truth of his position, as already *in Christ* brought nigh to God. And how real, how wondrous, a nearness is that! But in proportion to the believer's hearty appreciation of this nearness as the effect of redemption, will be his feebleness of desire and ineptitude for the enjoyment of that which feeds and gratifies the will either of the flesh or of the mind. A soul full of Christ *cannot* enjoy the world. It is impossible. But Christians are not always full of Christ. They should be so—they may be so. But, alas! too often it is with far different meat that the soul which He has bought is filled. What keeps us in the place of certain and conscious blessing is a watchful abiding in Christ by faith. And where spiritual declension has occurred, and the soul has become enfeebled through its wanderings from the only source of strength, its true and healthful tone can be effectually recovered by no other means than a recurrence to those springs of pure and unupbraiding mercy from whence, in its original discernment of the cross,

[7] Luke vii. 47.

it first drew the sweet water of life out of the fulness of the living God. There, and there only, amid the busy recollections of faithful but ill-requited mercies, will that true contrition of heart be realized, which is the chief moral element of all genuine communion with God.[8]

In the second verse, nonconformity to the world is pressed upon the conscience as a responsibility, attaching necessarily to those who, having been established in the liberty of Christ through the knowledge of His resurrection from the dead,[9] would, by a continued conformity to the maxims and practices of the present world, be practically falsifying their profession. Such a responsibility, however, can, as has been already said, be recognized only by an active and rejoicing *faith*, which, with a just appreciation of its calling, counts the present world a place of trial, and a sphere of fruitful service,[1] rather than a garden of delights.[2] True knowledge of God produces, as its result, a willing ignorance of the world. Not that indifference to secular life in its busier and more exciting forms, which is often the effect merely of constitutional temperament, and which may well

---

[8] Isa. lvii. 15.   [9] Chap. vi. *passim*.
[1] Luke xix. 13; John xii. 26.
[2] Wide indeed is the difference which exists between true Christian devotedness, and that thankless asceticism which forgets and dishonours the God who gives us all things richly to enjoy. To the free all things are lawful, and to the pure all things are pure. So far from the enjoyment of natural blessings being incompatible with spirituality of mind, it is the spiritual man alone who can enjoy them rightly. Natural pleasures are such as the world pursues, because it has not the Spirit. They are called in Scripture "the pleasures of sin," not so much on account of the immoral character or tendencies of some among them, as because they are followed in the spirit of natural wilfulness and insubjection to the truth of God. Their votaries are accordingly described as "lovers of pleasures rather than lovers of God;" His fear being hidden from their eyes.

consist with an entire absence of saving faith; but such a disregard of the world's habits and principles of action as is produced by practical holiness, and which still increases, as the man of God is more habitually conversant with the path of *life*. For the true service of God consists in a willing surrender of ourselves to the absolute disposal of His own good pleasure. The activities of the Spirit's energy, in forming and filling the mind of a believer, find their occupation, and take their direction, from the varied expression of the *will of God*, as it stands revealed in the word of truth. The present world[3] is the thing here warned against.

The reason is plain. It was to deliver us from this present evil world that Jesus died at the will of our God and Father.[4] Until the Lord return, whose right it is to possess all things, conformity to the world is enmity to the cross of Christ. For the course of this world is governed, not by the Spirit of God, who glorifies Jesus, but by the power of darkness, which rejected Him.[5] Satan is the prince and the god of this world.[6] He is judged, it is true, and the time is near when he shall be finally bruised under the feet of His children by the God of peace. But as yet he rules the world, and directs its ways. Its lively amusements and its serious pursuits are, equally with its grosser forms of vice, the ministers

[3] Αἰών is the word used, not κόσμος. We well know what we mean when we speak of the course and spirit of the *age*. This is just the meaning of "world" here. The contrast is between the drift and progress of the natural mind according to the current of the world's ways, and the distinct assertion of the will of God, as the regulating principle of ordinary life, on the part of those whose glory is to be in this world as servants of One whom the world knoweth not.

[4] Gal. i. 4.   [5] Luke xxii. 53.   [6] John xvi. 11; 2 Cor. iv. 4.

of his rule. He governs the world by the natural lusts of men—the desires of the flesh and of the mind. The world, therefore, stands, *in all its forms*, in perpetual contrariety to the truth as it is in Jesus.[7] Separateness, consequently, from its fellowship, and nonconformity to its maxims and its ways, must always be the result of spiritual energy in the soul.

To prove the perfect will of God is the calling and responsibility of a child of God. What is requisite for this end is here stated to be the renewing of the *mind*.[8] "Be ye transformed by the renewing of your mind, that ye may prove," &c. The mind of nature is reprobate, as already has been shown;[9] but a believer has the mind of Christ. With respect to the instrumentality of thought and judgment, the faculties of the mind, like the members of the body, may be used either for good or for evil, for holiness or for sin. Now, the natural and ceaseless tendency of every man's mind is *from* God, and towards the world in some shape. But there is in a Christian a power of government competent to the control and management of that which is naturally averse from God, so as to turn it into an instrument of obedience to His will. This power is the living Spirit of God and of Christ. There is, moreover, another thing to be remembered. The Christian is himself a new creature. It is not only true that the Spirit dwells in the heart of a saint, producing thence the cry, "Abba, Father." The man is himself renewed. There is an "inner man," which the Holy Ghost may and does strengthen, indefinitely, as to the measure of its comprehension of Divine things,[1] and which may

[7] 2 Cor. vi. 14–18. [8] νοῦς. [9] Chap. i. 28. [1] Eph. iii. 16.

be renewed by the same blessed Spirit day by day,[2] but which we must not confound with the power that thus acts upon it.

Now it is the possession of this new nature, this distinct principle of life, (quite separate from, and incongruous with, that which is of the old nature,) that renders the Christian accessible to the warnings or the exhortations, in a word, to the ministry generally of Divine truth. But, side by side with this new nature, and on every side encompassing it, there is found the old man still; dead, as we have seen, *in truth*, according to the effectual judgment of God in the cross, but living still in fact, and ever striving for the mastery of the believer's way.

The word of exhortation is intended, by its action on the conscience of a Christian, to quicken the energies of his inner man to the more effectual assertion of the glory of God; by like-mindedness to Christ,[3] and consequent subjection to the Father. True Christian conduct is not that negative holiness only, which consists in abstinence from moral evil in obedience to the commandments of God. It is the fruit and expression of an energy which has its birthplace in the soul's communion with God in Christ,[4] and which, in a thorough and happy consciousness that its own interests and those of the Master which it serves are identical, seeks its end in the positive accomplishment of His will. It is, therefore, a progressive thing. Every real believer has been sanctified once for all to God, through the precious blood which has washed him, and the Spirit which has sealed him; as now no longer his own, but pertaining

[2] 2 Cor. iv. 16.   [3] Phil. ii. 5.   [4] 1 John iv. 19.

to Him who has bought him with a price. But there is another sense in which a Christian is said to be sanctified, namely, as the result of single-hearted devotedness to the Lord, which, making *Him* the sole object of life and action, is withdrawn more and more from harmful contact with evil, whether in the Church or in the world. Dissociation, in the power of a word-enlightened conscience, *from all evil*, is the just effect of the sanctification of the Lord Himself in the heart.[5] A Christian who walks thus is said to be a vessel *sanctified*, and meet for the Master's use, and prepared unto every good work.[6] Conscience thus becomes the regulating spring of all true service, reäcting with healthful effect upon the faith by which alone we stand.[7]

So intimate a connection subsists between the mind and conscience, that what defiles one defiles the other also.[8] The natural object of a believer's contemplation is Christ; and where the Lord is kept steadily before our faces, a moral conformity to His perfections is always in some measure the result. As it is elsewhere written: "We all, with open face beholding, as in a glass, the glory of the Lord, *are changed* into the same image from glory to glory, as by the Spirit of the Lord."[9] If, however, faith be suffered, through inaction, to lose sight of this its proper object, other and nearer ones never fail to engage the mind's attention. Spiritual indifference is the result of worldly preöccupation. A careless or inactive Christian thinks only of himself, and thus has no mind left for Christ.

---

[5] 1 Pet. iii. 15.   [6] 2 Tim. ii. 21.
[7] "Holding faith, *and* a good conscience; which some having put away, concerning faith have made shipwreck." (1 Tim. i. 19.)
[8] Tit. i. 15.   [9] 2 Cor. iii. 18.

His conscience ceases to act healthfully, as the consequence of this. A dulling of every spiritual sense follows as the inevitable effect, because, God not being present continually to the mind, the thoughts are taken up with other things in His absence. Thus, while fundamentally the soul remains fast in Christ, there is a practical moving away from the hope of the Gospel, because the mind and affections are no longer occupied with the only things which can nourish and invigorate that hope.[1]

The renewing of the mind, then, is the thing here insisted on. All the old ideas and motive principles which once swayed the judgment, while as yet the knowledge of God had no place in the heart, have now to be exchanged for new ideas, new views, new intents, and new objects, which appear and are contemplated in the light which that knowledge affords. A Christian's glory, as a new man in Christ, is that he is capable of pleasing God. As they that are in the flesh *cannot* please God, because the carnal mind is enmity against Him, so the believer, because he is in the Spirit, cannot *but* please God, if only he walk as that blessed Guide would lead. The measure of a Christian's walk is Christ. "To me, to live is Christ," said he whose exhortation is now under our eyes. To follow him, as he followed Christ, would be to share his own happy consciousness of having walked unto well-pleasing before God.[2]

The thing which Satan endeavours to infuse into the minds of those who are established in the grace of the Gospel, and no longer doubt their personal acceptance, is a wrong judgment with respect to their

[1] Col. iii. 1–4. [2] 2 Cor. i. 12.

condition, not as sinners, but as *saints*. If ever the soul is allowed to meditate upon its blessings and its privileges apart from Christ, the effect is invariably to render a man self-complacent, even though he may be fully conscious that his blessings are the effect of pure grace. It was a forgetfulness of this that brought on the Corinthian saints so searching and humiliating a rebuke, when with kingly pretensions they were exhibiting the ignorance and foolishness of babes.[3] Thinking of *Christ* brings me in spirit *before God*. Thinking of what I am only, as a partaker of Christ, unless my thoughts proceed far enough to perceive the *end* of my redemption, and to find it to be God, uplifts rather than humbles; because no thought of acquired blessing is, in itself, sufficient to set the soul in its true place before God. We must know not only that we *are* blessed, but how, and why, and where we are thus blessed. Now, it is *in* Christ that a believer is the favoured, because beloved, object of Divine regard. The Father's eye rests *there* upon the children of His love, in the fulness of that peace and welcome with which He joys for ever in the one Beloved.

A soul kept watchfully in the presence of God, through its constant communion with the blessed Person and the finished love of Christ, will surely be kept lowly. But the apostle knew how far this is from being the necessary consequence of a man's being in Christ. He knew this as taught of God, who would teach him, for our sakes, the solemn lesson (making Satan himself the instrument of imparting it[4]), that no man in the body of sin can bear the

[3] 1 Cor. iv. 8, *seq*.   [4] 2 Cor. xii. 7.

weight of Divine blessing, unless kept still abiding, in the spirit of his mind, under the holy though gracious eye of Him with whom we have to do.[5]

The manner in which, in the verse which follows (verse 3), he introduces his direct warning is striking. "I say, *through the grace given unto me, to every man,*" &c. If he speaks, it is as the oracles of God,[6] while that which he delivers has an inclusive application to himself no less than others. It is as one who, having himself obtained mercy,[7] now keeps his course as a true follower of Christ, through the sustaining power of His grace,[8] that he seeks thus, with the authority of an apostle and the heart of a fellow-servant, to direct his brethren in the way. With respect to the point of his exhortation, it is to sobriety of judgment and lowliness of mind. The will of God being the object of Christian service, real devotedness must consist in depreciation and denial of self. But a Christian is a prepared servant of God. He has his *measure* of faith. The danger therefore is, that if he does not fall asleep through indolence, he will outrun the bidding of the Lord at the spur of his natural will.

Under the mask of godly zeal and desire, commodious place is often found for the action of the fleshly mind. Pretensions are easily asserted, and to the outward eye *maintained*, which are not really to the glory of God, because they are unsustained by faith. The possession of all the gifts of the Spirit is no sufficient qualification for truly acceptable service, if the habitual position of the soul be not that of faith-

---

[5] Heb. iv. 12–16; 1 Pet. i. 15–17.   [6] 1 Pet. iv. 11.
[7] 2 Cor. iv. 1.   [8] 2 Cor. i. 12, iii. 5, xii. 9.

ful dependence upon God. Where He is duly remembered, there is always an adjustment of the work to the power which has been received, or which faith reckons on as available in Christ. A man finds his true place among his fellow-servants when he has found it first before the Lord. Esteeming, then, others better than himself, he may find that the active exercise of love, according to the measure of the faith that is given to him, has brought already a harvest of blessing and honour to his share, through the intrinsic virtue of the Name in which he wrought; while he thought only of sowing, with long patience, that the Lord Himself might reap, in the harvest ripened by His own gracious blessing, the fruitful abundance of His praise.

Verses 4–9. The apostle, having laid down the principle of individual conduct above stated, proceeds, in what follows, to view more largely the subject of Christian service under a twofold aspect. It is treated, first, in its relation to the position of the Christian as a member of the one body of Christ; and secondly, with respect to his separate calling, and the responsibilities which attach to him personally as a man in Christ. It is under the former of these heads that the subject is principally regarded in the present chapter. In the fourth and fifth verses the unity of the Church as the body of Christ, and the constituent relationship of every Christian, both to the entire body and to each of the several members composing it, are stated and illustrated. The doctrine which is here presented is in a high degree important to any one by whom the perfect will of God is accepted as the present aim of life.

We must remark in the first place, that what is here stated is an *unalterable truth*. We, being many, *are* one body in Christ. We are, if believers, every one members one of another. The question before us, it must be remembered, is Christian service. The direction of the Spirit of God as to one great sphere of this service is based upon a statement of the unity of the body of Christ, and of the Christian's consequent relation to that one body, and to all other Christians whatsoever, in regard to their several participation in the same constituent membership.[9] This is an established truth, which neither time nor circumstance can destroy. The practical recognition of it, on the part of the believer, will be according to the paucity or abundance of his own communion with God in the truth itself.

An apprehension of the unity of Christ's body, as a positive revelation of the Spirit of grace, places the believer's conscience under the government of that doctrine as a portion of the truth by which he is to be practically sanctified.[1] The utter dissolution of the outward structure of the Church, through the folly and sin of man, does not at all affect the principle here stated. A Christian may, indeed, look in vain in the present day for the corporate unity of the Church of the living God, the pillar and ground of the truth. Nevertheless, the truth which man has

[9] The doctrine of the unity of the Church, as the body of Christ, is treated most fully in the Epistle to the Ephesians; where the Church is not only viewed in its finished blessing in heavenly places in Christ, but is set upon its foundations and shown forth to view as the habitation of God through the Spirit upon earth. The same subject is again presented, though not from the same point of view, nor with the same immediate object, both in the Epistle to the Colossians and the First Epistle to the Corinthians.

[1] John xvii. 17.

dishonoured remains as at the first. It remains a witness, indeed, of the general apostasy of the professing Church, but for the guidance also and comfort of those who, in any day of darkness, and under all circumstances of discouragement, are willing to confess and not deny the *whole* truth of God. There is not a Christian alive in Christ who has not a claim upon the affection of all saints. As it is the quickening power of the God of grace which puts a man in Christ, not at the desire of his natural will, but by the effectual working of the Divine good pleasure, through the faith of the Gospel; so also, as a Christian, he has an interest, both of affection and of debt, in all who are partakers with him of like precious faith. Would God that the gracious obligations of love in the Spirit were felt and acknowledged by us, according to their value in the scale of truth! The factitious ties of special membership, which now draw Christians more apart from each other in proportion to the strength of those ties, would then be set aside and replaced by the one living bond of perfectness, according to which the true unity of the Spirit may alone be practically confessed.[2]

In close connection with the doctrine of the unity of the body, we have next brought before us the subject of Christian ministry, so far as it pertains to the Church itself as the sphere of its exercise (ver. 6–9).

The source and power of this ministry—elsewhere more fully stated, where the sovereignty of the Divine presence and the distributive grace and energy of the Holy Ghost in the Church are in question[3]—are here intimated only by the general reference which

[2] Col. iii. 15; 1 John ii. 10.   [3] 1 Cor. xii.-xiv.

is made (verse 6) to *God*, as the bestower of grace and gift. The question of ministry is viewed in this chapter, not so much with reference to the individual responsibilities of the servant to his Master, as in connection with the doctrine of membership in the body. What the Church is to *itself* is here the apostle's subject, and not what it is to the world. The believer, thus, while always retaining untouched his own proper and exclusive relation to the Lord, whether in respect of blessing or responsibility, is here brought practically within the proper sphere of his privilege and service, as a member of the one body.

The body is the thing to be lived for and laboured for, because it is *Christ's*. One's own blessing and comfort are not the just measure of spiritual desire and attainment, but the will of God. But God's object is the Church. The gifts of His love, and the operations of His power, are for the edifying of the body of Christ, for the accomplishment of the perfect man, the attainment effectually of the measure of the stature of the fulness of Christ.[4] Hence, the heart-interest of every one who is spiritual will be the well-being of God's saints as such. It is for this, moreover, that we are responsible, inasmuch as we are, as God's workmanship, severally members one of another, being settled each into his appointed place in the body, according to the tempered unity of Divine adjustment, as it has pleased Him whose workmanship the body is.[5]

The same Holy Spirit that reveals to the believer the richness of his portion, as personally blessed in

[4] Eph. iv.   [5] 1 Cor. xii. 24.

Christ, acts also upon his heart and conscience by means of the word which makes manifest the perfect will of God. Subjection, therefore, of mind to the Spirit of Christ would surely produce, as its result, a measure of communion with the thoughts of Christ, which ever have the Church as their object. Christ loves the *Church*, and not only the souls individually which compose it. The remembrance of this opens to the soul of a Christian a new and special range of service, quite distinct from the line of personal faithfulness which he has to follow, as a witness for Christ in the world. The Lord has a claim upon him, not only for a holy walk in the presence of his fellow-men, that the way of truth may be glorified,[6] but also for an obedience to His new and special commandment. His joy is in His people in proportion to their practical like-mindedness to Him.[7]

With respect to the sphere of this ministry, it is the *Church of God*, without reference to locality or circumstance. Being a gift[8] from God, it must, if rightly exercised, be independent of all human control. The holder of the gift is responsible for its use to Him who gave it, and to Him alone. The condition, moreover, of its effectual operation is immediate and conscious dependence upon God; for at no time can any ministry be exercised, with profit to the minister, unless faith is in actual exercise toward God. The possession of a gift is not in itself sufficient for the accomplishment of profitable ministry.[9] A gift may be really present, yet utterly misused. It will be so, when the soul is not kept watchfully in

---

[6] Matt. v. 16; 1 Pet. ii. 12.   [7] John xv. 9–12.
[8] Χάρισμα.   [9] 1 Cor. xiv. *passim*.

the presence of the Giver of the gift. It is according to the practical nearness of the soul to God that efficacy for any service is acquired. The spring of it all is devotedness to Christ, and to the Church for His sake: "ourselves your servants for Jesus' sake,"[1] as he said whose more abundant zeal is our pattern and, too often, our shame.

The varied distribution, also, of ministerial gift is to be noted.[2] God has ordained, for the ministry of His grace, not one channel of supply, but many. The distinction between office and gift is quite clear. The latter is antecedent to, and qualifies for, the former. A man cannot fulfil the office of a teacher who has not received ability from God to teach. But if he has his ability from God, he has also full authority to exercise that, in responsibility to Him, which He has conferred for the accomplishment of His own will in the edifying of the Church. Where the Spirit of the Lord is, there is *liberty*, not only from the bondage of an evil conscience, but from all other restraints than that of His own presence.[3] But the abiding resting-place of the Spirit of the Lord is the Church of God. It is a habitation of God through the Spirit.[4] Although, therefore, the Holy Ghost might, and certainly sometimes did, confer a spiritual gift by some intermediate channel, as through an apostle;[5] or by a special indication of Divine choice might select by prophecy, and qualify for special service in the Church by a mediate communication of peculiar gift,[6] yet it is manifest that the distri-

[1] 2 Cor. iv. 5.
[2] Comp. for this purpose, Eph. iv. 11–13, and 1 Cor. xii. 27–31.
[3] 2 Cor. iii. 17.   [4] Eph. ii. 22.
[5] 2 Tim. i. 6. See also *ante*, chap. i. 11.   [6] 1 Tim. iv. 14.

bution of such gifts was generally immediate, even as it was always at the sovereign will and direction of the Spirit of God that they were distributed and conferred. The premonitory caution already noticed[7] is a sufficient proof of this. The apostle evidently, in the present passage, regards membership and operative grace, according to the gift distributed to each, under the same point of view. Every member is necessary to the unity and completeness of the body, and each member has its own proper function, in harmony with the widely diverse yet equally-needed functions of the rest. Hence, while there is an enumeration here of certain ministries of a more demonstrative character and wider scope, as well as of public exercise, such as teaching, exhortation, &c., yet it is most instructive to remark how these more prominent and conspicuous ministries appear but as units in a crowd of spiritual energies which follow in detail, and which, along with the gifts of more extended power and more general effect, are the manifestation, in each particular case, of the *faith* which God has in measure apportioned to each member of the body.

True Christian ministry is a result of the Divine energy in the Church. It is not based on *man's* liberty to act as a member of the body. It is, on the contrary, the liberty of the *Spirit*, working according to the excellency of the perfect will of God, and in the sufficiency of *His own* power, through the special instruments of *His own* choice.[8] When a man, then, felt himself qualified to fulfil a certain ministry, the consciousness of power invested him at the same time

[7] Verse 3.   [8] 1 Cor. xii. 6–11.

with a responsibility to exercise the gift bestowed on him, to the glory of God. He became a debtor to his brethren according to the extent of the ability conferred. To fetter or obstruct this gift in its exercise, was to contend with God. Faith, however, and watchful dependence upon God, were absolutely necessary for the profitable exercise of the ministry, as they were also on the part of those ministered to, that God in all things might be glorified.[9] Blessing in result would doubtless be proportionate to the measure in which lowliness of mind and simplicity of dependence might enable God, who giveth grace to the humble, to act in power by means of the ministry of His own grace.

I must again and again remind the reader, that the Church of the living God consists of members themselves alive in Christ. Facts, alas! flow in upon us in overwhelming abundance, in proof of the non-existence in the present day of any such practical manifestation of the unity of Christ's living body, as that which is contemplated by the Spirit of God in the chapter before us. God's Church indeed still lives, and cannot die, because its life is Christ himself. Nor can a single living member be found *finally* wanting in the place which the creative grace of God has assigned to it. But while the aim of the Spirit's teaching is to bring the Church on earth into a faithful conformity to the perfect pattern in the heavens, how different has been the result! The living Church presents its visible unity nowhere to our view. There are living units in dead masses. There are spiritual exceptions to carnal profession.

[9] 1 Pet. iv. 11.

It has even come to such a pass, that by an inversion of the scriptural illustration,[1] the lump may now be taken to represent the flesh, and the little leaven the Spirit, in estimating the general features of professing society. Still, it is well to remember that truth is a permanent thing. That which the Spirit of truth portrays as the just expression of the mind of God, in describing the unity of the body of Christ, and adjusting the order of Christian service, remains (unaltered by the lapse of time, and unimpaired by the progress of corruption,) as the expression of the same mind still, respecting the selfsame things. The standard of Divine truth is incapable of change; nor may the conscience of a Christian, who desires to glorify God, adopt a lower measure than His perfect will.

Human innovations may have infringed and practically set aside Divine appointment; methodical arrangements of official place may have superseded the lively perception of the real presence and power of the Holy Ghost; faith, instead of being the necessary condition of Christian worship, and of the efficient ministration of the grace of God, may, by the substitution of words for power, and of form for life, have become no longer necessary, in the judgment of men, for the performance of "religious services." Such things may be, and have been. They have been witnessed in times past; and, alas! are still acquiesced in far and wide where Christ is outwardly acknowledged, and the Person of the Holy Ghost is not in word denied. But the question for the simple-minded believer is, not how far Satan may have been

[1] 1 Cor. v. 6, 7.

permitted to work his evil work of corruption through the folly and sin of man, but what says the still audible voice of the Spirit of God in the true and faithful witness of His word.

Nothing can ever change the nature of true Christian responsibility. It is in the light[2] which shews to the believer his position, as accepted and sealed in the Beloved, that he is expected here to walk. The very trial of his faith, in a day of prevalent apostasy, is his *continuance* in the things heard from the beginning, while on the part of the Church at large many things have been let slip.[3] Personal security is not the question here, but the glory of God as accomplished in the doing of His will. A Christian of to-day stands in the same relation to the living members of Christ's one body, *in all respects*, as was the case when this chapter was written. He may find, and indeed cannot but find, experimentally, that the true position of the Church has been practically abandoned long ago, and that impediments and obstructions present themselves at every step to the practical realization of the truth which he holds. Nevertheless, the truth itself is the thing to be acknowledged; for in the confession of His truth, we own *God*, and seek His glory. And if to a faithful assertion of this truth, there must needs be added a deep and large confession of the common sin; which has at length obtained such mastery, even in the hearts of God's saints, as to lead them to turn Christ's glory into shame, by boasting in the very institutions and sectarian divisions which most emphatically witness to the completeness with which the very idea of the

[2] Eph. v. 8.   [3] 1 John ii. 24; 2 Pet. iii. 2; Heb. ii. 1.

Church's unity has faded from their thoughts,[4]—if, moreover, the revival of truth bring with it the sense of feebleness and distress, because of the apparently hopeless difficulties which beset the simple and unhesitating declaration of the word as it is,—let the heart that loves Christ better than itself remember that the reformation of existing disorder is not proposed as the aim and duty of a child of truth, but *a cleaving to the testimonies of God.* God is the only true Reformer, and He works His work by our obedience to His will. To keep the word of God, to hold fast the traditions and commandments of the apostles of the Lord, is now more than ever the privilege, as well as responsibility, of the saints. The word of Christ's patience is the deposit of the Lord's love, for the proving of their faithfulness to Him. There are precious promises to such as keep this treasure without loss. "Hold fast that thou hast, that no man take thy crown,"[5] is the word of Him who stands ready to appear to the joy of them that look for Him. We may not diminish Christ in order to please Christians. A great deal of most precious truth may be habitually ministered and enjoyed on the part of those who yet remain in a position which, while professedly maintained in the Lord's name, is really at variance with the explicit testimony of His word.

At the present day, the instability of everything which men have constructed, and which may have

---

[4] Except as it is recognised necessarily as a thing existent in heaven. But the doctrine of Scripture respects the forming and maintaining of the one body *here below*, as the witness and expectant bride of Him who is, for her sake, gone on high.

[5] Rev. iii. 10, 11.

sheltered many souls beloved of God in time past (and which, doubtless, yet contain multitudes of His children), is being demonstrated in a way which must strike the least observant Christian. Nothing is capable of abiding the hour of shaking and of sifting but the pure truth of God. As the principles of Divine truth are eternal, so the forms of Divine doctrine are permanent and unchangeable, so long as they remain among the recorded testimonies of God, until the purpose for which they were revealed is effectually reached. Now, the ministration of the Holy Ghost as the Comforter, the Spirit of truth, is until the Lord, whose absence He supplies, be again revealed in glory. If, therefore, a Christian desire to glorify God as a servant of the truth, it must be in the unreserved and decided affirmation of what the Scripture reveals, and in the firm refusal to acquiesce in anything which, while it is not a confession of the perfect truth, yet occupies, in the eye of the world, the professed position of the Church of God. I believe, assuredly, that the very question which is now being put for the trial of the precious faith of God's saints is, whether they will or will not, in this day of boasted light and knowledge, give ear to the still unbroken Scripture of God's truth. May the believing enjoyment of the mercies of God, and of the endless consolations which are given us in Christ, strengthen the hearts of those who love Him to a genuine readiness to do His will. Then will *all* doctrine become yet more clear.[6] Then, too, will the sweet and more than compensating joy and blessing of Divine communion be more than ever enlarged

[6] John vii. 17.

and enjoyed in the soul of that Christian who, while girding the loins of his mind to bear the burden of all truth, even though he should find none to share it with him when all seek their own,[7] will find that in wholly following the Lord he has a strength, in the discernment of the Lord's joy, which he never could have had but for the possession of the very truths which may haply make him seem a man of strife, instead of peace, to them that are at ease in Zion.[8] Seclusion, when it is the effect of obedience, because it shuts us up with God, really enlarges the heart's affections more than ever towards the children of God.[9] Meanwhile, the exhaustless depths of His own sufficing blessedness, revealed by the Spirit in the Son of His love, become more than ever perceived and enjoyed in the soul that is thus exercised of Him.[1]

In the verses which follow the ninth, we have a wider reach of general precept addressed to the individual conscience of the Christian, not only with reference to his social obligations as a member of the

[7] Lam. iii. 28; Phil. ii. 20, 21.
[8] Jer. xv. 10, 19; Gal. iv. 16; Amos vi. 1.   [9] 1 John v. 1–3.
[1] It is necessary, in order to complete the mournful picture which but too faithfully presents itself to any one who views attentively the present condition of the Church in the light of Divine truth, to notice the attempts which, in these latter days, have been made by some whose eyes have been opened to the true nature and unity of the Church of God, to return to the position and resume the order which the grace of God originally established. That in the prosecution of such an endeavour, the very evils protested against might reäppear under new forms, was a danger perhaps but too little contemplated in the fresh enjoyment of that blessing which never fails to accompany any effort, however transient, to return to the "old paths." It was not, it may be feared, sufficiently remembered that a continuance of such blessing can be secured only by the constant exercise of *faith*. Even the soundest principles, when uncombined with faith and lowliness of mind, become mere instruments of human wilfulness, and are the most effective nourishment of spiritual pride. But let those who may have participated in this movement, and whose hearts may now be saddened by the too evident tokens of

household of faith, but with a view to a fuller manifestation of the life of Christ in his walk and conversation in the world. It would be inconsistent with the design of this work to dwell at length on these several precepts, well worthy as they are of the believer's closest study. It may, however, be remarked that the ninth verse presents to us in brief the end and summary of all spiritual exhortation, namely, pure-hearted, undissembled love in the Spirit,[2] preserved from degenerating into any lower or less comprehensive sentiment by the steadfast following of holiness. The admonitory teaching contained in the remainder of the chapter is a setting forth of what is looked for from believers, as no longer carnal but spiritual. Because they have the mind of Christ, and with it, also, the unction of the Spirit, there is expected from them both an ability to distinguish between things good and things evil, and a decision of choice in rejecting and abhorring the evil, while cleaving to that which is good.

failure which present themselves on every side, take courage still in the remembrance that no amount of failure on our part can either alter the truth of God, or exhaust the resources of His goodness. With the lowly there is wisdom, and a blessing for the poor in spirit. Aims once fondly cherished may have to be modified, or even quite abandoned, when a sounder knowledge of the Scriptures has discovered their futility. But if, instead of seeking to resuscitate the past, we are content to "hold fast and repent," we shall find experimentally, that they that think upon the Lord are thought upon by Him. To confess truth in the power of godliness, is always difficult; and is surely most so, at the close of a dispensation in which an empty *form* of godliness is the crowning provocation of a thoroughly apostate christendom. (2 Tim. iv.) But the Lord is with His people to the end. Their wish to work deliverance may be frustrated and rebuked by a practical experience of their helplessness; but He chastens whom He loves. We please Him while we keep His sayings, and if we suffer with Him, we shall also reign. They shall not be ashamed that wait for Him.

[2] 1 Peter i. 22.

The measure of compliance yielded on our part to the claims of the Spirit of grace, will be in proportion to the degree in which we are realizing and enjoying by faith the deeper truth out of which all these exhortations arise. Christian happiness is the result of Christian obedience.[3] On the other hand, Christian obedience is the fruit of faith and love. "If ye love me, keep my commandments,"[4] is the word of Him whose commandment is, that we love one another, even *as He has loved us*. The measure of love which He has meted to us, even while dead in our sins, is the appointed pattern of our love towards the brethren.[5] A heart that thinks worthily of the love of Christ to us-ward, will surely feel that life alone is the limit of its debt of love to the brethren. Brotherly love is put in Scripture as the one decisive test of a man's position before God. "We know that we have passed from death unto life, because we love the brethren. He that loveth not his brother abideth in death."[6] Where this love is in practical exercise, there every good work will be found abounding. Acts of kindness, the expression of particular sympathy, meekness and forbearance, quietness and gentleness, with such other kindred fruits of blessing as are here described, put themselves forth for the refreshment of Christ's weary brethren, where the Master's grace is so truly enjoyed, through the Spirit, as to become the reason and the motive of our walk among His saints.

Passing by many things without comment, I would dwell for an instant on the exhortation (verse 12) to

[3] John xiii. 17.
[4] John xiv. 17.
[5] 1 John iii. 16.
[6] 1 John iii. 14.

continuance in prayer. The prayer of a Christian, who has received the truth in power, is not for the deliverance of his own soul from wrath; for already he belongs to Christ, who *has* delivered him from that. This is, surely, clear to all who are, by the grace of God, capable of rejoicing in Christ Jesus. The end of prayer is to enlarge the soul's acquaintance with God, as the giver of more grace. Prayer is in itself the expression of habitual dependence upon God. A believer has already all things secured to him in Christ. But his position here is one of ceaseless dependence upon God for the true use and enjoyment of the blessing wherewith he is blessed. He *has* nothing in himself. He *is* nothing in himself. The effect of prayer is both to nourish in him that sentiment of reverence and godly fear which is so essential to genuine communion, and to enrich his soul with a more enlarged perception of the ability of God to bless with present effect, according to those boundless riches in glory which form the covenanted portion of His saints.[7]

Nor has prayer one object only. It is not chiefly for himself, or for his own, that a Christian, when praying in the Holy Ghost, makes known his requests unto God. It is for *all* saints that he is taught and encouraged, as a member of Christ's mystic body, to supplicate with perseverance.[8] Such prayer will most abound in the heart which is most conversant with the things of Christ, and most habitually subject to the *word of God*. It is by means of that word that the Holy Ghost directs and regulates the affections of the inner man. The

[7] Phil. iv. 9. [8] Eph. vi. 18.

specialty of any trial which may befall either the Church or an individual member of it, while it interests and commands the sympathies of Christ in His saints, turns to the profit and blessing of the soul thus exercised, by enlarging its experimental knowledge and enjoyment of Him with whom we have to do.

A watchful continuance in prayer is both the appointed prevention of Satanic malice, and the chief means of positive communion with God. Combined with thanksgiving, it is the outward expression of the faith of the inner man. Power for service flows as a result from prayer, for such power is the acting of God in sympathy with His own Spirit in us, who produces the desires thus expressed. The moving spring of prophetic energy of old was the prayer of faith.[9] *Jesus* prayed, before He called Lazarus from the grave. It was thus that He glorified God in His place of obedience. Refusing to act as from Himself, He called upon Him whom He came to glorify by perfect dependence in love. In the same spirit He could say, "The Father which dwelleth in me, He doeth the works." Solace to the wearied and buffeted spirit springs, too, from the same source. I need not pursue this further. I add only one consideration, that prayer is the inalienable *right* of a Christian. There is no time or circumstance (except actual sin) when a Christian may not pray. Prayer is, indeed, the proper touchstone of a believer's actions. Whatever cannot be done prayerfully had better not be done at all.

It may be noticed also, before closing these re-

[9] James v. 16, 17.

marks, that verse 14 opens another standing characteristic of our calling. A Christian is called to bless, and not to curse. His birth is of the blessed God, and he is called to inherit a blessing.[1] This is the vantage-ground which the Spirit of grace claims for the believer. Blessing is his condition. He is blessed with all spiritual blessings.[2] By his union with the Blessed One, he is already satisfied with favour, and full of the blessing of the Lord.[3] It is in the consciousness of this that he is called to walk, as one whose feet are shod with the preparation of the Gospel of peace. He is thus, while incapable of being enriched by the world, a vessel from which may flow the precious blessings of Christ, into the drought and weary bitterness of many a world-worn heart, whose fretting against the Lord[4] may be turned to prostrate adoration, by the gracious power of that Name in which it is the Christian's privilege to bless.

When God enjoins His children to overcome evil with good (verse 21), He is only calling on them to be imitators of Himself. For this is His way and His peculiar glory. The gift of His Son is the eternal witness of this; and if we are led of His Spirit, we shall walk with Him. May our feet be ever guided in that way of peace![5]

[1] 1 Pet. iii. 9.
[2] Eph. i. 3.
[3] Deut. xxxiii. 23.
[4] Prov. xix. 3.
[5] Eph. v. 1; 2 Thess. iii. 5.

CHAPTER XIII.

CONTINUING still his train of exhortation, the apostle opens the present chapter with a peremptory call for the believer's ready and unreserved[1] subjection to the actual possessors of power in the world. "Let every soul be subject unto the higher powers." The reason is immediately added: "For there is no power but of God; the powers that be are ordained of God."

The doctrine of this passage is of the utmost moment to a Christian whose end is to glorify God in obedience. We have to remember that a believer, as one called to confess Christ before men, is also to stand in the world as a witness for *God*. His glory, as well as responsibility, is to own God in all things. His true position in the world is that of a pilgrim and a stranger. Divine truth in Christ has opened heaven to him, not only as a hope to be realized in due time, but as his home in spirit *now*. We sit in Christ, in heavenly places, now.[2] Faith, taking the soul into the presence of God, according to the revelation of the present truth, finds its pleasant places of inheritance to be nothing less than the heaven which Christ now enjoys. .A Christian, therefore,

[1] Nothing being reserved but the paramount right of God to the obedience of His servant, when the commandments of men are found to be in collision with His declared will. [2] Eph. ii. 6.

because he belongs to heaven as a *citizen*,³ has no longer a place found for his name on the roll of the world's citizenship. His registry of franchise is the Lamb's book of life.⁴ He is a stranger here. But the same truth which has delivered him from the present evil world, and reconciled him to God with whom the world remains at enmity, marks out for him now the line and measure of his way, and furnishes him with governing principles of conduct while yet remaining *in* the world, although no longer of it.⁵

One of the chief privileges of a Christian is to have to do with God in everything. Being himself God's workmanship, he is never in his true place except when under the dominion and direction of His will. In all the circumstances and relations of life, his calling is to act or suffer for the *truth*, and by the power of *God*. The government of the world, in what manner soever it may be conducted, or in whose hands soever it may happen to be, is by the Christian to be referred to *God*. The powers that be are ordained of Him. Now the natural thought of man

---

³ 'Ημῶν γὰρ τὸ πολίτευμα ἐν οὐρανοῖς ὑπάρχει. (Phil. iii. 20.)
⁴ I do not forget the instances in which the rights of Roman citizenship were asserted by the apostle himself. Without examining here the circumstances of the case in each instance (though it is most needful to do so, if we would extract from these instances the special instruction which they contain), it is sufficient to notice the general principle of Scripture, that in the state in which a man is called of God, he is to remain. (1 Cor. vii. 20–22.) Privileges may attach to that state, which may stand a Christian in stead in certain emergencies. He may surely use these, if, by so doing, he contradict no commandment of God. But to *contend* for such privileges as personal *rights*, and, when they are questioned by the ruling powers, to endeavour forcibly to maintain them, is to quit the only relation in which the Holy Ghost sets the Christian towards the powers that be. This subject is further opened in the sequel.
⁵ John xv. 19, xvii. 16.

is far from this truth. To regard *himself* as the origin of his own honour, and his *will* as the fountain of his rights, is a characteristic trait of the natural man at all times. At the present day, we find on every side the assertion of this principle in the broadest terms.

The democratic sentiment which now exerts so commanding an influence upon the public mind in civilized Christendom is, in its full expression, the very contrary of the maxim here laid down for the guidance of the believer by the Spirit of God.[6] But it is not necessary to enter on a comparative examination of the various forms of government which prevail among men. Our question is with the relation in which the Christian stands, as a servant of God, to government and power of *any* kind in the hands of the authorities of this world.

With respect to this, it is well for us to bear in mind that the seat of government for the ruling of this world, as well as *all* worlds, is reserved for Christ.[7] He has, with His other titles of glory, that of "Prince of the kings of the earth."[8] The purpose of God, as we have noticed at an earlier page, is to set up His kingdom in the hands of Jesus, who shall reign, a priest upon His throne, before the face of the Most High. No form, therefore, of present government can really satisfy God's end, so long as Christ remains hidden with the Father, and expecting until His enemies be made His footstool. But, in the mean while, the *possession* of power or dominion

---

[6] It is perhaps hardly necessary to add that a despotic or irresponsible form of government is, while in the hands of sinful man, not less ineffectual than its opposite for working the righteousness of God.   [7] Ps. viii.; Heb. ii. 5–8.   [8] Rev. i. 5.

places the holder of it under an especial responsibility to God as His delegate. In administering rule and exercising power, he is administering and exercising that which belongs to God, and not to man. For "power belongeth unto God."[9] And again, "He is the Governor among the nations."[1] Nevertheless, the right of the ruler to the obedience of those ruled is secured to him by the sanction of God's own name. The Son of God both acknowledged and glorified by personal compliance this, with all other truth, in the days of His obedience on earth.[2] Cæsar has thus "his things," which are to be rendered duly unto him; and to refuse to acknowledge this due is to deny the sovereignty of God. This is a wide and general principle, addressing itself to the conscience of every man who owns subjection to God.

The thing which a Christian is expected to recognise is the eternal right of God in the distributive exercise of His own power. "For there is *no* power but of God." The will of man naturally resists and resents the imposition of arbitrary restraint. That man should be his own governor, is the aim and effort of those who deceive their own hearts, and those of others, with delusive promises of liberty, while yet ignorant of the truth which alone sets free. The cardinal idea of the human heart, so long as the man remains unregenerate, is the paramount value and importance of natural, personal *rights*. The glory and blessedness of a believer, on the contrary, is to be able to say, that the things which once he counted his chief gain are now become dross for the excellency of the knowledge of Christ Jesus *his Lord*.

[9] Ps. lxii. 11.   [1] Ps. xxii. 28.   [2] Matt. xvii. 24-27, xxii. 21.

The cross is the extinction of natural rights, as well as the discharge of natural responsibilities. By it the world is crucified to the believer, and he to the world.[3] A believer is Christ's freedman. He is the Lord's servant. He knows, therefore, no longer any man after the flesh. For he is placed by the Spirit of grace in totally new relations both to his brethren and to the rest of mankind.[4] His place in the world is to be as his Master, and that was ever to be the perfect servant of the perfect will of God.[5] "It is enough for the disciple that he be as his master, and the servant as his Lord." To walk as He walked is the hopeless[6] yet cherished ambition of the child of God.

But it may be asked, "Has a Christian, then, no duties to perform as a member of the human family, and has he not a place and functions in the social system of which he forms, even if involuntarily, a part?" Such a question would, however, be quite gratuitous. For it is in the several relations of human life and society, that a Christian is to adorn the doctrine of God his Saviour. A believer in Jesus is not called to be an eremite. His calling is to have his conversation *in the world*, according to the truth of the Gospel, and by the grace of God.[7] He is to act, in the various situations of human relationship, according to the will of God. The same things are to be done and discharged by the believer as by other men, in very many respects. But the

---

[3] Gal. vi. 14.   [4] 2 Cor. v. 16, 17.   [5] Isa. xlii. 1.

[6] Hopeless, except in remembrance of that boundless grace which works with omnipotent effect in those who, with wise knowledge of their personal nothingness, abide watchfully and prayerfully in Him. (2 Cor. iii. 5; xii. 10; and Phil. iv. 13.)

[7] 2 Cor. i. 12; Phil. i. 27.

motive principle in either case is utterly different. Policy, expediency, advantage, self-esteem, emulation, natural inclination or affection, hope or fear, with other motives, acting variously, according to circumstances and natural temperament, on the minds of men, form the regulating springs by which the general course of the world is governed and maintained. On the other hand, the Christian is to walk by *faith*, and with a conscience governed by the word of God.[8] Whether as a father or a child, a husband or a wife, a master or a servant, a subject, or in what other relationship soever he may be, it is *to* the Lord that what he does is to be done; it is *in* the Lord that all these relations are to be acknowledged.[9]

The point of view from which a Christain is taught to regard everything, whether heavenly or earthly, is the CROSS. His estimate of present things is to be taken from thence. But the world, viewed from thence, is a withered and a desolate thing. It is already a *judged* world.[1] A man in Christ is one who is, by faith, alive already from the dead. He is thus dissociated, effectually, from all that which is not standing in the power of redemption. The basis and condition of true Christian society, is *life* in the risen and ascended Christ. To recognise a fellowship on any other basis is to deny, in principle, the first truth of the Gospel. Hence the earnestness of the exhortation to separateness from the varied forms of natural evil which, in their aggregate, express "the world," elsewhere addressed to the believer's conscience.[2] Testimony, and not communion, is the

[8] 2 Cor. v. 7; Heb. xiii. 18.
[9] Col. iii. 18, 23; Eph. vi. 1-4; 1 Cor. vii. 22.
[1] John xii. 31.   [2] 2 Cor. vi. 14-18.

proper character of a Christian's intercourse with the world.

The spectacle which presents itself to the eye of a believer when, in our own times, he attempts a survey of the world around him, is widely different from that which met the view of a Christian in apostolic times. In the place of idolatrous heathenism, he sees professed Christianity. Instead of the sword of the magistrate being in the hands of the avowed haters of the name of Christ, authorities and powers nominally Christian are the guardians and conservators of a state of society which, in an outward sense at least, recognises, as a fundamental maxim, the authenticity and moral claims of revealed truth. In addition to this, there are found Christians who are really such, not only filling almost every variety of post and office in the system of the world's government, but intimately connected with, and contributing powerfully to, the furtherance of nearly all the leading schemes of social change and amendment, which so largely operate, for good or for evil, upon the generation of the present day. Deep and most real personal piety is frequently found united in the same person with laborious energy in the pursuit of objects which are valuable only within the precincts of natural life and experience, but which fade into vanity when viewed in the light of the resurrection from the dead. To be carnal, and to walk as men, does not of necessity imply such an indulgence of apparent sin as would render a godly Christian incapable of its toleration. The Christian who is not walking in Christ, *above* the maxims and principles of the world, must be acquiescing in and accommodating himself to the ways of men, so far as he has a common object with themselves.

It is the end of a man that determines his way. But a Christian's end is Christ. "To me to live is Christ."[3] He has not *many* characters to sustain, but *one*. To associate, for the sake of personal advantage, with those who love not the Lord, is to dishonour Him, and to bring the rebuke of His Spirit on our souls by declining the cross and departing from the place of testimony to His name. To enter into combination or confederacy with unbelievers, for the furtherance of objects common to all, is to forget that *no* object can exist for the heart of a spiritual man in separation from the glory of God as its end. But that glory can on our parts be asserted only by obedience to the truth; and it is the word of truth that denies community of interest to be compatible with the difference which God has established, permanently, between a Christian and the world.[4]

At the present day, a believer in Jesus finds himself invoked by a multitude of claims which, with more or less of speciousness, address his sympathies, and solicit his natural feelings and energies, as a man, and as a member of civilized society. It cannot be doubted, that very many of the temporal comforts and advantages which are now so largely enjoyed by ourselves are owing, in great measure, to the influence of Christian doctrine, directly or indirectly, on the masses of society. It is no unusual thing to hear men congratulating themselves on this fact, and drawing from it inferences as to the purpose

[3] Phil. i. 21. Compare 2 Cor. v. 15.   [4] 2 Cor. vi. 14–18.

and intent of the Christian dispensation, which, in very many instances, are such as to place the minds and consciences of those who accept them under *totally false impressions*, not only as to the true character of the times in which they are living, but with respect also to the declared counsel of God, as it regards both the Church and the world.

There is a Christianity in the present day, of large and general acceptance, in which the cross of Christ is really no element at all. To mind earthly things, instead of being regarded as a fatal symptom of reprobation,[s] which must needs fill with anguish the hearts of those who love the Lord indeed, is now sanctioned as a duty by multitudes who, nevertheless, are not slow to make outward profession of the name of Christ. This is, indeed, Satan's chief handiwork. To reduce the grace of God, which bringeth salvation through the redeeming blood of the Lamb, to a mere instrument of moral amelioration for the amendment and polish of this present world, is the last outrage but one which can be offered to the long-suffering holiness of God. When Christian truth, instead of being "mixed with faith," is carelessly adopted as a matter of opinion, it ceases to be the oracle of God, and Christ is already gone.

The certain tendency of most of the revolutionary changes in human society which are now in progress, is to work the natural mind more and more free from all restraint. But Christian opinions are no restraint, so long as they are simply such. A man's opinions are the creatures of his own mind, and are subject to himself. He may change them at his

[s] Phil. iii. 18, 19.

will, and even while still holding them, may violate their spirit in his practice to any conceivable amount.[6] *Truth*, held from God by faith, binds its possessor in heart and conscience to Him in whom he believes. The cross of Christ cannot be taken up as an opinion. The Gospel is to the believer the *power of God* unto salvation. The "Christian religion," as men speak, may, on the other hand, be thus viewed. It commonly is so, and being thus mentally adopted, is varied and coloured in its form and expression, according to the temperament of the mind in which it finds a place. And so it has happened, that the preaching of the cross has been, and now is, nearly as much an offence in Christendom as it was within the sphere of the ancient and idolatrous civilization, to which, in many respects, our own day presents so striking an analogy.

A simple-minded Christian is not deceived by names, so long as he is nourished by the sincere milk of the word. By such an one, the difference between flesh and Spirit, between God and the world, is not only confessed as a doctrine, but experimentally understood. He knows—and it is, indeed, a solemn consideration—that the truth of God in Christ, if it be not effectual through faith unto salvation in them that hear, is to the negligent and unbelieving a witness of condemnation, and a token of destruction.[7] The world has not become the friend of God, because it has borrowed the name and outward profession of Christ. If Jesus be not owned in truth, according to the witness and in the power of the Holy Ghost, the debased and misappropriated doctrines of the Gospel

[6] 2 Tim. iii. 1–5.   [7] 2 Cor. ii. 15, 16.

are but the spoils of God's dishonoured Son, for which inquiry will surely be made at the appointed time.

A Christian, because he is a child of God, the Possessor of heaven and earth, is free in all places and at all times. He is free, therefore, to use the world. There is not a convenience of modern device which may not, in its place, be gratefully acknowledged as a mercy, to the Father of mercies, if it meet some present need of a child of God. The very things which feed and inflame the natural pride of men, and the inventions whereby their dependence on God is rendered more and more remote, are capable of use to the glory of God in the hands of such as fear Him. For "to the pure all things are pure;" while, as it respects their title of enjoyment, "the earth is the *Lord's*, and the fulness thereof."[8]

There are blessings, for instance, and advantages of a high order attaching to an Englishman by natural birthright. Assuredly, no English Christian is insensible to such benefits, when they fall to his share as having his lot cast in this much-favoured land. The recognition of Divine mercy in a tranquil and well-ordered polity, where personal liberty and a large variety of desirable immunities are very generally enjoyed, is a daily obligation on the heart of every thoughtful Christian. But for men in Christ to be contending for such things as their *rights*—still more that Christians (as is often the case in the present day) should be endeavouring to compel[9] the

[8] Tit. i. 15; 1 Cor. x. 23-31.
[9] One of the most common and mischievous fallacies of the day is the assumed distinction in principle between moral compulsion and physical force. In either case it is *man's will* attaining its end by

ruling powers to their will—too surely indicates the loss of that separate standing of heavenly strangership which pertains to the believer as united to the risen Christ.

Liberty is the professed aim of such political movements as—tending upwards from the governed class—seek to control or to modify the existing order of government. Liberty of this kind is a thing to which men seem ever to be approximating, but which they never fully attain. It is a natural thing for the human mind to desire freedom from all outward restraint, because every man naturally refers his happiness to *himself* as its cause. Hence, the whole course and process of civil polity in the world is but a prolonged strife of separate interests. No fixed standard of right and truth is asserted. *God* is not owned in immediate relation to human government, and therefore the restless changes of human expediency are continually causing the form and pattern of the times to vary and to shift, according to the diverse influences which govern and direct the minds of men.

But that which the natural man grasps at vainly, as an ever-fleeing shade, the believer already possesses in full perfection in Christ. He is free. The home of his liberty is God himself in Christ. The supply of his necessities is from the Father of lights. The cross has taught him the end of *all* human per-

---

subduing an opposing force. God's word commands subjection *to Himself* in the person of the ruler. Revolutionary movement of any kind has its rise in the dissatisfaction of the governed party. A grievance is no sooner felt than it is sought to be removed. If refusal be given to a request, dictation by the moral force of expressed opinion is resorted to. Every day the quality of executive power is becoming less stable, from its virtual dependence on the will of the subject. Is this according to the mind of God?

fection, and he has already begun to look into the open vision of peace and glory, which the Spirit of liberty displays to the waiting patience of inquiring faith in the still increasing disclosure of the love of Christ.[1]

The present chapter contains a text (verse 2) which, if applied to much that has ranked very high in the recorded estimate of human worth, and laid the foundations in many instances of national glory, and upon which even men, themselves no strangers to Christ, have bestowed their praise, would prove instructively how little sympathy there is between the motives and ends of human action at its fairest, and the Divine leadings of the Spirit of God, whose single motive is to exalt Christ, and whose one end is the glory of God in the way of unreserved obedience to His will. Very much might be advanced in illustration of this, but I hasten to the sequel of our chapter.

The believer, if he would adorn the doctrine of God, must exercise himself so as to have a conscience void of offence.[2] He is to endeavour to walk blameless under the eye of the Master whom he serves. With the decision of political questions he has properly nothing to do. He has to submit himself to *every* ordinance of man for the Lord's sake.[3] God

---

[1] 2 Cor. iii. 18.   [2] Acts xxiv. 16.

[3] 1 Pet. ii. 13-15. The Scripture does not contemplate the Christian, I believe, anywhere as a ruler. The reason of this is not only the fact that at the time none such had embraced the faith, but rather, as it seems to me, the incompatibility of pure Christian principle, as a realized thing, with those maxims on which alone the world will consent to be governed. Flesh will not acknowledge Spirit; nor will the world obey Christ. A government conducted in the energy of the Holy Ghost and according to the truth of God, would be none other than the Church itself.

comes before him in the ordinances of men. The ruler is therefore a minister of God to him for good (verse 4). Upright conduct and peaceful following of that which is good would secure him the favour instead of the resentment of the power. Where men can only see themselves, a believer is privileged to see God. The enactments of the ruling government are stamped with the name and weighty with the sanction of God, in every case in which nothing is enjoined on him which renders obedience possible only by a breach of some Divine command. A law might be in its terms most unjust; yet is the Christian to obey it still, if personal inconvenience or suffering be the only evil consequence of obedience. In complying with an oppressive edict of man, he is rendering obedience to the will of God, who is not slack to recompense, even in this present life, the affliction of such as suffer for His name. If he resists, he not only dishonours God, who commands subjection, but renders himself obnoxious to a special judgment[4] at the hands of Him who is not mocked. All suffering of the kind above mentioned is an "affliction of the Gospel." It is something borne for the name of Christ; and the Spirit of glory and of God rests approvingly on them that suffer for His sake.[5]

But secular government is regarded, both here and elsewhere, less as a possible grievance than as a general blessing from the hand of God.[6] It is in the nature of a blessing when impartially administered,

---

[4] Κρῖμα, not κατάκριμα. "Damnation," as in the English Version, conveys quite a wrong idea.
[5] 1 Pet. iv. 14; 2 Tim. i. 8.   [6] 1 Tim. ii. 1, 2.

and is, as such, to be enjoyed and acknowledged to the praise and glory of God. The conscience of a Christian, although susceptible of appeals of a very different kind, is not regarded by the Spirit of God as above the necessity of warning with respect to his conduct as a man in the world. He is placed, with others, under the government of one who, as God's minister, is the dispenser to him of praise or blame, according to the manner of his outward life. For it is no impossible thing that a Christian, while in the flesh, may justly come, if not careful and vigilant, within reach of the arm of the secular power for correction. The judgment of the power would, in such case, be the visitation of God upon his ways.

It is not, however, for wrath alone, or chiefly, that he is called on to be subject, but for conscience' sake (verse 5). Submission, that is, was to be perfectly rendered, lest they should in any way even seem to confound the holy liberty of God's children with the natural licence of the flesh. For thus they would hinder the Gospel of Christ, by furnishing to the adversary a valid accusation, such as he loves to find, of their walk and conversation in the world.[7] They were to take good heed to this, lest the truth of God in Christ should for a moment, or in any one point, appear capable of identification with any of those movements of the natural will, which, under what disguise soever, always betray their true nature and source by aiming at earthly ends. Righteousness and pure dealing as before God must ever form the straight line and measure of the true believer's walk.

[7] 1 Pet. ii. 12.

Love may go beyond this, but can never either vary from or fall short of it.

Verses 6, 7, confirming and extending the general doctrine already laid down, carry the sanction of Divine command into all the specialties of detailed administration. The impositions, even if both burdensome and arbitrary, which a positive law of human government lays on its subject, are to be cheerfully submitted to and borne. Cæsar must have his dues. The Spirit of God still recognises them as such. A Christian, being personally on the ground of *grace* alone, has no personal *rights* which he may justly regard as infringed by such enactments. It is a thing both lovely and of good report, when, as a companion of the *patience* of Christ,[8] the believer is enabled thus to accept, without murmuring or disputing, the circumstances of his position as a stranger in the world which men call theirs, but which really belongs to them that are Christ's.[9] Submission, not grudgingly nor unwillingly, but cheerfully, as to the Lord and not to man, is the clear path of the Christian in these things. His obedience to the ordinance of man is itself a result of his perfect freedom from man. It is by such things that the doctrine of our Saviour-God is most effectively adorned.[1] These verses are, with the entire passage which precedes, of pointed application in the present day.

Verses 8–10 are pregnant with weighty exhortation. The injunctive prohibition with which the passage opens, passes presently into an affirmative precept of yet deeper and wider range. We are *not* to remain debtors to any man. We *are* to own still an unpaid

[8] Rev. i. 9. [9] 1 Cor. iii. 22, 23. [1] Phil. ii. 14, 15; Tit. ii. 10.

debt of love. With respect to the first of these, I only remark here, that there is no just argument to be drawn from this passage against a Christian's borrowing money, or anything else, on the free consent of the other party. The question is not about borrowing, but paying. If a thing be due, it is to be at once paid. But a loan, of course, is not due unless the set time of payment has arrived. A heedless borrowing, therefore, with no present prospect of restitution at the appointed time, is a breach beforehand of this express command. Christians do well to weigh carefully this counsel. No small dishonour has been cast on the precious name of Christ from the neglect of this. Faith never oversteps the bounds of right. But there is a burden of debt from which the Christian has neither the ability nor the desire to be free. He is bound in a firm bond to the perpetual love of the brethren, for the Master's sake. The real creditor in this case is the Lord Himself, while His sheep are the appointed receivers of His due.[2] It is the new commandment, addressed to the children of the true and perfect light.[3]

Love is here set as the seal of Christian service upon the heart and conscience of the believer, in the place of the letter of Law. The Law repressed and forbade evil: "Thou *shalt not* covet," &c. Grace, acting on the affections of the new man, calls forth into operative exercise desires which are eternally opposed to that evil selfishness which the letter vainly essayed to subdue. "Thou shalt love thy neighbour as thyself," was originally addressed to man in the flesh. Its fulfilment is possible only by those who,

[2] John xxi. 15–17.   [3] 1 John ii. 8–10.

being themselves new-born in Christ of the Father's love, are already members one of another according to the unity of the Spirit of life. The heart of a Christian, who is rejoicing in his portion by a lively faith, goes forth willingly to meet the commandments of God. They are not grievous to one who is himself " of God."

But, while every child of God is surely rooted and grounded in Divine love, there is large diversity of practical condition in those who are thus blessed. The Spirit of God may be able sometimes to speak of saints as no longer needing exhortation to love one another,[4] while to others He may have to address such words as, "Grudge not one against another, brethren, lest ye be judged;[5] behold, the Judge standeth before the door."[6] It is a humbling but needful thing that the word of exhortation should be addressed to a Christian in terms which indicate, not merely a possibility, but an *imminent danger* of his falling into ways and practices utterly at variance with the sound doctrines of faith. Holiness is the native atmosphere of the child of God. His inner man crieth out for God. Yet nothing is more certain than that prayerful watchfulness of self-government can alone secure him from the ways of evil. He has to watch and pray, *lest he enter* into temptation. Nothing can for a moment keep him but the gracious power of God. This power, though it surely acts in a measure far beyond the application of our desires in prayer, (or where should we be?) is a concurrent

---

[4] 1 Thess. iv. 9.
[5] The true reading in this passage seems to be, ἵνα μὴ κριθῆτε.
[6] James v. 9.

aid of the believer as he strives to keep the way of truth. We must have to do with God, as the companion of our way, the present upholder of our steps. Assuredly, the soul that is delighting itself in Him will need no quickening appeal to conscience, in order to restore it to the paths of righteousness. The fear of the Lord is a clean thing,[7] and the Spirit that leads the children of God, rests likewise upon them as the Spirit of that fear, that they may be quick of perception in the right ways of the Lord.[8] A legal spirit in a Christian may produce a punctual discharge of preceptive obligation, at the bidding of conscience; but such works are of little worth. The ready flow of devotedness in love can only come from a heart in which God dwells. A heart kept full of Christ, by faith,[9] finds no cause of regret but in the thought of the scanty measure in which he loves, who is himself so mightily beloved. Yet is he often the most fruitful, who most feels this sense of shortcoming and defect.

In the 11th verse we have a new and solemn accessory introduced in connection with the preceding exhortations. The nearness of the salvation, to the obtaining of which they had been appointed of God,[1] is now brought before their view as an additional stimulant to their hearts and consciences alike. The desire of that day of joy is intended to act with purifying effect on the ways of God's saints.[2] A believer, moreover, is expected to have knowledge of the *time*. The world takes no willing notice of the lapse of time, because the world's day is *now*. A

[7] Psalm xix.   [8] Isa. xi. 1, 2.   [9] Eph. iii. 17.
[1] 1 Thess. v. 9.   [2] 1 John iii. 3.

believer is a prisoner of hope in this body of death and corruption, expecting until his change shall come.

It is a remarkable fact, and one which harmonizes characteristically with the standing now assigned to the believer, as already risen with Christ, that *death*, in the New Testament, is never spoken of as the natural end and expectation of a Christian. The general principles are indeed laid down that, living or dying, we are the Lord's;[3] that to die is, to a believer, gain, because to depart and be with Christ is far better than to continue in the midst of toil and sorrow;[4] that death in Christ is no argument of hopeless sorrow to those who survive the departure of their brethren, seeing that the dead in Christ shall at His appearing first arise, before the bodies of the saints then alive shall undergo their change from mortality to life. But the one great object which the Spirit of God sets and keeps before the view of the Church in the word of truth, is *the revelation of the Lord from heaven.* We wait for a salvation which is *ready to be revealed* in the last time.[5] It was shown to the apostle Peter, that he should put off his tabernacle of flesh before the Lord's return.[6] The writer of the present epistle seems also to have had a similar intimation.[7] Moreover, the testimony of the Spirit with respect to the progress of that evil which, beginning while yet the apostles wrote, was to pass through more than one stage before its ultimate ripeness for judgment should be attained, clearly indicates that some undetermined space of time must

[3] Chap. xiv. 8.   [4] Phil. i. 20–23.   [5] 1 Pet. i. 5.
[6] 2 Pet. i. 13,`14.   [7] 2 Tim. iv. 6.

needs elapse before the promised and desired advent of the Lord in glory. Still, while the testimony of the Spirit measures with prophetic distinctness the progressive stages of the present dispensation, and furnishes the man of God with unerring counsel for the guidance of his steps,—in what scene soever of this drama of still deepening evil his lot may have been cast,—the truth which evermore presents itself to the eye of the believer, when he turns for solace from the stress of evil to those sure testimonies of God which make the spirit glad,[8] is the promise of the speedy coming of the Lord.

The truth now before us, how little soever it may have been owned and valued in the Church at large since first she left her early love, will be found, on an examination of Scripture, to occupy a very prominent place in the mind of the Spirit of God. From the day that Jesus ceased from the sight of men, because ascending into the light which no man can approach unto,[9] the date of the patience of His Church began. To wait for the Son of God *from* heaven became, from that moment, both the duty and the desire of those who not only knew the fact of their Master's presence there, but understood the purpose wherefore He was gone.

He had spoken of His return before the hour of His departure had arrived. Whether as the Son of man, invested with all majesty and dominion, and coming in the clouds of heaven;[1] as the unwelcome and unlooked-for Minister of vengeance against a hardened and apostate world;[2] as the righteous

---

[8] Psa. cxix. 14.
[9] Acts i. 11.
[1] Matt. xxiv. 30, xxv. 31.
[2] Luke xvii. 26–37.

Awarder of His servants' due, when suddenly returning to make inquest into His house;³ or, finally, as the faithful Redeemer of the special promise of His love, when, in preparing the hearts of the disciples for His departure, He spake of mansions in the Father's house, the preparation of which should occupy His care until He came again to receive them to Himself;⁴ in each and all of these characters had He taught, to them that heard Him, the doctrine of His second advent, while as yet He was among them in the days of His flesh.

The Holy Ghost sent down from heaven to be the witness to the Son, to the glory of the Father who has exalted Him and placed the name of Jesus above every name,⁵ declares the present readiness of Him whom now that Spirit reveals and preaches as a *Saviour*, to come forth at the appointed day to judge the world in righteousness.⁶ The Scriptural testimony in further proof of this I need not here repeat. But it is to the Church of God, the purified object of Divine affection, the bride whom the Comforter still labours by His teaching to make ready for her Lord's return, that the second coming of Christ is especially revealed and presented as a *hope*. To the mind of the Spirit in the Church this truth is continually present. It stamps its character accordingly upon all true worship during the absence of the Lord. The continual remembrance of the dying love of Jesus is kept with especial reference to this. "As often as ye eat this bread, and drink this cup, ye do show the Lord's death *until He come*."⁷ To be wait-

³ Matt. xxv. 19–30.　　　⁴ John xiv. 2, 3.
⁵ Phil. ii.　⁶ Acts xvii. 31.　⁷ 1 Cor. xi. 26.

ing for the Son of God from heaven, is the attitude in which the Church is placed, from the moment that it turns from idols to the knowledge and service of the living and true God.[8] "A little while," is the brief though indefinite line of time with which the Spirit measures, for them whose need is *patience*, the interval which still separates them from the unfulfilled desire of their souls.[9] I pass by the very many passages of Scripture yet unnoticed, in which this truth, so all-important to the Church, is treated, and return now to the present chapter, which presents, in its concluding verses, so striking and so practical an application of this doctrine.

There are two ways in which the promise of the Lord's coming is intended to act on the believer. First, to excite and stimulate his spiritual affections, augmenting thus the abundance of his labour of love for the Lord's sake; and secondly, as a warning to his conscience, since he is ever in danger of departing more or less from God by reason of the deceitfulness of sin.[1] Both these ends are contemplated in the exhortation before us. It was high time to awake, because the day was at hand; but that day was the day of their completed salvation and glory (verses 11, 12). They had need of further vigilance, for it was yet night, and the dangers of the night remained around them still. But deliverance was the near expectation of those who were thus aroused. They had not to seek afresh the evidence of their hope, and their title of blessing in the day that was so near. Because they had *believed*, they were already

---

[8] 1 Thess. i. 9, 10. [9] Heb. x. 36, 37.
[1] Heb. iii. 12, 13.

saved in hope, and the salvation of promise was daily drawing nearer to their sight. They stood already sealed and fitted, by the grace of God, for participation in the inheritance of the saints in light. They were already "of the day."[2] But they had to look diligently to their ways, that their conduct might be worthy of their hope.

It is because the condition of a Christian is perfect sanctification in Christ, that he is exhorted to be holy as God is holy, who has thus sanctified him in His Son. Salvation is the end and present hope of the saint, who has yet to wage his war of faith in conflict with the powers of darkness. That salvation,[3] which is a synonym of rest and glory, must not be confounded with the same word, when used, as it often is, to express the standing of the justified believer as already safe. "*He hath saved us*" is the triumphant reason of the hope which looks with patience for its vindication in glory at the revelation of Jesus Christ.[4] To these saints, therefore, at home, the constant shortening of the term of patience was to be a still recurring argument of watchfulness and hope. Each daily revolution in the flight of time, while it sealed to their hearts the sweet assurance of the still nearer advent of their salvation and their rest, added another incentive to a yet more earnest zeal. The way of pilgrimage had been long, but they were nearly at its close. With yet more watchful diligence, therefore, should they seek to cast aside whatever still remained as a weight or hindrance to their course.[5] They were on the eve of meeting God. They are

[2] 1 Thess. v. 8. [3] 1 Pet. i. 5; Eph. vi. 10. *seq*.
[4] 2 Tim. i. 9; Tit. iii. 5. [5] Heb. xii. 1.

warned therefore to put off every defilement contracted by the way, that their entrance into the place of His dwelling might be with both readiness and joy.[6]

The Christian is exhorted to put off, to thrust from him with effort, the works of darkness by which he is surrounded, and in which, without this vigilant decision, he is sure to be entangled. He has to cleanse *himself*, because already he is clean through the washing of the word of grace; to *keep*, by watching and by faith, those garments which are already whitened by the blood of the Lamb.[7]

Nor should he only seek to purify his way. He is called to put on the Lord Jesus Christ (verse 14). To cease merely from sinful practice is to present our souls as the objects of Satan's aim, whose temptations are not ended till we rest with God. To hide himself in Christ is the only safety of the saint. The flesh will have provision for its lusts, where the soul is not full fed on the satisfying portion of the Bread of life. Our daily exhortation is to put on Christ. Already we are *in* Him. We are planted in His likeness before the living God. But we are called to walk up and down in this present evil world in the holiness and power of that Name.[8] To put on Christ implies a divesting and denying of ourselves. A daily death to the world and its desires must accompany a living to the Lord. But the confidence of faith, which knows Him as the proper fountain of its joy, thinks that a gainful loss which must be foregone in order that the fuller light of life may shine.

[6] Comp. Gen. xxxv. 1–4; and 2 Pet. iii. 14.   [7] Rev. xvi. 15.
[8] Zech. x. 12; Col. ii. 6.

May the blessed Spirit of all truth so guide us into the love of God and the patient waiting for Christ, and so confirm our hearts in diligent and steadfast labour for His name, that when the voice of the archangel is heard indeed, we may be found of Him in peace, without spot and blameless in His sight.[9]

[9] 2 Pet. iii. 14.

CHAPTER XIV.

THE transition from the closing subject of the last chapter to that which the apostle now introduces is less abrupt than may at first sight appear. The strong exhortation to personal holiness and putting on the Lord Jesus Christ, if effectually obeyed, would induce, not only increased vigilance of personal conduct, but a diligent circumspection and watchful caution with respect to the admission of anything into the Church which might prove to be an evil communication, such as would only work corruption and defilement in the body of Christ. The operation of this principle of godly vigilance might, however, if untempered by the sound-minded wisdom and love of the Spirit, lead to the erection of a factitious standard of Christian fellowship, by which personal qualities, or the attainment of some presumed measure of doctrinal knowledge, might become the warrant of a man's reception into the Church, rather than his genuine recognition and enjoyment of the grace of God.

But this would have been a ruinous error; for it would have been virtually to lose sight of the Lord, whose name it is which is the title of entrance into His own house. It would have been a confounding of *knowledge*, which, in the mind of the Spirit, is an after-addition, with *faith*, which is the foundation on which it rests.[1] The basis of Christian fellowship is the grace of Christ—is Christ Himself. The cross is the common meeting-place of all who are sanctified by faith in Him. It is as *saved sinners* that men know one another in Christ, according to the grace in which they are themselves known of Him. The requisites, therefore, for Christian fellowship were faith and holiness. One who had been a thief to the moment of his conversion, was as fully received of the Lord, as he who might have been zealous in all works of human righteousness, while yet ignorant of the grace of God in truth.

But there was another point connected with the reception of new converts. The case might arise of those who made true profession of the name of Christ, and against whose admission into the Church no moral objection might be urged, while, on inquiry, it might appear that they were feeble or imperfect in the faith itself. The chapter before us opens with the direct expression of the mind of the Spirit as to this point.

Verse 1. "Him that is weak in the faith receive ye." Such is the plain and positive commandment of the Lord who knows His sheep, and whose will it is to reject none who truly come to Him.[2] It is the *believer* who is to be received, without reference to the degree or measure of his faith. With respect to this, there might be a large diversity. There are babes who have need of milk, as well as men who use strong meat.[3] The emergence of a believer's conscience from a state of legal bondage into the

[1] 2 Pet. i. 5. [2] John vi. 37. [3] Heb. v. 12–14.

perfect liberty of Christ might be, and often would be, in fact, a matter of time. But, in the mean while, the government of such a conscience was in the hands of the Lord, who had received its owner on the ground of *faith*. And so it is immediately added, "not to doubtful disputations," or, according to the margin, "not to judge his doubtful thoughts."[4]

An ignorant conscience is a very different thing from a defiled conscience. There were some, even in the apostle's time, who professed that they knew God, while in works they were denying Him. To such, as he tells us, nothing is pure, but both mind and conscience are alike defiled.[5] But widely different is the case of the man who, while under impressions perhaps most erroneous, and altogether remote from those which a fuller light would produce, yet walks in sincerity of purpose under such impressions, as under a yoke which *God* has placed upon his neck. It would, for example, be a proof of spiritual weakness if a Christian abstained from meats. But so long as his observance of this scruple was not obtruded on the conscience of other men, as a thing absolutely right, and therefore entitled to general observance, he was not to be despised on account of what might seem to the more established saint a bondage of conscience unworthy of the liberty of Christ (verses 2, 3).

But where the conscience of a believer is, in its intelligence, below the just appreciation of the truth which forms the standing of real Christian liberty

---

[4] Μὴ εἰς διακρίσεις διαλογισμῶν. "*Doch nicht zur Erregung zweifelnden Gedanken,*" as DE WETTE renders.
[5] Tit. i. 15, 16.

before God, there is a danger that his spirit will become censorious in proportion to the sensitiveness of his conscience. This opposite evil is, therefore, equally to be watched. For the moment individual conscience is set up as a standard by which to judge another's conduct, the Lord is thrust out of His true place. The judgment of declared evil is a different thing entirely. In such a case, it is the Lord who, by expressing His own judgment in the word, leaves nothing to the believer but an obedient fulfilment of His will. That word grants no immunity to an evil or defiled conscience. It deals with sin according to the truth and holiness of God.

Assuredly, the conscience is the immediate arbiter of good and evil to the man. But the only safe directory of conscience is the word of truth. Unless, then, a believer is walking in a way inconsistent with the declared commands of God, or is holding for doctrine things contrary to the truth, to reject him on account of paucity of faith, or of spiritual discernment or attainment, is to despise and reject the Lord Himself, who has received him in His grace. While, therefore, the entrance of allowed evil was to be watchfully resisted, and no pretext listened to which would serve as a cover for the introduction of the leaven of false doctrine into the temple of Divine truth,[e] the weak-hearted Christian, whose heart was right with God, though his joy might be but scant and feeble, because the light of God as yet shone dim within him, was to be received, according to the Spirit of liberty, into the Church in which that Spirit dwells. He was to be welcomed in the bowels of the

[e] 2 Cor. vi. 16.

love of Christ. He was to come among them, not to be questioned or directed as to his individual conscience, but to be comforted, and strengthened, and led onward, in the path of truth; to be owned according to the fellowship and power of that kingdom of God which is not meat and drink, but righteousness, and peace, and joy in the Holy Ghost.

The doctrine of this chapter is of much practical weight and importance at all times. For the gracious adjustment of Christian liberty within the Church of God will ever be a matter of difficulty, to be met and overcome only by the watchful recognition of *the Lord*, in the several members of His body, and by the mutual and habitual exercise of self-denial and of grace.[7]

The distinction between individual weakness of faith and consequent special observances for conscience' sake, and an active legal spirit which would *insist* on such observances, is clear in itself, but is to be carefully kept in view as a practical point. The one never goes beyond the individual conscience. Certain things are observed *to the Lord*, for conscience' sake. In the other case, the object is to place a yoke upon the necks of others, to spoil and hinder the liberty of Christ. But this is a thing to be resisted utterly wherever it occurs, as a positive work of Satan, and in no respect of God.[8] It is an evil of constant recurrence in the Church of God, and one which demands, therefore, incessant watchfulness. Its root can never be perfectly extracted or destroyed, for it

[7] Eph. v. 21; Phil. ii. 3.
[8] The havoc and desolation which have often been made within the nominal fold of Christ by the operation of this principle is too well known to need any special notice here.

lies deep in the natural constitution of the human heart. Yokes and bonds to bind again the consciences which Christ died to set free, are the incessant machinations of the enemy of light; who finds, alas! too ready a material, and too commodious a space, for his evil work in the natural heart. The Epistle to the Galatians is worthy of all attention with reference to this subject.[9]

To proceed with our chapter. Verses 4–6 assert powerfully the paramount claim of conscience in the Church of God, and assign to the Lord His true place of preëminence as the alone Judge of His servants' way, and the Maintainer of those whose hearts are given, in simplicity and godly sincerity, to the fulfilling of His will. The latter part of verse 4 is rich in reässuring comfort to the soul of the poor unprofitable servant, when judging himself on account of the faultiness of his work. He has no hard master to deal with. He shall stand in his lot in the coming day; for *God is able* to make him stand.[1] It is the Lord, whose interests are bound up in the prosperity of His servant. This is ever the true rest and ultimate resort of the exercised soul. The power of God is the wealth and confidence of those who love Him, under all circumstances. They know that their being called to serve at all is the result of their being already fully blessed of Him in *grace*.[2]

The caution in the following verse should not be lightly regarded: "Let every man be fully per-

---

[9] Compare also 2 Cor. xi. 12–15; Acts xv.
[1] I do not alter in the text the ordinary E. V., but all the best MS. authorities (including *Cod. Sin.*) read Κύριος instead of Θεός.
[2] Heb. ix. 14, xii. 28.

suaded in his own mind." A Christian is never rightly in a state of indifference as to anything. He is called to the exercise of a sound mind, before God, upon everything with which he is brought into present contact. He is to walk by faith: to stand with loins *girded*, not loose. Full persuasion, therefore, is expected as a precedent condition of his actions of what kind soever. The Lord is often dishonoured in this respect. Christians follow each other's example much more easily and naturally than they follow Christ. It is the characteristic of the wise man that he is able to render a reason for what he does. This wisdom is looked for from the Christian. As it is elsewhere said, "See that ye walk circumspectly, not as fools, but as wise," &c. Example is no reason in itself for imitation. We have to judge the work, and when we discern the faith which produced it, we are to follow *that*.[8] Thus God is glorified; for what is then done, is done to Him.

After giving, in verse 6, a picture of the peaceful harmony which prevails, amid the widest differences of personal judgment, where God is truly known and remembered, he expresses in brief the ruling principle and maxim of the life of God: "None of us liveth to himself, and no man dieth to himself" (verse 7),—a truth which forms the regulating spring of all fellowship that is really of the Spirit. The principle is a simple one, and has its root in the very ground-truth of Christian doctrine. The cross, which has terminated judicially the believer's mortal life, leaves now no other life but Christ Himself. *To* Him, then, he lives, for *in* Him he lives. He lives

[8] Heb. xiii. 7.

(verse 8) because he is the Lord's, not his own. He is Christ's by the eternal title of redemption—His own, at the paid price of His most precious blood. Yet, simple as this principle is, it demands for its practical observance the watchful, ceaseless exercise of self-denying grace. Meanwhile, the blessed truth (while its recital may well shame us because of our dull, and slow, and altogether inadequate exemplification of it) remains still in its undiminished power of sustaining comfort to the soul. Living or dying, we *are* the Lord's.

Verse 9. The special mention of the Lord's name as the owner, in absolute possession, of His chosen people, according to the special title of redemption, is now followed by a fuller and more comprehensive expression of Divine doctrine, in which the power and dominion of the Redeemer are asserted to their full extent: "To this end Christ both died and lived,[4] that He might be Lord both of the dead and living." It is evident that the general statement here made of the end and purpose of the death of Christ, though it contains in it the specialty of the Church's redemption, goes far beyond that truth. Christ died to establish His dominion over the dead; that *all* judgment, whether of the living or the dead, might be administered by Him who is the Son of man.[5] The resurrection has accordingly transferred the keys of death and Hades to the hands of Jesus;[6] for by means of death He destroyed him who aforetime had

---

[4] Ἀπέθανε καὶ ἔζησεν. Such is the reading now, I believe, almost universally received by critical inquirers. The *Cod. Sin.* concurs with the other MSS. of highest authority in omitting the intermediate words.

[5] John v. 22. [6] Rev. i. 18.

the power of death, that is, the devil.[7] Satan's power of destruction is therefore now delivered, with other trophies of victory,[8] into the hands of the great Captain of our salvation.[9] The day of ultimate resurrection will attest this, when, after the blessed harvest of the first resurrection shall have been safe lodged, a thousand years, in the barns of God's eternal rest, those who had no part in that resurrection shall come forth at the voice of the Son of man, to bear reluctant witness to the glory of His power as the Lord of the dead.[1]

There is a resurrection both of the just and of the unjust.[2] With respect to the latter, some further remarks seem desirable. The vindication of the character of God, as the Judge and Avenger of sin, is the occasion of this resurrection. It is the prelude to God's last act with respect to sin. Now the root of sin is the devil. And so. it is written, "The devil sinneth from the beginning." The fruit of his work is death, and man, from the day when he yielded to the tempter, has fed upon that bitter fruit. But the death of the body is not the *fulfilment* of death. That first death is but the decease of a life which sin has limited in death by the sentence of God, who first breathed life into the creature of His hands. This death of fallen man is in Scripture referred to the devil as the wielder, under Divine permission and control, of its power. But there is

---
[7] Heb. ii. 14. [8] Eph. iv. 8; Col. ii. 15.
[9] Faith sees it thus, because faith sees truth as it is revealed in Christ. Satanic power may wield mortal weapons, even against God's saints; but in such conflict, though they love not their lives to the death, they overcome him by the blood of the Lamb, and by the word of their testimony. (Rev. xii. 11.)
[1] Rev. xx. 12. [2] John v. 27–29.

another death to which he will himself be subject. The sinner and his work will alike be swallowed up of that second and eternal death.[3] Resurrection, which to the believer is an entrance into the endless life, in hope of which he passes now the time of his patience, will be the preparation, to the unwashed sinner, for that final death from whence there is no more hope of resurrection or release. The deceiver and his willing victim find fellowship of ever-during woe in· the lasting bondage of the second death. This fearful reality of finished death, instead of being a cessation from sentient existence, is the entrance of its subject into the condition of awarded punishment. It will be the ultimate result of that day of appointed judgment,[4] in which the unconfessed secrets of men's hearts will be discovered, and a portion measured out to each according to his deeds. Unforgiven sin will receive at that day the judgment, already denounced against it, of the wrath of God.

But the Judge of that day is Christ. The Man whom God hath raised up from the dead will vindicate the perfect righteousness of God, by the just award, according to truth, of the eternal judgment from of old ordained against sin.[5] It is a wondrous and a solemn thought that thus brings the wide domain of corruption under the direct sway of the Lord Jesus, placing the dark beginnings of death under His control, who alone as yet has truly tasted death in its full reality as the penalty of human sin. By the *grace of God*, He has tasted death for every

[3] Rev. xx. 10–15. [4] Heb. ix. 27.
[5] Acts xvii. 31.

man.⁶ He died, and now the utmost chambers of the grave are under the absolute mastery of His hand, to be unlocked in due time by the word of His power. Christ died, then, to establish thus His right of dominion over the dead. By dying He has made death evermore His own.⁷

But He has also lived again. He is alive according to the power of an endless life. Life and the living, then, are His. For His return from the dead was the manifestation of His Person as the Prince and Lord of life. Having descended into the lower parts of the earth, He has ascended far above all heavens, to fill the abodes of life and joy with His fulness as the Lord of life, even as He had reached in that fulness the deep extreme of all that death contains. His dominion over the living He will exercise in power, as well as His lordship over the dead. He will drive far away and utterly remove the shadow of death from the redeemed heirs of life, when, in the majesty of His power, He calls back their bodies of humiliation from the dust. He will enfold in the mist of everlasting darkness the self-destroyed recusants of mercy, and the ungodly corrupters of His grace, when the hour of their judgment shall have come.⁸ As Lord of the living and the dead, He will do what He will with His own. The full tide of blessedness which flows in upon the heart of the believer from this demonstration of the sovereignty in power of the Saviour and lover of his soul, need not be told

---

⁶ ὑπὲρ παντός, Heb. ii. 9. As to the true meaning of this expression, see *Notes on the Hebrews* in loc.

⁷ And therefore *ours* who believe. Wondrous, and mighty, and triumphant truth! (1 Cor. iii. 22, 23.)

⁸ 2 Peter ii. 17; Jude 13.

to those who by faith have found their portion in the Lord.

The 10th verse returns to the subject of conscience, and re-states the question put in the 4th verse. There is now, however, a new argument of forbearance brought forward, which takes its rise from the doctrine of Christ's lordship above stated. There is a *judgment-seat*, at which all Christians must appear. But let us carefully mark the distinction which the Scripture draws between the judgment which the Lord will pass upon His *servants*, because they are such, and have wrought for His name, and the judgment which will sit upon those whose chief and decisive condemnation will be their insubjection to the Gospel of the grace of God. Respecting the believer in Jesus it is said, that he shall not come into judgment, but that he *is passed* from death unto life.[9] These are the words of Divine assurance, uttered by none other than the Judge Himself.

If the doctrines of grace, with which the earlier chapters of this Epistle so richly abound, have been received in simplicity into the reader's heart, he will not·need a large digression, in this place, in proof of the essential difference which exists between the citation of the believer before the judgment-seat of Christ, for the adjudication of reward or loss, according to the quality of his work,[1] and the entering into judgment, on the ground of human responsibilities, by one who has to learn Christ for the first time when revealed as the Judge. As to these responsibilities, they have, in the believer's case, already been borne and met for him to the full by the grace of Him who

[9] John v. 24.   [1] 1 Cor. iii.

died, the Just for the unjust. We who believe have boldness, therefore, in the day when others fear, because our fear of condemnation has been exchanged for the Divine assurance of the Holy Ghost, that to them that are in Christ there now remaineth no *condemnation*.

Still, it is a solemn truth that a believer has an account to render up to God—to God in Christ. A Christian's present position in the world is that of *a man of God*. He is called to be and to act among men worthy of God. Moreover, he is especially, and by name, the servant of Christ the Lord. For this service he has a sufficiency, not in himself, but by the grace of God, and therefore in proportion to his faith.[2] The Holy Ghost is, to the believer, the enabling power of all obedience to the will of God. All things pertaining to life and godliness are already given to him through the knowledge of Him who has called him through glory and virtue.[3]

Now the Lord is not indifferent to the ways of His saints. He has spoken no word in vain; and most assuredly the slighted commandments of God will have their vindication in due time. "The Lord will judge His people," is the expression of a standing principle of the Divine government. We have already seen, in the 11th chapter of this Epistle, one fearful exemplification of this principle in the case of the lifeless body of mere nominal profession. But it

---

[2] Col. i. 10, 11; 2 Thess. i. 11, 12.
[3] 2 Pet. i. Διὰ δόξης καὶ ἀρετῆς. If, however, the reading ἰδίᾳ δόξῃ κ. α. which seems to have most MS. authority (including *Cod. Sin.*) be adopted, the proper rendering will be, "By His own glory and virtue." God, that is, Himself being the example of our way. (Comp. Eph. v. 1.)

applies to that which is truly alive to God as well as to that which lives only in name.

It is, however, necessary to make a distinction between the *works* of a Christian and his confessed sins and failings. With respect to the former, a man may be flattering himself most foolishly in his own eyes, and mistaking external bustle and activity for true devotedness to Christ. His estimate may be most faulty and erroneous as to the measure and quality of his service here.[4] He may be comparing himself with others, and may think, in self-complacent foolishness, himself to be something, to the disparagement of others who perhaps may be, to their surprise and his, exalted far above him in the day when the Lord settles finally His house. Nay, if he be looking at his service at all, except in order to judge and to amend it, he most certainly will form wrong conclusions as to his position. Looking steadfastly at the *Lord* alone keeps the heart full, and the spiritual judgment, as well as the conscience, clear. Devotedness will follow, and keep pace with, *love*. The apostle himself stands before us as the most perfect example of true Christian service. He could call on his brethren to be followers of him, as he followed Christ.[5] As one who spoke in Christ and before God, he was able to allege the testimony of his conscience as to his pure and faithful conversation. Nor does he hide from our knowledge the rule by which he walked. It was by the zeal of Christ. "Not I, but Christ," was the motto and the power of

---

[4] The epistles addressed by the Lord to the Churches are full of the deepest and most practical instruction on this point.

[5] 1 Cor. xi. 1.

his service. The love of Christ constrained him; and so the manner and the ordering of his conversation were ever, *by the grace of God.*[6] This kept him full of Christ, and therefore of love and Divine energy. Yet even he had to abide the award of that coming day, for the final approval of his service; nor did he venture to anticipate his Master's judgment, nor estimate beforehand the measure of his praise,[7] though he knew well that a crown of life and glory, a crown of *righteousness*, was ready in the Lord's hand to be placed upon his head. Nor is the crown for him only, but for all who love the appearing of the righteous Judge.[8] The confidence which remained always clear and steadfast in his heart, was founded solely on his conscious enjoyment of the grace of God.[9] That, therefore, which stayed his soul, and kept him busy with a glad and constant alacrity in the labour of love, is common to *all* saints, as alike partakers of Christ. Assuredly there shall be no shame to those who hold fast Christ as their confidence towards God, and whose only ambition now is to be acceptable to the Lord. Meanwhile, the word of needful caution is, "He that glorieth, let him glory in the Lord. For not he that commendeth himself is approved, but whom the Lord commendeth.[1]

On the other hand, the conscious sins and failures of a Christian are, when confessed, forgiven things, and therefore *forgotten* also by the mercy which remits them.[2] The faithfulness of God secures this.[3] Confession of sin, or of shortcoming, casts the matter

[6] 2 Cor. i. 12.
[9] 2 Cor. v. 5–9.
[7] 1 Cor. iv. 1–5.
[1] 2 Cor. x. 17, 18.
[3] 1 John i. 9.
[8] 2 Tim. iv. 8.
[2] Heb. x. 17.

confessed, with the person who confesses it, on the righteous advocacy of Jesus. The blessed Lord acts thus for the instantaneous removal of all that can defile or darken the conscience, or afflict the soul with a sense of guilty deficiency. It is for this very purpose that the priestly ministry of the Son of God has been ordained, that the once-purged worshipper might be sustained in the presence of God, notwithstanding his shortcomings of every kind, according to the fulness of that grace which flows evermore towards him, through the intercession of our great High Priest.[4] Peace thus is again restored to the conscience, while the heart yet retains its humbling sense of natural vileness. A personal appreciation of the power of restoring mercy effectually humbles and *keeps low* the soul.

But forgiven sin is no subject of the Lord's judgment at that day. Having acted as our Advocate, for the lightening of our faces when ashamed before God, we need not fear that He will then revive and reproduce the pardoned sin, to the denial of His own work and the contradiction of the perfect truth of God. It is a promise more than once declared in the Old Testament, for the reässuring and encouragement of God's true penitents, that their sins should not be *mentioned* to them any more;[5] and now that Divine redemption has effectually wrought what could not be attained by legal righteousness, such promises, with all other once *conditional* words of comfort, are become "yea and amen" to the justified believer in Jesus.[6] "Their sins and their iniquities will I

---

[4] Heb. iv. 14–16, and vii. 25. [5] Ezek. xviii. 22, and xxxiii. 16.
[6] 2 Cor. i. 20.

remember no more," is the testimony of the Holy Ghost, concerning the abiding state of God's mind in Christ towards believing sinners. But things once buried in oblivion by the grace of God (whose Spirit thus, by words so full of precious meaning, declares the Omnipotence of Love to extend even to the *forgetfulness* of what has been, in the present contemplation of what is), are surely not again to come into mind with Him who has already welcomed us, with perfect acceptance, in the Son of His love. Under the Law, there was provided, besides "the blood of bulls and goats," the "ashes of an heifer sprinkling the unclean;" a figure which shews forth the lasting virtue of the once shed blood of Christ. The worshipper once purged has no more conscience of sins, because he stands by faith, not upon lustral ordinances, but in the efficacy of sacrificial *truth*.[7] Unbelief may gather like a cloud over the heart, when self-condemned; but that cloud is dispelled, and God's abiding peace restored, the moment faith returns to its proper object, which is Christ. The eye of God, who is greater than our hearts, and knoweth all things,[8] rests in full complacency on Him who is gone into heaven for our sakes. What was outwardly effected under the Levitical ordinances by successive *acts*, is now inwardly tasted and enjoyed through our steadfast continuance in the *faith*.[9]

It is not, then, a second judgment of faults already judged in ourselves, and faithfully forgiven us of God, which awaits the believer at the judgment-seat of Christ. That place and hour are for the bringing

---

[7] *Notes on the Hebrews*, chaps. ix. and x.
[8] 1 John iii. 19–21, i. 9.   [9] Col. i. 22, 23.

to light the hidden things of darkness, and for the manifestation of *the counsels of the hearts;*[1] "and then," it is added, "shall every man have praise of God." Secret acts of love, and settled purposes of heart, uncommunicated to any mortal ear, will then come forth from the treasury of the Lord's remembrance, and receive the praise which He for whose sake these things have been devised and wrought will know well how to award. Then, too, will other purposes and acts, the doing or imagining of which may haply have fed with illusive expectations of reward the hearts of those whose minds were lofty because of knowledge, or falsely confident because of cumbrous service, be weighed and balanced at the beam of truth, and being found imperfect, will be cast aside. What once seemed gold or silver to the partial eye of its possessor will prove, perhaps, but wood or stubble, when submitted to the burning ordeal of God.

On the next two verses (11, 12) I only remark, that they form a striking testimony to the person of the blessed Lord. The Godhead of Christ is perhaps nowhere more strongly and directly stated. The passage from Isaiah here quoted has been noticed before, in connection with the subject of the glory of the risen Jesus as exalted and glorified of God.[2] There is a difference in the uses which the Spirit of God sometimes makes of the same passage of Scripture. Thus, in the present instance, the words of Isaiah are cited, not for the demonstration of the Lordship and dominion of Christ as that which He has received of God, but rather to affirm

[1] 1 Cor. iv. 5.   [2] Phil. ii. 10.

the proper glory of His person as essentially Divine. It is to *God* that we have to give account; each for himself accounting, and not for another, unto Him that trieth the hearts.[3] We may be sure that if our present thoughts of the grace wherein we stand do not lead us into the presence of God, we are not in our true position. To have to do with God is our calling now. "If our heart condemn us not, then have we confidence toward God. And whatsoever we ask, we receive of Him, because we keep His commandments, and do those things that are pleasing in His sight."[4] It is thus that an exercised heart and conscience make the prospect of appearing to give account to God a prospect of joy rather than of dread. For all who truly walk with God, already are made manifest to Him, and have no dearer wish than that their judgment should proceed from Him.[5] That they who judge themselves shall not be judged, is elsewhere laid down as a settled maxim of Divine government.[6] But do we always judge ourselves? This is a question which each believer should often put to his own heart. For it cannot be doubted, that *neglected* sins, habitual and contented carelessness, with all that savours of high minded self-complacency, must shew themselves again at that great day, to become fuel for the fire which will try the work of every man.[7] So also will there then be called up, for a final hearing and decision, a multitude of questions, which in the long day of

---

[3] There is, too, an account to be rendered, by such as take in hand to guide Christ's sheep, of the souls over which they watch. (Heb. xiii. 17; Acts xx.) The doctrine in the text is general.
[4] 1 John iii. 21, 22. [5] Ps. cxxxix.; 1 Cor. xv. 58; 2 Tim. i. 12.
[6] 1 Cor. xi. 31. [7] 1 Cor. iii. 13–15.

faith and patience, have divided saint from saint, and made (to our shame it must be said,) internal controversy to be a permanent condition of the Church. The question put in verse 3 of this chapter will not, until then, receive its perfect and conclusive answer. What we remember as penitents the Lord forgets; but He has a book of remembrance for all things, good or evil, which we have done and not repented, since we took His name as our own.[8]

Verses 13–15. The certainty of a coming judgment of the Lord upon His people's ways, imposes on them severally a new and especial responsibility, and that of a mutual kind. Instead of judging one another, they are exhorted to "judge this rather, that no man put a stumbling-block or an occasion to fall in his brother's way." Every Christian has a living interest in his brother, as a member of the body of Christ. As a consequence of this, he should be interested also in his brother's walk. He is to look diligently to himself and to his own conduct, lest, by too heedless a use of his liberty, he unwittingly become a hindrance in his brother's course. He is encouraged also to make straight paths for such as are *out* of the way.[9] The effects of the conduct of God's saints upon each other's walk, as those effects are made apparent in the day of the Lord, will alone discover to the full the value of maintaining godly circumspection—of keeping a conscience void of offence towards *man* as well as towards God. Meanwhile there is but one way of avoiding occasion of stumbling. Love of the brethren, if real, is a sure preservative from offence.[1] It ought to be an easy

[8] 2 Cor. v. 8–10.   [9] Heb. xii. 13.   [1] 1 John ii. 10.

thing to them who are born of love to walk in love. Yet, alas! it is here that the root of *all* difficulty lies. And sad indeed is the feeling which so often rises in the heart, while pondering the precepts of the Spirit of grace (founded as they are on the perfect testimonies of accomplished mercy), at the thought how little there is found the mind to care naturally for the estate of one's brethren. The complaint of the apostle has its echo through all time.[2] Nor will love have its perfect course until the mighty change from flesh to spirit, once wrought upon these bodies of humiliation, shall leave no longer anything of ours to be cared for; and we shall know, in the light of His pure joy, that when seeking the things of Jesus we were most effectually seeking *our own*.

The 14th verse is of importance. I regard it as superseding, to the Gentile Christian, the rescript of the Church at Jerusalem, so far as that related to the eating of meats offered to idols.[3] "I *know*, and am persuaded of the Lord Jesus, that there is *nothing* unclean of itself," &c. The conscience of a believer is expected to be adjusted to the truth in which he stands. A risen man is a *new* man.[4] The earth on which he tarries until his change come is the Lord's, with all the fulness which it contains.[5] He is free from *all* legal bondage. This truth was not brought fully forth while as yet the Lord's mercy lingered over Jerusalem, and the apparent throne of the

[2] Phil. iii. 20, 21.
[3] Even the prohibition with respect to things strangled, founded as it appears to be on Gen. ix. 4, I should regard as no longer binding on one who draws the daily aliment of his soul from the shed blood of the Lamb. But as to these things, we do well to heed the general caution in the text.
[4] Col. iii.   [5] 1 Cor. x. 25–29.

Spirit's government was in the Church assembled there. The proper apostolate of the Gentiles was but beginning in the person of Paul, who was himself the bearer of the decrees ordained of the apostles and elders which were at Jerusalem.[6] But we have here, and elsewhere in his epistles, an estimate of things founded on the now declared and manifested setting aside of law and ordinance *of every kind;* because Christ, as the life, the second Adam, the *beginning,* the first-born from the dead, as well as the substance of all Jewish ordinance, is now clearly made known as a present truth. The position of the Church, as already raised in Him from the dead, was preached among the Gentiles; who were to find in that Gospel of the grace of God which revealed to them their *heavenly calling,* the maxims and precepts which should regulate their earthly walk.[7]

Still, conscience should always determine practically our way. "To him that esteemeth anything to be unclean, it is unclean." And love, which is the bond of perfectness, would keep a man who walked by that rule from grieving his brother's conscience with his liberty of meats (verse 15). It is to be remarked, that the exercise and privilege of personal liberty is founded on individual faith. It is thus a *private* matter strictly. It is a constituent part of that perfect blessing in liberty which makes the believer free and happy anywhere and everywhere, in the remembrance that he is both personally Christ's, and that he sees, and touches, and uses nothing that is not Christ's. Where, therefore, a Christian is associated with others, this conscious feeling of liberty

[6] Acts xvi. 4.   [7] Col. ii. 20–23.

(though ever held firmly fast in his heart) is to be tempered in practice by the mightier principle of love. He is not to think of himself, but to have respect to the state and requirements of those with whom he is associated, or before whom he walks.

Edification is to be his end. But the first condition of this is self-denial. The importance which the Spirit of God attaches to this is evinced by the strong language found at the close of this verse. What does not edify or build up, does pull down and destroy. A doubtful heart is the constant associate of a violated conscience. But conscience is often injured through the evil force of example, and when this is long persisted in, it necessarily becomes dulled and hardened in its temper. A false and carnal boldness, far different, indeed, from the confidence of faith, is noted by the Spirit as a natural result to the consciences of our fellow Christians, where liberty is the only rule, and spiritual expediency is left out of our account.[8] But to put conscience aside is to expose faith to shipwreck.[9] It is a ruinous thing. To blunt conscience is practically to lose Christ. He cannot reveal Himself where His claims are deliberately set aside to please the flesh. The importance of the principle here enforced cannot be overrated. The declension and

[8] 1 Cor. viii. *passim*, spec. 10, 11; 1 Cor. vi. 12.
[9] 1 Tim. i. 19. The life of every Christian is hid with Christ in God, and therefore secure from ultimate loss. He is preserved in Jesus Christ. (Jude 1.) The apostle's question is not here with the ultimate loss or safety of the soul which really belongs to Christ, but to show that all is gone when conscience is let go. Gone, that is, as far as the Christian is himself concerned; but where we fail, there God still abideth faithful. Yet, in stating the principle, he shows (and it is a most solemn consideration) that the carelessness of a Christian may harden a sinner to his destruction.

corruption so generally observable in large bodies of Christians, after a while, arise mainly from failure on this point. Love is succeeded by mere imitative action, and outward consistency becomes a wretched substitute for the effectual work of faith.

But to proceed. The admonitory caution in the 16th verse is succeeded, in the one following, by a moral definition of the kingdom of God. It is *not* meat and drink; it *is* righteousness, peace, and joy, in the Holy Ghost. What God owns is spirit, and not flesh. But meat and drink are not of the Spirit, but of the flesh. They are things to be used to God, if used at all. Essentially, they are neither of blame nor of praise;[1] but if not used in subjection to the truth which is above them, they surely work evil, and not good. On the other hand, the undisturbed sway of God is known by three tokens here given. Where God is enthroned in the conscience according to the truth of the Gospel, there will be found righteousness, and peace, and joy in the Holy Ghost. Meats and drinks can establish no heart before God. They may, and often do, disturb and unsettle, but it is grace alone which can establish, strengthen, and settle, the soul.[2] Verse 18 applies itself searchingly, yet with comfort, to the individual heart. It is well for a Christian to ask himself often *how* and in what things he is serving Christ; otherwise, zeal may sometimes injure rather than profit. Nothing is either pleasing to God, or profitable to men, which is not done in the power of this kingdom of God. So long as a believer is realizing the presence and leaning on the power of God, he will surely be acting

[1] 1 Cor. viii. 8. [2] Heb. xiii. 9; 1 Pet. v. 10.

rightly, if he act at all. For *God* will then act by him, and in him, to the fulfilment of His own will. When He is not thus kept in mind, things right in themselves turn often to a mischievous result, because it really is the fleshly will that is at work, instead of the Spirit of God.

I do not examine minutely the remaining verses. The reïteration of the principle (verses 20, 21) attests its intrinsic importance in the eye of the Spirit of God. But in verse 22 we are furnished with a decisive test by which genuine spiritual liberty may be at all times distinguished from its counterfeit, carnal wilfulness. "Hast thou faith? Have it to thyself *before God.*" There is a careless assumption of privilege, founded on doctrinal liberty, which is quite a different thing from faith. The faith here spoken of is a fruit of the Spirit.[3] It is not justifying faith in Christ, but one of its results, discovering itself practically according to the measure of the justified believer's communion with the Lord. This faith is a *home* joy of the soul. It abides within, choosing the privacy of the presence it loves best.[4] Faith of this kind courts no observation, and makes no boast of privilege. It is shewn in its effects, and these effects are always according to God, and therefore for blessing to others. The light and liberty enjoyed within may enable one thus blessed to help forward with more effect the lagging steps of those who need some guide to clear them, it may be, from the mazy ground in which they are bewildered. Meanwhile, it is the heart's pure peace and blessedness to be thus fully filled with Christ.

[3] Gal. v. 22.   [4] Prov. v. 15–19.

But there is another point connected with this. The presence of God is the only place where faith can really act. But God is *light;*[5] in that light therefore is everything to be weighed before it can be rightly allowed under the plea of liberty. Conscience thus becomes the monitor and guide of faith. Else mere persuasion of self-will might easily usurp the place of genuine faith toward God. And so it is added: "Happy is he that condemneth not himself in the thing that he alloweth." A weighty sentence, and full of needed caution, such as may temper and regulate the flow of Christian liberty, lest, ceasing to be restrained within the conscious limits of godly fear, it should degenerate to mere self-pleasing, and the license of the natural will.

The chapter closes with a yet stronger enforcement of the principle under review.[6] A Christian is a man of faith. If he ever walks according to a lower principle, he dishonours the standing which he occupies. Nothing that he does can be merely indifferent; it is an act either of obedience or of sin: that is, he is either pleasing God or himself. Hesitation, therefore, or doubt as to any course, is a sufficient reason for abstaining from it. The moment there is a question as to the nature or quality of a step proposed, the path is already closed to the believer. For faith can go nowhere without God. Actions which do not satisfy the conscience before Him are always wrong. God leads in the way of

---

[5] John i. 5.

[6] The connection between these verses is very clear. We are self-condemned if we eat, or otherwise act, *doubtfully.* κρίνων in verse 22, is about equivalent in force to κατακέκριται in verse 23. For further illustration of the principle, see 1 John iii. 19–21.

uprightness. The light which He *is* is radiated through the word into the heart that lives upon Him. The consideration of the large amount of action in which a saint may be engaged, with, perhaps, *no thought at all* as to its true nature or intent, is a truly solemn one when taken in the light of this passage.

It will be seen, that though the particular instance stated in this verse is a religious scruple with respect to meats, the principle which it illustrates is one of the widest description. Yet we must be on our guard against a *fretful* conscience. Light is the healthful atmosphere of conscience. But grace is the ground on which the soul of the believer rests. The *word of grace* is the medium through which the light which is to shew to him his path is communicated to a child of God. That the children are *free*[7] is the Divine assurance of Him who alone had the right of sonship in that house of liberty into which He has now brought the believing heirs of promise, until, by His finished work of grace and truth, He had himself secured eternally that liberty to them.[8] May we, then, who believe, *stand fast* in that liberty with which Christ has made us free.[9]

[7] Matt. xvii. 26.   [8] John viii. 32–36.   [9] Gal. v. 1.

CHAPTER XV.

THE present division of these chapters is not a happy one. The first seven verses of chapter xv. conclude the subject which immediately precedes, and should not have been separated from their context. At the 8th verse there is a change in the subject, as we shall presently see. Meanwhile let us follow the apostle to the close of his exhortation.

Verse 1 assigns to the "strong" their true place and service in the Church of God. Their strength, if it be really such, has here a labour matched with its degree. There is a tender and yet powerful appeal in this passage, addressed to the true sympathies of the inner man, which is well fitted to check and abase that natural highmindedness which, even in a godly man, is ever ready to assert itself. We are to have *faith* to ourselves. We are to be *strong* for others. Looking on the burdens and infirmities of his brethren, a believer who is really "strong in the Lord, and in the power of His might," finds suited occasion for the exercise of that strength in ministering to the infirmities of the weak.[1] This is a work which, because it calls for patience, and forbearance, and diligence; because, too, its fruit often lies long hidden, and its present effect may seem, to those who

---

[1] Eph. vi. 10; Gal. vi. 1, 2.

judge by appearances, to be little more than a vain spending of labour, is one of no attraction to the natural mind. With many kinds of Christian service natural elements easily mingle; and, where they enter, always deteriorate, if they do not utterly corrupt, the blessing of the work. But with the patient labour of love the flesh can have no part. It can oppose and resist it; and so indeed it does, because at every step it finds itself thwarted in its natural course of self-pleasing; but *further* such a work it never can. The Christian, because he is a vessel of the *grace of God*, is exhorted not to please himself. For he is not his own. But the services expected from him are not those of involuntary compulsion. The Spirit, to whose leading the children are committed, seeks rather to excite them to the willing devotedness of love. He lays down, indeed, His Divine principles, as the guiding maxims of Christian conduct; but preceptive direction is sustained, and the believer invested with power for its accomplishment, by a continual reference to the person of Christ Himself. It is *faith* only that can work by love.[2]

Accordingly, after laying down for us this rule of charity, as the bond of fellowship within the Church of God (verse 2), he adds the commanding motive which the grace of the Lord Jesus Christ supplies, with an ever-increasing force and effect, to the inner man, as the believer is personally growing in the knowledge of Him. "For even Christ pleased not Himself; but, as it is written, The reproaches of them that reproached thee fell on me." The glory of that blessed One was to be the servant of the Father's

[2] Gal. v. 6.

will, and the minister of the desperate necessity of poor sin-ruined man: "The Son of man came not to be ministered unto, but to minister, and to give His life a ransom for many."[3] It was not for Himself that He came into the world; nor was it for His own pleasure that He remained in it. For the world, in which He was the "Man of sorrows," could be no place of rest or happiness to Jesus. He tarried there awhile, and as a Stranger, only that He might fulfil the word of God. He was sent, and He obeyed. That which was good in the Father's sight rejoiced the Spirit of the lonely Son of God.[4]

We have seen in the foregoing chapter, how the Spirit of God sets forth the Divine majesty of Christ, as Lord both of the dead and the living, and how the prospect of their appearing at His judgment-seat is made to bear upon the conscience of His servants. But now the blessed One, who in that day is to judge our work of what sort it is, comes before our view as the pattern of the way in which that work is to be done.

It is the happy privilege of a believer, that there is nothing taught or commanded him of God, which is not presented to his conscience in immediate connection with the Person of the Saviour. We are called to learn *Him*, that the mind which was in Him may also be in us. The disciple, as he meditates the Master's sayings with desire of practical conformity to Him, finds strength renewed for more abundant service, when he calls to mind that every precept which directs his conscience proceeds from One who has already saved him in Himself. The grace in-

[3] Matt. xx. 28.   [4] Matt. xi. 25, 26.

effable of Jesus, who, although the hand which was nailed with pain and ignominy to the cross was the hiding of Almighty power,[5] yet suffered in weakness, and with the utterance of that loud cry of sore distress, which told of a heart broken under the sense of God's desertion,[6] is the subject which the Holy Ghost now sets before His people's view, in order to produce in them a *Christian* frame and temper, in the true sense of the word. The contradiction of sinners, which in the patience of His perfect love the Lord of glory willingly endured against Himself, is the living lesson which is spread before the Christian as a learner in the school of God. The grace and patience, which in their completed triumph in the Cross, have wrought for us our endless peace, are reflected in us only as we know the morally transforming power of His presence. The believer learns to deny himself, when he perceives in the self-denial of the Son of God the immediate condition of his own redemption. Christian self-denial is a fruit borne only through the energy of Christian love. Christian love, again, is but the reverberate echo of the love of God in Christ to us-ward who believe. We love Him because He first loved us.[7]

It was the zeal of God's house that ate up the strength of the Man of God's delight. But the parent of that zeal was the knowledge of the Father's love, which filled the heart of His eternal Son. Under the likeness of a servant, He abode still in that love;[8] dwelling in and proving its delight, in continual obedience to the Father's will. It was this

[5] Hab. iii. 4.
[6] Matt. xxvii. 46.
[7] 1 John iv. 19.
[8] John xv. 10.

divine and perfect fellowship in love that made all toil and suffering endurable to Jesus. He leaned upon that love for the present solace of His grief. He looked to its bright end of joy, and drew from thence persuasion of triumphant endurance, when in immediate prospect of the cross.[9] Jesus bore the cross, because He loved the Father.[1] With that love there was indeed united a kindred sentiment, though looking to a widely different object. For Jesus loved His *own*. Yet the energy of His love was manifested ever in the form of perfect service to the God whom He was born to serve.[2] Made in the likeness of a servant, He was *obedient* unto death.[3] The cross was the tremendous, and yet, to the perfect devotedness of the obedient One, the acceptable expression of the Father's will. For love lives only to perform the will of love; while the horror of that great darkness was soon to be forgotten in the brightness of His everlasting joy.[4] Now the witness of these things is given for our sakes. They are written, not only for the furtherance of our joy, and the confirmation of our hope, but also for the fashioning of our hearts and ways "as obedient children," according to the pattern of the perfect Truth.

The quotation from the Psalms, contained in the 4th verse, gives the apostle an occasion of settling the minds of the saints at Rome, and of all believers, as to the true value and bearing of the Old Testament Scriptures. Questions might arise, and probably had already arisen, as to the continued validity and authority of Jewish Scripture, now that the full

[9] Heb. xii. 2. [1] John xiv. 31. [2] Gal. iv. 4, 5.
[3] Phil. ii. 7, 8. [4] Heb. xii. 2.

and especial revelation of the truth had been made by the Lord and the apostles of His word.[5] Already he had quoted largely from the Old Testament in the course of his argumentative demonstration of Christian doctrine, and the exposition of God's dispensational dealings in which the nation of Israel held so conspicuous a place. Now, however, there is a direct reference made to the Old Testament, as to that in which the Christian is to search for and discover Christ not less than in the New. It is presented to the believer as entirely *his own;* as written for him and for his sake. This is important, because it enables the Christian to lay distinct claim to *all* Scripture as his own. But while this is so, he is cast, for a right perception of the relative bearing of each part, and its more or less immediate application to the Church, on the Spirit of God, which is given to them that believe—to lead and to direct them, as the Spirit of truth, into *all* the truth.[6] Acting upon the children's understandings as the "Spirit of a sound mind," He thus enables them to discriminate

[5] How early these questions arose, and how earnestly the father of lies laboured to break the unity of Scripture, is well known to students of Church history. Nor need the modern Christian be reminded of the efforts so assiduously made with a similar object by the gnostic theology of the present day.

[6] John xvi. 13. ὁδηγήσει ὑμᾶς εἰς πᾶσαν τὴν ἀλήθειαν. The Scriptures testify of Christ. The Old Testament, equally with the New, is the word of Christ which is to dwell richly in the saints. (Col. iii. 16.) Yet how needful to distinguish between the widely differing character and object of the varied testimonies of the One Spirit. Christ is the unity of Divine truth. But to conclude from this that the Church is the unity of the Divine work and purpose in redemption would be to err most injuriously. Yet this error has prevailed, and yet does prevail, over many Christian minds. But where this is the case, the word of God is sure to be more or less dishonoured by perversion from its just intent. This remark applies to much which goes under the inappropriate name of "spiritualization," when used with reference to the exclusive Christian appropriation of Scripture properly Jewish.

between the widely differing though kindred topics of Divine revelation.[7] The word of the Old Testament is, then, placed on an equal level with that of the New. Both are the testimony of the same Spirit, and both alike belong to the children of God. They were written for us Christians, though doubtless not for us alone.

The Scriptures are presented here to the believer as the means and practical supply of patience, of comfort, and of hope. They are so because they are the word of God, who is alone the minister of these things. He is the God of patience, and the God of consolation (verse 5), even as He is the God of hope. He is to be sought and inquired for, as such, in the word of His own grace. And here it is only necessary to repeat, that what is given to us is the *entire* word. The habit of partial selection which is so common among Christians is an injury to their own souls, as well as a neglect (rather *because* it is a neglect) of the gracious provision which the Father of lights has furnished for the necessary instruction of those who are His children in the midst of the darkness of this world.[8] Such an acquaintance only with the

[7] Phil. i. 9; 2 Tim. i. 7.

[8] A mind really subject to Scripture, as the *word of God*, will find no difficulties where those who are destitute of faith discover them at every step. Such an one will easily distinguish between the primary intention of much of that which was written aforetime, and its lasting power and significance as the living voice of *God*. God, who spake to the fathers by the prophets, now speaks to us by His Son. (Heb. i. 1, 2.) But the true Light which now shines, not only demonstrates the intrinsic unprofitableness of the legal ordinances, but turns the former testimonies to the new and happier purpose of unfolding more abundantly, by means of their elaborate variety and minuteness of detail, the fulness of that grace and truth which came by Jesus Christ. While this principle is illustrated in all the books of the New Testament, it is in the Epistle to the Hebrews that it receives its largest and most striking exemplification. See *Notes on the Hebrews*, passim.

word of Scripture as suffices to keep the springs of salvation fairly within the soul's view, is not sufficient for the complete equipment of the man of God; for it may be safely said, that a just appreciation of the word of God is impossible where the soul of a believer is not sufficiently established in the grace of the Gospel to enable him to see, and understand, and feel, that his individual salvation in Christ is the *beginning*, and not the *end* of his calling. His justification and sanctification in Christ are the preparation by which he is made ready now to know the will of God, to become a partaker, through the Holy Ghost, of a wisdom and knowledge which it is the portion of the heirs of promise only to possess, and the revelation of which is now made to such as a mystery, according to the wisdom and prudence of the God of grace.[9] Hope, then, will abound, with comfort and patience, according to the diligent simplicity of our faith in pondering the whole word of Christ, and thus increasing in the knowledge of God.

Verses 5–7. The end of individual growth and blessing is union in the practical fellowship of the truth enjoyed. Praise, one-minded and one-toned, offered to God in the perfect knowledge of Him as the Father of our Lord Jesus Christ, is the comeliest fruit of the one blessed Spirit by whom both Jew and Gentile, in the unity of the New Man, alike have access as the true and acceptable worshippers of His name.[1]

God, then, is glorified (verse 7) by our mutual reception of one another in the faith and power of the name of Christ. Personal knowledge of the Saviour

[9] Eph. i.   [1] Eph. ii. 15–18.

is thus laid as the basis of Christian communion and fellowship. "*As* Christ has received us," so are we to receive one another. To receive on a lower ground than this, by substituting mere verbal recognition of doctrine for living faith, would be to exchange the communion of the Holy Ghost for the agreement of human opinion, and to forget that "living stones" can alone be used for the construction of the temple of the living God. To add to the Divine conditions of life and holiness further requirements, as necessary to communion, would be to grieve the Spirit of grace, and to glory in man rather than in the Lord; turning thus the perfect liberty of the grace of God into an evil bondage to the will of man.[a] They were to receive one another. The strong were to receive the weak, the weak the strong. The Jew was to acknowledge the Gentile; the Gentile to rejoice together with the Jew, as an equal partaker of the grace of Christ. Christ had received them both alike to the glory of God. God was thus glorified in them, as alike vessels of His own mercy. The cross, which annihilates for the believer all fleshly distinctions (because it is the dissolution in death of the flesh itself), was their preparation for the glory which they looked for as their portion, through the knowledge of

---

[a] It may not be superfluous, in the present day of general laxity in doctrine, to remind the reader that the holiness of a believer's standing is the holiness of *truth* (Eph. iv. 24); that "the fruit of the Spirit is in all goodness, and righteousness, and *truth*" (Eph. v. 9); that the toleration, therefore, of unsoundness in doctrine is utterly repugnant to the first principle of Christian communion, the condition and the power of which is the presence of the Spirit of Truth. To receive into Christian fellowship one unsound in doctrine, would be to receive him, not to the glory of God, but to His highest dishonour, by refusing to distinguish between the Spirit of Truth and the spirit of Error. (1 John iv. 1–6.)

Jesus as the Resurrection and the Life. They were, then, to know one another, not after the flesh, but after the Spirit, "according to Christ"[3] (verse 5), and by thus honouring the name of Jesus, they would be truly giving glory to God.

At the 8th verse, the apostle takes up a new subject, though not without its connection with what has just preceded. The doctrine already laid down of their common acceptance, in the way of grace, does not interfere with the question of the separate calling of the Jew and the Gentile. To the former, the sending forth of Jesus was the proof and witness of the faithfulness of God, who redeemed in the person of His Son the promises made to the fathers. "Jesus Christ was a minister of the circumcision *for the truth of God*, to confirm the promises made unto the fathers." How these promises, confirmed and secured in the person of Christ, will have their eventual fulfilment in their destined objects, we have already seen. On the other hand, the Gentiles were to glorify God for His *mercy* (verse 9). As strangers to the covenants of promise, they had been taken up in the way of pure and unsought grace and mercy.

The passages which are quoted in succession in the following verses (9–12) deserve careful attention. They are here quoted in order to attest the unity of Scripture as the word of Christ. If the passages be examined, there is not one of them which has yet received its complete fulfilment. The first in the series might appear at first sight an exception, but it is not really such.[4] A careful examination of the several places from whence these extracts have been

[3] Κατὰ Χριστόν.   [4] See *Notes on the Psalms*.

made, will show that in every case the object before the mind of the Spirit is not only the glorified person of Christ, but that person and that glory in their special and yet future manifestation in connection with the accomplishment of *earthly* promise. They relate to the effects to be produced hereafter upon the nations of the world by the earthly reign of Immanuel, as the true Son of David, the anointed King of Israel. The quotation from Psalm cxvii. 1, is clearly an utterance of the grateful celebration of Israel's new-born joy and blessedness, when reïnstated in the favour of Jehovah according to the fulfilment of His loving-kindness and His truth. Filled themselves, and satisfied, with the merciful kindness of the Lord, they call on the Gentiles to share their joy, and to echo their praise. As it is written in the preceding verse, "Rejoice, ye Gentiles, *with* His people."

We have already considered, in a former chapter, the present condition of the nation, and have seen how its restoration to the mercies of the Lord is made dispensationally to attend the issue of the present work of God among the Gentiles, during the time when they are enemies, as concerning the Gospel, for the Gentiles' sake.[5] The passages here quoted are, in fact, all of them Millennial passages. Yet have they a fulfilment in principle even now. The grace which is to have its triumphant manifestation in the kingdom of the glorified Messiah, is already the ground of the believing Gentile's confidence and joy. The Person of the Lord, in whom all the promises of God are yea and Amen, is the one great subject of the

[5] Chap. xi. 26.

Spirit's present testimony in the word. Thus, while clearly discriminating between the differing and often contrasted portions of the perfect truth, the well-taught Christian is already in possession of that which makes all Scripture directly applicable to the furtherance of his own proper blessing, as an heir of *all*.[6]

Christ being known through the Spirit as the substance of the promises, the believer can place himself, by anticipation, in that day when the root of Jesse shall be manifested as the ensign of the nations,[7] and when the Gentiles will rest under the sway of that sceptre of Peace and Righteousness, which shall then be held, as the rod of fruitful blessing, in the hand of the glorified Son of David, the God of the whole earth. The Gentiles will in that day hope in Him who is the desire of all nations. But the *now* believing Gentile knows that hope already, in a yet higher and more abundant measure of blessing. The day which brings the earthly hope of Jew and Gentile within their reach, shall witness the heavenly glory of those who now trust in Christ; of those who, relatively to the pervading reign of Millennial blessing, are said to have *fore-hoped* in Christ,[8] and for whom that special blessing is reserved which belongs only to those who, not having seen, have yet believed.[9] For it is in the light of the glorified Church, the reigning bride of the Lamb, that the restored and justified people of Israel, and the nations of the

---

[6] Rev. xxi. 7; 1 Cor. iii. 21–23.

[7] Isaiah ix. 10–16. The apostle's quotation is not from the Hebrew original, but from the Septuagint.

[8] Eph. i. 12. Εἰς τὸ εἶναι ἡμᾶς εἰς ἔπαινον τῆς δόξης αὐτοῦ τοὺς προηλπικότας ἐν τῷ Χριστῷ.

[9] John xx. 29; 1 Peter i. 8, 9.

world which share the blessing of Israel, will rejoice in that day.

The Person of Christ is the hope of the believer now. The same Person will be the hope of the nations hereafter, when His dominion shall be to the ends of the earth. Kings and nations, rulers and tribes, will then acknowledge, in the day of *His power*,[1] the name which as yet is known only to "the election," who are called to bear His reproach, and to confess His shame as their glory until He come. The transition from the 12th to the 13th verse is not so well appreciated by an English reader, who is not aware that the last word in verse 12 should be "hope," and not "trust." The God of hope is invoked to fill them with all joy and peace in believing, that they may *abound* in hope by the power of the Holy Ghost. This is a very full expression when its connection with the foregoing passages is seen. The Gentiles will laud and magnify the name of Jesus in the day when the kings of the earth shall sing in the ways of the Lord, because the displayed majesty of His glory is great.[2] Very full will be the cup of blessing which, in that day, will satisfy the desires of the nations who stand in the blessing of the seed of Abraham.[3] But that day is not yet. The night which precedes it is indeed far spent, and the day is at hand; but as yet the creature waits in earnest ex-

[1] It is in one sense already the day of His power. All power has been committed to Him of the Father, power in heaven and power in earth. (Matt. xxviii. 18.) To the Church, which knows Him as its Head, this is a realized truth. The Holy Ghost is the witness of it, and faith is the means of its appreciation. But it is to faith alone that this is now revealed. While we see Jesus crowned with glory and honour, we see not yet all things put under Him. For that He awaits the day appointed of the Father.

[2] Psalm cxxxviii. 4, 5.   [3] Gen. xii. 3.

pectation for the manifestation of the sons of God. Until then, the sieve of vanity contains the nations of the earth, in readiness for that last shaking,[4] which shall produce as its result the apparent presence in glory of Him who, having borne up from of old the pillars of creation, will then manifestly be known as the One whose hand establishes, in the sure fulfilment of recorded *mercy*, that which must first be shaken in the righteous judgment of His truth.

But in the mean while, the believer, as a child of hope, and an anointed heir of promise, has out-spread before him in the word of truth the wide domain of the patrimony of the Son of God, the Heir of all things. The Holy Ghost is given to him to be the witness and revealer of this, and of his personal interest in it all as a joint-heir with Christ. The God and Father of the Lord Jesus Christ, the giver of the inheritance, thus becomes the God of the believer's hope. This hope, which is Christ Himself, comprises, as one of its specific expectations, the fair scene of Millennial promise. The dispensation of the fulness of times, when earth as well as heaven shall be held under the confessed dominion of Christ, is, to the disciple of the Holy Ghost, the first bright page of the exhaustless volume of promise. It is the first of the *ages* which are yet to come.[5] And who shall tell the number of those ages, which are to have their course in everlasting witness of the exceeding riches of that grace of God; the most glorious expression of which is His kindness towards the *Church*, whose present calling is to suffer with His world-rejected Christ?

[4] Hag. ii. 6, 7, 21–23; Heb. xii. 25–27.   [5] Eph. ii. 7.

There is thus to the believing Gentile now a more *abundant* hope, which corresponds with the abundance of the grace in which he stands.[6] For his calling is not to rejoice with Israel, the earthly people of the Lord, but to rejoice in hope of that glory which is his appointed and expected portion as made already *in Christ* a participator, in hope, of the heavenly as well as earthly inheritance of the saints in light. The power of the Holy Ghost is the means of creating and sustaining this more abundant hope. It is that Spirit which alone can draw forth for the believer's comfort the marrow and fatness of those sure testimonies which are the appointed nourishment of the heirs of promise. While, therefore, this verse (13) is full of comfort to the heart of a Christian, when considered simply as a corroborative addition to the word of reconciliation which confers on the believer the sure hope of *personal* salvation, as a forgiven sinner, it goes much further than this. It is intended rather to raise and fill our souls by a just perception of the nature and dimension of the hope of our calling, that both joy and peace might permanently fill the hearts of those who, by abiding in the faith, hold fast the beginning of their confidence as justified "partakers (or fellows[7]) of Christ,"[8] and who look, therefore, to be with Him and be like Him in the day when His glory is revealed.

Verse 14 expresses the apostle's happy persuasion of the effectual working of the Spirit among them, to the abundance of those fruits of refreshment and works of holiness and love, which should make for

[6] Chap. v. 17. [7] μέτοχοι. Heb. i. 9, iii. 1, 14.
[8] Heb. iii. 14.

the furtherance of their common joy, and their growth unitedly toward God. And it may be noticed how strong, though incidental, a protest is here implied against clerical or other limitations of the active power of the Spirit in the Church. Nothing but the most unfettered liberty of ministry is compatible with the language of this verse. The *knowledge* with which the apostle desires to find his brethren filled was not to lie idle in the hearts which had received it;[9] while a part of God's *goodness* is the ability which He confers, at His good pleasure, upon the members of Christ's body, to edify each other through the word of His own grace.[1]

Verses 15–17. In referring to the Apostolate of the Gentiles as that which, being his especial calling by the grace of God, emboldened him to address the saints at Rome, he again places the present dispensation of Gentile mercy in a striking light, as contrasted with that which is to come. Instead of the Lord Christ, on His throne of government, demanding and receiving the homage of all nations, we have His chosen servant fulfilling his mission as an ambassador of grace by publishing to all alike the word of life, and of deliverance from a world already judged. The result of this ministry was to bring nigh unto God with acceptance the Gentile offering which was sanctified by the Holy Ghost.[2] This ex-

[9] 2 Pet. i. 8.   [1] 1 Pet. iv. 11.
[2] Paul was a minister (λειτουργός) of Jesus Christ. His service was the ministry of the Gospel. The result of this was the acceptance of the Gentile offering sanctified by the Holy Ghost. The Church is an offering acceptable to God. At Pentecost this had its first exemplification, when the Holy Ghost descended upon the saints. Dispensationally, as we learn from chapter xi., that which was once a pure lump becomes a loathing and offence at the end—to be cut off

pression I understand to refer primarily to the election of grace, but in a wider sense to extend to the dispensational standing of the Gentile Church, as occupying the position and enjoying the privileges of the people of God. He had, then, a boast (verse 17) in the things of God. This was a confidence which pertained to him simply by the grace of God, which had made him to be what he was, according to His will. His rejoicing, then, was still *in Christ*,[3] whose chosen messenger he was.

The two verses which next follow (18, 19) pursue the same topic. It was Christ who wrought in him; and that not in word only, but in deed. Mighty signs and wonders had enforced, with Divine power of attestation, his faithful preaching of the word of grace. Of such things therefore he would freely speak, that the Lord might be magnified who had wrought the work. For he was not ashamed of His message. Of other things he would not dare to speak, for it was enough for him to be occupied with that which the Master had specially intrusted to his charge. Borrowing nothing from the sanction or cooperation of the other apostles, he stood before the brethren in the confident assurance that they would acknowledge him according to his work. Moreover, he knew that there were false apostles as well as false brethren, and he hastens thus to lay his credentials (albeit this marvellous epistle itself might, as an exposition of the doctrine of Christ, have appeared sufficient proof of apostolic power) before them, that

as a sapless branch from the root of promise. With respect to this meaning of the expression "offering," a good illustration may be found in Numb. viii. 11–21.

[3] Ἔχω οὖν καύχησιν ἐν Χριστῷ Ἰησοῦ τὰ πρὸς Θεόν.

U

if any urged upon them similar claims, they might have as it were a security against deceptive pretensions, in the possession of the genuine lineaments of an apostle of Christ.[4]

In the 19th verse there is a descriptive statement of the bounds within which the power which wrought by him had confined itself up to that time. From Jerusalem, and in a circuit as far as Illyricum, he had fully preached the Gospel of Christ. The passage is remarkable. When we remember the specialty of the apostle's dispensation among the Gentiles, and compare our Lord's words,[5] respecting the character and objects of the evangelical ministry which was to intervene between the ascension and the second advent, there appears no warrant for limiting the terms here used.[6] The testimony as to these parts was fulfilled. Wherever the apostle preached, a prominent topic in his testimony was the near approach of the day of judgment. Wherever the testimony was accepted, and believers were gathered to the name of Jesus, the speedy coming again of the Son of God from heaven was ministered as their characteristic hope in the midst of a hopeless, because Christless, world. The accomplishment, then, by the apostle, of his mission in any given district left nothing more to be *necessarily* done. The work was finished; so far, that is, as the fulfilment of the Lord's word respecting the Gospel of witness was

---

[4] These lineaments are more fully traced in the Epistles to the Corinthians. The complete figure and living portraiture, however, of this most Christ-like of Christians and least imitable of apostles, is only to be collected in its several features from an attentive and prayerful study of the entire body of his writings, and from the Acts.

[5] Matt. xxiv. 14.

[6] Πεπληρωκέναι τὸ εὐαγγέλιον τοῦ Χριστοῦ.

concerned. The Lord might tarry still. He *did* tarry, and lingers even yet, because His suffering is long, and He waits with much forbearance while the record of His goodness is, because still despised, but hardening a careless world in the ways of its destruction.[7]

But I regard this passage as one which, rightly considered, utterly confounds and disallows that perilous notion (itself the offspring of the Church's declension from its proper standing and true expectation) which leads men to regard the apostles as simply *founders* of churches, and leaders in the work of Gospel testimony. They were this, undoubtedly. But the sure word of Scripture, if carefully heeded, will convince us that the ideas of permanence[8] and improving progress are both of them opposed *exactly* to the plainest expression of the truth of God, respecting the proper calling and prospective dispensational character of the Church of God in the world.[9]

On the next five verses (20–24) I have not much to remark. The jealous zeal of the servant, whose boast was to do not the work of another, but his own, still conspicuously appears. From verse 22 we may gather a practical lesson of value. He had long desired to visit Rome, and the idea of personally

[7] 2 Pet. iii. 9, 10.
[8] Permanence, that is, in an earthly position. Instead of this, its place, although enthroned above in Christ, is here that of waiting expectation till He come. (Eph. i. 3; 1 Thess. i. 10.)
[9] In one of the last epistles of this apostle (Col. i. 23), he speaks of the Gospel having been preached "to every creature which is under heaven." When we remember that the unwearied labours of the other apostles, which we know were in a different direction and in different localities from those of Paul, were concurrent with his own, this expression seems capable of acceptation as a simple statement of fact, as it regarded the then known world. Ecclesiastical historians have already noticed this.

carrying the Gospel into that vast metropolis of spiritual death may have stirred his mind with ardent longing. But he had to abide the Lord's pleasure as to the time, the distribution, and the manner of his work. He should see Rome in due time; yet not as he had thought and wished, but as the Lord had willed in the perfect wisdom of His counsel. Conflict between inclination and duty is a thing of everyday occurrence with a tried servant of Christ. "If I yet pleased men, I should not be the servant of Christ,"[1] was the word of this most susceptible yet most steadfast of servants. Least of all, if *self* be pleased, can a man hope to be used of God. We see, in verse 24, how large and wide were the anticipations of future labour, which filled the mind of this devoted and unwearied apostle. Whether these anticipations were fulfilled in the instance of the Spanish journey is unknown. The preparation, however, which he proposes to make for it is worth our attention. He would not willingly go thither *alone*. He would carry with him some remembrance of the brethren at Rome. He would gather, from a respite of toil spent in the sweet and precious fellowship of the Spirit, a measure of fresh strength and courage to proceed still further on his dangerous yet welcome way.

Apostolic labour, like every other species of ministry, is the fruit of personal responsibility to the Lord. It must, therefore, be exercised without conference with flesh and blood. Yet it is the happiness of the servant to find his hands strengthened and his way cheered by the cordial sympathy and prayerful

[1] Gal. i. 10.

aid of his brethren. For the work is the work of the Lord, and in that work all have their common interest, and all are exhorted to abound.[2] How necessary to his help and comfort in labour Paul felt the prayers of the saints to be, appears from the frequency with which he calls on them in all his epistles for such aid. Nor was it only or even chiefly for his sake, but rather for their own, that he sought thus to excite and keep alive in them a constant interest in the work of the Lord. For he well knew that their true prosperity of soul depended much on the singleness of zeal with which their hearts were occupied with the things of Jesus Christ.

Verses 25–28 announce his contemplated journey to Jerusalem, and the objects with which that journey was to be made. It was a strong and steadfast purpose of heart which made him still persist in the endeavour to accomplish that enterprise, so remarkable in its accompanying circumstances, and of such eventful result. The prospect of bonds and imprisonment did not deter him. We have the circumstances which preceded and accompanied, and the consequences which followed, this visit to Jerusalem, detailed in the Acts of the Apostles. At present I only notice the remarkable language in verse 27. The Jew's preëminence is fully asserted here. Nor, indeed, does he ever lose it, in any just estimate of *natural* comparison, though, when the cross is known in its power, all fleshly distinction is set aside. But salvation is of the Jews.[3] The spiritual things are theirs; for theirs is the Christ. The believing Gentile, while rejoicing in a light which utterly trans-

[2] 1 Cor. xv. 58.   [3] John iv. 22.

cended the national Jewish blessing,[4] had still to remember that it was the despised and forfeited blessing of the Jew which had become thus to him the opening of the gates of salvation and of praise. They were enemies, as concerning the Gospel, for the Gentiles' sake.

But not only so. The believing remnant of Israel, who by the grace of God had trusted in Christ, formed the original nucleus of the Church, which, though characteristically Gentile, because formed by a testimony which the nation at large had rejected, received both its name and its anointing at Jerusalem. Thus, while the effectual work of God wrought by the Cross to the dissolution of Jew and Gentile alike, that *one new Man* might appear in the risen Christ,[5] grace would ever lead the Gentile believer to acknowledge in his Jewish brethren a preëminent title to his sympathy and aid. He would be thus recognising God in the sovereignty of His wisdom and counsel. Mindful of the abundance of that mercy which had for a while forsaken its ancient channel, and descended as a mighty stream of blessing to the world,[6] he would remember that the place of the Gentile, as a receiver of blessing, is, in the Divine order, ever a *mediate* place. As it is written before, "To the Jew first, and also to the Gentile."[7]

Verse 29 expresses his confidence as to the effect of his wished-for visit to Rome. He knew that when he came it would be in the fulness of the blessing of Christ.[8] He knew this, first, because he was well

---

[4] The heavenly calling, and the riches of the glory of God's inheritance in the saints, being the distinctive portion of the Church.

[5] Eph. ii. 15.   [6] Chap. xi. 12–21.   [7] Chap. ii. 10.

[8] All the best MSS. (including *Cod. Sin.*) omit the words τοῦ εὐαγγ. τοῦ.

aware of the nature of the dispensation committed to him,[9] and what its fruits would be when faithfully ministered and gladly received;[1] but, secondly, because after so long a deferring of his desire, the *time* seemed really come. Let us carefully observe, that his being an apostle was not in itself sufficient to secure a blessing as the result of his visit. For this he must wait on God. With him there could be neither yea nor nay.[2] He was God's servant; and by His grace he had wrought, and for His counsel he had waited, as it respected the fulfilling of His will in the countries in which he had been labouring. Now, therefore, he feels *free* to undertake this further enterprise of love.

There was, however, one intervening engagement on his hands. The journey to Jerusalem, which (whether rightly or no I hesitate to say) was so settled a purpose in his mind, alone remained to be performed before he set out, free in body and zealous in desire, to enter on his new and untried field of evangelical labour at Rome and in Spain. That he felt misgivings as to the results of this journey is apparent from the earnestness with which he calls upon the saints at Rome to further him with their prayers (verse 30).

He had, indeed, other fears than those which respected his personal safety. He dreaded lest by any means Satan should successfully act on the natural pride and prejudices of the saints at Jerusalem, and thus render them unwilling to accept the aid of their European and Gentile brethren. The preservation, on the part of Jewish Christians, of the unity of the

[9] Eph. iii. 1–8.   [1] Col. i. 4–6.   [2] 2 Cor. i. 17.

Church, as a practical reality, depended on this. The Gospel itself was involved in the consequence of a refusal of unreserved fellowship and coëqual standing and privilege to their Gentile brethren. Now the reception of pecuniary aid by one Church at the hands of another, is a very complete and entire recognition of practical fellowship, founded on the confessed unity of the body. Grace alone in the receivers would prevent the intrusion of natural feeling, to the hindrance of this blessing. Yet upon the maintenance unbroken of this truth depended the efficiency of the Church, as a testimony of God in the world. This was a matter which needed something more than apostolical power to arrange and prosper it. Besides, though an apostle to the Gentiles, he had not any special claim upon the obedience of the Jewish saints. He felt, therefore, that the preservation and cementing of the unity of the Spirit in the bonds of peace, and love, and mutual confidence, must result from the active and prayerful energy of that Spirit's love in the brethren themselves. The saints at Rome had not been concerned in this movement in Macedonia and Achaia, yet were they interested in its results. For, as having been all baptized into one body, and as having all drunk into one Spirit, the object of their interest and the just measure of their spiritual sympathies was the *body of Christ*, and not one part of it alone. He reckons, therefore, upon this active liveliness of spiritual affection on their parts, while writing to those whom he had never yet seen face to face.

Nor were the dangers which threatened his personal safety either few or small. When he prayed for deliverance from the unbelieving Jews (verse 31), he was conscious of the terrible energy of that perfect hatred of Christ, which in his own case had once made the blood of the saints a pleasant spectacle to his eyes. How the event of this visit to Jerusalem turned, in the Lord's hand, to the accomplishment of his desires respecting Rome, I will not pause now to recount. An attentive consideration of what has been recorded as to these things in the Acts of the Apostles,[3] will largely repay the reader who studies the word of God, not for information simply, but as that which is altogether profitable for the perfecting of the man of God.[4]

Verses 32, 33, close the main body of the epistle. They are noticeable now only as again reminding us of the state of conscious dependence upon God in which the apostle lived. His office was no security for his person. He held not his life as an apostle by any fixed tenure as to the appointed number of the days of his service. This, had it been so, would doubtless have acted mischievously on his flesh as a man. Its direct tendency would have been to withdraw him from that state of dependence on the Lord, which is the sole condition either of personal blessing in communion or of effectual power in service.[5] May he be in this, as in all other things, the heeded pattern of our ways.

[3] Acts xx. xxviii.   [4] 2 Tim. iii. 16, 17.   [5] John xv.

CHAPTER XVI.

THIS concluding chapter of the epistle stands apart from the rest of the work, and possesses a character and an interest peculiarly its own. It is a kind of postscript, the epistle having been closed by the valedictory sentence at the end of the last chapter. We shall find it, however, well worthy our careful attention.

Verses 1, 2. "I commend unto you Phœbe," &c. The sister here mentioned by name may possibly have been sent, or have voluntarily gone to Rome on some matter which affected the Church assembled at Cenchrea. The nature of the relation in which she stood to the Church of which she is here called "a servant,"[1] as well as that of the particular matter, if such there were, in which she was charged or had undertaken to act for them while at Rome, is quite unknown, and is entirely immaterial. Private and personal business of some sort would rather seem, from the second verse, to have been the occasion of

[1] Phœbe is called a διάκονος τῆς ἐκκλησίας, κ. τ. λ. This proves nothing as to her position. Because, though there may possibly have been female διάκονοι in an official sense in the Church, there is certainly no passage in Scripture which clearly exhibits the term in that sense. In the text it may simply be intended to express the general character of this devoted woman. On the other hand, the inference from this verse that she was a "deaconess" is not at all absurd.

her presence in the city at this time; though she may possibly also have been the bearer of this epistle. Being there, she was to be received in a manner worthy of saints,² whom it became to welcome and succour one another in the Lord.

But besides the claim upon their common charity and kindness which attached to her as a member of the one body of Christ, Phœbe had others which she could not urge herself, but which in an especial manner entitled her to their affectionate esteem. For she was one whose praise was already in the Church elsewhere as a succourer of the saints. The apostle therefore hastens to put upon her that comeliness in their eyes which would make, not for the puffing up of the fleshly mind, or the kindling of jealousy or selfish emulation, but for the furtherance of practical communion, through a ready discernment of the grace and love of the Lord as it shone forth from the individual members of the body, and gave its light in the house for the comfort and blessing of all.

With this view it is, too, that he connects his own name so pointedly with that of Phœbe, and with the many others who are expressed by name as his fellow-labourers and helpers in the course of this chapter. He was eagerly watchful to take all occasion of bringing such under the notice of the saints. Ever jealous in the highest degree for the *doctrine*, because jealous for the Lord, he never suffers his apostolate to become a pedestal on which to display himself. To him to live was *Christ*. What was wrought in him by the grace of Christ he made no secret of,

---

² In another passage, where those who had gone forth to preach Christ are the subjects of commendation, the expression is different. Such were to be received ἀξίως τοῦ Θεοῦ. (3 John 6, 7.)

that the Lord, to whom the excellency of the glory pertained, might have His praise. On the same principle of single-hearted devotedness, where he saw the abundance of that grace and power displaying itself in others, he found equal cause of glory and of joy. Utterly refusing to acknowledge in any shape the vain pretensions of worldly-minded men to individual credit or distinction, he delighted, on the other hand, to discover and openly to commend the work and way of those whose aim seemed less their own things than the things of Christ.[3] The root of this feeling was grace. Personal experience, through faith, of the living God as our portion, can alone produce and sustain that thorough disinterestedness of heart which finds an unmixed joy in the honour which, for the Lord's sake, is put on other men.

Verses 3, 4. Priscilla and Aquila are distinguished according to their work. There is a blending of personal affection with a higher and more solemn feeling, which connected itself with his calling and position as the apostle of the Gentiles, beautifully apparent in this greeting. He owed them his life; and joyfully proclaimed that debt, to their praise, and for their worthier esteem in the Church of God. But how does this smaller, and in a manner more natural, though most precious feeling, become enlarged and sobered into solemn thanksgiving to God, when the value of the life thus rescued is perceived! The expression, "*all* the Churches of the Gentiles," is as bold as it is full. Yet it was even so. To none other had the Lord committed the apostolate of the Gentiles than to Paul. He had found indeed,

---

[3] Phil. ii. 1-5.

fellowship in that work, and delighted to acknowledge it. Nevertheless, to him it pertained to sustain the burden of all the Churches,[4] and to fill up that which remained of the afflictions of Christ for His body's sake—the Church.[5] None but Paul could do *that*. *With* him others might share in part the burden, but it was given to him peculiarly to bear, by the especial grace of God.

On the expression, "the Church that is in their house," I make a brief remark. The term "Church" in the New Testament is used in three senses only. First, it signifies the one body of Christ, the aggregate of those living stones which form the habitation of God through the Spirit. Secondly, local assemblies of united worshippers, themselves severally recognising the unity of the body, and kept asunder by local distance alone, are called Churches.[6] And, lastly, the same name is sometimes given to the diminutive assembly of a man's own household, where that house was kept for the Lord, and its roof gave shelter to any small number of the flock of God, who might habitually meet there for purposes of social worship. The beauty and the gracious power of this last expression, implying as it does the assured enjoyment in such domestic assemblies of all that fulness of blessing which flows from the recognition of the presence of the Lord, as the life and light of His own house,[7] are as apparent as they are precious.

---

[4] 2 Cor. xi. 28.   [5] Col. i. 24.
[6] But vainly will search be made in the word of God for a passage which would justify a sectarian position in the Church of God. A local Church was the Church of God in a place.
[7] Comp. Heb. ii. 12, and iii. 6.

I shall not linger over each of these greetings, though I heartily recommend my reader to do so. It is well, however, to bear in mind that we read in this chapter, as in the rest of the epistle, the language of the *Holy Ghost*. The remembrance of this suggests one general reflection with respect to the varied salutations contained in this chapter. The delicate adjustment of praise, according to a discrimination which refuses to confound labouring in the Lord with labouring *much* in the Lord, and which, while greeting all in love unfeigned, sets some conspicuously in the light, that all might see and approve with joy that which till then had perhaps remained unnoticed or unknown, is a circumstance full of instructive force. It affords, perhaps, to the Christian understanding, a readier explanation and illustration of the doctrine, already stated,[8] of future reward and loss, than any other part of Scripture. That there are such differences of reward and loss, as well as that there are wide diversities of place and function in the kingdom whose glory is so soon to be revealed, is most sure. The Spirit of God, when declaring to us the truth as it is revealed in its perfection in Christ, presents the Church in its unspotted perfectness before God as an object of our common faith. All believers are there seen unitedly presented on the ground of redemption, and the assured and everlasting favour of God is affirmed to be the indefeasible possession of every heir alike. The same Spirit, when speaking *to* the saints concerning their ways, as the Spirit of testimony in the Church, because He acts still as the Spirit of *truth*, gives a varying testimony

[8] *Ante*, chap. xiv.

according to the actual state of that which He describes. Thus, in the present instance, some were to be honoured especially because of their more abundant labours and more diligent devotedness. Others were noted by no mark of personal approbation, while saluted equally in the love of Christ. Surely, no question ever suggested itself, either to the mind of the apostle or to those whom he addressed, as to their perfect equality in spiritual fellowship as alike saved by grace.

So will it doubtless be in that day. No saved child of grace shall find his portion in the kingdom less than royal. For by one Jesus Christ shall they all reign in life.[9] Nor will the worship which the more honoured guest of that feast of eternal charity shall receive, in the presence of them that sit at meat with Him,[1] be other than an increase of the joy of all, where emulation and an evil eye shall have no place, because the former things shall then be wholly passed away.

To return to the chapter before us. It is most interesting, and discovers to us a very precious trait of Christ in the apostle, to notice how assiduously he labours thus (and he is speaking in the Spirit), to turn the hearts of the several saints to each other. Certain individuals were to be saluted publicly, whose names and whose value had perhaps been little known before. The end of this was the more perfect communion, the closer knitting together in love of the saints addressed. Nothing is more easily deranged than Christian fellowship. The moment the principle of esteeming others better than ourselves is

[9] Chap. v.   [1] Luke xiv. 10.

practically lost sight of, the mainspring of happy fellowship is gone.

The mention of Epœnetus and Stachys, with the adjunct of "beloved," while the name of the Lord is not expressed, seems to indicate that these were personal friends of the apostle. Brotherly love contains all saints. But within that limit there is room for specialty of personal intimacy, without prejudice to the wider sentiment which includes it. Epœnetus was indeed doubly dear, as being the first link of that long chain of tender and enduring association which bound him, as a father in Christ, to so many in Achaia.[2]

The kinsmen of the apostle are not overlooked. With respect to the expression, "of note among the apostles" (verse 7), I feel uncertain as to its precise meaning. I think, however, that the term apostle is here applied in a lower sense, to the Lord's messengers indifferently.

Rufus is saluted as "chosen of the Lord" (verse 13). So were they all. I should suppose that this particular style of address was used in order to meet some doubt or difficulty in his mind on the subject of election. There is nothing improbable in such a supposition. Certainly, such a greeting would do much to confirm in the faith a tried spirit, whose mind Satan might haply have been assailing and darkening on this point. Much, too, would it tend to the encouragement of such an one that an apostle

[2] Rather in *Asia*, as I believe, taking this word in its limited application, as used in the New Testament. Τῆς 'Ασίας is now generally accepted by critical editors in this passage instead of τῆς 'Αχαίας. This reading (confirmed as it has lately been by the *Cod. Sin.*) removes at once the difficulty which might otherwise be felt with respect to 1 Cor. xvi. 15.

of the faith should claim with such emphatic tenderness a brother's place in his regard. And so the greeting here addressed to Rufus is extended "to his mother and to mine."

In the three succeeding verses the same strain of salutation, both general and particular, is continued. Those whom he personally knew he mentioned carefully by name. For others he expresses a no less earnest love, although he knew them only by the common yet endearing name of "brethren." To believe that they were Christ's, was to feel for them a hearty and unfeigned love. Nor does he forget the affectionate desire which others felt towards the saints at Rome, while forward to express his own. Speaking in the Holy Ghost, and understanding well the manner of that love which is of God, and which formed the very life of each true member of the unity of Christ, he can truthfully convey to them the general salutation of "the Churches of Christ." In each of those local assemblies there abode that one and self-same Spirit which bore witness of the oneness of the body to which all belonged. The instincts of that Spirit are everywhere the same. They tend to the conscious uniting in the bond of perfectness of all who are partakers of the one true Bread.[3]

Verses 17–19. Faithfulness and vigilance in keeping themselves pure are here insisted on in immediate connection with the subject of practical fellowship. Unquestionable soundness of doctrine is a condition of Christian communion entirely indispensable.[4] Moral corruption is equally to be abhorred and avoided. For holiness and truth are the two regu-

[3] Col. iii. 14; 1 Cor. x. 17.   [4] 1 John i. 7.

lating springs of all intercourse in the Spirit. In the present instance, corruption of doctrine is the danger chiefly warned against. This is, indeed, ever the most dangerous, because the most *insidious* evil, and the most readily communicative of injurious effect. The effects, too, of false doctrine are far less easily removed in ordinary cases, than a vicious habit of a moral kind. False doctrine, because it dishonours Christ by setting a lie in the place of Himself who is the Truth (for let the ramifications of error be what they may, they *all* touch Christ directly or indirectly), deteriorates, of necessity, the whole tone of the man in whose mind it finds acceptance. The light within him is already dimmed. Accepting the fallacious guidance of his own understanding, instead of following the light of life,[5] his path, if persisted in, will surely lead him to the ditch.[6]

But it is in its contagious effect upon a company of Christians that the presence of false doctrine is to be chiefly dreaded. With respect to this, every obedient believer is both forewarned and forearmed. He has learned the truth, and he has an unction from the Holy One whereby he is to hold fast that which he has received, and to continue in the things which he has heard and learned. He must abhor evil. He must strive to keep himself practically pure. Even if the Church should sanction what is evil, or refuse to judge it, he is individually responsible still. For his obedience is due to the Lord, and not to the Church. He is to be *wise* as to this. For neglected warning will leave him else a prey to the very delu-

[5] John viii. 12; Prov. iii. 5.
[6] Matt. xv. 14; Prov. xvi. 25, xxvi. 12.

sion which at first he may, perhaps, have clearly estimated, but forborne to shun or to denounce.

The character of evil, against which the warning is here given, is defined with great breadth of expression; while there is sufficient precision in the terms employed to furnish believers at all times with available counsel in similar cases. Anything which on any pretence led the souls of God's sheep away from Christ, was to be shunned. It might not amount, perhaps, to a patent heresy; but on pretence of refinement of exposition, or of a deeper investigation of the more recondite mysteries of the faith, an imposing claim might be set up to the attention of those who were eager to advance in the knowledge of Divine truth. This is an ancient device of Satan, and one which he continually practises in the Church. The moment our minds are accustomed to regard the truth of God as an *abstruse* subject, we are in danger of falling into some snare of this description. The word of God is never abstruse, in the ordinary sense of that term. There are, indeed, things hard to be understood, even in the writings of our apostle.[7] But the difficulty arises partly from the subject being the unsearchable way of God, and partly from the fact that our minds are usually pre-occupied by erroneous notions on the subjects which are handled by the Spirit of truth. Now the teacher of the way of truth is *God Himself*, who pours His instruction only into the obedient ear, concealing from the wise and prudent that which He reveals to babes.[8] Childlike patience, waiting upon Him, and pondering, not so much with effort of mind as with simplicity of

---

[7] 2 Pet. iii. 16.   [8] Isa. l. 4; Matt. xi. 25.

sober-minded faith, the sure testimonies of God, finds nourishment in that which the unlearned and unstable man wrests, in his impatience, to his own destruction. It is the very erroneous notion that intellectual effort is the first condition of a proper understanding of Scripture, which leads so many persons, who are had in reputation among men as clever theologians, into paths of inquiry which conduct only to fields of profitless disquisition, to the exhaustion rather than enrichment of the soul. Scientific theology (in popular phrase) is no sure or safe exponent of the truth of God.[9]

They were to be on their guard against the insidious entrance of corruption. It was not enough for them to be simple and pure in mind; they were to be vigilant as well. They were to be wise concerning that which is good, and simple concerning evil (verse 19). Guilelessness of character, unaccompanied by watchfulness toward God, would expose them to the craft of the deceiver.

But (verse 20) the time of their watching and their patience would be short. The adversary, meanwhile, who eyed them and who sought their life, was fierce, and cunning, and very strong. Moreover, he was, as it were, ubiquitously present at their steps. It is he who contends in heavenly places[1] against the entry of the believer into that sphere of blessing, into which the Spirit of adoption already leads him as no longer a stranger in the house of God; seeking ever, as the accuser of the brethren, to cast his own

---

[9] How frequently, in the present day, it leads its infatuated disciples to conclusions utterly repugnant to the doctrine of Christ, is but too well known to those who are conversant with the subject.

[1] Eph. vi. 11, 12.

dark shadow upon the pure surface of those consciences which the precious blood of Christ has purged. It is he who, as the ruler of the darkness of this world, sets in array the native animosity of the flesh to the Spirit, and stirs up the men who are after his own heart to oppose and oppress such as confess the love of the Father in the name of the Son. It is he, too, who, as the deceiver, the mock-preacher of Christ, the pretended angel of light, sows within the field which is Christ's the tares of destruction, which grow side by side, to the marring of the crop, with the true wheat of the garner, until the time of harvest be arrived.[2] It is the same ever-vigilant adversary who, when not heard as a roaring lion, is even yet more to be dreaded for the serpentine subtlety which deceives the whole world, and which, but for the faithful guardianship of the true Shepherd, would doubtless lure back again to their destruction the very sheep who had once escaped through the knowledge of His name.[3]

All these, and manifold other modes of evil warfare, are possessed and practised by Satan against the believer. But the God of peace is *for* him. The standard of the battle is the name of Jesus, which in heaven is now known and honoured, because of the eternal victory already won in the hour of His bruising by the grace of God. God's face, which in Christ is towards the reconciled people of His redemption, is against their adversary. He has sworn to put out the memory of Amalek from under heaven. He wages a war with him from generation to generation until then.[4] Meanwhile, the word of promise is, that

[2] Matt. xiii. 24–30.   [3] 2 Pet. ii. 20; John x. 27–30.   [4] Ex. xvii.

He will *shortly* bruise this dreaded foe under *our* feet, even as he has been and is prostrated under the feet of Christ.

The first resurrection will be the fulfilment of this word. Each successive pilgrim who departs to be with Christ, knows a full cessation from the molestation of this enemy, as well as from the burden of this mortal tabernacle. But the bruising of the evil one himself is to be a manifested thing.[5] The day of glory will reveal it, which is to display the prepared thrones of that kingdom, which already is known in promise as the pledged gift of the Father's pleasure, to the sharers of the reproach of Christ. Until then, the grace of the Lord Jesus Christ is with them, to keep them that they may be presented faultless in that day.

At the 21st verse he again pauses to introduce into his Epistle the several messages of love in the Lord which fill this and the two following verses. Perfect, happy fellowship, far indeed removed from magisterial distance, characterized the intercourse of the apostle with those whom he delighted to own as brethren beloved, and as fellow-labourers in the husbandry of God. And so he inserts everything that could minister to comfort or edifying, on one side or the other. His Epistle is the channel through which Timothy, Sosipater, and others, convey their love in union with his own to these distant brethren, to whom it is probable they were as little known, personally, as himself. Tertius, his willing Scribe, and who from his name was probably of Italy, salutes them also in the Lord. In the names which follow,

[5] Rev. xx.

and which close this interesting list, the three degrees of opulent ease, of official distinction, and of modest obscurity, appear to be severally represented in the common fellowship of grace. This large-hearted Gaius was also probably one of the few at Corinth who received baptism at the hands of Paul.⁶ Quartus from his name, was possibly less known at Corinth than at Rome.⁷

Verses 25-27. We come now to the remarkable doxology which finally closes this most full, most weighty, and, in every sense, most precious Epistle. These concluding verses are in a high degree important. We have, first, the general commendation of the saints to God, as the Omnipotent establisher and preserver of that which He had Himself produced by the word of His power. But there is an especial mention made of the Gospel (which the apostle here calls his own), in connection with the mystery of God, which should by no means be overlooked.

The mystery here mentioned is said to have been kept secret since the world began.⁸ What this mystery is we find from the passage before us. It is the preaching of Jesus Christ among the Gentiles. That is, the doctrine of Christ which is now preached in the Epistles of Paul among the Gentiles, opens to the believer a calling quite distinct in many of its characteristic features from any that had preceded it. Dis-

⁶ 1 Cor. i. 14.
⁷ The repeated benediction in verse 24 of E. V. is probably a gratuitous addition: *all* the best MSS. being without it.
⁸ Κατὰ ἀποκάλυψιν μυστηρίου χρόνοις αἰωνίοις σεσιγημένου. A strong and clear expression, which plainly shows that, although the letter of the revealed word of God may have contained hidden in it the truth of the mystery, yet it formed no part of the revelation of the Holy Ghost to the saints of God until the time arrived to bring it forth, and to minister it *now* among the Gentiles.

tinct, even, in some important respects, from that which the first testimony of the Spirit to the name of the ascended Jesus opened to those who, in Jerusalem, hastened to save themselves from the untoward generation among whom they dwelt.

It differed in this, that while the forgiveness of sins was as freely preached through the precious blood of the Lamb, from the first moment that Peter had his mouth opened to address the murderers of Christ,[9] as it was by the apostle Paul, yet the preaching was, for the time, limited in its scope to the natural seed of Abraham, and was characterized by a direct appeal to Jewish national promise as that which, being already secured in the Person of the glorified Jesus, awaited only the repentance of the nation for its full manifestation to take place. Instead of something kept secret from the foundation of the world, Peter pointedly refers to the testimonies of the prophets, who, they well knew, had spoken before of the things to which he then bore this fresh and divinely authenticated testimony. With respect those who received believingly the word of grace, they became immediately a part of the Church of God.

Such was the beginning of the Gospel, as it was preached among men in the power of the Holy Ghost sent down from heaven. But the special standing and calling of the Church—its true nature and its proper hope,—these things, although in one sense included in the *Name* which was preached from the first, were not made the subject of distinct revelation until the Lord was pleased, on the foreseen rejection

[9] Acts iii. 17–26.

of the last witness of His long-suffering to Jerusalem, to turn away definitively from Israel, in order to take from the *Gentiles* a people for His name. I refer the reader to the 11th chapter, and to what has been noted there, for a fuller view of this subject. In the mean time, I add a few words as to what the Scriptures reveal with respect to the distinctive blessings of the Church standing, as brought fully out by the apostle Paul.

The Gospel which was intrusted to his ministry was not the Gospel of the *kingdom* only. The subject of his testimony was the Person of Christ in them, the hope of glory,[1] and their inheritance in Him according to the mystery of God.[2] This mystery was something more than the preaching of salvation to Gentiles as well as Jews. It included that, but extended much further. The fellowship of Jew and Gentile, in the common blessings of redemption upon earth, was no secret to the Old Testament prophets. But there was now revealed in the Gospel the union *in Christ* of the two, as alike quickened by the Holy Ghost, through faith, into the knowledge of the *heavenly calling*.[3] The present subject of testimony is the formation, in the risen Son of God, of *One new Man;* the old man, whether Jew or Gentile, having first, by the cross of Jesus, come to its end in judicial death.[4] This was the new thing which God, who fore-ordained it from eternity, had kept hidden from the sons of men, until the light shone forth from the

---

[1] Col. i.   [2] Eph. i.
[3] Heb. iii. 1; Phil. iii. 14.
[4] Evidently this was involved in the first preaching of the cross; but it was reserved for the apostle to bring it clearly to light. This subject is more fully examined in my *Notes on the Ephesians*.

glory of the ascended Christ, in which alone it could be seen and known.

It is Christ, then, glorified in heaven, hidden in God, and believed on through the Spirit in the world, which is the mystery here spoken of.[5] This had never been declared in former ages. Scripture indeed contained its constituent truth, but not as a manifested doctrine, nor even as an expressed promise. That is to say, the manner of its present revelation, in the calling and anointing of the Church, was no subject of ancient prophetic testimony. The Son of God, now manifested to the eye of faith, upon the Father's throne, and presented to the believer as the Hope of glory, is the revelation of the hidden and previously silent mystery of God. That silence was broken by the voice of the Spirit, sent down to declare the glory of Christ as the immediate portion in hope of His disciples. He is revealed now as the exalted Man, the second Adam, the appointed Heir of all things; the Head moreover, and *especially*, of that body which now, from among the Gentiles, is brought into the fellowship of the Son of God.[6]

Meanwhile, the Scriptures of the prophets[7] were

---

[5] Closely connected with this is the doctrine of the Church as the bride of the Lamb. That subject, however, cannot be examined in this place. See the previous note.

[6] The Jew finding his place in that body, not as a matter of inherited privilege, but by the grace of God, which meets him in the cross as a lost *man*.

[7] διά τε γραφῶν προφητικῶν, κ. λ. It has been thought by some, that by this expression the apostolic epistles were intended (especially those of Paul), and *not* the ancient prophets. To this view I cannot accede, because I think that it is contradicted, not only by numerous other passages, but by the apostle himself at the very opening of this Epistle. (Chap. i. 2; compare Acts xxviii. 23.) How Paul used and relied on the Jewish prophecies as authentic aids and confirmations of his own apostolic testimony, must surely be evident to any careful reader of this Epistle. (See especially chaps. iii. and xv.) Of the

the means by which the Holy Ghost opened and alleged the truth of His blessed Person, wherein the mystery is contained. It was by the commandment of the everlasting, the *only wise God*, that this was now done.[8] He had caused His perfect word to be so written, that it should not only present the ordered detail of His dealings with Israel, and the record of blessings hereafter to flow through them to the Gentiles, but should likewise become a voucher

critical reasons alleged in support of the above view, I will only say, that they appear to me of no value whatever. It is indeed true—and the truth is of much importance—that the apostolic writings are also prophetic in their character. It is also evident that in another place the apostle gives peculiar prominence to the prophetic gifts of the Spirit in the founding and edification of the Church.¹ (Eph. ii. 20, iii. 5; comp. 1 Cor. xii. 28.) But such a view as the one above stated tends evidently to remove the Old Testament Scriptures from that place, in the estimation of modern Christians, which they so manifestly held in the minds and hearts of the apostles. (Comp. 2 Tim. iii. 16; 2 Pet. iii. 2.) The fact is, *all* Scripture is in one sense prophetic, until the end of all things is attained. A type is but another form of prophecy; and we have only to turn to the latter part of Ephes. v. in order to see a perfect example of the way in which the living voice of the Holy Ghost expands, *by means of* the ancient oracles, that mystery which, as a direct revelation, had been withheld from ages and generations, until the fitting moment had arrived, and the chosen messenger was found. It may be further noticed, with respect to the term προφητικός, that the only other passage in which it occurs is 2 Pet. i. 19, where the Old Testament prophecies are expressly meant.

[8] In Acts xiii. 46, 47, we have a striking example of the manner in which the voice of ancient prophecy became, to an inspired apostle, the immediate commandment of the Lord: "For so hath the Lord commanded us, saying, I have set Thee as a light to the Gentiles," &c. The first utterance of prophecy is not always the disclosure of a present truth; but at the appointed time the vision speaks. The prophets were not always in the secret of the things which they disclosed. (Dan. xii.; Habak. i. 3; 1 Pet. i. 10–12.) While, however, I feel no doubt that the Old Testament prophecies are chiefly, if not exclusively, intended by the apostle in this passage, it is most needful to remember that the New Testament Scriptures, and especially the Epistles, are a prophetic warning as well as testimony to the nations. God, who as the God of Israel spake *of* the Gentiles to His people, now speaks *to* them in the Gospel of His Son. Futurity is now no longer an enigma, but a definite assurance *to mankind at large*, of happiness or misery, according to their reception or rejection of the words of God.

and witness of the heavenly mystery of the Church's calling, during the suspense of the still-remembered promises once made to the fathers. Thus the things which God had spoken in His earlier testimonies,[9] although receiving, by means of apostolic ministry, this new and marvellous addition, are in perfect harmony with what is now revealed. As Gospel grace establishes the Law,[1] while superseding it for the believer, so the chief honour of the prophets is that they so spake, both of the Person of Christ, His sufferings, and His glories, as to furnish, when the building time arrived, the suited materials for laying the foundations of God's everlasting house.

An incarnate Christ was the subject of primal promise. The seed of the woman was foretold before the seed of Abraham and of David was especially defined. All this has been fulfilled by the first advent of the Lord. But the accomplishment of the blessings which were to flow from Him to the nations, by the terms of the promise, has been frustrated hitherto, as has been shown.[2] Nor will it take effect until the appointed channel of the world's full blessing is reöpened by the restoration of Israel, in the plenitude of gracious favour, to Immanuel's land.

A regnant Christ, triumphing in the victory of righteousness as the God of the whole earth, is no mystery. It was a constant burden of the ancient prophecy. But the Son, glorified in heaven as the Head of His own Church, and awaiting upon the Father's throne the time for His kingdom to be established, is the mystery of blessedness already opened to the eye of faith, and which shall presently

[9] Heb. i. 1.　　[1] *Ante*, chap. iii. *ad fin*.　　[2] Chap. xi.

be realized in all its results of perfected glory, when the long night of patience shall for ever have vanished into the cloudless day of His appearing.[8]

May the only wise God be the refuge and stability of the reader of these Notes until that day, and in that day his exceeding great reward.

[8] 2 Sam. xxiii. 2–7; Rev. xxii. 16, 20.

THE END.

www.ingramcontent.com/pod-product-compliance
Lightning Source LLC
Chambersburg PA
CBHW071433300426
44114CB00013B/1410